LINES
OF
FIRE

Books by Ralph Peters

Nonfiction

Endless War
Looking for Trouble
Wars of Blood and Faith
New Glory
Never Quit the Fight
Beyond Baghdad
Beyond Terror
Fighting for the Future

Fiction

Hell or Richmond
Cain at Gettysburg
The Officers' Club
The War After Armageddon
Traitor
The Devil's Garden
Twilight of Heroes
The Perfect Soldier
Flames of Heaven
The War in 2020
Red Army
Bravo Romeo

Writing as Owen Parry

Fiction

Rebels of Babylon
Bold Sons of Erin
Honor's Kingdom (Hammett Award)
Call Each River Jordan
Shadows of Glory
Faded Coat of Blue (Herodotus Award)
Our Simple Gifts
Strike the Harp

LINES
OF
FIRE

A RENEGADE WRITES ON
STRATEGY, INTELLIGENCE, AND SECURITY

RALPH PETERS

STACKPOLE
BOOKS

Copyright © 2011 by Ralph Peters

First published in paperback in 2013 by
STACKPOLE BOOKS
5067 Ritter Road
Mechanicsburg, PA 17055
www.stackpolebooks.com

Printed in the United States of America

First paperback edition

10 9 8 7 6 5 4 3 2 1

Front cover photo by Lance Cpl. Christopher M. Burke
Cover design by Tessa J. Sweigert

ISBN-13: 978-0-8117-1112-8
ISBN-10: 0-8117-1112-9

Library of Congress Cataloging-in-Publication Data

Peters, Ralph, 1952–
  Lines of fire : a renegade writes on strategy, intelligence, and security /
Ralph Peters.
    p. cm.
  ISBN-13: 978-0-8117-0588-2 (hbk.)
  ISBN-10: 0-8117-0588-9 (hbk.)
  1. United States—Military policy. 2. National security—United States. 3.
Military art and science. 4. Strategy. 5. World politics—21st century. I.
Title.
  UA23.P694 2011
  355'.033573—dc23
                          2011016188

*To all the troops who died
while generals dithered*

Contents

Introduction

Making Mud Pies in the Sty

The opportunity to gather the worthiest essays and articles from decades of assaults upon the keyboard should have brought me satisfaction. Instead the drill has been painful: It rubbed my snout in my failure to change the minds that mattered in our government or at the upper ranks of our military. Reviewing thousands of pages of efforts to make a difference drove home how futile it is to attempt to interest Washington without a corporate checkbook.

My writing prospered in the marketplace, while being reviled by all the right people. Soldiers and Marines at the action level valued it, and both extremes of the political spectrum accused me of belonging to the other. So far, so good. But no sculpted sentences, serious analysis, or firsthand evidence could persuade a prospering, self-congratulatory establishment that the world might not conform to its desires. The hallmark of our diplomats and generals in my time has been the refusal to think honestly about the transformations of our age; the first have not moved much beyond the Congress of Vienna, and the second dream of refighting bygone wars with shiny new toys. Whether Taliban hillbillies or Georgetown graduates, men cling to what they know. And much that Washington "knows" is bluntly wrong. But the price of our leaders' illusions is paid by others: In our time, when diplomats blunder or generals lose their wars, the consequence is promotion and a book deal. Why should they change?

When there are no penalties for playing it safe and failing, there are few incentives to take bold steps to win: A military that can go through a decade of wars without losing a single general on the battlefield isn't much of a fighting organization.

We are governed from a city built on a swamp, where, despite superficial partisan divides, conformity is valued above all: New ideas mortify. Faced with revolutions and counterrevolutions around the world, our leaders and their acolytes cling to the *ancien regime*, confident that they themselves won't face the guillotine. As I write these lines, yet another wave of crises—the flash-mob revolutions in the Middle East and North Africa—leave our government bewildered and behind: *Those* people weren't supposed to act like that. But the truth is that our leaders did not even know who "those people" were.

In the midst of postmodern wars against men of premodern mentality, we dare not even name our enemies accurately. In Washington, from the Department of Justice to the Central Intelligence Agency, there are no such creatures as "Islamist terrorists." Religions that have endured for thousands of years, outlasting countless empires and deciding the fates of billions, are deemed to have no grip on human affairs. Discussing religion is . . . awkward. So our leaders pretend faith away.

Faced with opponents who sacrifice the innocent to their god, our generals study atheist guerrillas. To cope with fanatical killers with global ambitions, we turn to courts of law meant for common criminals. Pirates terrorize shipping lanes, while we wring our hands over their legal status. And all parties on the Potomac still insist that stability can be assured by supporting tyrants and that infernally corrupt governments are bound to reform if only we treat them respectfully. We mouth admirable principles for which we won't lift a finger.

If we must be hypocrites, we should at least apply some intelligence to the task.

As a soldier, then as a civilian, it has been my fate to watch defense contractors rob the taxpayer, abetted by pliant legislators and swinish retired generals who value golf-club memberships above the lives of our troops. I stand by my remark of two decades ago: "Our military could defeat any other military, but we can't beat Lockheed Martin." As for outsourcing military tasks to the defense industry, it's been a cancer, not a cure. Watching the occupation of Iraq turn into a looting orgy for American contractors may have been the most disheartening public experience of my life. We paid civilian thugs to murder jaywalkers.

The intelligence world, in which I worked for years, was always sluggish. Of late, though, it has gone into reverse gear, with timid managers insisting that analysts must footnote the future before it can be briefed to decision makers. Undervaluing humans, we continue to chase technologies to address a global crisis of the soul. No satirist could better lampoon our intelligence chiefs than they do themselves.

We buy military junk based on doctored threat assessments. Serious intelligence work is squelched in favor of studies so bland they cannot be challenged. Think tanks avoid thought. Legislators from both parties praise our troops, then pander to defense contractors. Washington's revolving door is made of solid platinum. And the raucous world beyond our shores, brimming with dangers and opportunities, goes ignored except when it explodes. Our leaders have made art forms of ignorance and greed.

For me, writing is a compulsion, not a choice, and I'm grateful for the extraordinary opportunities I've had to publish: I've had my say, and the rest was up to others. Still I can't help regretting that the warning flags a number of us raised over the decades went resolutely ignored. And our soldiers died, committed to ill-conceived missions that, even if improbably successful, would change nothing for the better. Even when we did great things, such as deposing Saddam Hussein, we did them poorly. The world is hungry, angry, passionate, hopeful, frightened, and anxious for us to live up to our professed values. Our answer is to build outhouses in Afghanistan.

I still have great faith in the United States of America: We will continue to be the dominant power throughout the twenty-first century. But we suffer a crisis of leadership that goes beyond party politics or service affiliations. We are led by men of more ambition than virtue, of tremendous energy and cramped imaginations. Our wealth and power permit their mediocrity.

I always wrote what I believed to be true, without regard for reward, approval, or penalty. As for the enduring value of the work, the reader may judge.

—Ralph Peters
February 25, 2011

The New Warrior Class

Parameters

Summer 1994

The soldiers of the U.S. Army are brilliantly prepared to defeat other soldiers. Unfortunately, the enemies we are likely to face through the rest of this decade and beyond will not be "soldiers," with the disciplined modernity that term conveys in Euro-America, but "warriors"—erratic primitives of shifting allegiance, habituated to violence, with no stake in civil order. Unlike soldiers, warriors do not play by our rules, do not respect treaties, and do not obey orders they do not like. Warriors have always been around, but with the rise of professional soldieries, their importance was eclipsed. Now, thanks to a unique confluence of breaking empire, overcultivated Western consciences, and a worldwide cultural crisis, the warrior is back, as brutal as ever and distinctly better armed.

The primary function of any civilization is to restrain human excess, and even Slavic socialism served a civilizing mission in this regard. But as the restraints of contemporary civilization recede and noncompetitive cultures fracture, victim-states often do not have the forces, and the self-emasculated West does not possess the will, to control the new warrior class arising in so many disparate parts of the world. We have entered an age in which entire nations are subject to dispossession, starvation, rape, and murder on a scale approaching genocide—not at the hands of a conquering foreign power but under the guns of their neighbors. Paramilitary warriors—thugs whose talent for violence blossoms in civil war—defy legitimate governments and increasingly end up leading governments they have overturned. This is a new age of warlords, from Somalia to Colombia, from Afghanistan to the Balkans. In Georgia an ex-convict became a kingmaker, and in Azerbaijan a warlord who marched on the capital with a handful of wheezing armored vehicles briefly became prime minister. In Chechnya, on the northern slopes of the Caucasus, a renegade general carved out the world's first state run entirely by gangsters—not the figurative gangsters of high Stalinism, but genuine black marketeers, murderers, drug dealers, and pimps—and then his tribal followers defeated the Russian army. Their warriors are the source of power for such chieftains, and the will of the populace, enervated and fickle, matters little when it matters at all.

This essay briefly considers who these new warriors are in terms of their social and psychological origins and examines the environment in which they operate. The objective is to provide an intellectual passport into the warrior's sullen world for U.S. military officers and defense analysts, who, given their cultural and professional conditioning, would much rather deal with more conventional threats. This is an alert message from a very dark place.

Most warriors emerge from five social pools that exist in some form in all significant cultures. These pools produce warriors who differ in their individual implacability and redeemability. This differentiation is key to understanding warriors—who outwardly may appear identical to one another—and helps identify human centers of gravity within warrior bands or movements.

First-pool warriors come, as they always have, from the underclass (although their leaders often have fallen from the upper registers of society). The archetype of the new warrior class is a male who has no stake in peace, a loser with little education, no legal earning power, no abiding attractiveness to women, and no future. With gun in hand and the spittle of nationalist ideology dripping from his mouth, today's warrior murders those who once slighted him, seizes the women who avoided him, and plunders that which he would never otherwise have possessed. Initially, the totemic effect of a uniform, however shabby and incomplete, and the half-understood rhetoric of a cause lend him a notion of personal dignity he never sensed before, but his dedication to the cause is rarely as enduring as his taste for spoils. He will, however, cling to his empowering military garb. For the new warrior class, many of whose members possess no skills marketable in peacetime, the end of fighting means the end of the good times.

The longer the fighting continues, the more irredeemable this warrior becomes. And as society's preparatory structures such as schools, formal worship systems, communities, and families are disrupted, young males who might otherwise have led productive lives are drawn into the warrior milieu. These form a second pool. For these boys and young men, deprived of education and orientation, the company of warriors provides a powerful behavioral framework. These are the foot soldiers of the expanding revolution or insurrection, the masses in the streets, yet their commitment, initially at least, is the weakest. Although some second-pool warriors can ultimately be gathered back into society, their savagery increases with the duration and intensity of the conflict. The average warrior who takes up a Kalashnikov at age thirteen is probably not going to settle down to finish out his secondary school education ten years later without a powerful incentive.

The third pool contains the opportunists, the entrepreneurs of conflict, whose great strength is their cynicism. When it is profitable or otherwise advantageous, they may speak beautifully of the greater cause—but their real cause is their personal gain in power, money, influence, and security. Although such men can often be "converted" by a display or application of power, they will be your allies only as long as you are strong, strict, evidently committed for the duration, and intrusive. In their own cultural context, these men generally possess the best and most varied intelligence networks of all the warrior groups, since they are not constrained by faction or even local morality. They will even operate beyond the blood ties of family, clan, or tribe that often limit the effectiveness and broader appeal of warrior groups. They are masters of timing and surprise. Often touched with a dark genius, these chameleons are immeasurably dangerous—and the most likely type of warrior to be underestimated as mere criminals or vulnerably corrupt. When the interest of Western actors fades, their lack of core values and sense of maneuver can leave these third-pool warriors—true warlords—in control of cities, regions, and entire countries after the men of conviction have served their purpose and been killed by us or through betrayals.

The fourth pool of warriordom consists of the patriots. These may be men who fight out of strong beliefs in ethnic, religious, or national superiority, or those who have suffered personal loss in the course of a conflict that motivates them to take up arms. Although these warriors are the easiest to reintegrate into civil structures—especially if their experience of violence is relatively brief—some of these men, too, will develop a taste for blood and war's profits (all of the warrior pools, or categories, are porous, and men can float between them or manifest multiple characteristics simultaneously). These "patriotic" warriors are the most individualized psychologically, and their redeemability depends on character, cultural context, and the depth of any personal loss, as well as on standard characteristics such as goal achievement in their conflict and perceived postwar opportunities for jobs and other societal rewards. Even when they are our enemies, they are heroes to their kind, and many a Western military policy has foundered on our inability to see the appeal of the upright man who hates us and who is willing to kill or be killed to drive us from his tormented land.

Dispossessed, cashiered, or otherwise failed military men form the fifth and most immediately dangerous pool of warriors. Officers, NCOs, or just charismatic privates who could not function in a traditional military environment, or who have emerged from a dissolving military establishment, these men bring other warriors the rudiments of the military art—just enough to inspire faith and encourage folly in many cases, although the fittest of these men become the warrior chieftains or warlords with whom we must finally cope on the battlefield, or in the jungles, streets, and sewers. These warriors are especially dangerous, not only because their skills heighten the level of bloodshed, but also because they provide a nucleus of internationally available mercenaries or gunmen for future conflicts. Given that most civil wars begin with the actions of a small fraction of the population (less than 1 percent might actively participate in or support the initial violence), any impassioned assembly of militants with cash will be able to recruit mercenary forces with ease and spark "tribal" strife that will make the brutality of Africa in the 1960s seem like some sort of Quaker peaceable kingdom.

The mercenary trend is also on the rise in Western employ, and the advent of butchers' bands masked as corporations, from Eurasia to South Africa, demands constant scrutiny. A logo and a business card do not legitimize international murder.

Paradoxically, while the warrior seeks to hold society out of equilibrium for his own profit, he thus prevents society from offering him any alternative to the warrior life. In our century of massive postwar demobilizations, most receiving governments retained sufficient structure to absorb and assist their ex-soldiers. Helpfully, the soldiers of the great armies of the West rarely tasted war's spoils as does the warrior; rather, soldiers experienced war's sacrificial side. But the broken states in which warriors currently control the balance of power do not have the infrastructure to receive veterans and help them rebuild their lives. In many cases, the warrior's roots have been torn up, and since he is talented only at violence, his loyalty has focused on his warlord, his band of fellow warriors, or, simply, on himself. Even if the miracle of peace should descend permanently on the ruins of Yugoslavia, Liberia, Lebanon, Cambodia, or El Salvador, the survivor states will be unable to constructively absorb all the warriors who have fallen away from civilized norms—and the warriors themselves often have no real interest in being absorbed. In the Caucasus and Afghanistan, in Nicaragua, Haiti, and Sri Lanka, warriors without wars will create problems for a generation, if not longer.

In the centuries before the rise of modern professional armies, the European world often faced the problem of the warrior deprived of war. In the sixteenth century—another age of shattered belief systems—disbanded imperial armies spread syphilis and banditry across the continent, and the next century's Thirty Years War— waged largely by warriors and not by soldiers as we know them—saw the constant disbanding and re-formation of armies, with the *Soldateska* growing ever more vicious, unruly, and merciless. Arguably modern Europe's greatest trauma, the Thirty Years War formally ended in 1648, but its warriors continued to disrupt the continent until they found other wars in which to die, were hacked to death by vengeful peasants, or were hunted down like beasts by authorities who finally had caught their breath. Today's warriors have a tremendous advantage over their antique brethren in the struggle for survival, however: the West's pathetic, if endearing, concern for human life, even when that life belongs to a murderer of epic achievement.

For the U.S. soldier, vaccinated with moral and behavioral codes, the warrior is a formidable enemy. Euro-American soldiers in general learn a highly stylized, ritualized form of warfare, with both written and customary rules. We are at our best fighting organized soldieries that attempt a symmetrical response. But warriors respond asymmetrically, leaving us in the role of redcoats marching into an Indian-dominated wilderness. Despite the valiant and skilled performance of the U.S. Army Rangers, our most significant combat encounter in Mogadishu looked much like Braddock's defeat. Russian regulars were first "Little Big Horned" in Tajikistan by tribesmen who slipped across the Afghan border, then Moscow's draftees and professionals alike were massacred in the streets of Grozniy by archetypal warriors. The asymmetries of conflict in Northern Ireland cancered the British military for three decades, and peace is yet a fragile hope. Around the world, conventional military establishments are discovering their limitations.

While the U.S. Army could rapidly devastate any band of warriors on a battlefield, few warlords would be foolish enough to accept such a challenge. Warriors usually stand and fight only when they know or believe that they have an overwhelming advantage. Instead they snipe, ambush, mislead, and betray, attempting to fool the constrained soldiers confronting them into alienating the local population or allies, while otherwise simply hunkering down and trying to outlast the organized military forces pitted against them. U.S. soldiers are unprepared for the absolute mercilessness of which modern warriors are capable, and they are discouraged or prohibited by their civilian masters and their own customs from taking the kind of measures that might be effective against members of the warrior class.

The U.S. experience with warriors in Somalia was not a happy one, but the disastrous UN experience in Yugoslavia was worse. Imagining that they could negotiate with governments to control warrior excesses, the United Nations and other well-intentioned organizations pleaded with the men in suits in Belgrade, Zagreb, and Sarajevo to come to terms with one another. But the war in Bosnia and adjacent regions had degenerated to a point where many local commanders obeyed only orders that flattered them. It took a local military shift—a far more important factor than NATO aircraft—to bring an exhausted pause to the fighting. Now American soldiers patrol a landscape made safe for ethnic cleansing and belatedly hunt down warriors to bring them to court years after their excesses. Even if our efforts succeed beyond reasonable expectation, gunmen, gangs, and black marketeers will haunt the Balkan passes and urban alleys for years to come.

On the West Bank of the Jordan and in Gaza, the newly legitimized Palestinian authorities face formidable problems with two lost generations, unskilled or deskilled, whose heroes answer offers of dialogue with terror and for whom compromise appears equivalent to prostitution. Without the Intifada, many Palestinians, from teenagers to the chronologically mature, have no core rationale for their lives. At a virtually immeasurable cultural remove, Irish Republican Army terrorists remain heroes for men and women who prefer a lush myth of the past to the sober demands of the future. In Sri Lanka, many Tamil rebels will never be able to return to productive lives in a settled society—nor will many of the Khmer Rouge, Kashmiri separatists, Peruvian narco-Marxists, Mexican drug "cowboys," Angola's UNITA rebels, or any of Africa's other clan-based warriors masquerading behind the rank and trappings of true soldiers. Even in the United States, urban gang members exhibit warrior traits and may be equally impossible to reconcile to civilized order as it is generally valued in Euro-America. For the warrior, peace is the least desirable state of affairs, and he is inclined to fight on in the absence of a direct, credible threat to his life. As long as the warrior believes that he can survive on the outside of any new peace, he will view a continuation of warfare through criminal means as the most attractive alternative. And there is good reason for the warrior to decline to lay down his arms—the most persistent and ruthless warriors ultimately receive the best terms from struggling governments. Indeed, they sometimes manage to overthrow those governments and seize power when the governments tumble into crisis after failing to deliver fundamental welfare and security to the population.

In addition to those warriors whose educations—however rudimentary—were interrupted, men who fall into the warrior class in adulthood often find their new situation far more pleasant than the manual labor for subsistence wages or chronic unemployment to which peace had condemned them. The warrior milieu allows pathetic misfits to lead lives of waking fantasy and remarkable liberties. Unlike organized militaries, paramilitary bands do not adhere to rigorous training schedules, and when they need privies, they simply roust out the locals at gunpoint and tell them where to dig. In the Yugoslav ruins, for instance, many of the patriotic volunteers (identical, whether Serb, Croat, or Bosnian Muslim) found that war gave them leisure, choice, and recognition, as well as a camaraderie they had never known in the past. The unemployed *Lumpenproletarier* from Mostar or Belgrade could suddenly identify with the action-video heroes he and his comrades admired between raids on villages where only women, children, and old men remained.

In Armenia, during a period of crisis for Nagorno-Karabakh, I encountered a local volunteer who had dyed his uniform black and proudly wore a large homemade swastika on his breast pocket, even though his people had suffered this century's first genocide. The Russian mercenaries who rent out their resentment over failed lives almost invariably seek to pattern themselves after Hollywood heroes, and even Somalia's warlords adorned themselves with Anglo nicknames such as "Jess" or "Morgan." This transfer of misunderstood totems between cultures has a vastly more powerful negative effect on our world than the accepted logic of human behavior allows. But then, we have entered an age of passion and illogic, an era of the rejection of "scientific" order. That is exactly what the pandemic of nationalism and fundamentalism is about. We are in an instinctive, intuitive phase of history, and such times demand common symbols that lend identity and reduce the need for more intellectualized forms of communication. Once warriors wore runic marks or crosses on their tunics—today they wear T-shirts with Madonna's image (it is almost too obvious to observe that one madonna seems to be as good as another for humanity). If there were two cultural artifacts in any given bunker in the Bosnian hills, they were likely to be a blond nude tear-out and a picture of Sylvester Stallone as Rambo. Many warriors, guilty of unspeakable crimes, develop such a histrionic self-image that they will drop just about any task to pose for a journalist's camera—the photograph is a totem of immortality in the warrior's belief system, which is why warriors sometimes take the apparently illogical step of allowing snapshots of their atrocities. In Renaissance Europe (and Europe may yet find itself in need of another renaissance), the typical *Landsknecht* wanted money, loot, women, and drink. His modern counterpart also wants to be a star. Worldwide, the new warrior class already numbers in the millions. If the current trend toward state softening continues, the opening decades of the new millennium may see more of these warriors than soldiers in legitimate armies in the struggling regions of the world. Although exact figures will never be available, and statistics junkies can quibble endlessly as to how many warriors are really out there, the forest looks dark and ominous enough without counting each last tree. And perhaps the worst news comes right out of *Macbeth*: The trees are moving.

Warrior-mercenaries always moved. Irishmen fought for France and Hungary, Scots for Sweden and France, and Germans sold their unwashed sword arms to everyone from Palermo to Poland. Swiss mercenaries still guard the pope. But today's improved methods of travel allow warriors deprived of "their" war to fly or drive to the next promising misfortune. Mujahedeen from Afghanistan, so recently adored by Americans, have turned up in Azerbaijan, and Russian brawlers with military educations have fought in Bosnia, Croatia, Georgia, Nagorno-Karabakh, Tajikistan, Africa, and Latin America and as enforcers for the internationalizing Russian mafia. One of the most intriguing characters I met in the Caucasus was an ethnic Armenian citizen of Lebanon who had been trained by the PLO in the Bekaa Valley to fight Turkic Azeris in Karabagh. The Azeri warriors he faced had been trained by entrepreneurial Russians and exasperated Turks, and reportedly by Iranians and Israelis. In Bosnia, mustered-out Warsaw Pact soldiers served in the same loosely organized units as adventure-seeking Germans and Frenchmen. Yugoslavia and the wars on Russia's crumpled frontiers have been vast training grounds for the warriors who will not be content without a conflict somewhere. While most warriors will attempt to maintain their privileges of violence on their own territory, within their own linguistic groups, the overall number of warriors is growing so quickly that even a small percentage migrating from trouble spot to trouble spot could present a destabilizing factor with which we have yet to reckon.

The U.S. Army will fight warriors far more often than it fights soldiers in the future. This does not mean that the Army should not train to fight other organized militaries—they remain the most lethal, although not the most frequent, threat. But it would be foolish not to recognize and study the nasty little men who will haunt the brutal little wars we will be called upon to fight within the career span of virtually every officer reading this text.

There are quite a few realistic steps we might take to gain a better grasp on these inevitable, if unwanted, opponents. First, we should begin to build an aggregate database that is not rigidly compartmented by country and region. We may deploy to the country where Warlord X has carved out his fief, or we may meet him or his warriors on the soil of a third-party state. The future may create allegiances and alliances that will confound us, but if we start now to identify likely players, that drab, laborious, critical labor may pay significant dividends one day. As a minimum, if we start files on warrior chieftains now, we will have richer background files on a number of eventual heads of state. Such a database will be a tough sell in a time of shrinking staffs and disappearing budgets, and analysts, accustomed to the luxury of intellectual routine, will rebel against its challenge and uncertainty. But in practical terms, studying potential opponents of this nature now will pay off on two counts: First, when we fight, we will be more likely to know whom we're fighting; second, the process of compiling such a database will build human expertise in this largely neglected field.

We also need to struggle against our American tendency to focus on hardware and bean counting and attack the more difficult and subtle problems posed by human behavior and regional history. For instance, to begin to identify the many fuses under the Caucasus powder keg, you have to understand that Christian Armenians, Muslim (and other) Kurds, and Arabs ally together because of their mutual legacy of hatred toward Turks. The Israelis support Turkic peoples because Arabs support the Christians (and because the Israelis are drawn to Caspian oil). The Iranians see the Armenians as allies against the Turks but are torn because Azeri Turks are Shi'a Muslims. And the Russians want everybody out who doesn't "belong." Many of these alignments surprise U.S. planners and leaders because we don't study the hard stuff. If electronic collection means can't acquire it, we pretend we don't need it—until we find ourselves in downtown Mogadishu with everybody shooting at us.

We need to commit more of our training time to warrior threats. But first we need to ask ourselves some difficult questions. Do we have the strength of will, as a military and as a nation, to defeat an enemy who has nothing to lose? When we face warriors, we will often face men who have acquired a taste for killing, who do not behave rationally according to our definition of rationality, who are capable of atrocities that challenge the descriptive powers of language, and who will sacrifice their own kind in order to survive. We will face opponents for whom treachery is routine, and they will not be impressed by tepid shows of force with restrictive rules of engagement. Are we able to engage in and sustain the level of sheer violence it can take to eradicate this kind of threat? Recent experience says no. Yet that answer may prove transient as administrations change and nontraditional threats multiply.

Although there are nearly infinite variations, the warrior threat generally requires a two-track approach—an active campaign to win over the populace, coupled with irresistible violence directed against the warlords and the warriors. You cannot bargain or compromise with warriors. You cannot "teach them a lesson" (unless you believe that Saddam Hussein or General Aideed learned anything worthwhile from our fecklessness in the clinch). You either win or you lose. This kind of warfare is a zero-sum game. And it takes guts to play.

Combatting warriors will force us to ask fundamental questions about ourselves as well as about our national and individual identities and values. But the kind of warfare we are witnessing now and will see increasingly in the future raises even more basic issues, challenging many of the assumptions in which Western culture indulges. The breakdown of Yugoslavia alone raised issues that have challenged philosophers and college freshmen since the first professor faced a lecture hall. What is man's nature? Are we really the children of Rousseau and of Benetton ads, waiting only for evil governments to collapse so that our peaceable, cotton-candy natures can reveal themselves? Or are we killing animals self-organized into the disciplinary structures of civilization because the alternative is mutual, anarchic annihilation? What of all that self-hobbling rhetoric about the moral equivalency of all cultures? Isn't it possible that a culture (or religion or form of government) that provides a functional combination of individual and collective security with personal liberties really does deserve to be taken more seriously than and emulated above a culture that glorifies corruption, persecutes nonbelievers, lets gunmen rule, and enslaves its women? Is all human life truly sacred, no matter what crimes the individual or his collective may commit?

Until we are able to answer such questions confidently, the members of the new warrior class will simply laugh at us and keep on killing.

The Culture of Future Conflict

Parameters

Winter 1995–96

The computer will not replace the book, and postmodern forms of conflict will not fully replace conventional war. We will, however, experience a bewildering expansion of the varieties of collective and factional violence. The computer expands our possibilities and alters methods of working and organizing. So, too, the worldwide crisis in systems of social organization and belief broadens the range of challenges to global, regional, and local order. States and military establishments that restrict their preparations, initiatives, and responses to traditional patterns will pay for their fear of the future in blood, money, and quality of life.

Although man and his failings will remain at the center of war and conflict, a unique combination of factors will precipitate and shape events. At least into the seventeenth century, Western man believed that planetary and stellar conjunctions were responsible for disasters on the earth. Today, we face a constellation of crises much closer to home with profound strategic and military implications. The warning comet is already with us as we approach a dark new century.

Future wars and violent conflicts will be shaped by the inabilities of governments to function as effective systems of resource distribution and control, and by the failure of entire cultures to compete in the postmodern age. The worldwide polarization of wealth, afflicting continents and countries, as well as individuals in all countries, will prove insurmountable, and social divisions will spark various forms of class warfare more brutal than anything imagined by Karl Marx. Poststate organizations, from criminal empires to the international- izing media, will rupture the integrity of the nation-state. Niche tech- nologies, such as postmodern means of information manipulation and dissemination, will provoke at least as often as they produce and will become powerful tools of conflict. Basic resources will prove inadequate for populations exploding beyond natural limits, and we may discover truths about ourselves that we do not wish to know. In the end, the greatest challenge may be to our moral order.

The incompetence of the state has been demonstrated along fault lines from the former Yugoslavia and desperate North Korea to Congo/Zaire and Liberia. The "state" as we revere it is a cultural growth and must develop organically—where it has been grafted it rarely takes. The Euro-American and East Asian state's civility as well as its authority rely on expanding wealth, on a perceived com- munity of interests that allows public compromise or acquiescence, and on individual and collective senses of responsibility. In many of the "states" that presently hold seats in the United Nations, per capita wealth is declining, there is no community of interests, nor is there an individual sense of responsibility for the common good. Even in Western states, the vital sense of generalized responsibility is deteriorating as interest groups promote factionalization and citi- zen expectations grow excessive and wantonly selfish.

In many "accidental states" shaped hastily in the recession of empire, state structures survived only through their ability to apply internal violence. Today even these oppressive construct-states are breaking down as burgeoning populations make state-sponsored violence against their own citizens statistically ineffectual. Simulta- neously, thanks largely to the temptress Media, worldwide citizen expectations of government have wildly surpassed the abilities of government to deliver (the gray area between possibilities and needs/wants is the age-old breeding ground of organized crime and political radicalism). This is true of the United States and of Algeria. Fortunately for us in the United States, our government's ability to deliver generally exceeds requirements, if not expecta- tions. In Algeria, government shortcomings have led to a cultural struggle that has engulfed the state and threatens to destroy it.

Cultural failure has many historical precedents, from the collapse of the Hittite empire to the destruction of the Aztecs, but there has never before been a time when a single dominant culture and its imitators have threatened to overwhelm every other major culture on earth. Even in the great age of European empire, most of the conquered peoples remained free to practice their own religions and lifestyles, blissfully unaware of a seductive alternative model. Today, thanks to the distribution of addictively Western films, videos, television, and radio to even the most obscure and hopeless backwaters, there is an unprecedented worldwide awareness of relative physical and cultural poverty within non-Western cultures. Western models of behavior and possession—often misunderstood—create crises of identity and raise appetites that local environments cannot sate. Increasingly, we live in a world where the Flintstones meet the Jetsons—and the Flintstones don't much like it. When they try to imitate our performance, they fail, except in the case of gifted individuals. When they try to secede from the West, they fail again. In the end, there is only rage.

Wealth polarization is worsening after a century of limited progress toward equalization. The United States and a few other adept nation-states have entered a wealth-generation cycle for which there is no predictable end, despite intermittent trade squabbles and recessions. But the nature of postmodern competition is such that membership in this club is closing. Although some disciplined, culturally predisposed states may eventually join the rich West-plus, they will be exceptions. The value of manual and mass labor is plunging in a world of surplus population, while the skills necessary for successful economies and desirable jobs increasingly rely on the total environment in which the individual lives and learns, from infancy forward. In the past, fortunate individuals could jump from premodern to modern. But the gap between premodern and postmodern is too great to be crossed in a single leap. The economically vibrant jobs of the next century will demand "transcendent literacy": the second-nature ability to read, write, think abstractly, and manipulate information electronically. This fateful shift is already creating painful dislocations in our own country and threatens to create an expanded and irredeemable underclass. Its effect on the non-Western world will be to condemn states, peoples, and even continents to enduring poverty.

Social division is the obvious result of the polarization of wealth. Although most of the world's population has always been condemned to poverty, a combination of religious assurance, ignorance of how well others lived, and hope for a better future more often than not curbed man's natural rage at wealth discrepancies. Now the slum dwellers of Lagos are on to the lifestyles of the rich and famous, while hopes of prosperity even for a future generation dwindle. In the West-plus, this bifurcation into skilled and well-off versus unskilled and poor has created archipelagoes of failure in a sea of success. The rest of the world contains only fragile archipelagoes of success in vast, increasingly stormy seas of failure. Occasionally, the failures attack us at home, staging events, such as the World Trade Center bombing, that are as spectacular as they are statistically ineffective. More often, these unmoderns take out their inchoate anger on the nearest targets—rival clans or tribes, citizens of minority religions or ethnicities, or their own crumbling governments. Intermittently, these local rages will aggrieve our extraterritorial welfare—primarily our economic interests—and we will need to intervene. In the twentieth century, the great wars were between ambitious winner-states. In the coming century, the routine conflicts to which we will be party will pit those same winner-states, now reconciled, against vast "loser" populations in failed states and regions.

The rise of the anti-state in various forms has been and will be the result of the failure of governments to cater to basic needs and to satisfy expanding desires. The anti-state can take many forms, from media conglomerates that determine what the world should know, through much-maligned peace-preferring multinational corporations, to webs of criminality expanding across oceans, enterprise disciplines, and cultures. In the world of the anti-state, international criminals often cooperate more effectively and creatively than do states. Criminal enterprise mirrors legitimate enterprise in its focus on secure profits, but its "integrity" exceeds that of the greatest multinationals because the criminal anti-state has a galvanizing enemy: the state fighting for its life. It is in the adaptive nature of the postmodern anti-state that it can develop a symbiotic relationship even with a formal government it strategically penetrates, as criminal anti-state webs have done in Russia, Nigeria, Mexico, and numerous less-spectacular examples.

Anti-states also take the forms of premodern structures, such as tribal or religious identifications. At the high end of development we are witnessing the birth of new "tribes" based on skills, wealth, and cultural preferences. As with the old, enduring tribes, the geographic domain of these new communities rarely matches the contours of existing state borders.

We are entering an era of multidimensional, interpenetrating structures of social control, wealth allocation, and even allegiance. The decline of the state, real or relative, accelerates under *knowledge assault*, as new structures of knowing outpace the ability of traditional governments to process and respond to information. The modern age was the age of mass efficiencies. The postmodern age is the age of mass inefficiencies, wherein bigness equals clumsiness and lethargy. Ours is increasingly an age of neoanarchic "cellular" accomplishment that, at its best, gives us enhanced microchips and, at its worst, turns the world's cities into criminal harbors. Reduced to the fundamentals, we face a conflict between blood ties and knowledge ties. Ours is a world whose constituents may lurch backward as well as forward, but in which nothing can remain unchanged.

Decisive technologies, from the birth control pill to the computer, have exploded traditional forms of organization, behavior, and belief in our lifetimes. Technology can lead to enhanced environmental mastery—but it can also lead to fatal dependencies. The best example of this pits the computer against the television. A skilled computer user is an active "techno-doer." Unless he or she is particularly creative, this computerist is the postmodern blue-collar worker, the new machinist. This computerist adds value in the classic sense enshrined by Marx, Keynes, and Schumpeter. On the other hand, the passive television viewer, especially one possessing a VCR, confuses us because we imagine that he or she is mastering technology. On the contrary, the technology is mastering the human. The passive "techno-user" adds no value and may even lose operative abilities and initiative. This is not an attack on television in general, which can be a powerful tool for the dissemination of information; rather, it is a warning that technology consumers do not necessarily become technologically capable. *A society must produce techno-doers*, and all technologies, active and passive, must find a healthy integrative level. Otherwise, the force of technology is destructive, if deceptively comforting in its amusement value. Dangerous for segments of our own society, this addictive passivity can be fatal to noncompetitive cultures.

Rich issues also arise out of our attempts to redefine "military technology" in the postmodern age, but there is one respect in which all relevant branches of Westernness, from the military through business, are alike. Increasingly, we take our entire environment with us when we go. From techno-gypsies working their laptops in jungle backwaters to the military that fought Desert Storm, we are learning to insulate ourselves as never before from the inefficiencies of the non-West. This is the first, unavoidable step toward an enclavement of our civilization that excludes the noncompetitive.

Resource scarcity will be a direct cause of confrontation, conflict, and war. The struggle to maintain access to critical resources will spark local and regional conflicts that will evolve into the most frequent conventional wars of the next century. Today, the notion of resource wars leads the Westerner to think immediately of oil, but water will be the fundamental need of some states, anti-states, and peoples. We envision a need to preserve rain forests, but expanding populations will increasingly create regional shortages of food—especially when nature turns fickle. We are entering the century of "not enough," and we will bleed for things we once could buy.

Gross overpopulaton will destroy fragile possibilities for progress in much of the non-Western world, and much of this problem is the West's fault. Our well-intentioned introduction of relatively crude concepts of sanitation and disease control, combined with our determination to respond generously to local famines, has allowed populations to explode. Changes in public health so small a Westerner would not notice them can have spectacular effects in underdeveloped societies. For instance, reductions in infant mortality can occur swiftly, but it takes generations for societies to adjust to the value-challenging concept of family planning—and some refuse to adjust. Thus, populations increase geometrically as behavior lags behind technology. These population increases lead to greater urbanization, as the countryside and traditional structures cannot support the additional surviving offspring and the city appears to offer economic opportunity and a more attractive lifestyle. But few economies outside of the West-plus can create jobs as quickly as they are creating job seekers. Even rates of economic growth that sound remarkable leave Third World countries with ever-greater unemployed and underemployed masses. The result is an even further breakdown of traditional structures and values. In the end, the only outlet for a lifetime's frustration is violence.

Present and future plagues are the current nightmares of choice on the bestseller lists and movie screens of the United States. The general scenario has a new disease exploding out of its previously isolated lair in the Third World and hopping a flight to Gringoland, where it behaves with the random destructiveness of an inner-city teenager. Certainly, this is a plausible scenario, and one against which we must guard. But the real threat to this planet's future may be just the opposite: Disease is one of nature's many corrective mechanisms. *Our battle against disease may prove too successful,* resulting in populations that the earth's resources cannot sustain and precipitating literally endless human misery and conflict. Whereas the pandemics of the past were tragic for countless individuals, they were only rarely tragic for societies or cultures—and never for mankind as a whole. Indeed, epidemic disease may have been our dark, unrecognized friend, not only as a population regulator but also as a catalyst for dynamic change. Certainly there has never been a single disease, not even the oft-cited Black Death, that seriously threatened to wipe out mankind—only human beings know how to do that.

So what does it all mean? There will be fewer classic wars but more violence. While conventional war will remain the means of last resort to resolve interstate confrontations, the majority of conflicts will be asymmetrical, with a state or coalition of states only one of the possible participants. The rise of nonstate threats is a tremendous problem for Western governments and militaries, because we are legally and behaviorally prepared to fight only other legal-basis states—mirror images of ourselves—at a time when state power and substance are declining worldwide.

"Survivalists" in North America have it exactly wrong. While they fear a metastasizing, increasingly intrusive, globalizing state, the world is fracturing, and our own government has less control over the behavior of its citizens than at any time during the twentieth century. *The survivalists fear excessive lawfulness, when the problem is exploding lawlessness*—or the inability to enforce existing laws. While our state occasionally falters, foreign states are collapsing, and we face constituencies of the damned, of the hopeless, from whose midst arise warrior classes for whom peace is the least rewarding human condition. As we in the West enter the postmodern age, much of the non-West (starting at the borders of the former Yugoslavia) looks like the Trojan War with machine guns and, perhaps eventually, with nuclear weapons.

What will future conflicts look like? Traditional forms of warfare will remain, with the Middle East and the Asian landmass as their primary cockpit, but these conventional wars will be supplemented with new and hybrid forms of conflict. *Civil wars*—usually distinctly uncivil in their conduct—are a growth industry, as cultures and societies attempt to resolve their threatened, globally incompetent identities. Although these civil wars will intermittently threaten Western interests, rule-bound military interventions will not be able to bring them to closure. Today many human societies are cultural ecosystems striving to regain equilibrium, often through gruesome civil wars. The introduction of powerful foreign elements only further upsets the equilibrium and guarantees exaggerated bloodshed after the intervening power has withdrawn.

Dying states will resort to violence against their own populations in last-gasp efforts to maintain power, spawning expanded insurgencies. Elsewhere, state inefficiencies and the lack of ethnic or cultural harmony will spark revolts and terrorism. Massive criminal insurgencies are a new method of challenging the state through violence. In Southeast Asia's Golden Triangle and in the Andean Ridge, drug-lord insurgencies moved from defying laws to denying great tracts of territory to the state. In Russia, a confluence between organized crime and government in lucrative spheres constitutes a quiet criminal coup. Nigerian criminality looks to exceed oil income as the primary revenue of the state in the future. In the past, insurgencies were easy to recognize—the rebels marched on the presidential palace. Today, some of the most threatening criminal insurgencies in the non-West will be conducted by officials already *inside* the presidential palace. We cannot respond to such top-down insurgencies under international codes of law designed for a world run by Woodrow Wilsons.

Aftermath instability is already a pernicious problem and will worsen. In the wake of high-level agreements to resolve conflicts, most broken states or territories cannot reabsorb the human detritus left behind by waves of violence. With a previously inadequate infrastructure further degraded by conflict, even individuals who desire to live in peace often cannot find shelter or adequate food, much less employment. For those who have become habituated to violence and its quick rewards, postconflict societies often have nothing to offer that can wean these warriors back to constructive patterns of behavior. As populations expand and hatreds deepen, we will find that, although a swift, determined military intervention may bring a formal end to some conflicts, informal conflict will persist indefinitely, destroying any hopes for local societal healing.

Intercultural struggles, with their unbridled savagery, are the great nightmare of the next century, and a great deal has been written about them, either warning of the "Clash of Civilizations" à la Huntington or, in outraged, well-intentioned responses, assuring us that everybody will get along just fine if the West sends money. While we may dread the moral and practical issues that intercultural competition poses, this struggle is already upon us, with parties hostile to the West forcing the issue to the extent of their still-limited competencies. If present conflicts evolve toward open warfare, this could be the defining struggle of the next century—as ideological competition was for the twentieth century. The question is whether we can manage such conflicts with nonmilitary means or whether they will deepen and spread until they require a general military response. At present, it appears likely that our military will find itself drawn into intercultural struggles in future decades—if only because it will be impossible to appease challengers bent on supplanting us, punishing us, or destroying us. If there is a single power the West underestimates, it is the power of collective hatred.

Cataclysm response will continue to demand military participation. Traditional natural disasters, short of world plagues, are ultimately manageable and do not fatally divert military resources. Man-made cataclysms are another matter. Even peacekeeping is a form of cataclysm response—and a very expensive one. Further, the proliferation and terrible condition of nuclear facilities in much of the Northern Hemisphere make Chernobyl look like a precedent rather than an anomaly. We also will see a growing cross-fertilization between cataclysm and conflict, with one feeding on or aggravating the other. Whereas past wars often spread famine or plague in their wakes, we may be entering a period of renewed spoils-taking or even wars of annihilation. From Kuwait to Rwanda, the comfortable modern boundaries between man-made and natural disasters have already begun to break down in postmodern confusion.

The strategic military implications are clear—at least in part. But those implications can be more easily discussed than practically addressed. First we will see an *expeditionary West*, condemned to protect its distant interests. Given our finite resources, we will have to weigh national interests against human interests, asking ourselves whether to intervene for humanitarian reasons and whether our national interests may be contrary to non-Western human interests. We are not going to get off easily in the conscience department. We often will have to redefine victory in an era of unwinnable wars and conflicts. Sometimes the dilemma will be whether there is an advantage to an intervention that only delays resolution. We may have to recast traditional military roles when faced with criminal insurgencies or foreign corruption so wildly out of control it threatens our national interests. We will face a dangerous temptation to seek purely technological responses to behavioral challenges—especially given the expense of standing forces. Our cultural strong suit is the ability to balance and integrate the technological with the human, and we must continue to stress getting that balance right. We must beware of wonder weapons that offer no significant advantage in a changing world.

There are practical military considerations as well. We will fight men who do not look, think, or act like us, and this can lead to a dangerous dehumanizing of the enemy, just as it will make it more difficult for us to understand him. We will fight in cities, and this brutal, casualty-prone, dirty kind of combat will negate many of our technological advantages while it strains our physical and moral resources. Technology will continue to pile up new wonders, but we will find that there are sharp limits to what technology can add to our effectiveness in asymmetrical conflicts. The quality of leaders and soldiers will become even more important as we fight in smaller increments, whether on an "empty" postmodern battlefield or in the overcrowded, dysfunctional cities of failing states. We will encounter unprecedented densities of noncombatants stranded in the maelstrom of urban combat. And we will try, whenever possible, to cocoon our forces in "movable fortresses"—not classic fortresses with physical walls but transferred environments with electronic, missile, and fire barriers, antiseptic support environments, and impenetrable information structures. This will work best in conventional warfare, but our efficacy in setting the terms of involvement will deteriorate the farther down the scale of organized conflict we must descend. No matter how hard we try to take our world with us, we will still find that we sometimes must fight the enemy on his ground, by his rules. This is the hardest form of combat for the United States, because our own rules cripple us and, at worst, kill us.

The new century will bring new weapons, and some of those weapons will bring moral dilemmas. For example, suppose that discoveries in fields as seemingly diverse as evolutionary biology, neurology, complexity studies, advanced sonics, computerization, and communications allowed us to create a "broadcast weapon" that could permanently alter human behavior without causing physical harm. We would immediately face protests from concerned parties to whom it would, paradoxically, be more humane to kill an enemy than to interfere with his or her free will.

Other new weapons will require the military to expand its skill range, and leader-to-led ratios will need to be increased in favor of low-level leaders, because of the new skills required by technological advances and because of the compartmentalization effect of urban combat and the dispersion of the conventional battlefield. The oldest forms of warfare, such as in-close individual combat, will coexist with over-the-horizon cyberspace attacks. And again and again, we will face well-intentioned interlocutors who insist that, since the military never did that, it shouldn't be allowed to do it now. An enduring tension between expanding missions and traditional strictures will hamper military operations. We will face repeated situations in which we are asked to send our soldiers into conflicts for which they have been physically well trained but in which the rules we impose on them leave them practically defenseless. We must learn as a country to identify that which we truly need to achieve, and then to assess honestly the necessary means of getting to that achievement. It is the duty of our military leadership to inform that debate.

What will our twenty-first-century world look like? For the successful, it will be an age of nontraditional empires. The United States in particular, and the West in general, currently possesses a cultural and business empire that touches all parts of the globe. It is far more efficient and rewarding than any previous form of empire has been. The Russian Federation is trying to build an empire on the cheap, in a less benign form, in which regional political, military, economic, and resource hegemony takes the place of large armies of occupation, waves of colonization, and expensive local administrations. Traditional colonies have disappeared not because of liberation ideology but because they were ultimately unprofitable and too difficult to manage. The new empire largely manages itself.

As noncompetitive regions decline, wealth enclaves will emerge, primarily in the West-plus. The "colonies" of the future will be controlled economically and "medially," not politically, and will focus on resources and markets. The political and then the military arms of West-plus governments will become involved only when business encounters disadvantageous illegal behaviors or violence—today the flag follows trade. West-plus governments will police physical and digital "safe corridors" for resource extraction, general trade, and information ranching, but in failed countries and continents, the West-plus will be represented primarily by postmodern traders.

The great dangers that could spark broad conventional wars will be resource competition and cultural confrontations—or a volatile combination of both, which could arise, for instance, in the Persian Gulf–Caspian Sea macroregion. Worldwide social bifurcation will lead increasingly to a triage approach to diplomacy, aid, and interventions, and a sobered West will prove necessarily selective in its military deployments, concentrating on financial interests and lifestyle protection.

By the middle of the next century, if not before, the overarching mission of our military will be the preservation of our quality of life.

Our Soldiers, Their Cities

Parameters

Spring 1996

The future of warfare lies in the streets, sewers, high-rise buildings, industrial parks, and sprawl of houses, shacks, and shelters that form the broken cities of our world. We will fight elsewhere, but not so often, rarely as reluctantly, and never so brutally. Our recent military history is punctuated with city names—Tuzla, Mogadishu, Los Angeles, Beirut, Panama City, Hue, Saigon, Santo Domingo—but these encounters have been but a prologue, with the drama still to come.

We declare that only fools fight in cities and shut our eyes against the future. But in the next century, in an uncontrollably urbanizing world, we will not be able to avoid urban deployments short of war and even full-scale city combat. Cities have always been centers of gravity, but they are now more magnetic than ever before. Once the gatherers of wealth, then the processors of wealth, cities and their satellite communities have become the ultimate creators of wealth. They concentrate people and power, communications and control, knowledge and capability, rendering all else peripheral. They are also the postmodern equivalent of jungles and mountains—citadels of the dispossessed and irreconcilable. A military unprepared for urban operations across a broad spectrum is unprepared for tomorrow.

The U.S. military, otherwise magnificently capable, is an extremely inefficient tool for combat in urban environments. We are not doctrinally, organizationally, or psychologically prepared, nor are we properly trained or equipped, for a serious urban battle, and we must task organize radically even to conduct peacekeeping operations in cities. Romantic and spiritually reactionary, we long for gallant struggles in green fields, while the likeliest "battlefields" are cityscapes where human waste goes undisposed, the air is appalling, and mankind is rotting.

Poor state or rich, disintegrating society or robust culture, a global commonality is that more of the population, in absolute numbers and in percentage, lives in cities. Control of cities has always been vital to military success, practically and symbolically, but in our postmodern environment, in which the wealth of poor regions as well as the defining capabilities of rich states are concentrated in capitals and clusters of production-center cities, the relevance of nonurban terrain is diminishing in strategic, operational, and even tactical importance—except where the countryside harbors critical natural resources. But even when warfare is about resource control, as in America's Gulf War, simply controlling the oil fields satisfies neither side.

The relevant urban centers draw armies for a slew of reasons, from providing legitimacy and infrastructural capabilities, to a magnetic attraction that is more instinctive than rational (perhaps even genetically absorbed at this point in the history of mankind), on to the fundamental need to control indigenous populations—which cannot be done without mastering their urban centers. We are entering a new age of assaults on cities, but one in which the siege techniques would be largely unrecognizable to Mehmet the Conqueror or Vauban, and the parameters incomprehensible to our own greatest conquerors of cities, Ulysses S. Grant and Winfield Scott.

Consider just a few of the potential trouble spots where U.S. military intervention or assistance could prove necessary in the next century: Mexico; Colombia; the subcontinent with an expansionist, nuclear India; the Arabian Peninsula; Brazil; or the urbanizing Pacific Rim. Even though each of these states or regions contains tremendous rural, desert, or jungle expanses, the key to each is control of an archipelago of cities. The largest of these metropolitan areas have populations in excess of twenty million today—more specific figures are generally unavailable as beleaguered governments lose control of their own backyards. Confronted with an armed and hostile population in such an environment, the U.S. Army as presently structured would find it difficult to muster the dismount strength necessary to control a single center as simultaneously dense and sprawling as Mexico City.

Step down from the level of strategic rhetoric about the future, where anyone with self-confidence can make a convincing case for his or her agenda. Survey instead the blunt, practical ways in which urban combat in today's major cities would differ from a sanitary anomaly such as Desert Storm or the never-to-be-fought third European civil war in the German countryside, where we pretended urban combat could be avoided, and for which so much of the equipment presently in our inventory was designed.

At the broadest level, there is a profound spatial difference. "Conventional" warfare has been horizontal, with an increasing vertical dimension. In fully urbanized terrain, however, warfare becomes profoundly vertical, reaching up into towers of steel and cement and downward into sewers, subway lines, road tunnels, communications tunnels, and the like. Even with the "emptying" of the modern battlefield, organizational behavior in the field strives for lateral contiguity and organizational integrity. But the broken spatial qualities of urban terrain fragments units and compartmentalizes encounters, engagements, and even battles. The leader's span of control can easily collapse, and it is very, very hard to gain and maintain an accurate picture of the multidimensional "battlefield."

Noncombatants, without the least hostile intent, can overwhelm the force, and there are multiple players beyond the purely military, from criminal gangs to the media, vigilante and paramilitary factions within militaries, and factions within those factions. The enemy knows the terrain better than the visiting army, and it can be debilitatingly difficult to tell friend from foe from the disinterested. Local combat situations can change with bewildering speed. Atrocity is close-up and commonplace, whether intentional or incidental. The stresses on the soldier are incalculable. The urban combat environment is, above all, disintegrative.

The modern and postmodern trend in Western militaries has been to increase the proportion of tasks executed by machines while reducing the number of soldiers in our establishments. We seek to build machines that enable us to win while protecting or distancing the human operator from the effects of combat. At present, however, urban combat remains extremely manpower intensive—and it is a casualty producer. Although a redirection of research and development efforts toward addressing the requirements of urban combat could eventually raise our efficiency and reduce casualties, machines probably will not dominate urban combat in our lifetimes, and the soldier will remain the supreme weapon. In any case, urban warfare will not require substantial numbers of glamorous big-ticket systems but great multiples of small durables and disposables whose production would offer less fungible profit margins and whose relatively simple construction would open acquisition to genuinely competitive bidding.

Casualties can soar in urban environments. Beyond those inflicted by enemy action, urban operations result in broken bones, concussions, traumatic-impact deaths, and, with the appalling sanitation in many urban environments, a broad range of septic threats. Given the untempered immune systems of many of our soldiers, even patrol operations in sewer systems that did not encounter an enemy could produce debilitating, even fatal, illnesses. One of many potential items of soldier equipment for urban warfare might be antiseptic biosheathing that coats the soldier's body and closes over cuts and abrasions as well as wounds. Any means of boosting the soldier's immune system could prove to be a critical "weapon of war."

Urban warfare differs even in how "minor" items such as medical kits and litters should be structured. Soldiers need new forms of "armor"; equipment as simple as layered-compound knee and elbow pads could dramatically reduce the sort of injuries that, while not life-threatening, can remove soldiers from combat for hours, days, weeks, or even months. Eye protection is essential, given the splintering effects of firefights in masonry and wood environments, and protective headgear should focus as much on accidental blows from falls or collapsing structures as on enemy fire, on preserving the body's structural integrity as much as on protecting against ballistic threats.

Communications requirements differ, too. Soldiers need more comms distributed to lower levels—down to the individual soldier in some cases. Further, because of loss rates in the give-and-take of urban combat, low-level comms gear should not be part of the encrypted command and control network. Radios or other means of communication do not need extended range, but they must deal with terrible reception anomalies. Even a "digitized" soldier, whose every movement can be monitored, will require different display structures in the observing command center. This is the ultimate three-dimensional chessboard at the tactical level.

On the subject of command and control, the individual soldier must be even better trained than at present. He will face human and material distractions everywhere—it will be hard to maintain concentration on the core mission. Soldiers will die simply because they were looking the wrong way, and even disciplined and morally sound soldiers disinclined to rape can lose focus in the presence of female or other civilians whom they feel obliged to protect or who merely add to the human "noise level." The leader-to-led ratio must increase in favor of rigorously prepared low-level leaders. Whereas higher-level command structures may flatten, tactical units must become webs of pyramidal cells capable of extended autonomous behavior in a combat environment where multiple engagements can occur simultaneously and in relative isolation in the same building. Nonsensical arguments about the Wehrmacht making do without so many NCOs and officers on the battlefield must be buried forever; not only is the German military of the last European civil war ancient history, but it lost decisively. Our challenge is to shape the U.S. Army of the twenty-first century.

Personal weapons must be compact and robust, with a high rate of fire and very lightweight ammunition, but there is also a place for shotgun-like weapons at the squad level. Overall, soldier loads must be reduced dramatically at the edge of combat, since fighting in tall buildings requires agility that a soldier unbalanced by a heavy pack cannot attain; further, vertical fighting is utterly exhausting and requires specialized mobility tools. Soldiers will need more upper body strength and will generally need to be more fit—this includes support soldiers as well.

Ideally each infantry soldier would have a thermal or post-thermal imaging capability—since systems that require ambient light are not much good thirty meters below the surface of the earth. Also, an enhanced ability to detect and define sounds could benefit the soldier—although he would have to be well trained to be able to transcend the distracting quality of such systems. Eventually individual soldiers may have tactical equipment that can differentiate between male and female body heat distributions and will even be able to register hostility and intent from smells and sweat. But such devices will not be available for the next several interventions, and we will have to make do for a long time to come with soldiers who are smart, tough, and disciplined.

The roles of traditional arms will shift. Field artillery, so valuable elsewhere, will be of reduced utility—unless the U.S. military were to degenerate to the level of atrocity in which the Russians indulged themselves in Grozniy. Until artillery further enhances accuracy, innovates warheads, and overcomes the laws of ballistic trajectories, it will not have a significant role in urban combat divisions. Because of attack angles and the capabilities of precision munitions, airpower will prove much more valuable and will function as flying artillery. Mortars, however, may be of great use, given their steep trajectories. More accurate and versatile next-generation mortars could be a very powerful urban warfare tool.

The bulk of tactical firepower will need to come from large-caliber, protected, direct-fire weapons. This means tanks, or future systems descended from the tank. Although today's tanks are death traps in urban combat—as the Russians were recently reminded—the need for protected, pinpoint firepower is critical. Instead of concentrating entirely on obsolescent rural warfare, armor officers should be asking themselves how the tank should evolve to fight in tomorrow's premier military environment, the city. First, the "tank" will need more protection, and that protection will need to be distributed differently—perhaps evolving to tuned electronic armor that flows over the vehicle to the threatened spot. Main guns will need to be large caliber, but ideally will be able to fire reduced-caliber ammunition as well, through a "caliber tailoring" system. Crew visibility will need to be greater. The tank will not need to sustain high speeds but will need a sprint capability. Further, the tank will need to be better integrated into local intelligence awareness.

Although the need for plentiful dismounted infantry will endure, those soldiers will intermittently need means for rapid, protected movement. But this does not necessarily mean mechanized infantry; rather, it may demand armored transport centralized at the division level on which the infantry trains, but that does not rob the infantry of manpower in peacetime or in combat.

Engineers will be absolutely critical to urban combat, but they, too, will need evolved tools and skills. The vertical dimension is only part of the challenge. Engineers will need to develop expanded skills, from enabling movement in developed downtown areas to firefighting. Demolition skills will be essential but will be a long way from blowing road craters. Tomorrow's combat engineers may have to drop twenty-story buildings on minimal notice under fire while minimizing collateral damage.

Aviation is vital to mobility, intelligence, and the delivery of focused firepower in urban environments, but as Mogadishu warned us, present systems and tactics leave us highly vulnerable. Rotary-wing aviation for urban combat does not need great range or speed but demands a richer defensive suite, great agility, and increased stealthiness.

Military intelligence must be profoundly reordered to cope with the demands of urban combat. From mapping to target acquisition, from collection to analysis, and from battle damage assessment to the prediction of the enemy's future intent, intelligence requirements are far tougher to meet in urban environments than on traditional battlefields. The utility of the systems that paid off so richly in Desert Storm collapses in urban warfare, and the importance of human intelligence (HUMINT) and regional expertise soars. From language skills to a knowledge of urban planning (or the lack thereof), many of the abilities essential to combat in cities are given low, if any, priority in today's intelligence architecture. Although leaders are aware of these shortfalls, military intelligence is perhaps more a prisoner of inherited Cold War structures than is any other branch—although field artillery and armor are competitive in their unpreparedness for the future.

Military intelligence is at a crossroads today and must decide whether to continue doing the often irrelevant things it does so well or to embrace a realistic future that will demand a better balance between systems and soldiers in a branch particularly susceptible to the lure of dazzling machines. Try templating an irregular enemy unit in urban combat in the center of Lagos after twenty-four hours of contact. This does not mean that high-tech gear and analytical methodologies are useless in urban environments. On the contrary, innovative technologies and organizational principles could make a profound difference in how military intelligence supports urban combat operations. But we would need to shift focus and explore radical departures from the systems we currently embrace.

Military police and civil affairs troops will continue to play the important roles they played in urban interventions during the twentieth century, but psychological operations (PSYOPS) units, long a stepchild, will surge in importance and may ultimately merge fully with military intelligence to enhance synergy and efficiency. Especially given the potential for electronic population control systems in the next century, PSYOPS may function as a combat arm, even if not credited as such.

Even supply is different. While deliveries do not need to be made over great distances, soft vehicles are extremely vulnerable in an environment where it is hard to define a front line and where the enemy can repeatedly emerge in the rear. All soldiers will be fighters, and force and resource protection will be physically and psychologically draining. Urban environments can upset traditional balances between classes of supply. There may be less of a requirement for bulk fuel, but an intervention force may find itself required to feed an urban population or to supply epidemic-control efforts. Artillery and antitank guided missile expenditures might be minimal, while main gun and infantry systems ammunition consumption could be heated. Urban combat breaks individual and crew-served weapons and gear, from rifles to radios, and masonry buildings are even harder on uniforms than on human bones. Soldiers will need replacement uniforms far more often than during more traditional operations. Unfortunately, we also will need more replacement soldiers, and all combat support and combat service support troops are more apt to find themselves shooting back during an urban battle than in any other combat environment.

Where do we begin to prepare for this immediate and growing challenge? There are two powerful steps we ought to take. First, the U.S. Army should designate two active divisions and at least one National Guard division as urban combat divisions and should begin variable restructurings to get the right component mix. Rule one should be that the active divisions are not "experimental" in the sense of nondeployable, but remain subject to short-notice deployment to threatened urban environments. This would put an incredible stress on the unit and, especially, on the chain of command. But today's U.S. Army cannot afford to have any divisions "on ice," and this pressure would drive competence. Two such divisions is the irreducible initial number, since one urban combat division would be rapidly exhausted by the pace of deployments.

Most of the divisional artillery would be shifted to corps level, while engineers at all levels would be increased and restructured, including the addition of organic sapper platoons to infantry battalions. Composite armor and mechanized elements would be added to light forces at a ratio of one battalion (brigade) to four, with a longer-term goal of developing more appropriate and readily deployable means of delivering direct firepower and protecting the forward movement of troops. Innovative protection of general transport would be another goal. Military intelligence units would have to restructure radically and would need to develop habitual relationships with reserve-component linguists and area specialists. Aviation would work closely with other arms to develop more survivable tactics, and each division would gain an active-duty PSYOPS company. Signalers would need to experiment with low-cost, off-the-shelf tools for communicating in dense urban environments, and an overarching effort would need to be made to create interdisciplinary maps, both paper and electronic, that could better portray the complexity of urban warfare. The divisions' experience would determine future acquisition requirements.

But none of the measures cited above is as important as revolutionizing training for urban combat. The present approach, though worthwhile on its own terms, trains soldiers to fight in villages or small towns, not in cities. Building realistic "cities" in which to train would be prohibitively expensive. The answer is innovation. Why build that which already exists? In many of our own blighted cities, massive housing projects have become uninhabitable and industrial plants unusable. Yet they would be nearly ideal for combat-in-cities training. Although we could not engage in live-fire training (even if the locals do), we could experiment and train in virtually every other regard. Development costs would be a fraction of the price of building a "city" from scratch, and city and state governments would likely compete to gain a U.S. Army (and Marine) presence, since it would bring money, jobs, and development—as well as a measure of social discipline. A mutually beneficial relationship could help at least one of our worst-off cities, while offering the military a realistic training environment. The training center could be at least partially administered by the local National Guard to bind it to the community. We genuinely need a National Training Center for Urban Combat, and it cannot be another half measure. Such a facility would address the most glaring and dangerous gap in our otherwise superb military training program. We need to develop it soon.

In summary, an urbanizing world means combat in cities, whether we like it or not. Any officer who states categorically that the U.S. Army will never let itself be drawn into urban warfare is indulging in wishful thinking. Urban combat is conceptually and practically different from other modes of warfare. Although mankind has engaged in urban combat from the sack of Troy to the siege of Sarajevo, Western militaries currently resist the practical, emotional, moral, and ethical challenges of city fighting. Additional contemporary players, such as the media and international and nongovernmental organizations, further complicate contemporary urban combat. We do not want to touch this problem. But we have no choice. The problem is already touching us, with skeletal, infected fingers. The U.S. military must stop preparing for its dream war and get down to the reality of the fractured and ugly world in which we live—a world that lives in cities. We must begin judicious restructuring for urban combat in order to gain both efficiency and maximum effectiveness—as well as to preserve the lives of our soldiers. We must equip, train, and fight innovatively. We must seize the future before the future seizes us.

Spotting the Losers

Seven Signs of Noncompetitive States

Parameters

Spring 1998

When you leave the classroom or office and go into the world, you see at first its richness and confusions, the variety and tumult. Then, if you keep moving and do not quit looking, commonalties begin to emerge. National success is eccentric. But national failure is programmed and predictable. Spotting the future losers among the world's states becomes so easy it loses its entertainment value.

In this world of multiple and simultaneous revolutions—in technology, information, social organization, biology, economics, and convenience—the rules of international competition have changed. There is a global marketplace and, increasingly, a global economy. Although there is no global culture yet, American popular culture is increasingly available and wickedly appealing—and there are no international competitors in the field, only struggling local systems. Where the United States does not make the rules of international play, it shapes them by its absence.

The invisible hand of the market has become an informal but uncompromising lawgiver. Globalization demands conformity to the practices of the global leaders, especially to those of the United States. If you do not conform—or innovate—you lose. If you try to quit the game, you lose even more profoundly. The rules of international competition, whether in the economic, cultural, or conventional military field, grow ever more homogeneous. No government can afford practices that retard development. Yet such practices are often so deeply embedded in tradition, custom, and belief that the state cannot jettison them. That which provides the greatest psychological comfort to members of foreign cultures is often that which renders them noncompetitive against America's explosive creativity—our self-reinforcing dynamism fostered by law, efficiency, openness, flexibility, market discipline, and social mobility.

Traditional indicators of noncompetitive performance still apply: corruption (the most seductive activity humans can consummate while clothed); the absence of sound, equitably enforced laws; civil strife; or government attempts to overmanage a national economy. As change has internationalized and accelerated, however, new predictive tools have emerged. They are as simple as they are fundamental, and they are rooted in culture. The greater the degree to which a state—or an entire civilization—succumbs to these "seven deadly sins" of collective behavior, the more likely that entity is to fail to progress or even to maintain its position in the struggle for a share of the world's wealth and power. Whether analyzing military capabilities, cultural viability, or economic potential, these seven factors offer a quick study of the likely performance of a state, region, or population group in the coming century. These are the key "failure factors":

- Restrictions on the free flow of information.
- The subjugation of women.
- Inability to accept responsibility for individual or collective failure.
- The extended family or clan as the basic unit of social organization.
- Domination by a restrictive religion.
- A low valuation of education.
- Low prestige assigned to work.

Zero-Sum Knowledge

The wonderfully misunderstood Clausewitzian trinity, expressed crudely as state-people-military, is being replaced by a powerful new trinity: the relationship between the state, the people, and information. In the latter phases of the industrial age, the free flow of quality information had already become essential to the success of industries and military establishments. If the internationalizing media toppled the Soviet empire, it was because that empire's battle against information sharing had hollowed out its economy and lost the confidence of its people. When a sudden flood of information strikes a society or culture suffering from an information deficit, the result is swift destabilization. This is now a global phenomenon.

Today's "flat-worlders" are those who believe that information can be controlled. Historically, information always equaled power. Rulers and civilizations viewed knowledge as a commodity to be guarded, a thing finite in its dimensions and lost when shared. Religious institutions viewed knowledge as inflammatory and damnable, a thing to be handled carefully and to advantage, the nuclear energy of yesteryear. The parallel to the world public's view of wealth is almost exact—an instinctive conviction that information is a thing to be gotten and hoarded, and that its possession by a foreign actor means that it has been, by vague and devious means, robbed from oneself and one's own kind. But just as wealth generates wealth, so knowledge begets knowledge. Without a dynamic and welcoming relationship with information as content and process, no society can compete in the postindustrial age.

Information-controlling governments and knowledge-denying religions cripple themselves and their subjects or adherents. If America's streets are not paved with gold, they are certainly littered with information. *The availability of free, high-quality information and a people's ability to discriminate between high- and low-quality data are essential to economic development beyond the manufacturing level.* Whether on our own soil or abroad, those segments of humanity that fear and reject knowledge of the world (and, often, of themselves) are condemned to failure, poverty, and bitterness.

The ability of most of America's workforce to cope psychologically and practically with today's flood of data and to cull quality data from the torrent is remarkable—a national and systemic triumph. Even Canada and Britain cannot match it. Much of Japan's present stasis is attributable to that nation's struggle to make the transition from final-stage industrial power to information-age society. The more regulated flow of information with which Japan has long been comfortable is an impediment to postmodernism. While the Japanese nation ultimately possesses the synthetic capability to overcome this difficulty, its structural dilemmas are more informational and psychological than tangible—although the tangible certainly matters—and decades of educational reform and social restructuring will be necessary before Japan returns for another world-championship match.

In China, the situation regarding the state's attempt to control information and the population's inability to manage it is immeasurably worse. Until China undergoes a genuine cultural revolution that alters permanently and deeply the relationship between state, citizen, and information, that country will bog down at the industrial level. Its sheer size guarantees continued growth, but there will be a flattening in the coming decades, and decisively, China will have great difficulty making the transition from smokestack growth to intellectual innovation and service wealth.

China, along with the world's other defiant dictatorships, suffers under an oppressive class structure, built on and secured by an informational hierarchy. The great class struggle of the twenty-first century will be for access to data, and it will occur in totalitarian and religious-regime states. The internet may prove to be the most revolutionary tool since the movable-type printing press. History laughs at us all—the one economic analyst who would understand immediately what is happening in the world today would be a resurrected German "content provider" named Marx.

For countries and cultures that not only restrict but actively reject information that contradicts governmental or cultural verities, even a fully industrialized society remains an unattainable dream. Information is more essential to economic progress than an assured flow of oil. In fact, unearned, "found" wealth is socially and economically cancerous, impeding the development of healthy, enduring socioeconomic structures and values. If you want to guarantee an underdeveloped country's continued inability to perform competitively, grant it rich natural resources. The sink-or-swim poverty of northwestern Europe and Japan may have been their greatest natural advantage during their developmental phases. As the Shah learned and Saudi Arabia is proving, you can buy only the products, not the productivity, of another civilization.

States that censor information will fail to compete economically, culturally, and militarily in the long run. The longer the censorship endures, the longer the required recovery time. Even after the strictures have been lifted, information-deprived societies must play an almost hopeless game of catch-up. In Russia, it will take at least a generation of genuine informational freedom to facilitate an economic takeoff that is not founded hollowly upon resource extraction, middleman profits, and the looting of industrial ruins. Unique China will need even longer to make the next great leap forward from industrial to informational economy—we have at least half a century's advantage. Broad portions of the planet may never make it. We will not need a military to deal with foreign success, but to respond to foreign failure—which will be the greatest source of violence in coming decades.

If you are looking for an easy war, fight an information-controlling state. If you are looking for a difficult investment, invest in an information-controlling state. If you are hunting a difficult conflict, enter the civil strife that arises after the collapse of an information-controlling state. If you are looking for a good investment, find an emerging or "redeemed" state unafraid of science, hard numbers, and education.

A Woman's Place

Vying with informational abilities as a key factor in the reinvigoration of the U.S. economy has been the pervasive entry of American women into the educational process and the workplace. When the stock market soars, thank Elizabeth Cady Stanton and the suffragettes, not just their beneficiary, Alan Greenspan. After a century and a half of struggle by English and American women, the U.S. economy now operates at a wartime level of human-resource commitment on a routine basis.

Despite eternally gloomy headlines, our country probably has the lowest wastage rate of human talent in the world. The United States is so chronically hungry for talent that we drain it from the rest of the planet at a crippling pace, and we have accepted that we cannot squander the genius of half our population. Even in Europe, "overskilling," in which inherent and learned abilities wither in calcified workplaces, produces social peace at the cost of cultural and economic lethargy, security at the price of mediocrity. The occasional prime minister notwithstanding, it is far rarer to encounter a female executive, top professional, or general officer in that mythologized, "more equitable" Europe than in the United States. Life in

America may not be fair, but neither is it stagnant. What we lose in security, we more than compensate for in opportunity.

While Europe sleepwalks toward a thirty-five-hour workweek, we are moving toward the thirty-five-hour day. The intense perform-ance of our economy would be unattainable without the torrent of energy introduced by competitive female job candidates. American women revolutionized the workforce and the workplace. Future social and economic historians will probably judge that the entry of women into our workforce was the factor that broke the strangle-hold of American trade unions and gave a new lease on life to those domestic industries able to adapt. American women were the Japan-ese cars of business-labor relations: better, cheaper, dependable, and they defied the rules. Everybody had to work harder and smarter to survive, but the results have been a spectacular recovery of economic leadership and soaring national wealth.

Change that men long resisted and feared in our own country resulted not only in greater competition for jobs but also in the cre-ation of more jobs, and not in the rupture of the economy but in its assumption of imperial dimensions (in a quirk of fate, already priv-ileged males are getting much richer, thanks to the effects of femi-nism's triumph on the stock market). Equality of opportunity is the most profitable game going, and American capitalism has realized the wisdom of becoming an evenhanded consumer of skills. Despite serious exclusions and malignant social problems, we are the most efficient society in history. When Europeans talk of the dignity of the working man, they increasingly mean the right of that man to sit at a desk doing nothing or to stand at an idling machine. There is a huge difference between just being employed and actu-ally working.

The math isn't hard. Any country or culture that suppresses half its population, excluding them from economic contribution and wasting energy keeping them out of school and the workplace, is not going to perform competitively with us. The standard counter-argument heard in failing states is that there are insufficient jobs for the male population, and thus it is impossible to allow women to compete for the finite incomes available. The argument is archaic and wrong. When talent enters a workforce, it creates jobs. Compe-tition improves performance. In order to begin to compete with the

American leviathan and the stronger of the economies of Europe and the Far East, less-developed countries must maximize their human potential. Instead, many willfully halve it.

The point isn't really the fear that women will steal jobs in country X. Rather, it's a fundamental fear of women—or of a cultural caricature of women as incapable, stupid, and worrisomely sexual. If, when you get off the plane, you do not see men and women sitting together in the airport lounge, put your portfolio or treaty on the next flight home.

It is difficult for any human being to share power already possessed. Authority over their women is the only power many males will ever enjoy. From Greece to the Ganges, half the world is afraid of girls and gratified by their subjugation. It is a prescription for cultural mediocrity, economic failure, and inexpressible boredom. The value added by the training and utilization of our female capital is an American secret weapon.

Blaming Foreign Devils

The cult of victimhood, a plague on the least successful elements in our own society, retards the development of entire continents. When individuals or cultures cannot accept responsibility for their own failures, they will repeat the behaviors that led to failure. Accepting responsibility for failure is difficult, and correspondingly rare. The cultures of North America, Northern Europe, Japan, and Korea (each in its own way) share an unusual talent for looking in the mirror and keeping their eyes open. Certainly there is no lack of national vanity, prejudice, subterfuge, or bad behavior.

But in the clutch we are surprisingly good at saying, "We did it, so let's fix it."

In the rest of the world, a plumbing breakdown implicates the CIA and a faltering currency means that George Soros—the Hungarian-born American billionaire, fund manager, and philanthropist—has been sneaking around in the dark. Recent accusations of financial connivance made against Mr. Soros and then against the Jews collectively by Malaysia's Prime Minister Mahathir only demonstrated that Malaysia's ambitions had gotten ahead of its cultural capacity to support them. Even if foreign devils are to blame—and mostly they are not—whining and blustering does not help. It only makes you feel better for a little while, like drunkenness, and there are penalties the morning after.

The failure is greater where the avoidance of responsibility is greater. In the Middle East and Southwest Asia, oil money has masked cultural, social, technical, and structural failure for decades. The military failure of the regional states has been obvious, consistent, and undeniable, but the locals sense—even when they do not fully understand—their noncompetitive status in other spheres as well. It is hateful and disorienting to them. Only the twin blessings of Israel and the United States, on which Arabs and Persians can blame even their most egregious ineptitudes, enable a fly-specked pretense of cultural viability.

In contrast, Latin America has made tremendous progress. Not long ago, the gringos were to blame each time the lights blinked. But with the rise of a better educated elite and local experience of economic success, the leadership of Latin America's key states has largely stopped playing the blame game. Smaller states and drug-distorted economies still chase scapegoats, but of the major players, only Mexico still indulges routinely in the transfer of all responsibility for its problems to Washington, D.C.

Family Values

After the exclusion of women from productive endeavors, the next worst wastage of human potential occurs in societies where the extended family, clan, or tribe is the basic social unit. Although family networks provide a safety net in troubled times, offering practical support and psychological protection, and may even build a house for you, they do not build the rule of law, democracy, legitimate corporations, or free markets. Where the family or clan prevails, you do not hire the best man (to say nothing of the best woman) for the job, you hire Cousin Luis. You do not vote for the best man, you vote for Uncle Ali. And you do not consider cease-fire deals or shareholder interests to be matters of serious obligation.

Such cultures tend to be peasant based or of peasant origin, with the attendant peasant's suspicion of the outsider and of authority. Oligarchies of landed families freeze the pattern in time. There is a preference for a dollar grabbed today over a thousand dollars accrued in the course of an extended business relationship.

Blood-based societies operate under two sets of rules: one, generally honest, for the relative; and another, ruthless and amoral, for deals involving the outsider. The receipt of money now is more important than the building of a long-term relationship. Such societies fight well as tribes but terribly as nations.

At its most successful, this is the system of the Chinese diaspora, but that is a unique case. The Darwinian selection that led to the establishment and perpetuation of the great Chinese merchant families (and village networks), coupled with the steely power of southern China's culture, has made this example an exception to many rules. More typical examples of the *Vetternwirtschaft* system are Iranian businesses, Nigerian criminal organizations, Mexican political and drug cartels, and some American trade unions.

Where blood ties rule, you cannot trust the contract, let alone the handshake. Nor will you see the delegation of authority so necessary to compete in the modern military or economic spheres. Information and wealth are assessed from a zero-sum worldview. Corruption flourishes. Blood ties produce notable family successes, but they do not produce competitive societies.

That Old-Time Religion

Religion feeds a fundamental human appetite for meaning and security, and it can lead to powerful social unity and psychological assurance that trumps science. Untempered, it leads to xenophobia, backwardness, savagery, and economic failure. The more intense a religion is, the more powerful are its autarchic tendencies. But it is impossible to withdraw from today's world.

Limiting the discussion to the sphere of competitiveness, there appear to be two models of socioreligious integration that allow sufficient informational and social dynamism for successful performance. First, religious homogeneity can work if, as in the case of Japan, religion is sufficiently subdued and malleable to accommodate applied science. The other model—that of the United States—is of religious coexistence, opening the door for science as an "alternative religion." Americans have, in fact, such wonderful plasticity of mind that generally even the most vividly religious can disassociate antibiotic drugs from the study of Darwin and the use of birth-control pills from the strict codes of their churches. All religions breed some amount of schism between theology and social practice, but the American experience is a marvel of mental agility and human innovation.

The more dogmatic and exclusive the religion, the less it is able to deal with the information age, in which multiple "truths" may exist simultaneously, and in which all that cannot be proven empirically is inherently under assault. We live in a time of immense psychological dislocation—when man craves spiritual certainty even more than usual. Yet our age is also one in which the sheltering dogma cripples individuals and states alike. The price of competitiveness is the courage to be uncertain—not an absence of belief, but a synthetic capability that can at once accommodate belief and its contradictions. Again, the United States possesses more than its share of this capability, while other societies are encumbered by single dominant religions as hard, unbending, and ultimately brittle as iron. Religious toleration also means the toleration of scientific research, informational openness, and societal innovation. "One true path" societies and states are on a path that leads only downward.

For those squeamish about judging the religion of another, there is a shortcut that renders the same answer on competitiveness: examine the state's universities.

Learning Power and Earning Power

The quality of a state's universities obviously reflects local wealth, but even more important, the effectiveness of higher education in a society describes its attitudes toward knowledge, inquiry versus dogma, and the determination of social standing. In societies imprisoned by dogmatic religions, or in which a caste or class system predetermines social and economic outcomes, higher education (and secular education in general) often has low prestige and poor content. Conversely, in socially mobile, innovative societies, university degrees from quality schools appear indispensable to the ambitious, the status conscious, and the genuinely inquisitive alike.

There are many individual and some cultural exceptions, but they mostly prove the rule. Many Indians value a university education highly—not as social confirmation, but as a means of escaping a preassigned social position. The privileged of the Arabian Peninsula, on the other hand, regard an American university degree (even from a booby-prize institution) as an essential piece of jewelry, not unlike a Rolex watch. In all cultures, there are individuals hungry for self-improvement and, sometimes, for knowledge. But statistically we can know a society, and judge its potential, by its commitment to education, with universities as the bellwether. Not all states can afford their own Stanford or Harvard, but within their restraints, their attempts to educate their populations still tell us a great deal about national priorities and potential. Commitment and content cannot fully substitute for a wealth of facilities, but they go a long way, whether we speak of individuals or of continents.

Any society that starves education is a loser. Cultures that do not see inherent value in education are losers. This is even true for some of our own subcultures—groups for whom education has little appeal as means or end—and it is true for parts of Latin America, sub-Saharan Africa, and the Arab world. A culture that cannot produce a single world-class university is not going to conquer the world in any sphere.

America's universities are triumphant. Once beyond the silly debates (or monologues) in the liberal arts faculties, our knowledge industry has no precedent or peer. Even Europe's most famous universities, on the Rhine or the Seine, are rotting and overcrowded. We attract the best faculty, the best researchers, and the best student minds from the entire world. This is not a trend subject to reversal; rather, it is self-reinforcing.

Yet there is even more to American success in education than four good years at the "College of Musical Knowledge." The United States is also far ahead of other states in the flexibility and utility of its educational system. Even in Europe, the student's fate is determined early—and woe to the late bloomer. You choose your course, or have it chosen for you, and you are more or less stuck with it for life. In Germany, long famous for its commitment to education, the individual who gains a basic degree in one subject and then jumps to another field for graduate work is marked as a *Versager,* a failure. In the U.S. system, there are second, third, and fourth chances. This flexible approach to building and rebuilding our human capital is a tremendous economic asset, and it is compounded by the trend toward continuing education in midlife and for seniors.

A geriatric revolution is occurring under our noses, with older Americans becoming "younger" in terms of capabilities, interests, and attitudes—and much more apt to continue contributing to the common good. In the early decades of the next century, many Americans may hit their peak earning years not in their fifties but in their sixties—then seventies. This not only provides sophisticated talent to the labor pool but also maintains the worker as an asset to, rather than a drain upon, our nation's economy. For all the fuss about the future of Social Security, we may see a profound attitudinal change in the next generation, when vigorous, high-earning seniors come to regard retirement as an admission of failure or weakness, or just a bore. At the same time, more twenty-year-old foreigners than ever will have no jobs at all.

Investments in our educational system are "three-fers": They are simultaneously investments in our economic, social, and military systems. Education is our first line of defense. The rest of the world can be divided into two kinds of societies, states, and cultures— those that struggle and sacrifice to educate their members, and those that do not. Guess who is going to do better in the hypercompetitive twenty-first century?

Workers of the World, Take a Nap!

Related to, but not quite identical with, national and cultural attitudes toward education is the attitude toward work. Now everyone has bad days at the office, factory, training area, or virtual workplace, and the old line "It's not supposed to be fun—that's why they call it work," enjoys universal validity. Yet there are profoundly different attitudes toward work on this planet. While most human beings must work to survive, there are those who view work as a necessary evil and dream of its avoidance, and then there are societies in which people hit the lottery and go back to their jobs as telephone linemen. In many subsets of Latin American culture, for example, there are two reasons to work: first to survive, then to grow so wealthy that work is no longer necessary. It is a culture in which the possession of wealth is not conceptually related to a responsibility to work. It is the get-rich-quick, big-bucks-from-heaven dream of some of our own citizens. The goal is not achievement but possession, not accomplishment but the power of leisure.

Consider any culture's heroes. Generally, the more macho or male-centric the culture, the less emphasis there will be on steady work and achievement, whether craftsmanship or Nobel Prize–winning research, and the more emphasis there will be on wealth and power as the sole desirable end (apart, perhaps, from the occasional religious vocation). As national heroes, it's hard to beat Bill Gates. But even a sports star is better than a major narco-trafficker.

Generally societies that do not find work in and of itself "pleasing to God and requisite to Man" tend to be highly corrupt (low-education and dogmatic-religion societies also are statistically prone to corruption, and if all three factors are in play, you may not want to invest in the local stock exchange or tie your foreign policy to successful democratization). The goal becomes the attainment of wealth by any means.

Workaholic cultures, such as those of North America north of the Rio Grande, Japan, South Korea, and some other East Asian states, can often compensate for deficits in other spheres, such as a lack of natural resources or a geographical disadvantage. If a man or woman has difficulty imagining a fulfilling life without work, he or she probably belongs to a successful culture. Work has to be seen as a personal and public responsibility, as good in and of itself, as spiritually necessary. Otherwise, the society becomes an "evader" society. Russia is strong, if flagging, on education. But the general attitude toward work undercuts education. When the characters in Chekhov's *Three Sisters* blather about the need to find redemption through work, the prescription is dead-on, but their lives and their society have gone so far off the rails that the effect is one of satire. States and cultures "win" just by getting up earlier and putting in eight honest hours and a little overtime.

If you are seeking a worthy ally or business opportunity, go to a midlevel government office in country X an hour before the local lunchtime. If everybody is busy with legitimate work, you've hit a winner. If there are many idle hands, get out.

Using This Knowledge to Our Advantage

Faced with the complex reality of geopolitics and markets, we must often go to country X, Y, or Z against our better judgment. Despite failing in all seven categories, country X may have a strategic location that makes it impossible to ignore. Country Y may have an internal market and regional importance so significant that it would be foolish not to engage it, despite the risks. Country Z may have resources that make a great deal of misery on our part worth the sufferance. Yet even in such situations, it helps to know what we are getting into. Some countries would devour investments as surely as they would soldiers. Others just demand savvy and caution on our part. Yet another might require a local ally or partner to whom we can make ourselves indispensable. Whether we are engaging militarily or doing business in another country, it gives us a tremendous advantage if we can identify four things: their image of us, their actual situation, their needs, and the needs they perceive themselves as having (the four *never* connect seamlessly).

There are parallel dangers for military men and businessmen in taking too narrow a view of the challenges posed by foreign states. An exclusive focus on either raw military power or potential markets tells us little about how people behave, believe, learn, work, fight, or buy. In fact, the parallels between military and business interventions grow ever greater, especially since these form two of the legs of our new national strategic triad, along with the export of our culture. (Diplomacy is a minor and shrinking factor, its contours defined ever more rigorously by economics.)

The seven factors discussed above offer a pattern for an initial assessment of the future potential of states that interest us. Obviously, the more factors present in a given country, the worse off it will be—and these factors rarely appear in isolation. Normally a society that oppresses women does so under the aegis of a restrictive dominant religion that also insists on the censorship of information. Societies lacking a strong work ethic rarely value education.

In the Middle East, it is possible to identify states where all seven negatives apply; in Africa, many countries score between four and seven. Countries that formerly suffered communist dictatorships vary enormously, from Poland and the Czech Republic, with only a few rough edges, to Turkmenistan, which scores six out of seven. Latin America has always been more various than *Norteamericanos* realized, from feudal Mexico to dynamic, disciplined Chile.

Ultimately our businesses have it easier than our military in one crucial respect: business losses are counted in dollars, not lives. But the same cultural factors that will shape future state failure and spawn violent conflicts make it difficult to do business successfully and legally. We even suffer under similar "rules of engagement," whether those placed on the military that dictate when a soldier may shoot or the legal restraints under which U.S. businesses must operate, imposing a significant disadvantage vis-à-vis foreign competitors.

As a final note, the biggest pitfall in international interactions is usually mutual misunderstanding. We do not understand them, but they do not understand us either—although, thanks to the Americanization of world media, they imagine that they do. From megadeals that collapsed because of Russian rapacity to Saddam's conviction that the United States would not fight following his invasion of Kuwait, foreign counterparts, rivals, and opponents have whoppingly skewed perceptions of American behaviors. In the end, military operations and business partnerships are like dating—the advantage goes to the player who sees with the most clarity.

We are heading into a turbulent, often violent new century. It will be a time of great dangers and great opportunities. Some states will continue to triumph, others will shift their relative positions, many will fail. The future will never be fully predictable, but globalization means the imposition of uniform rules by the most powerful actors. They are fundamentally economic rules. For the first time, the world is converging toward a homogeneous system, if not toward homogeneous benefits from that system. The potential of states is more predictable within known parameters than ever before.

We have seen the future, and it looks like us.

Our New Old Enemies

Parameters

Summer 1999

Our enemies of the future will be enemies out of the past. As the U.S. armed forces put their faith and funding behind ever more sophisticated combat systems designed to remove human contact from warfare, mankind circles back to the misbehaviors of yester-year. Technologies come and go, but the primitive endures. The last decade of this millennium has seen genocide, ethnic cleansing, the bloody rending of states, growing religious persecution, the ascendancy of international crime, an unprecedented distribution of weaponry, and the persistence of the warrior—the man of raw and selfish violence—as a human archetype. In the 1990s, our Gulf War was the sole conventional conflict of note. Both lopsided and inconclusive, it confirmed the new military paradigm: the United States is unbeatable on a traditional battlefield, but that battlefield is of declining relevance.

We have failed to ask the most basic military question: *Who is our enemy?* Our ingrained response when asked such a question is to respond with the name of a country—ten years ago it was the Soviet Union, while today China is the answer preferred by lazy analysts and defense contractors anxious to sell the unnecessary to the uncritical. We are desperate for enemies who make sense to us, who certify our choices and grant us clarity of purpose. But the age of warfare between states is waning—it may return, but it is not the pre-eminent military challenge of the coming decades. We must ask that question, "Who is our enemy?" on a much deeper level. We must study the minds and souls of violent men, seeking to understand them on a level that our civilization has avoided for two thousand years. We can no longer blame atrocities and the will to violence on the devil, or on mistaken ideologies, or even on childhood deprivations. None of the cherished explanations suffice. In this age of technological miracles, our military needs to study mankind.

Morally, the best among us may be those who argue for disarmament. But they are mistaken. The heart of the problem is not the weapon, but the man who builds and wields it. Were we to eliminate all weapons of mass destruction, as well as every last handgun and pocketknife, the killers among us would take up wooden clubs or rocks. The will to violence is within us—it is not merely a function of the availability of tools.

Man, not space, is the last frontier. We must explore him.

It should not surprise us that religions have done a better job of locating man's desires and impulses than have secular analysts, whether Hegel, Freud, or media critics. Religions handle the raw clay, and only those that address all of man's potential shapes survive. We are defined by the full range of our desires and behaviors, not only by those worthy of emulation. Successful religions grasp our totality (and our fears). Whereas social orders are concerned with surface effects, religions look within. And every major religion has a prohibition against killing. There would be no need for such rules were man not a killer by nature.

In the Judeo-Christian heritage, there is a commandment that believers credit directly to the writing finger of God: "Thou shalt not kill." Think about that. Overall, the ten commandments did a remarkable job of cataloging human frailty. As behavioral rules they are as valid for today's techno-civilization as they were for the dreary near-Orient of three thousand years ago. Those prohibitions acknowledged the most destructive things that we humans are apt to do, and they warned us not to do them. The warning not to kill was the bluntest commandment.

For the moment, lay aside the concept of the Old Testament as a sacred book and consider it as a documentary of human behavior: It is drenched in violence, and its moral tenets arose in response to a violent world. It begins with the plight of two refugees—Adam and Eve—and moves swiftly to the fratricide of their children. In book after book, we encounter massacre, genocide, ethnic cleansing, rape, plunder, kidnapping, assassination, ineradicable hatreds, and endless warfare. The fall of civilizations is reported with a merciless eye, and cities vanish with a terse comment. It sounds like the twentieth century: Humanity is consistent.

Historians, however, are inconsistent. Today we have moved away from our earlier view of civilization as a process of constant improvement, with Western civilization as man's crowning achievement. Yet the most vociferous multiculturalists and antimodernists, who imagine virtue in all that is foreign, still insist thoughtlessly that humankind is perfectable, if only we would take the latest scholarship on the mating habits of aborigines more seriously. I do not believe that man has improved. There is no evidence for it. Are we better than Christ, the Buddha or Mohammed, than Socrates, Ulug Begh, Maimonides, or Saint Francis? Fashions, conveyances, medicines, communications, and the sophistication of governmental structures have all evolved. Man has not. Man is the constant. Saddam is Pharoah, and Cain will always be with us.

I have chosen religious texts and figures as examples because you know them and they resonate. Is there a more powerful cautionary myth for a military man than that of Cain and Abel? Throughout both testaments, we encounter violent actors and soldiers. They face timeless moral dilemmas. Interestingly, their social validity is not questioned even in the Gospels. Although the New Testament is often ambivalent toward soldiers, the thrust of the texts is to improve rather than abolish the soldiery. It is assumed that soldiers are, however regrettably, *necessary*. In Luke, soldiers approach John the Baptist asking, "What shall we do?" John does not tell them to put aside their arms. Rather, he answers them, "Rob no one by violence or by false accusation, and be content with your wages." Would that the generals and admirals involved in procurement might heed that advice today.

The Bible does not sugarcoat man's nature. Belief is not required—read it as a document and you will get a better picture of the very human enemies our soldiers will face in the next century than any work of contemporary scholarship or speculation provides. From child warriors to fanatics who revel in slaughter, man's future is written in man's past.

Still, if you are uneasy with the Old Testament as a catalog of human behaviors, substitute another work, the *Iliad*. It is the fountainhead of our civilization's secular literature. That epic begins with an argument over raping rights, proceeds through slaughter and betrayal, and has genocide as its goal. It is about the wreckage of Yugoslavia.

In our staff and war colleges, we still read Thucydides—not for the history, but for the immediacy. Has there been another historian since the Greek twilight who matched his wonder at man's stubborn imperfection, at his ineradicable nature?

Literature is history with the truth left in. I believe that we can profit from the study of the classical texts as never before. The veneer of civilization—so recent and fragile—is being stripped from much of the world. The old problems are today's problems—and tomorrow's. If we want to know "Who is our enemy?" we must look within.

I believe that mankind is a constant in a changing world. We love the familiar and find change hard. The conflicts in which our military will engage in the coming years will have many topical causes; at bottom, however, there will be only two: man's nature, and the impact of change upon him.

The Muezzin and the Microchip

Whether or not we as individuals believe in a divine being, we can recognize religion as the most supple and consistently effective behavior-modification tool available to mankind. Now if you study religions—and the soldier who does not know what his enemy believes fights blindly—you will find that virtually all of them have two myths in common: a creation myth, and the myth of a lost golden age. The need for a creation story to explain our origins is self-evident—it responds to the adult counterpart of the child who wants to know from whence his little sister came. But the myth of a lost golden age, of the white and shining temple before the fall, is directly relevant to understanding our enemies.

We live in an age of unprecedented change. This is statistical fact. Never before has so much happened on so many levels with such breathtaking speed. Developments in a wide range of disciplines tumble over one another in a practical and psychological avalanche. Whether we speak of social structures and gender relations, medicine, communications and the utility of information, the changing nature of work and wealth, convenience and the shape of the inhabited landscape, or the sheer revolution of choice available to our citizens, our society has undergone a greater degree of intense and layered change than has any human system in history. It is a tribute to the robustness of our civilization that we have coped so well with change thus far. Other civilizations and cultures (and some individuals everywhere) are less resilient and are not coping effectively; in fact, they are decaying. And the decay of a culture is the human equivalent of the decay of atomic particles.

We live in an age when even the most adept, confident man or woman feels the earth shifting underfoot. In the parlance of strategic theorists, change is destabilizing. In the experience of the human being enduring it, change is confusing, threatening, and often hurtful. In the great scheme of things, most change turns out to be positive for most people. But it is only rarely so perceived.

Especially as we grow older, our eyes play tricks on us—we are more likely to see that which is lost than that which is gained. How often do we hear our colleagues, friends, or relatives complain about the passing of the good old days or how much better things were under the old boss (forgetting how that boss was resented during his or her tenure)?

Experience is of two kinds: that which we undergo, and that which we remember. Those "good old days" were not better. If man has not developed much, his (and certainly her) opportunities have. But we long for the certainty of that which we have known, suffered, and survived—especially when it lies at a safe distance. When I was a kid, a drugstore in my hometown displayed a poster showing a little boy lowering a bucket into a well. The print read, "Remember how sweet the water was from the old well? It was the leading cause of typhoid fever." I have never encountered a more succinct description of man's relationship to change. In our memories, we sweeten the waters of the past and erase the dirt and the sickness from the myths we make of our experience.

Men fight for myths, not for truth.

Those myths of the lost golden age are most seductive in turbulent times. In the ferocity, confusion, and competition of the moment, we *need* to believe that things were not always so hard or so unfair, that there was a time of greater kindness and justice, when man's better qualities prevailed—and that such an epoch might return, if only we take the correct actions. Whether a radicalized mullah aching to turn back the clock to the days of the great caliphs, or a weekend militiaman in the Midwest longing for the surety of a misremembered childhood, the impulse to believe that times were better once upon a time is universal.

The experience of change and the consequent impulse to gild the past are timeless elements of the human saga. I wrote above that we live in an age of unprecedented change. This is true. Yet it is also true that men and women in past ages have lived through times of then-unprecedented change. They, too, have felt the earth shake beneath their feet and heard the heavens rumble. Accounts of the early days of the locomotive and telegraph are packed with wonder and warning. An early weapon of mass destruction, the crossbow, was outlawed in its time by secular authorities and by the pope. Poets have always wept over the prosaic nature of their own ages, when the beauty of the past lay murdered by the practical. Can we imagine the shock to the people of the ancient Middle East upon the arrival of bronze weapons? How the villager must have recoiled from the stench and temptation of the rising city. The first wooden cask would have excited mockery and the insistence by the old guard that wine was meant to ferment in clay pots, and that was that. The potato, the most revolutionary food in modern history, terrified Europeans when it was first imported, inspiring the belief that it caused leprosy, among other diseases. The information is lost to us now, but try to imagine the shock that the first laws codified by a state had on ancient populations governed until then by custom and by fear of the supernatural. For that matter, imagine the shock that a legitimate, enforced code of law would have on Russia or Mexico today.

With man's inherent fear of change, it is astonishing how intensely we have developed our civilizations, if not ourselves. We have changed the world—but all we have changed about ourselves are our table manners.

The longing for the preservation or resurrection of an old order, real or fantastic, is the key to understanding much of the world's disorder. Even when our enemies are not personally motivated by the fear of change, it is the fears of their neighbors that grant those enemies opportunity. Wrapping themselves in the cloak of this convenient cause, they exploit any rupture between the governing and the governed, any gulf between a prospering "progressive" elite and the stagnating ranks of believers or traditionalist masses. The men who guide their followers to massacre understand the power of a call to the banner of nationalism or an appeal to tribal supremacy or an invitation to do some god's cleansing work with fire and sword. Demagogues capitalize on the sense of a trust betrayed and the "evil" of the new. They are geniuses of blame. All their failures, and the failures of all their followers, will forever be the fault of someone else.

Men will fight to the death to cling to a just-bearable past rather than embrace a less certain future, no matter its potential.

In periods of great change, human beings respond by turning to religion and resuscitating tradition. In the age of science, the frightened turn to belief. Perhaps the truest of all our clichés is that "ignorance is bliss." Men and women do not want to know. They may be pleased to learn of the misfortunes of their neighbor—confessional television shows have their roots in tribal whispers—but they do not want to know that their way of life, of belief, of organizing, learning, producing, and fighting is a noncompetitive bust. The greatest impact of this information age is that it makes the global masses aware of their inadequacy.

At the height of the British Empire, the average imperial subject had no idea how his rulers lived. Today, the poor of the world's slums have awakened to the lifestyles of the rich and famous, courtesy of television, film, video, radio, cassettes, the self-justifications of kinsmen who have gone abroad and failed, and appalling local journalism. They do not, of course, grasp our reality. But they believe they do. The America they see is so rich and powerful it must be predatory. It *must* have robbed them to grow so rich. It has no right to be so rich. And it is unjust that they should not be so rich.

The media create instant myth. An illusion of America arrives, courtesy of lurid television serials, exaggerating Western wealth, ease, and sexuality. There is no mention of the sufferings of our ancestors on the long road to contemporary prosperity, or even of the workaday lives of average Americans today. It is as if our riches had fallen from the skies. It is an unbearable spectacle to those who have not.

At the same time, those who watch from abroad, appetites growing, find themselves less and less able to compete with the American juggernaut. Economic structures, the decline in the relative value of muscle power, educational inadequacies, social prohibitions and counterproductive customs, the ineffectiveness of civil law—these things and more constrict the potential of other cultures to compete with the West: the United States and our most culturally agile allies. Even cultures that appeared poised to break out to near equivalence with us, such as those of Southeast Asia, hit cultural ceilings—and such ceilings are made of iron, not glass.

Most analysis of the current plight of the Asian "tigers" focuses on economic issues, but the underlying problem is cultural: The human infrastructure could not support the level of success already achieved, let alone that which was desired. The most disappointing and worrisome aspect of the near collapse of Asian economies was not the financial losses but the alacrity with which the disappointed states, leaders, and people blamed foreigners for their misfortunes, when the problems were transparently homemade. Some also blamed their own minorities, especially the overseas Chinese. In Indonesia, we saw the return of ethnic pogroms. Even our South Korean allies responded to economic crisis with a tantrum of xenophobia. Hatred and revenge are always more satisfying than a sense of responsibility for one's own failure.

When nations and their underlying cultures fail to qualify in today's hypercompetitive world, they first complain. Then, if there is no turnaround, they kill. Iraq did not invade Kuwait in a burst of self-confidence, but from fear of economic decline and future inabilities. Tomorrow's enemies will be of two kinds—those who have seen their hopes disappointed, and those who have no hope. Do not worry about a successful China. Worry about a failing China.

And even a failing China is unlikely to become the threat defense charlatans would have us believe. China is culturally robust. Our most frequent opponents will rise from cultures on the rocks. In our grim century, Russia and Germany grew most dangerous after systems of cultural organization failed. Above all, this means that the Islamic world will be a problem for the foreseeable future, since it is unprepared to deal with the demands—and mandatory freedoms—of the postmodern age. Beyond that faded, failing civilization, watch out for other change-resistant cultures, from tribes and clans to states that never shook off feudal, agrarian mentalities (such as Mexico, or Russia and its determination to be a regional spoiler). None of these will threaten our homes; abroad, however, they will threaten our preferred order and the extraction of the wealth that pays for our homes.

Contrary to the myths of the old, pitiful Left, the United States did not build its new cultural-economic empire on the backs of the world's workers and peasants. But thanks to the information age, we will expand that empire at the expense of failing cultures, since the world insists on devouring our dross. The Left understood neither the time line nor the dynamics of history. And today's shriveled Left—hardly more than a campus entertainment—still gets one thing hugely wrong: the notion of an American determination to impoverish others. The United States prefers *prosperous* markets—starving masses don't buy much software (and they really do work on the Western conscience). But we cannot force people to be successful.

Those who fall by the wayside in global competition will have themselves, and their ancestors, to blame.

Sherman, Set the Way Back!

With the antimodern tide of fundamentalism that has swept away regimes and verities over the past two decades, we have come to accept, once again, that religious belief can turn violent. Yet, when we analyze our opponents, we insist on a hard, Joe Friday, "just the facts" approach that focuses on numbers, hardware, and perhaps a few of their leaders. We maintain a mental cordon sanitaire around military operations, ignoring the frightening impact of belief on our enemy's will and persistence. We accept the CNN reality of "mad mullahs" and intoxicated masses, yet we do not consider belief a noteworthy factor when assessing our combat opponents. Yet only plagues and the worst personal catastrophes excite the religious impulse in man to the extent that war does.

The interplay of religion and military violence deserves books, not just a few paragraphs. But begin with that which we know. In vague outline, we are all familiar with the Great Indian Mutiny, when the British East India Company's native levies, both Muslim and Hindu, reacted to a rumor that their new cartridges had been soiled with pig fat or beef lard by rising up and slaughtering their overlords. While any Marxist will tell you that there were structural factors at play in the Sepoy Mutiny and that the cartridges were but a catalyst, the fact remains that the most savage experience of the Victorian era was the butchery of the Mutiny—first the atrocities committed against British men, women, and children, then the slaughter perpetrated against the native population by the British, which was crueler still.

The Indian Mutiny offers only a hint at the religious violence once extant in the British Empire. London's imperial history offers an interesting study for today's problems; the overwhelming impact of industry-backed regiments against native masses, the shattering of established orders, the spiritual dislocations of the defeated—all this is replaying around us and will play on into the next century at fast-forward speed. Notably, Britain's most embarrassing defeats of the nineteenth century were dealt the empire not by other organized militaries but by true believers—whether the ferocious holy warriors of Afghanistan or the devout Calvinist Boers. Again and again, resistance to British influence or rule rallied around a religious identity, whether following the Mahdi in the Sudan or, in our own century, struggling to recreate Israel or a united, independent Ireland. Our own national introduction to imperial combat involved a Chinese revivalist order, the "Fists of Righteousness," or Boxers, and in the Philippines, the impassioned Muslim Moros proved a far tougher enemy for us than the conventional Spanish military.

And what of the impact of belief *within* armies? It is a war-movie truism that the frightened and dying turn to the chaplain, but if we argue individual cases, we might conclude that this is evidence of desperation, not of a genuine propulsion toward belief. Yet consider our own bloodiest conflict—the Civil War. It saw a widespread religious revival in blue ranks and gray—although as the South's condition worsened, the intensity of religious fervor in the Confederate armies grew extreme. Although it is unfashionable to say so, there is ample evidence that, for many on both sides, this was a holy war. Certainly the hungry, ill-clothed men in the Army of Northern Virginia fought with the determination of martyrs. Stonewall Jackson *entered* the war a religious extremist and fought with a holy warrior's dedication. Sherman was a secular fanatic produced by an age of belief. His march from Atlanta to the sea, then northward through the Carolinas, was a crusade executed with a religious fervor, if without religious rhetoric. When we examine contemporary letters and reports, it is clear that God was very much with both sides.

This is an ancient phenomenon. Return to the *Iliad*. Read differently and more closely this time. Don't skim the long passages detailing sacrifices or the name-dropper poetry about squabbling gods. Look at what Homer tells us about belief in the ranks. The book begins with Agamemnon's defiance of the ordained order of things—a middle finger thrust up not only at Achilles but also at the gods. The Greek forces suffer for it. Plague sweeps them. The Trojans briefly turn the tide. *And the Greeks respond in terms of their religion.* The first step is not a new battlefield strategy, it is a religious revival. Even the king must be called to order. Penitence is in. Sacrifices must involve real sacrifice. Certainly the return of Achilles to the fight boosts morale, but the Greeks also experience a renewed sense that the gods are on their side. Meanwhile, in threatened Troy, an otherworldly fatalism takes hold, dark prophecies ring out, and Priam and his people search for an explanation of their impending fall in the will of the gods.

Of course, we do not read the *Iliad* that way. It is not our habit; we shy away from manifestations of faith, suspecting or ignoring them or, at best, analyzing them in the dehydrated language of the sociologist. But if we want to understand the warriors of the world, and the fury that drives them, we had better open our minds to the power of belief.

In our own Western cultural history, the fiercest military brutalities and the most savage wars were fought over faith, whether Crusades or defensive wars against Muslims, campaigns of suppression against dissenting Christians, the great religious wars of the sixteenth and especially seventeenth centuries, or the twentieth century's world wars between secular religions.

Now our history is playing out in other flesh. When Indonesian rioters murder Chinese merchants, or when the Sudanese Muslims who hold power butcher and enslave the Christians in their country's south, their behavior is not inhuman. On the contrary, it is timelessly human.

Beware of any enemy motivated by supernatural convictions or great moral schemes. Even when he is less skilled and ill equipped, his fervor may simply wear you down. Our military posture could not be more skewed. We build billion-dollar bombers, but we cannot cope with bare-handed belief.

The Shaman and the Gangster

If the intoxicated believer is one very dangerous extreme in the range of our enemies, the other is the man utterly free of belief or fear of the law or civilizing custom. When you encounter them together—the saint and the cynic in league—you have the most dangerous combination on earth. True believers and opportunists are a dynamic match, as many a successful televangelist instructs us. You see it in a sloppy fashion with Saddam and his belated attention to Islam, but also in the alliance between the current set of Kremlin bandits and the Orthodox Church.

From Algeria's religious terrorists to politicians anywhere who align themselves with religious movements whose convictions they privately do not share, it is often difficult for us to determine where the prophet ends and the profiteer begins, how much is about faith and how much about grabbing power. In such cases, we tend to err on the side of cynicism, preferring to impute base motives to our enemies (even as we imagine that those enemies are somehow redeemable). But slighting either side of the equation, the human potential for cynicism or for belief, brings us only half answers. In conflict, the saint and the cynic can complete each other without consciously understanding why their alliance works so well. Together, they combine the qualities of the cobra and the chameleon.

The most difficult thing for Americans in (and out of) uniform to face may be that even the most powerful military can, at most, briefly alter outward behaviors. We subdue belief only by killing the believer. From Somalia to Bosnia, the opportunist will bow to the threat of lethal power—until you turn your back. But no display of might will change the essence of either the man driven by God or the man driven by greed.

We have entered another age when empires begin to learn their limits. Although America has—and will maintain—informational dominance, we cannot dictate which information will be accepted and acted upon by foreign populations. We can flood them with our culture, shock them into doubt, sell them our wares—but we cannot make them behave as we would like, unless we are willing to commit brutalities on a scale that would destroy our own myth of ourselves.

Certainly, if sufficiently provoked, we are capable of killing plentifully and with enthusiasm. But such events are exceptional. In their balance and wisdom, the American people will fight genuine enemies, but they would not countenance the unprovoked slaughter of foreign populations over distant misbehaviors. The mark of our civilization's greatness is a simple but rare one: At this point in our social development, we would rather do good than evil, so long as it doesn't cost too much. It is a surprisingly rare quality.

In other regions of the globe, there is less interest in the inviolability of the individual. We face enemies whose sole motivation to refrain from killing is the fear of being killed. Nothing else moves them. It is difficult for Americans, with our lack of historical knowledge and our fuzzy notion of the validity of all cultures, to grasp the richness of hatred in this world. For all of our alarm over crime, most Americans live in an astonishingly safe environment. We are not threatened, and we behave cooperatively and corporately. But our safety is both the result of and contributor to our insularity. We lead sheltered lives. And we imagine that the rest of the world is just like us, only less privileged.

Hatred

The rest of the world is not like us. For all of our lingering prejudices, we have done a remarkable job of subduing our hatreds. Perhaps it is only the effect of wealth bounded by law that makes us such a powerful exception to history, but our lack of domestic faction is a miracle nonetheless. We are indescribably fortunate—but our good fortune has lulled us into our primary military and diplomatic weakness: We do not understand the delicious appeal of hatred.

We cannot understand how Serbs, Croats, and Bosnian Muslims could do that to each other. We cannot understand how Hutus and

Tutsis could do that to each other. We do not understand how the Chinese could do that to the Tibetans. We do not understand how the Armenians and Azeris could do that to each other. We do not understand how the tribes of Sierra Leone or Liberia could do that to each other. We do not understand how India's Hindus and Muslims could do that to each other. We do not understand how the Russians and Chechens could do that to each other. We do not understand how Haitians, Somalis, Colombians, Mexicans, Indonesians, Sri Lankans, Congolese, Burundians, or the Irish could do that to each other.

Over the years, I have written about "warriors," the nonsoldiers, from guerrillas to narco-traffickers, whom we encounter and fight. In the past, I stressed the importance of recognizing five types of warriors: the scum of the earth, the average Joe who is drawn into the conflict as it drags on, demobilized military men, opportunists, and true believers. Now I worry about only two of these sources of conflict—the opportunists and the believers, the gangsters and the godly, the men unrestrained by morals and those whose iron morality is implacable. They are the centers of gravity. The others are swept along by the tide.

Man, the Killer
Of all the notions I have advanced over the years, the only one that has met with consistent rejection is the statement that men like to kill. I do not believe that all men like to kill. At the extreme, there are those saintly beings who would sacrifice their own lives before taking the life of another. The average man will kill if compelled to, in uniform in a war or in self-defense, but has no evident taste for it. Men react differently to the experience of killing. Some are traumatized. Others simply move on with their lives. But there is at least a minority of human beings—mostly male—who enjoy killing. That minority may be small, but it does not take many enthusiastic killers to trigger the destruction of a fragile society. Revolutions, pogroms, genocides, and civil wars are made not by majorities, but by minorities with the acquiescence of the majority. The majority may gloat or loot, but the killing minority drives history.

Violence is addictive. Police know this. That's where the phrase "the usual suspects" comes from. In our society, the overwhelming majority of violent acts are committed by repeat offenders. Statistics would make us a violent nation; in fact, we are a peaceable people until aroused. The numbers are skewed because we have failed to deter recidivists.

Spouse and child abusers do not do it once—they repeat. Sex offenders—and sex crimes are all crimes of violence—are notorious repeat offenders. Most barroom brawls are begun by the same old troublemakers. Even in combat, when mortal violence is legal, most enemy combatants killed in close fighting appear to be killed by a small number of "high performers" in our ranks. Throughout history, many a combat hero has had difficulty adjusting to peace.

We reject the evidence of the human enthusiasm for violence because it troubles us and undercuts the image we have created of perfectible man. But violence has an undeniable appeal. Certainly, for the otherwise disenfranchised, it is the only response left. Perhaps the psychologists are right that much violence is a cry for help. But what both of those arguments really say is that violence, however motivated, is gratifying and empowering.

Religions and civilizations may be seen as attempts to discipline mankind, to trim our worst excesses. Traditionally, religions and civilizations acknowledged mankind's propensity for violence and imposed appropriate strictures. Certainly no religion or civilization has believed that it could ignore violent behavior as peripheral. Yet our contemporary American approach is to treat violence as an aberration, the product of a terrible misunderstanding. It is the mentality of the born victim, of the spouse who believes every weeping apology, of the social worker who believes in the mass murderer's rehabilitation. Our willful denial of the full spectrum of man's nature, from the sublime to the beastly, is a privilege of our wealth. It is not a privilege that will be extended to our soldiers.

Look at the wreckage of this decade. Can we pretend that the massacre of half a million Rwandan Tutsis by their neighbors was carried out as a laborious chore? On the contrary, reports from the scene describe murderers intoxicated by their deeds. When we consider the ingenious cruelties perpetrated daily in Algeria, can we believe that the killers are forced to commit those atrocities against their inclinations? Will we pretend that the dead of Srebrenica were the victims of reluctant hands?

A meaningful sense of humanity demands that we ask hard questions about the nature of man. Military effectiveness in the coming decades will make the same demands. It will be terribly difficult for us. Our noble, unique elevation of the individual's worth is ill suited to a world in which our opponents regard the masses who follow them as surplus capital.

The American Myth of Peace

A corollary to the universal myth of a lost golden age is the recurring myth of the peaceable kingdom, where the lion lies down with the lamb and the spear is broken in two. This has long been a powerful myth in the American grain, carried from Europe in the first ships that sailed for New England. In those northern colonies, many of the early settlers belonged to dissident Protestant sects out to replicate the kingdom of God on earth. Many were pacifists or had strong pacifistic inclinations. They had been oppressed, and, although they would become oppressors in their time, their experiences had condensed their vision of a just, ideal world to a diamond hardness.

Our founding parents fled Europe's dynastic struggles convinced that such wars, and by extension all wars, were ungodly. Later they fought the Indians, then the French, then the British, then their hemispheric neighbors, then much of the world. But they never accepted war as being in the order of things. War was a terrible, unnatural misfortune, perpetrated by despots and madmen or spawned by injustice. But it was not a core human endeavor.

From that heritage we Americans have developed our ahistorical belief that all men want peace, that all conflict can be resolved through compromise and understanding. It leads to the diplomatic equivalent of Sunday-night snake handling—faith in the power of negotiations to allay hatred. Because we are privileged and reasonably content with our corner of the planet, we find peace desirable. There is nothing wrong with this. The problem arises when we assume that all other men, no matter how discontented, jealous, disenfranchised, and insulted, want peace as well. Our faith in man is, truly, a blind faith.

Many human beings have no stake in peace. They draw no advantage from the status quo. We see this even in our own fortunate country.

A disproportionate share of crime is committed by those with the least stake in society—the excluded and marginalized with little or nothing to lose. In this age of accelerating change, we, too, suffer from extreme fundamentalism concentrated at the lower end of the social spectrum (though not at the bottom among the drug-wrecked *Lumpenproletariat*). Consider the crimes that trouble us most. Gang crime occurs between those with the least to gain or lose from the social order the rest of us cherish. The Oklahoma City bombing was the work of a man who felt rejected by the society around him, who felt *wronged*. The repeated bombings of planned parenthood clinics consistently prove to be the work of low-skilled males who have turned to aggressive religious beliefs in which tolerance is intolerable. Dangerous true believers and violent opportunists are very much with us even in our own homeland.

We are, however, well positioned to moderate their excesses. Neither right-wing militias nor extreme fundamentalists are going to take over our country in the foreseeable future. But much of the world is less fortunate. Where there is less opportunity (sometimes none) and the existing, comforting order shrivels, human beings want validation and revenge. They cannot accept that their accustomed way of life is failing and that they are failing individually because of the behaviors to which their culture has conditioned them. They want someone to blame, and then they want revenge on that someone. A leader, secular or religious, has only to preach the gospel of foreign devils and dark conspiracies—to absolve his listeners of responsibility for their own failures—and he will find a willing audience.

Humans do not want change. They want their customs validated. They want more material possessions, but they do not want to alter their accustomed patterns of behavior to get those things. This is as true in America's inner cities as it is in the slums of Karachi or Cairo.

Again, many human beings thrive on disorder. When the civil war ends, the party is over. Many of the difficulties in Bosnia today stem from warriors who built thriving black-market and criminal networks during the fighting and do not want to let go of them. Often those who do the bulk of the fighting are men ill equipped to prosper in peace. The gun is their professional tool. When they grow convinced by, or are at least cloaked in, nationalist or fundamentalist religious beliefs, they are vulnerable only to greater force. In Russia, much of the citizenry longs for the rule of law—even the harsh law of the past. But those who have enriched themselves during Russia's new "time of troubles" like the system just the way it is. Although our Department of State does not believe it, it is difficult to convince a prospering gangster that democracy and the rule of law will work to his advantage. Around the world, from Uganda to Abkhazia, it is difficult to persuade those whose only successes in life have come from the gun in their hand that they should hand over that gun. Being a warlord, or just the warlord's retainer, is a far more attractive prospect than digging a ditch for a living or, worse, failing to find work as a ditchdigger.

We profit from peace. Our opponents profit from conflict. It is as fundamental a mismatch as the one between our forces and theirs. When they try to play by our rules, whether in the military or economic sphere, we demolish them. When, however, we are forced to play by their rules, especially during military interventions, the playing field is not only leveled—it often tilts in their favor.

When we drive the warriors into a corner or defeat them, they will agree to anything. When our attention is elsewhere, they will break the agreement. Their behavior, natural to them, is unthinkable to us. And then they massacre.

We pride ourselves on our rationality, while avoiding reality. If we are to function effectively as diplomats and soldiers, we need to turn a dispassionate eye on mankind. We need to study the behavior of the individual and the mass, and to do it without stricture. We cherish the fiction that technology will be the answer to all our dilemmas. But our enemies know that flesh and blood form the irresistible answer to our technologies.

Troy and Jerusalem

Another cliché with a core of truth is that Americans are the new Romans, proprietors of a (near) universal empire based on engineering and codification. Certainly we guard the walls of our civilization against new barbarians. But the mundane parallels are more intriguing. First, even when the Romans behaved cruelly at the height of empire, it was a measured policy. Second, their military was tiny in proportion to the range of their empire, and their legions, while rarely defeated, were often astonished by the savagery of their opponents. Third, the Romans so cherished their civilized image of themselves that it blinded them to barbarian strengths.

Fanatics brought Rome down. We associate the fall of Rome with Alaric and the Visigoths and a jumble of other warrior peoples who swept in from the north for long weekends (as German tourists do today). But Rome's decline was slow, and the empire rotted from within. Romans loved the law—even under the worst emperors, the rule of law never disappeared entirely—and they grew convinced that peace was the natural order of things. Their judges sought equity and order, and their legalisms crippled them.

Let us return to our beginning and consider the New Testament. We are made in the image of Pilate the Roman. On his fateful day, he was annoyed, briefly, by a minor case he just wanted to put behind him. He did not understand the matter and did not even believe that it lay within his purview. He was baffled and annoyed by the local squabbles, failing to appreciate the social and religious complexities involved—and the greater implications. Jesus was beneath the consideration of Rome's threat analysts. Pilate just wanted the problem to go away. Capable of insight, cruelty, and greatness on other occasions, on the most important day of his life, the Roman was caught drowsing. He is the classic representative of empire, the patron saint of diplomats.

We can almost smell the heat of the day and taste the dust. Imagine Pilate's impatience with his translator and his disbelief that the shabby, battered figure before him could be the cause of such a fuss. There simply was not enough of a challenge in evidence to excite a Roman governor and gentleman of great affairs. When a perfunctory attempt at arbitration between the locals failed, Pilate "washed his hands" of the prisoner's fate, anxious to move on to serious business, or maybe just to lunch. He did let his soldiers do a bad day's work, but only because the Romans kept a careful monopoly on capital punishments.

Pilate was a symbol of weakening Rome and growing Roman self-doubt. He served at Rome's apogee, yet the cancer was already there. His descendants, preferring debate to decision, would be no match for the fanatics who could kill the sober and the just without blinking. Pilate stuck to the letter of the law, and the law damned him.

As empires fall—and I am not suggesting that our own empire will fall anytime soon—the people of the empire return to religion, to cults, to blood ties. Christianity, a liberating mystery religion of the suffering classes, had to struggle during the heyday of empire. But when the decline became impossible to deny, the new religion, with its revolutionary rhetoric, prospered. In prospering, it further accelerated the decline of the old order. The repressions were too little too late, and they were a counterproductive tool to wield against the followers of that particular creed. Rome turned scolds into martyrs. The Roman threat analysts had failed again.

The Romans were chronically late to respond to challenges in the age of the lesser Caesars. They loved stasis and remembrance. The destruction of Solomon's Temple in Jerusalem and the suppression of the Jewish kingdom were not signs of remaining imperial strength but signs of weakness, frustration, and decline. In its confident years, the Roman Empire had been absorptive and tolerant. For centuries, these qualities lent strength and co-opted new subjects—but ultimately, core identities and commitments to the Roman idea became fatally diffuse and diluted. It was those who refused to be absorbed and who rejected toleration, from the brute German tribes to the true believers from the eastern provinces, who outlasted the greatest empire the earth knew until our own century.

Rome's greatest failure was its inability to understand the changing world.

We can measure historical climates by reading the growth bands of a tree stump. We can measure the climate of a culture by noting its religious revivals or the advent of a new religion—each marks a time of great stress on the society. In 1999, we are living in the most passionately religious age in centuries. The future looks ferocious.

Leaving aside the threat from weapons of mass destruction, however, the United States appears invulnerable for the foreseeable future. Terrorists might annoy us, but we will triumph. We will, ultimately, find the strength of will to do what must be done. The problems raised in this essay affect the average, prosperous American citizen little, if at all. But it is the soldiers of our new empire, the men and women who serve in our expeditionary forces and deploy to subdue enemies we neglect to understand, who will pay the cost of our ignorance. They will still win, when allowed to do so. But more of them will suffer and die for lowered returns because of our unwillingness to face the complexity of mankind.

Come back now to Troy. Read that great poem one more time, without the prejudices we have learned. You will find that the triumphant Greeks were the devious, the barbarous, the murderous. The Trojans were the urban, civilized, and tolerant. Troy stood for learning, piety, and decency. Its mistake was to humiliate implacable barbarians, without the will to destroy them. The Trojans fought to be left alone in their comfortable world. The Greeks fought for revenge, spoils, and the pleasure of slaughter. The Greeks won. Ulysses, who finally inveigled a way through the city gates, was the first great Balkan warlord. Murdered King Priam was a decent man who watched the war from behind his walls and had to beg for the return of his son's mangled body. He was presidential in his dignity.

We are not Trojans. We are far mightier. We rule the skies and seas and possess the power to rule the land when we are sufficiently aroused. But we have not learned to understand, much less rule, minds and hearts and souls. The only moral we need to cull from the *Iliad* is that it is foolish to underestimate the complexity and determination of the killers from the other shore.

The American Mission

Parameters

Autumn 1999

We, the American people, have reached the end of a two-and-a-half-century crusade that defined us and changed the world as profoundly as any event in history. For a quarter of a millennium, we fought empires. Now those empires are gone—every one—and we do not know what to do with ourselves. Our present enemies are vicious, but small. They cannot excite us to a new national purpose. The United States is suffering from victory.

Pentagon officials struggle to justify the purchase of $350 billion worth of unnecessary aircraft, while our diplomats sleepwalk through atrocity and our foreign policy is an incoherent shambles. None of our outward-looking institutions has grasped the dimensions of change. We need to break 250 years of habits we did not even realize we had. Our national cause, never articulated or even consciously realized, was to break the imperial hierarchies that held mankind in bondage. In 1989, as the last and worst of the old empires fell, we won a complete victory, and found ourselves unprepared for the fractured world the struggle left behind.

The verities and cherished villains are gone, and we have entered an age of small-scale evils. We crave a great, new American mission, and policy circles feel confusion and malaise in the new threat vacuum. The mightiest American foreign policy tradition is gone—a tradition that predated our existence as a country. We are a people formed in opposition, and that opposition was always to empire. Now there is no mightiness to oppose, no galvanizing evil, but only hard-to-locate countries where bloody shreds of mankind butcher neighbors.

We began under English dominion, opposing the French empire in a struggle that culminated in the mid-eighteenth century. If America's independence began at Lexington and Concord, it found its inspiration on the Plains of Abraham before Quebec, where colonial militiamen learned how easily an empire might fall. Next, we fought the greatest empire of the age, Britain itself, to champion the political and economic rights of man. A first war drove the British out, while a second confirmed their relegation to the Canadian margins of our continent.

Then we fought the Mexican empire and cut it in half. Our subsequent Civil War was an internal purge, cleansing from our soil the last European notions of hereditary authority and human subjugation. It was an Americanizing bloodbath that ended the first phase of our anti-imperial struggle, consolidating the physical shape of the United States we know.

The second phase of our crusade began with the Spanish-American War, a globe-spanning conflict whose brevity and relative lack of suffering have always obscured its importance. This time, we not only defeated a European empire, but destroyed it. It was not a local revolution against colonial overlords, but an international assault upon colonial possessions. No matter that Spain's imperium was little more than a carcass—this was a watershed in history, the death knell for the old European empires. The Spanish-American War was noteworthy, too, because it was our first war against a distant "evil empire." Spain's treatment of its Cuban and other colonial subjects both moved us and gave us an excuse to grasp its treasures. It proved an addictive model.

Japan observed the low price we paid, then emulated us half a dozen years later, when it attacked the other decayed European empire with dominions in East Asia, the Czar's Russia. Japan won brilliantly, then launched itself as an upstart empire that would end forty years later, in humiliation, on the deck of an American battleship.

The First World War was a conflict of discontents that were not ours, a hacking off of Europe's diseased limbs by the afflicted body itself. That great European civil war fatally weakened the remaining empires, while spawning new ones. America's late entry aligned us against three more empires: the Second Reich of Germany, Austria-Hungary, and the Ottoman Empire. Although we hardly engaged the latter two, we guaranteed their destruction.

In the Second World War, America saved the world from unspeakable tyrannies. This is an unfashionable, but absolutely accurate way of putting it. For all the valor of crumpled Britain and agonized Russia, the United States decided the outcome. In doing so, we destroyed the Japanese and Nazi-German empires, as well as the operetta empire of Fascist Italy. Fatally weakened, the British and French empires collapsed of their own weight after the war. Only the Soviet incarnation of the Russian empire, a domain of figurative and literal darkness, remained to represent the imperial idea of human subjugation.

In 1945, we found ourselves guarantors of a world we barely knew. It is not surprising that we made tragic mistakes, but that we made so few. During the Cold War, the complexity of our struggle increased. The force of arms proved weaker than the force of ideas—ours or theirs. In Korea, then Vietnam, we found ourselves engaged with a grisly empire of ideology. Yet the populations against whom we fought were fighting their own anti-imperial struggles. The United States fought anti-imperial wars against anti-imperialists fighting to expand a totalitarian empire. The Cold War was an age of paradox and moral erosion—as dark as it was cold—overshadowed by the ever-present threat of nuclear cataclysm.

At the end of this last struggle, those who believed that man should govern himself from below had defeated those who believed that man must be governed from above. In that sense, 1989 marked not the end of a mere quarter millennium of human history, but the climax of man's entire previous history of governance. Certainly many a local tyranny remains around the world, but they will not prosper. The future belongs to citizens who control their own governments. All else is a vestige.

When the Berlin Wall fell, we were triumphant and at a loss. We opened the door to mankind's future, but closed the door on who we had been for so long. Along the way, we had become an empire ourselves, if of an unprecedented kind. Ours is an empire of culture and economic power, not of military occupation and physical enslavement. Nonetheless, the nation that defined itself as David has become the last Goliath.

We destroyed the old world, but lack a useful vision for a new order. Since 1989, too much of humanity has failed to live up to our ennobling rhetoric. Our victory over the last of the old empires unleashed forces we failed to anticipate, zealous butchers wrapped in religion and ethnicity. Perhaps all that is left to us is a long minding of brute children.

We destroyed or helped destroy eleven empires in this 250-year epoch, while the remaining few—Portuguese, Dutch, Belgian—died of decay. The fundamental difficulty remaining, apart from mankind's innate tendencies, is that those empires twisted the world into unnatural shapes. Although the empires are gone, the treacherous boundaries they established remain. Empires drew borders based not upon popular preference or human affinities, but as a result of conflicts, competition, and compromise with other empires. Often, borders were defined in ignorance of local affairs or even of geographical detail. Lines inked—or sometimes crayoned—upon a map determined the fate of millions. Those borders remain a plague upon our times.

The United States, history's most powerful force for human liberation, now finds itself in a perverse and ill-considered position. Due to inertia and the fears of bureaucrats, we have slipped into the role of defending inherited, utterly dysfunctional imperial borders. Our Department of State, administrations drawn from both parties, lawyers, and academics all oppose "violations of sovereignty" and even the most logical and necessary amendments to borders. Future historians will be amazed at America's actions across the past decade. One administration initially tried to convince the Soviet Union to remain together, while successive administrations opposed the breakup of Yugoslavia, an entity as unnatural as any cobbled-together state could be. In our addiction to stasis and our obsession—for it is nothing less than that—with "inviolable" interstate boundaries carved out by imperial force in a different age, we are putting ourselves on the side of the empires we destroyed. America thoughtlessly supports oppression because we find the lines on the map familiar and convenient. The ghosts of kaisers, kings, and czars must be howling with glee in hell.

We must rethink this blind and destructive policy. Instead of using our might in vain attempts to force those who hate one another to live together—our "no-divorce" approach to foreign policy—we should lead the way in developing mechanisms to amend borders peacefully—or as peacefully as possible. Of course this will be difficult to do, for many of those in power profit from the present arrangement, and the sufferings of the powerless do not move them. And justice will be relative, for the redefinition of many borders will involve population transfers: Even when statistically just, such changes will prove unfair to many individuals. Amending borders is not a formula for a perfect world, only an approach to improve the present one and lessen slaughter.

The alternative is ethnic cleansing, genocide, and violence without end. We cannot force a man to love his neighbor. And, most important, redrawn borders and population transfers work. Those conducted at the end of World War II in Europe resulted in the longest period of peace in European history—until the disintegration of Yugoslavia, where borders had *not* changed.

Certainly the least mention of just borders will bring howls from every scruffy dictatorship in the United Nations. But should the nation that changed human history for the better and shattered the imperial model quake at the protests of Balkan thugs, African strongmen, or Asian authoritarians?

Of course, it will not be possible to impose effective changes in every case. Strategic interests will have their due, while some demands for independence arise only from a minority of the championed minority. At times, the ethnic mixing will be too complex, the claims too layered and contradictory. And in some cases the local populations will still have to settle their differences in blood. There will be no universal formula for success. Each case will have its own dilemmas. Yet who believes that the present system is functional, or acceptable, or decent? As we prepare to enter a new millennium, it is time to discard those foolish prejudices that have come to pass for wisdom in world affairs. Bad borders will change. The only question is how those changes will occur.

Our American mission is not over. Although it is ever a temptation to withdraw from this troubled world and celebrate our own wealth and comfort, isolation is an impossible dream. The world is now too much of a piece, its interlocking systems too complex and binding. American interests are everywhere, or nearly so. We are condemned to work for global betterment.

This does not mean our current penchant for plunging thoughtlessly into random crises that happen to get our attention is a wise one, or that we must engage always and everywhere. On the contrary, a consideration both of where our greatest national interests lie and of what is actually achievable (and affordable) should always shape our web of policies—economic, diplomatic, and military. But there are two worthy goals that we might bear in mind:

First comes the practical matter of borders. We must either foster the creation of mechanisms to fix those that do not work or at least side with those seeking self-determination and not with dying, repressive regimes that cling to every inch of their "sovereign" territory. This world is changing, whether we like it or not. A fundamental change is occurring in the forms, shapes, and sizes of statehood, reflecting national downsizing in the aftermath of empire and the simultaneous development of transnational modes of cooperation. Although horrified diplomats and professors declare the impossibility of changing borders, they are wrong. Borders are already changing, from Colombia's internal borders to the inevitable independence of Kosovo, from Central Africa to Indonesia. Our current position is at best naive. Because we do not support the legitimate aspirations of other human beings to live peaceably among those for whom they feel a natural affinity, we find ourselves time and again on the wrong side of history. It is time to come to our senses and lead the way to freedom once again.

The second worthy goal is support of universal human rights. The present administration, despite its deplorable failure to pursue that goal, began with appealing rhetoric. Long after the glare of scandal has dulled, America's enduring support for monstrous dictatorships will fascinate those who study our history. The mechanics of the present administration's failure were simple. Coming to office with a genuine desire, but not a commitment, to support human rights, the administration quickly found that it owed too much to too many interest groups—support for human rights was not compatible with business or diplomatic convenience. Early on, during a meeting of the National Security Council staff, the decision was taken to "give" Burma/Myanmar to the human rights advocates to appease them—anathematizing it for its human rights record and banning new American investment—while continuing to conduct business as usual with more important states such as China and Saudi Arabia, where human rights abuses were and remain far worse.

Support for human rights need not involve constant engagement on all fronts, with U.S. troops deployed each time a bully kicks a dog. Rather, we simply should consider this moral and practical factor when making diplomatic decisions. Strategic requirements will not always allow us to put human rights first in every case and country. But their consideration must never be fully absent. Further, dependable support for human rights—and a range of penalties for abusers—would bring our country both renewed respect and practical advantage. Respect for basic human rights forms the basis for both sound policy and good business. The partner state that respects the needs and aspirations of its own citizens is apt to be a dependable partner, but the dictator always comes down in the end.

We have too often been on the wrong side of a popular revolution. We no longer have even the excuse of Cold War polarities to explain our penchant for supporting oppressors. When the Russian government slaughtered tens of thousands of its own citizens in Chechnya, we hastened to assure Moscow of our unreserved friendship. In the Balkans, we cut deals with dictators time and again, only to watch the torrent of blood expand. In Indonesia, we clung to yesterday's corrupt regime even as the people pulled it down. Especially in the Middle East, we kowtow to regimes that oppress and abuse women, torment and even kill those of different faiths, and utterly reject democracy. These are inexplicable cases of the strong allowing the weak but intolerant to set the terms of engagement. We garner no respect, but are despised for our hypocrisy and fecklessness. We desecrate our heritage each day.

Americans attempt to defeat proposals they do not like by simplifying them to death. The propositions sketched above will be misinterpreted—purposely—as a call for sending in the Marines, or launching a quixotic global crusade, or even supporting the bogey-man of world government. I advocate none of these things, but only an intelligent approach to change, a moral stance where one is pos-sible, and a recognition that wishing away the desires of oppressed populations will not keep foreign borders intact.

As for sovereignty, it is the privilege of the just, successful state. Any state that butchers, or even oppresses, its own population for-feits any claim to sovereign rights. Recently, we heard repulsive argu-ments that attempts to stop mass murder and ethnic cleansing in Kosovo infringed on sovereign territory. By that logic, Hitler would have been acceptable had he killed only German Jews. States exist to protect and benefit their populations. That is the rationale for these United States. Shall other human beings be condemned in order to keep our atlases intact and our embassy receptions on schedule?

If a state cannot control criminality, terrorism, or ecological dev-astation on its own territory and those problems adversely affect its neighbors—or the entire planet—may it still claim sovereignty? This is the argument of kings, not of the common man. At present, we pretend that ineffective or even criminal regimes are legitimate because we "know no other way." It is time to forge another way.

This world is one in which we cannot stand alone. While we must protect our own sovereignty, which is legitimate, earned, and beneficial to all, we must also recognize the need for teamwork. NATO served American interests well—and still does, despite that organization's need to evolve. The United Nations, pathetic, inept, and indispensable, has also brought us more advantages than disad-vantages, from providing an umbrella for some necessary actions to giving discontented minor states the illusion of a voice. But NATO is a regional alliance, and will not span the globe. The United Nations remains ineffective in the clinch, not only because of its dreadful bureaucracy (which may, in fact, be a blessing, since it pre-vents the organization from doing much damage), but because it is too inclusive. No organization in which backward, vicious regimes, such as those of China or Russia, have veto power will change much of anything—least of all unjust borders, a digestive ailment from which both these gobblers of minorities suffer.

It is time to form a Union of Democratic Nations, of globe-span-ning, like-minded states whose people live under the rule of law and choose their own leaders. We need a grand alliance that can act—diplomatically, economically, and, when necessary, militarily—for global betterment. Such an alliance would include only true democracies, such as most European states, our own country, and others such as Japan, South Korea, Brazil, Argentina, Chile, Israel, South Africa, and the sturdy English-speaking states down under and to our north. It would exclude false democracies, such as Russia or Malaysia. Corrupt democracies and those in which religious prejudice or ethnic favor is dominant would also be excluded, until they reform. This would leave out for now India and Pakistan, Mexico and Nigeria. The purpose would be to unite in an alliance those states whose behavior has earned them the right to support positive change in troubled regions.

It would also have to be an open alliance, in which a two-thirds majority and not unanimity would be required for action, and in which no member would be required to participate in a specific embargo or deployment against its will. It would, in short, be truly democratic and utterly voluntary. Such an alliance might even prove capable of timely action. At a minimum, it would be the richest, most powerful, and most desirable club in the world.

On the threshold of a new millennium, Americans can be proud. We have led the world a long way out of the darkness. But there are still miles to go. We destroyed the old hierarchies that wasted human aspirations and talents as surely as they squandered human blood. We broke the tradition of rule by fiat that stretched from Babylon to Moscow. It is hard not to see these United States as blessed and chosen.

We are very fortunate. And with good fortune comes responsibility. We are condemned to lead. This means we must stop clinging to the past, whether antiquated notions about the sacrosanct nature of a butcher's borders or the belief that what goes on beyond our neighbor's customs barrier does not concern us. It is not a matter of seeking "foreign entanglements," or compromising our own hard-won freedoms, but of doing what is best for ourselves as well. A world in which men and women live freely and enjoy secure rights is the world in which our own greatness is likeliest to endure.

The Human Terrain of Urban Operations

Parameters

Spring 2000

Tasked with urban operations, soldiers think of buildings. The initial mental image is of physical forms—skyscrapers or huts, airports and harbors, size, construction density, streets, sewers, and so on. Planners certainly are interested in the population's attitudes and allegiances, but cities are more likely to be classified by their differences in construction than by the variety of their populations. This focus on "terrain" leads to the assumption that military operations would be more challenging in a Munich than in a Mogadishu. But the latter "primitive" city brutally foiled an international intervention launched with humanitarian intent, while "complex" Munich whimpered into submission at the end of the fiercest war in history. The difference lay not in the level of physical development, but in the human architecture.

While the physical characteristics of the assaulted or occupied city are of great importance, the key variable is the population. At its most obvious, the issue is simply whether the citizenry is hostile, indifferent, or welcoming. Too often, the evaluation of the flesh-and-blood terrain, of the human high-ground, ends there. Yet few populations are ever exclusively hostile, or truly indifferent, or unreservedly welcoming. Man's complexity is richer than any architectural detail. It is, finally, the people, armed and dangerous, watching for exploitable opportunities, or begging to be protected, who will determine the success or failure of the intervention.

Types of Cities

Analyzing the "human architecture" of a city begins with the recognition that there are three broad types of "mass terrain." For military purposes, cities can be classed as hierarchical, multicultural, or tribal. This imperfect system of classification does not offer a basis for command decisions—only a starting point for understanding the operational environment into which the force will be thrust. It can, however, provide early warning of the intractable nature of the problems that may await even an initially welcome peacekeeping force.

Hierarchical Cities

Hierarchical cities are those we Americans know. Chains of command operate within a broadly accepted rule of law. The citizens assume at least minimal responsibilities, from the payment of taxes to patterns of public behavior. In return, they expect that they will not be routinely cheated by government or merchants, that the light switch will turn on the light, that water will come from the tap, and that the police will provide a reasonable degree of protection without unreasonable intrusions into personal lives.

Apart from the technological aspects and the unusual degree of freedom enjoyed by Americans, the hierarchical city is a traditional form, stretching back to the dawn of history. Cities of the past were more repressive, of course, but chain-of-command cities, governed by a generalized consent or acquiescence and with popular respect for the rules of interaction, are mankind's great success story (the herding of cats on a mammoth scale). From Athens, Greece, to Athens, Georgia, such cities have provided men and women with the highest degree of well-being available in their ages. Sometimes repressive, elsewhere delightfully liberal—when not libertine—the common denominator of successful cities is a sense of unified popular identity, which is far more important than legal specifics. (A common Western fallacy is to imagine that liberal laws are an end unto themselves; in fact, most populations have preferred restrictive laws impartially administered to exemplary constitutions corruptly applied. A law's consistent observation is generally more important than its inherent quality, and the first purpose of law is certainty.)

Militarily, hierarchical cities, with their united citizenries, can provide bitter, prolonged resistance to an attacker. Paradoxically, they can be the easiest to govern once occupied—if the population recognizes its interests lie in collaboration. At the close of World War II, the cities of Germany and Japan contained populations recently committed to total war, yet they proved docile and easy to govern by constabulary forces. The citizenry must see the advantage in cooperation; once convinced, its homogeneity eases successful reconstruction, both physical and behavioral. It has always been easier to govern Paris than to take it.

Multicultural Cities

Multicultural cities, which have little to do with the fantasies of liberal arts faculties, are those in which contending systems of custom and belief, often aggravated by ethnic divisions, struggle for dominance. They are, by their nature, cockpits of struggle. Chains of command in government offices draw willing obedience only from their partisans, while groups that do not identify with those in power must be coerced into desired behaviors and will act subversively until a reaction defines the limits of what is tolerable. To those ignorant of local affairs, the multicultural city may resemble the hierarchical city, with its mayor or other administrator and its formal institutions. But real power is diffused beyond legal agencies into ethnic networks, religious and resistance organizations, and crime syndicates whose leaders usurp much of the authority and some of the functions of the "legitimate" government.

Multicultural cities, even in the best of economic times, squander creative energies and human capital on social struggles aimed at revising the balance of power. True multiculturalism of this sort is centrifugal, intolerant, and ultimately destructive. North American cities, even the most ethnically diverse, remain hierarchical—multiethnic, but not multicultural—while those that most closely approach the multicultural "ideal" described here tend to be the least safe and least prosperous. Successful cities require a community of values; multicultural cities may produce successful individual neighborhoods, but the sum is always less than the parts. Where cultural confrontation pits alternative value systems against each other, the city declines—no matter the relative merit of the contending values. Cities are, above all, cooperative ventures (with laws to protect the dull against the anarchic impulses of the creative), and require general agreement as to the social blueprint to be followed. Diversity may thrive within the cooperative, as it does in so much of North America, and may gradually reshape the society from the inside (although the opening of a Chinese restaurant does not presuppose the public's acceptance of Confucian values). But when cultural differences create a sense of assault on group values from the outside, the city is headed for riots at best and, at worst, genocide.

Perhaps the preeminent example of a multicultural city today is Jerusalem, with its irreconcilable differences between Jews and Arabs, whose beliefs, values, and ambitions are profoundly at odds. In this classic model, order is maintained only by the forcefulness of the more powerful faction, buttressing the hatreds of the group excluded from authority (and, by extension, from prosperity and social mobility). When a numerically inferior group holds a larger group or groups in thrall, the situation is especially volatile. The Israelis, with their settlement policies, attacked this problem long ago. Another recent example comes from East Timor, where a minority of Islamic Indonesian occupiers had oppressed and deprived the Catholic Timorese. The values of the two communities were bluntly incompatible (especially when overlaid with Indonesian fantasies of imperial grandeur).

Multicultural cities tend to develop along what Samuel Huntington has called the "fault lines" between civilizations—those marches and frontiers where dominance shifts between groups over centuries (and sometimes more swiftly). South Africa's harsh growing pains center largely on its multicultural cities, where British, Afrikaner, and native African cultural systems collided. When the restraining British hand lifted from the Indian subcontinent, the massacres inflicted on one another by Hindus and Muslims covered their cities with gore and disfigured their nascent states. Now cities such as Lahore and Delhi have returned, limping, to hierarchical status, but continue to suffer under the multicultural legacy of corruption and factionalism, aggravated by value systems ill-suited to modernity. Other urban areas, from Istanbul to its old polar opposite, Vienna, have devolved back into hierarchical cities more successfully as empires collapsed, civilizational fault lines shifted, and "foreign" elements were expelled or moved on. Even in the best cases, however, the transition periods from multicultural flowering back to monocultural roots are unstable, often bloody, and disquieting to foreign observers.

The continual, generally peaceful cultural evolution in the United States suggests that healthy, prosperous societies can change by elective accretion, but that cultural amalgamation bluntly does not work. Secure in their sense of identity, the populations of hierarchical cities can learn from new arrivals, while multicultural cities barricade themselves—sometimes literally—against intercommunal exchanges. Even in the United States, the immigrant groups that excited the most resistance and proved slowest to assimilate were those who arrived quickly, in large numbers, creating a perception of threat to the established order and its values. Numbers matter, perhaps even more than do racial differences, as the long struggle of Irish Americans toward equality compared to the comparatively easy acceptance of Korean Americans suggests. And overt conformity to societal norms may be even more important than religious conformity in gaining acceptance, except in the most demagogic and primitive cultures. The group established as social hegemon wants, above all, obeisance to its values and cherished behaviors.

Statistically, there are surprisingly few multicultural cities at any given time, since they are inherently unstable. Reversion to monocultural hierarchy—or destruction—is the norm: Turkish Izmir or vanished Troy (a close reading of *The Iliad* suggests that the Trojans drew their support from inherently unstable intercultural alliances, while the Greeks arrived in a state of dynamic cultural coalescence). Unless the city falls to an external power, its less powerful population groups inevitably are massacred, expelled, or forcibly assimilated, whether in the cities of Silesia, Andalusia, or India at the hour of independence from British rule. The ugly fact about the devolution of multicultural cities back into ethnically or confessionally harmonious ones is that the population transfers usually bring stability and peace.

From the military standpoint, multicultural cities can be easy to conquer—with the aid of oppressed minorities as a fifth column—but difficult to administer after peace has been established. If you have made allies of one group, they will expect to dominate after the victory or intervention. Western notions of equitable treatment and the rule of law strike the population as risible, if not as an outright betrayal. Peace can be imposed, but not even a generation of occupation will convince the opposing groups to behave "like us." In cultures where compromise is, literally, unthinkable, the peacekeeping adventure will see a constant jockeying for favor and usually a hardening of physical divisions between groups. The citizens of all factions will be looking beyond the presence of the peacekeepers to the renewed struggle, violent or otherwise, for hegemony. Often, the nominal government imposed by the occupier or peacekeeper will have less real power than ethnic leaders, militia commanders in mufti, religious leaders, or mafiosi. The primary interests of each faction will be to exploit the power of the constabulary force for partisan purposes, to exploit gaps in the force's knowledge of the local situation for advantage, to shield illicit activities from the force's awareness, to consolidate power within the group, and, finally, to corrupt key elements of the force to facilitate prohibited behaviors and to undermine competitors. The primary challenge for a Western military operating in a multicultural city is to get at the facts—and the facts never hold still.

There are also plentiful exceptions to the proposition that multicultural cities are easy to conquer. If the population group with which you are allied is powerless or unwilling to fight, you may face absolutely furious resistance from the enraged majority or urban hegemon. The first battle of Grozny, in Chechnya, was a striking example of this. If the divisions cut so deep that the antagonist is willing to fight a scorched-earth (or leveled-building) war—including the massacre of the minority or weaker group that has bound its fate to you—the intervention force faces extreme combat challenges that will be resolved as much by a question of will as by objective military capabilities. In general, a declared or perceived partisanship on the part of peacemaking or peacekeeping forces prior to deployment creates a window of slaughter, during which the threatened group accelerates ethnic cleansing operations, as in Dili, Pristina, or Freetown. Peace operations resemble other military operations in that, so often, speed saves lives—but swift intervention is one of the rarest acts of the international community. The world reacts to horror, but refuses to anticipate it.

Regarding other multicultural cities of the collapsed Soviet empire, most in Central Asia are losing ethnic European populations, although the situation varies from state to state, but Europeans have not been the objects of violent outbreaks; rather, outside of Tajikistan, the ugliest instances of violence have erupted between indigenous nationalities in Central Asia's Fergana Valley. In Afghanistan, a war of liberation degenerated into an ethnic civil war, and the dominant Taliban movement is willing to lay waste cities in order to "purify" them ethnically and religiously, rendering them monocultural with a vengeance. The number of unresolved issues and artificial states between the Black Sea and China's western provinces make this area the least predictable in the world. No one can foresee whether it will drowse or erupt—but Russia's greatest challenges in the coming decades are likely to arise on its frontiers, not on the financial spreadsheets of Western banks. The Russian Federation is the new "sick man of Europe," and, just as the collapse of the Ottoman Empire was triggered by events in Sarajevo, a dusty former city of that empire, so Moscow may face crises sparked in cities it once occupied, from Kiev through Baku to Tashkent. Indeed, Russia's large, creaking military, its loan-gobbling financial squalor, and its inability to control its remaining territories make it resemble the Ottoman Empire, but with rotting nukes. At a minimum, Russia's future military efforts will offer the West a laboratory in which to study the problems of urban operations, from the festering ulcer of Chechnya to terrorism in Moscow itself.

For the peacekeeping or constabulary force, the most promising environment is a formerly multicultural city that has been, regrettably, ethnically "cleansed." Problems will be directly proportionate to the extent to which status quo antebellum differences remain unresolved: Sadly, the more thorough the ethnic cleansing, the better the chances for the city's recuperation. The best hope for recovery in Dili, East Timor—difficult in any case, because of the ravages of violence and longstanding poverty—will be the complete departure of Indonesians who arrived after 1975. Although it remains to be seen, the hideous ethnic cleansing in the Caucasian cities of Baku, Sumgait, and Stepanakert—multicultural for generations, when not centuries—may eventually result in regional pacification.

The deprivation of the object of hatred is a powerful force for peace. This is an unattractive concept for Westerners. It is also true.

Tribal Cities

Tribal cities, the most difficult urban environments for peacekeeping operations, are growing in size and number around the world. Based upon differences in blood, but not in race or, necessarily, in religion, ethnic conflicts in this environment can be the most intractable and merciless. One of the many paradoxes of our time is that the greatest expression of human sophistication, the city, increasingly draws in those with primitive, blood-based allegiances. As traditional rural societies grow overpopulated and impoverished, the lure of the city disproportionately draws young males—society's most volatile population slice—seeking opportunity, adventure, and reinvigorated identity.

Whether in Mogadishu, Kigali, Dushanbe, or Karachi, violence between those of the same race and similar or identical religion has ruptured governments even where its remoteness has kept it off the television screen. While Tutsis and Hutus in Rwanda might differ in appearance to the tutored eye, they are not civilizationally different. In Mogadishu, peacekeepers could not tell the difference between clans without obvious cues. In Tajikistan, you have to know the *individual* with whom you are dealing. And in Pakistan, where the city of Karachi veers between ungovernable and barely governable phases, the city's explosive growth in the Independence period was based upon the relocation of religiously identical and ethnically indistinguishable "brothers" from the rest of the subcontinent. Now the brothers have turned fratricidal. Around much of the world, the tribe, once banished from the liberal vocabulary, has returned with a vengeance. It is mankind's basic killing organization.

Perhaps the most startling "tribal" conflict of our time has been the series of wars in the former Yugoslavia. While some might declare this a multicultural conflict based in religious and civilization differences, that is to subscribe to the rhetoric of Milosevic and Tudjman. The region's multicultural phase climaxed a century ago; since then, the local populations have blurred into a gray similarity. The day-to-day cultures of Orthodox Serbs, Croatian Catholics, and

Bosnian or Kosovar-Albanian Muslims had converged to the degree that the urban Serb and urban Muslim, in Sarajevo or Pristina, had more in common with one another than either did with his rural counterpart. Religion was discounted, a dusty relic, until revived by demagogues. Ethnicity was an old scar, not a present sore.

Although couched in terms of civilizational conflict, the battles and atrocities in the Balkans have had more in common with those in Somalia or Rwanda than with the epoch-making struggles between Ottomans and Byzantines, or czar and sultan. At the same time, we are seeing a phenomenon the West had assumed to be impossible in our "enlightened" age: These Balkan tribes that had largely lost their primitive identities are re-creating them, and doing so with bloody exuberance. We know more about the atmosphere of Mars than we do of the ties for which men kill.

Tribal cities, from Sarajevo to Freetown, pose difficulties for intervention forces or peacekeepers on multiple levels. On the most basic level, it often takes long experience for outsiders to tell members of the contending factions apart when they fail to pro-claim—or try to disguise—their identities. It is especially hard to crack tribal and clan cultures for intelligence purposes, and com-batants vanish easily into the "sea of the people." But perhaps the greatest difficulty lies in the peculiar depth of hatred clan fighting and tribal traditions bring to bear on a conflict. Interracial pogroms erupt and quickly subside, but tribal hatreds are robust and endur-ing. There is no will to compromise, no sense of shared advantage through cooperation—except perhaps briefly against outsiders, such as peacekeeping forces. The pattern appears to be that the more similar contending factions appear to foreign observers, the more savagely they will oppose each other.

We seem to be moving from an age of imperialist genocide—European against African or Native American, Japanese against Chinese or Korean, Arab against African (the oldest enduring genocidal tradition, lingering in Sudan)—to a period of genocide against familiars, shifting from slaughter between civilizations to the slaughter of neighbors. The Germans lit the fire, with their mas-sacre of the Jews who had immeasurably enriched German society over the centuries and who regarded themselves as every bit as Ger-man as any *Kanzler*. Now we see the new model of massacre from

East Central Africa to the Caucasus to the Balkans. Except in the Arab and Persian Islamic world, where the style of hatred lags behind, hatred of the family next door has replaced the fear of the distant, different devil.

Our knowledge of ourselves is too primitive to allow us to understand why this change in humanity's choice of victims is taking place at this time, and we cannot know if it is a psychological response to history or a biological reaction to proximity or something else entirely, but the focal point of ever more contemporary violence—and the likeliest scene of future violence—is the city.

Comprehending Cityscapes

Cities are far more complex organisms than any text can suggest. Suffice to say that the greatest illustration of the human ability to self-organize shows in the daily functioning of cities. The myriad actions required to make Manhattan go are no more subject to complete regulation than they are to thorough quantification. Law is the foundation from which human activity is elaborated, but even the most voluminous codes have failed to foresee the inventiveness of human behavior. The countless individual actions that sum to urban life defy logic in their ability to interact constructively. Anarchy should follow; instead we get Florence, Sydney, and Boston.

Yet for all the marvels in even a poorly functioning city, there are worrisome trends. Obviously the increasing size and number of cities pose practical challenges for urban operations. Even in the smoothest operation, cities consume troops; in combat, they devour armies. We look back on a century in which a rural world became an urban one, and the practical and psychological changes are not yet fully apparent. The urbanization of the world's masses will require centuries of adjustment.

Whether or not civilizations are in crisis, they are certainly under pressure to evolve. Some are better suited to change than are others. The problems for Western militaries will overwhelmingly arise in traditional societies that cannot or will not adapt. In our desire to please all and offend none, we fail to recognize that the civilizational difference between the antagonists in Desert Storm was greater than that between Spaniards and Aztecs, or between the British military and the Mahdi's horde.

The world is not becoming an even, equitable place, but a sphere of deepening fissures, some of which may prove unbridgeable. At a time when even the rich states of Europe are falling two generations behind the United States militarily, and when global economic competition is far fiercer than at the height of the Industrial Revolution, fragile states will not be able to support their unwieldy cities with hope, or jobs, or infrastructure. Look to those cities for conflicts.

This essay offers a crude framework for thinking about the military nature of cities. Doubtless, there are more insightful ways to frame the problem; the model here proposed should spark debate, not pass as a prescription. In an age of urban operations, with many more to come, we must think more deeply and clearly about this environment than we have done. A cold appreciation of the environment and firm resolve often will be of greater help than any technologies or even numbers. Above all, this brief discussion seeks to drive home the point that the center of gravity in urban operations is never a presidential palace or a television studio or a bridge or a barracks. It is always human.

The Plague of Ideas

Parameters

Winter 2000–01

People sense, in these disordered times, that more has changed than words have yet expressed. Ours is a restless, unsettled age, straining between unprecedented hopes and old terrors, bounded on its shining edge by possibilities undreamed of even by our younger selves and on its darker horizon by vast, enduring misery worsened by rekindled hatreds. A world order that defined half a millennium, the age of European imperial domination, ended with the collapse of the Soviet incarnation of the Russian empire, and no unitary political system will replace it in our lifetimes.

We have entered a long, inchoate interlude, in which the concentration of wealth and military power in a minority of nations obscures the centrifugal nature of contemporary change. This is an age of breaking down, of the destruction of outgrown forms, of the devolution of power. The process of building again atop the ruins and reorganizing our societies will occupy us at least through the new century. We can be sure of little, only this: The speed of change is without precedent; for the first time in history, change has come to the entire globe, if to differing degrees and with radically different results; and no state or society can rely solely on past forms to shape the future.

Comfortable security models and industrial-age warfare between competing powers seem as obsolete as Marxism, while, in much of the world, even the legacy of statehood left behind by the old empires is under threat. Ideological and physical control over populations crumbles relentlessly in every lagging state, and hatreds and blood ties bind where law cannot. Authority sputters, increasingly ignored wherever humans find it inconvenient. Although the evidence had never fully disappeared, across the last decade the world's ruling and educated classes began rediscovering the primitive nature of man and his unattractive tendencies when civilized constraints are brushed aside. We, the long empowered, do not know what to do.

In these eruptive times, thoughtful men and women have voiced concerns about new or resurrected threats that ignore or exploit national boundaries, both those of robust states and borders that are little more than a pretense hoping for a bribe. Whether speaking of organized crime in its countless mutations, of terrorism, of epidemic disease, of financial manipulations, or of the assaults of digital anarchists, those who would alert us do good service. Yet the greatest "transnational threat" is the closest kin to our brightest hopes. Of all the dangers globalization brings, none is so immediate, so destabilizing, and so irresistibly contagious as the onslaught of information—a plague of ideas, good and bad, immune to quarantine or ready cures, under whose assault those societies, states, and even civilizations without acquired resistance to informational disorders will shatter irreparably.

Global Infection

Several years ago—an antique age by technology's present measure—Americans enjoyed a brief infatuation with books and films about horrific diseases that, once unleashed, might ravage middle-class neighborhoods. While sober attention must be paid to even the least chance of new pandemics, whether sparked by global-man's intrusion on remote territories, or spread by adept madmen or by the decay of biological warfare facilities in the former Soviet Union, the alarmists missed the epoch-defining symptoms erupting in front of their faces: For the first time in history, thanks to a dynamic constellation of communications tools, ideas can spread to the world's masses more quickly than epidemic disease.

Historically, disease outpaced data, with ideas lagging far behind. Rumors might precede the first fever in a village, but a serious plague reached more human beings far more swiftly than any abstract concept ever did. Disease moved at the speed of human travel—the same velocity as the rawest information. Ideas were, statistically, far slower. One traveling merchant or sailor, or simply a rat conveyed by ship, might infect a hundred overnight, and thousands within a week, but no saint or prophet ever persuaded men in truly epidemic numbers at epidemic speed. Concepts, to say nothing of true ideas, need explication, digestion, comparison, and practical experimentation before they find more than a transient, intoxicated acceptance. But disease did not rely on persuasion. Ideas moved at the speed of a man's feet, then of his beast of burden, next of his caravan or caravel, then of his automobile or passenger aircraft, only to arrive at rejection far more often than not. Disease did not offer choices.

Persuading people to accept a new belief, whether regarding the path to salvation or the efficacy of hygiene, required fortuitous historical timing, reserves of patience greater than any single lifespan, and sacrificial single-mindedness—to say nothing of the ruggedness and adaptability of the idea itself. Until the meridian of the European Renaissance, the Roman church was able to label every reform movement within its geographic sprawl a heresy and to suppress it before it could overturn anything beyond local hierarchies—since the church's enforcers could move as swiftly as any dissenting missionaries, as well as moving in considerably greater numbers. The creed riding on the back of a mule could not outpace a powerful bureaucracy.

Then the first information revolution struck, that of the book or broadside sheet printed cheaply on a movable-type printing press, fortifying the Protestant Reformation by enabling the spread of its timely ideas beyond the scope and speed of bureaucratic response. The book still moved at the speed of the human's means of transport, and it could not spread its "infection" with the vigor of the Black Death, but the equation had begun its long shift. The Reformation was the crude dress rehearsal for today's "information revolution."

Elsewhere, numerous societies, even entire civilizations, managed to seal themselves against contagious information from foreign parts. Japan, an island nation, is a classic example of a state that successfully turned its back on the world for centuries until external forces, empowered by informational synthesis, grew irresistible. China, vast and ever porous at the edges, nonetheless managed, through the power of its culture and the culture of its power, to hold the greater world at bay for thousands of years, its long introspection punctuated occasionally by invasions that were quickly digested. Self-satisfaction and perceived sufficiency, a sense of order perfected, made for a world within a world. Today's China, with its exposure to the greater world increasing hyper-geometrically, is a new entity—its evolving qualities akin to a chemical compound transferred from a vacuum chamber into the open air. Whether or not the reaction will be explosive remains to be seen.

Even in late-Renaissance Europe, Spain, the apotheosis of a Counter-Reformation regime, managed to close not only its own borders but those of its then-incomparable empire to unwanted influences and the information explosion of the early modern era— but, given its strategic integration into the European system, with destructive results. Self-deprived of the nourishing strains of Moorish and Jewish culture, and militantly opposed to northern Europe's secular innovations, Spain's vibrant culture stiffened and slowed, its economy withered (enervated by vast annual welfare checks from the New World's silver mines), its statecraft grew impotent, its military slowly decayed, and the population lost the impetus to modernity. Theories that blame the Spanish decline on excessive military spending mistake the symptom for the disease: Spain was an early casualty of the first, primitive information revolution, as various information-resisting regimes are of today's deluge of data.

Information and Wealth Formation

Indeed, the fates of European states and peoples from the sixteenth century forward provide a rudimentary model for the successes and failures in today's world, when postmodern economies—not the governments lagging behind them—shape the rules of global interaction and even the United States cannot pretend to be a hermetic fortress. Consistently, those nascent European states that had the most liberal information policies dramatically outperformed those states or regions where the Counter-Reformation clamped down hard not only on religious dissent but on the sciences in their fumbling, haunted childhoods.

The most informationally liberal European state of its day, the Dutch Republic, prospered astonishingly even as it fought expensive wars to achieve and guarantee its independence. Only after a civil war permanently destroyed the darker powers of kingship and assured essential informational freedoms did more-populous, better-protected England outstrip Holland in wealth and power. Meanwhile, Italy, the cradle of the Renaissance, grew static, even backward, under the book-banning, idea-fearing, comforting, and comfortable tyranny of the Counter-Reformation. Corrupt and hypocritical, somnolent and cruel, outwardly pious and privately lascivious, silver-age Italy resembled today's Iran, becoming, literally, a masked culture.

Inevitably, the greatest Western thinker about the power of information to drive change emerged in the British Isles in the guise of a political economist. Adam Smith, with his invisible hand of the marketplace, described two centuries in advance why the United States will continue to outperform mainland China, despite the astonishing energies the Chinese people bring to bear. Certainly, others have recognized the greater dimensions of Smith's revelation implicitly— most recently Thomas Friedman in his incisive book, *The Lexus and the Olive Tree*—but it needs to be stated explicitly: Adam Smith confined his observations regarding the self-correcting force of that "invisible hand" to free markets because, in his day, the economic sphere was the most liberal sphere within Britain (a situation reversed, with pathetic consequences, in the middle of the twentieth century and only put back to rights under Margaret Thatcher). Certain political and social truths could not yet be uttered, but the market increasingly was allowed to speak its mind from London to Glasgow and Edinburgh. Describing the capitalism he knew and could foresee, Smith intuited the dynamics of the information age precisely.

That invisible hand applies not only to the trader's domain, but to virtually every aspect of a healthy human society. Mature, informationally open societies, such as today's English-speaking nations of Western culture, are self-correcting, not only economically but socially, culturally, and politically. Citizens consummate change before bureaucracy can stymie it. The people vote not only with their wallets, but with each minor, mundane choice. Self-improving through dynamic trial and error, learning from the results of countless unfettered actions, these societies confound competitors with the speed with which they can innovate, seemingly defiant of physical principles equating mass with inertia.

Above all, states whose behavioral contours are determined by that invisible hand are practical. The past is preserved in museums, not in confining cultural strictures. Free societies guided by the aggregate effects of individual choices are not only the highest expression of human—and humane—attainment to date, they are far and away the most efficient. While their defense establishments, behaviorally distinct and informationally crippled, limp behind, states that do not constrain the flow of data nonetheless generate sufficient wealth to allow for a startling degree of military waste.

In these successful societies, the efficacy and worth of ideas are determined in the same way that the price of a household object is arrived at. Societal rules are not enforced from above or inherited uncritically from buried generations, but are selected and constantly refined from below by the living. The results are not only high-quality goods at low prices, but adaptive individual and collective behaviors that allow the population, statistically, to maximize its human potential.

The culturally liberal nations of the West are, in many-layered senses, marketplaces of ideas (to the dismay of intellectuals on the right and the left, with their totalitarian instincts). The citizens of such states have acquired, over generations, if not centuries, the internal compass necessary to navigate through the storms of information confronting them today. While a minority of citizens from the underclass and aberrant performers who make headlines with statistically irrelevant acts may believe that which is false or even lunatic, the average citizen makes highly effective economic, moral, and cultural calculations on a daily basis. Simply put, the good citizen has been culturally educated to pass the true-and-false tests of everyday life. He chooses what works best, then makes it work better.

This is no small thing. The most threatening aspect of today's information revolution is the power of comforting but false information to infect populations that lack the instinct for empirical reality that enables the West and key East Asian states to outperform the rest of humanity. Whether we choose as our examples the Gulf

War, the economic competition of the Cold War, or the comparative successes of the two Korean states, it is absolutely clear that the side that deals with facts and freedom clobbers the side that indulges in fantasies and repression.

Instead of being self-correcting, societies deficient in the ability to discriminate between different qualities of information grow self-deluding, embracing reassuring myths—or comforting rumors—instead of adjusting to embarrassing realities. This is true not only of individuals and states, but of entire civilizations today. Serbia, the Russian Federation, and various sub-Saharan African and Middle Eastern countries offer trenchant examples. When an informationally inept population must compete with one that is informationally adept, the deficient state or region always loses.

Over the past few decades, the West often had to listen to self-adoring lectures from Asian tyrants whose informationally sluggish countries were achieving impressive growth rates. But those states were developing so quickly because they finally had entered the industrial age two centuries after it began. Meanwhile, the United States and a few like-spirited nations, derided as irresolute and faltering, took a deep breath and plunged into the post-industrial information age. The "social laxity" decried by authoritarians proud of a handful of new factories turned out to be the cultural foundation for the creation of fabulous wealth and power. Now societies with undereducated, informationally stunted populations and a litter of smokestack industries find themselves left behind again, their national economies dwarfed by the revenues of individual Western corporations. Populations that make running shoes for populations that design computer networks have won the global economic booby prize.

Cholera and the Telegraph Key

Returning to the greatest familial establishment in economic and political history, Britain and the United States, the nineteenth century saw the beginning of the second information revolution, that which has accelerated and expanded so dramatically in our lifetimes. The first of the great cholera pandemics barely preceded the advent of the telegraph, and the latter was able to report news of later outbreaks ahead of their arrival. This was a critical step in the emancipation of information from the tyranny of physical transport. While it was an inefficient and inadequate tool for transmitting ideas, the telegraph could move limited amounts of data over great distances at a comparatively low cost.

A stunning innovation in its day, the telegraph nonetheless remained only the crudest precursor of the information dissemination devices of our time, since it was an easily controllable device, subject to governmental oversight in various forms, as well as to moral codes, physical infrastructure limitations, cost restraints, and the limited volume of data it could transmit. Better suited to deliver orders than insights, it remained a tool of the already empowered echelons of society, although its benefits increasingly reached the average citizen in the form of brief personal messages and the from-the-scene dispatches that accelerated the newspaper's phenomenal expansion in the nineteenth century. Of note, the English-speaking countries fostered the private development and use of telegraph networks, though with state backing at crucial points, while continental states favored greater governmental control—initiating a crippling monopolistic pattern in communications that still hampers Europe today, although the advent of wireless communications and international pressures are finally breaking down these antique inhibitors.

Likewise, when the telephone appeared, with its hint of anarchic possibilities, English-speaking nations were more likely to permit the private sector to exploit the technology—which the private sector did more swiftly and efficiently—while European states generally preferred state monopolies on communication, imposed as soon as each new means matured. When the radio crackled to life, both market democracies and repressive regimes saw its potential, although they read its utility differently. At one extreme, the United States adopted a liberal licensing program that diffused a large degree of communicative power to localities, while, at the other, the Soviet Union and Nazi Germany centralized control of the first broadcast medium. In the United States, the radio voice might speak *to* the government, but in the gathering European darkness the voice on the radio spoke *for* the government.

Radio marked the early adulthood of our information revolution. For the first time, *ideas* could be disseminated to the masses, along with unadorned information and entertainment (simultaneously, feature films and newsreels hinted at the power of today's media, although they reached much smaller audiences than did radio). Given our contemporary challenges, it is worth noting that the initial masters of the communication of ideas over the airwaves were men with messages of hatred, just as the internet has become a forum for hate speech, delicious delusions, and conspiracy theories today. Hitler may have been a poor strategist in the end, but he was a master of the broadcast medium.

Even in the United States, the early days of radio were marred by populist—and popular—demagogues, from racist politicians to men of the cloth who ranted against all things foreign in terms far fiercer than those used by more recent profiteers and panderers of the airwaves. It was not unlike the broadcast environment in many less-developed countries today. Only under the stress of worldwide depression, then of world war, did the voices of liberal democracy come into their own—one thinks, inevitably, of the incomparable Winston Churchill and of the savvy Franklin D. Roosevelt, whose physical disability might have marred his effectiveness in the soon-to-come day of television, but who was perfectly pitched for his fireside chats over the radio waves.

Yet even radio was subject to laws, regulations, and, everywhere, ultimate state control. A small station in the midst of America might broadcast bigotry, as some still do today, but there are lines the disembodied voice may not cross. In wartime, underground stations might appear, or pirate broadcasts from offshore might enliven a peace, but radio is ultimately controllable, given the ease with which it can be monitored and its dependence on licensed frequencies.

In fact, the information revolution of our time has not been a straight-line march of progress. Television was, in one sense, a step backward in informational freedom, even as it increased phenomenally the amount of information it conveyed by adding the visual element pioneered by the cinema. While bringing images of a greater world to remote populations and capable of communicating sophisticated concepts through multisensory effects, television is a much more expensive endeavor than radio for those who want to originate a signal, to say nothing of offering attractive programming. With the television age came a reassertion of governmental control over broadcasting virtually everywhere, with corporate wealth a secondary filter in market democracies, and that control is only now experiencing a gradual breakdown with the advent of the cheap satellite dish.

Still, the synergy attained by all these communication means, as well as from teletypes and facsimile machines, voice and video cassettes, satellite communications, cell phones, and wireless, handheld computers, began to reach critical mass as the twentieth century drew to a close. Increasing global prosperity, though uneven in its distribution, meant the proliferation of receivers—first radio sets, then televisions, then computers that, joined to the internet, finally gave the common man a broadcast means of his own. The informational floodgates opened. Even comparatively simple devices destabilized societies, from the Soviet bloc to struggling states freed of both the colonial yoke and colonial order.

Ideas can now travel more swiftly than any human being—or disease. The global AIDS epidemic illustrates the point. An unknown sickness (admittedly slow-acting) appeared nearly simultaneously at different points on the globe, with fearsome initial results. But local infection rates and trends quickly diverged. In informationally adept, self-correcting societies, even libertine subcultures acquired the information about the disease necessary to modulate and then dramatically reduce rates of infection. In informationally deprived or self-mythologizing societies, the epidemic has raged on, devastating entire generations, states, and regions. In Africa, where idea transference remains a slow process due to both infrastructural and educational deficiencies, the disease moved classically along trade routes, its impact, scope, and nature initially unrecognized, then long denied. Meanwhile the United States hyperbolized its own epidemic and waged multiple aggressive educational campaigns, resulting in transmission rate declines in those social groups that were informationally aware and responsive to fact-based arguments.

Today, we still hear heartbreaking denials of medical evidence from African leaders dumbfounded by the AIDS epidemic's implications, while, in the United States, the disease has been confined largely to micro-groups within social subgroups that are unwilling to alter self-destructive behaviors. Clearly, the ready availability of factual information correlates to low rates of infection, even adjusted for cultural proclivities and radically different levels of medical infrastructure. Today vastly more people are aware of the causes of the disease known as AIDS than will ever contract it. Compare that to the centuries ravaged by the Black Death or, more appropriately, syphilis. It is a contemporary truism that a previously unknown disease might reach New York City at the speed of a jet aircraft. But information spans the globe at the speed of light.

The Internet and Foreign Devils

Just as those ignorant of the sources of infection are more likely to contract AIDS, societies ignorant of global realities are more likely to become victims of the plague of ideas ravishing our world. Troubled, faltering, humiliated societies—and failed individuals everywhere—are more likely to be seduced by lies or comforting myths than are the successful, and the dark side of the information revolution is that it makes a vast spectrum of very bad, stunningly false ideas and notions available to those seeking an impersonal reason for personal failure. Whether speaking of individuals or entire cultures, the successful have a healthy immunity, while the failed and failing are candidates for infection. And yet, establishing a cordon sanitaire is as impossible as it is, ultimately, undesirable.

With a sure grip on the past, Jacques Barzun has noted that since the appearance of the railway, mankind has been forced to learn a greater physical dexterity in everyday life to avoid harm from ever faster-moving, more powerful, and more numerous machines. But twenty-first-century men and women must add to that skill a dramatically increased intellectual suppleness to avoid being maimed by our informational juggernaut. Only a minority of the earth's population is prepared.

Certainly the information revolution has spread many good ideas. It is historically positive in its effect, breaking the hold of tyrants and shining the light of knowledge into long-curtained worlds, while enabling phenomenal economic performances. Awareness is liberating—but the challenge is to prevent the free-but-frightened from volunteering for an even more dangerous bondage. Different cultures at different levels of development respond differently to the flood of information increasingly available in even remote corners of the planet. Cultures that perceive themselves as making progress display a better collective sense of true and false than those that feel themselves threatened or sense that they are falling behind. As with individuals, the successful are usually willing to accept criticism and learn new techniques that reinforce their success, while the faltering grow increasingly sensitive to criticism, self-doubting, defensive, and close-minded.

Over two centuries ago, Johann Gottfried Herder remarked that encounters between cultures excite self-awareness in those cultures. Today, collisions between cultures infect weaker cultures with self-doubt (loud assertions of superiority are the symptom indicating that the disease has entered a critical phase). We live in a world where the success stories are increasingly evident to all, while the fear of failure haunts the majority of the world's population. That fear may manifest itself as rabid pride and spur aggression, but we must not mistake the terrorist's or tyrant's desperation for anything other than what it is: fundamental, inarticulate terror. Spite, hatred, and fitful violence are hallmarks of decline. They are the responses of frightened men who cannot bear the image in the mirror held up by the globalization of information. They imagine, as do children, that they have a choice in their fate, that they can refuse to see what they cannot endure. But the choices confronting information-resistant societies are not really choices at all.

The Brand-X Challenge

Consider the dilemma of Country X. Formerly the colony of a European power, its autocratic government sponsors a restrictive interpretation of the national religion, retains control of all decisions it considers significant, attempts to regulate the information to which its citizens have access, and is baffled that its recently booming economic growth has withered. Its official statements blame an unjust "neo-colonial" economic order for its weakening currency. Intelligent, but aging and increasingly out of touch, its leaders recognize with chagrin that countries they had heckled as yesterday's powers are not only resurgent, but growing wealthier and more dominant by the minute. Its citizens are split between the better-educated, who want greater personal and political freedoms, and the rest, who want a better material life but are more or less comfortable with the customary social and moral strictures. Corrupt elites and young people hungry for global culture form the statistical fringes. Younger technocrats within the government attempt to persuade the leadership that economic progress depends on more open policies, including an opening of the society to a liberalized flow of information, but the leadership is reluctant to risk the loss of any control.

The leadership of Country X imagines it faces a dilemma, but really it faces an inevitability. Better than the bright, young technocrats, the old leaders sense that once the informational floodgates are opened a crack, the pressure of the informational waters will force them open the rest of the way. They fear (rightly) that greater awareness of the world will bring with it demands for change and (wrongly) that it will bring a moral collapse. They worry (rightly) that a general availability of information will erode their monopoly on power and reveal their shortcomings, while worrying (wrongly) that the Western-dominated internet and the rest of this suspicious "information revolution" is just a return of colonialism in disguise, even a plot to dominate their country and its culture. The leaders *think* they have a choice between continuing to restrict the flow of information and opening those floodgates.

Strengthening the dikes no longer works. Faced with the global torrent of information, you either learn to swim or you drown.

The leadership's only choice, to the extent Country X has one, is between letting the economy and society go hungry for the informational nutrition it needs to have even a hope of competing globally or accepting a threatening loss of authority. And the lesson of liberalization that authoritarian regimes draw from the events of the last decade is that, once begun, the pace and scope of liberalization cannot be controlled. So the leadership argues and dithers, making cosmetic attempts at alternative reforms and reassuring themselves with state banquets. Meanwhile, the plague of ideas has already infected the population to a greater extent than the old men realize.

Except in the cases of utterly failed states, such as North Korea, the march of information is relentless. Attempts to block its progress result only in collapsing competitiveness and a delay in beginning the long, imperfect process of educating the country's citizens to tell fact from fiction. The choice isn't between prolonging an idyll and risking change, but between a belated attempt to secure a global niche and a decline into obscurantism likely to end in prolonged violence and general incapability. Leaders who convince themselves that they can preserve rigid informational hierarchies refuse to see the signs that those hierarchies are already eroding underneath them. Soon enough, they will have no credibility and no effective means to halt the disintegration of social order and the state they cherish.

And what of that charge of neo-colonialism? Is it any more than the demagogue's incitement of a restive population to blame foreign devils for local faults?

The global information revolution is explosive, insidious, irresistible, and destructive of traditional orders. It increases Western cultural and economic dominance, at least for the present. It is the enemy of all hierarchies except the hierarchy of merit. But it is not a new form of imperialism.

An End, and a Beginning

We stand at the bare beginning of the post-colonial era. Following five hundred years of European colonial domination of the world, much of it involving physical occupation, we have hardly begun the process of recovery from colonialism's deformations and the digestion of its legacies, both positive and negative. The old colonial world is still in a disintegrative stage, wrestling with faulty borders agreed on in distant capitals and with the inheritance of the European-model nation-state itself—which may prove to be the most fateful legacy of all. Now that the last of the great physical empires is gone, the mini-empires left behind in the colonial wake—artificial states such as Nigeria, Congo, the Russian Federation, the former Yugoslavia, Iraq, Pakistan, Indonesia, and, perhaps, India—are breaking apart or struggling to develop a sustainable political order.

We will be fortunate if the worst of the imperial legacies can be overcome by the end of the new century, and there is no doubt whatsoever that many of today's disorders may be laid at the doorstep of those vanished European empires. Yet it grows increasingly counterproductive to blame colonialism for today's poor choices. We may blame nineteenth-century conferences in Berlin when Africa's borders provoke and exacerbate bloodshed, but no one can fault Europe (or the United States) when the leader of a state that has been independent for half a century looks the other way when his own citizens are massacred because of their religion or ethnicity, or when he stages show trials of potential rivals that alienate the greater world and its investors, or when he imagines that national ignorance is not only bliss, but economically productive.

Despite the fact that we will all wrestle with colonialism's legacies for many decades to come, there is no further utility, if there ever was any, in obsessive, paralyzing accusations. To blame is to enjoy oneself at the expense of achievement. Europe no longer has a colonial problem. Except for the occasional military intervention or embassy evacuation in a legacy state unable to function responsibly, Europe has washed its hands of any serious responsibilities left over from the colonial era, while concentrating on business (and while business practices can be devastating, they are not synonymous with imperialism). If anything, backward, protectionist elements in Europe worry about becoming the victims of a "hyper-power" America they have conjured as their own imperialist threat, forgetting that real imperialism is bloody, commanding, possessive, physically present, economically outmoded, and a very poor business model.

Imperialism is also purposeful. But the global information revolution is creatively anarchic, subject to that invisible hand, not to the hands of statesmen who can barely send an e-mail. Indeed, had the marketplace been allowed to determine the course of the European colonial adventure, many lands would never have been occupied, or would have been handed back to their occupants far sooner. There were certainly exceptions, but, overall, imperialism was about vanity more than it was about sound economics. The United States, for its part, willingly suffers no end of public humiliations as long as the business side of the relationship is good. Above all, as the Soviet Union finally realized in its death throes, old-fashioned imperialism is simply too costly. When merchants traveled the world to trade, the risks made perfect economic sense. But when armies followed, the results rarely paid a return—or did so with destructive results, as in the case of Spain's colonial bounty.

Imperialism is an expensive boot on an impoverished neck. The information revolution is a boot in the backside of those who move too slowly. The age of Western imperialism is over. But the triumph of the knowledge-based economy has barely begun.

Perhaps the best thing we in the West can wish for the many states (logical or illogical in their geographic contours), cultures, and civilizations that endured imperialist occupation or suffered its lesser attentions would be that they might gain a level of intellectual sobriety that would allow them to assess colonialism's legacies honestly, both the bad and the good. For there was much good done, as well, if some of it was incidental. Independence will be mature when former colonies can acknowledge their debt to those imperial powers that left behind an educated civil-servant class, traditions of law-based government, at least the shadow of democracy, physical infrastructure that still functions, and that ultimate enabler of the information age, the English language. After the honest weighing up, those states and peoples have to move on, to look forward and not pick eternally at yesterday's sores. But the chances are not good for such an objective evaluation: Blame is too addictive and comforting. Blame is the heroin of dying regimes.

I'll Close My Ears, I'll Shut My Eyes . . .

The consequences when governments wage a hopeless struggle to restrict the flow of information to their populations may be varied, but they are all bad. The plague of ideas affects even countries such as the United States, Germany, and England, spreading ludicrous, exculpatory beliefs among the underclass and leading to occasional acts of violence—but it does not impede progress on any front for the majority of the citizens, nor does it threaten the government. For most citizens of informationally adept states, the abundant availability of data and the access to a swift flow of ideas are every bit as empowering as television commercials sponsored by high-tech firms would have it. But in societies that, literally, believe what they want to believe because they have not developed the discriminating mechanisms that prevent self-delusion, the information explosion leads to other types of explosions, some of them bluntly physical. Only an informed population has any hope of developing successfully on any front in the new millennium.

The ignorant believe lies. This is a fundamental truth in all cultures, illustrated by the universal appeal of rumors and the alacrity with which men and women believe the worst of their neighbors. Now, much current repression—in mainland China, for example—is based upon a misreading of the fact that those denied global frames of reference will embrace local fantasies. The problem is that the informationally deprived won't necessarily believe the lies the leaders in the capital city want them to accept. Far too many heads of state and ruling cabals, worried about the durability of their regimes, have muttered along with the exhortations of religious fundamentalists in the hope of renewing their appeal to the masses. This is disastrous—for the population, for progress, for the economy, for minorities, and, more often than not, for the leadership that opened the lid on this worst of Pandora's many dreadful boxes. Playing the ethnic nationalist card is almost as bad, and occasionally more direct in its incitement to violence. When, as in Suharto-era Indonesia, the leadership panders to both nationalist and religious elements, the state is torn apart.

The collapse into obscurantism initially appeals to much of the public in underdeveloped states, as well as to their misguided, selfish leaders. Yet the infatuation rarely lasts—witness the internal struggles in Iran today. While opening the gates wide to today's torrent of information destabilizes traditional structures if they are unsound and lack the required suppleness to adapt to contemporary needs, attempting to keep those gates shut is far, far more dangerous. An informationally naive population has a better chance of adjusting to the shock effect of informational freedom than to continued deprivation in a changing, inevitably intrusive world. The upheaval delayed is only intensified, and the time lost cannot be recovered. Iran has lost a quarter century, Burma and North Korea twice as long, and even states such as Saudi Arabia, which may appear successful to some, are brittle, hollow, and unprepared for the changes globalization will force upon them (today's oil-rich states are the postmodern equivalents to imperial Spain, stunted by their addiction to single-source "free" wealth). The populations of such states literally do not know what to believe, and, given human nature, many of their citizens are apt to believe the worst. Even Russia, which has pretended for three centuries to be Western, is a land of wild, inopportune beliefs.

As noted above, some information always seeps through. In the absence of trustworthy comparative data, it is almost always misinterpreted. Worse, comforting rumors and messages of hate have the power of an incantation where countering data is not readily at hand. The peasant or proletarian is unlikely to believe the droning messages from Beijing, but may well believe lies far more dangerous and more pleasing.

Nor must the debilitating information be outright lies—it may come as messages of faith assuring believers that all of their failures and lacks are the fault of the infidel abroad and the minority in their midst. The appeal to *believe*, to submerge yourself in the comforting promises of extreme, exclusive religion (comforting as much for the damnation promised to your enemies as for the salvation promised to you), is, of course, timeless. Indeed, the will to faith seems to exist in people everywhere. But the vigorous resurgence of the most intolerant varieties of fundamentalism—Muslim, Christian, Jewish, and Hindu—is demonstrably a product of the decades-long process of globalization and the threatening (to the less capable, the weak, the fearful) flood of information sweeping over the planet.

Extreme religious fundamentalism, like oppressive ethnic nationalism, is not an indication of a strong faith or shining conviction. On the contrary, the human being of deep, abiding faith can afford to be tolerant in thought and deed, to question and be questioned. Those who are comfortable with their deity are comfortable with their neighbors. They are also open to change, once they are convinced of its utility. Doctrinally rigid fundamentalism is always a symptom of insecure faith. This age of resurgent belief is really one of explosive doubt.

Those who feel compelled to force their vision of God upon others are trying to convince themselves, thus their ferocity. The possibility that alternative paths to salvation exist isn't an affront to their God, but a personal threat to them. We see it in the cruel cleric everywhere, and in the villager who murders the neighbor converted away from the old faith, in the unemployed American who attacks a "Godless" family-planning clinic, in the warrior who insists that God Himself denies rights to women, and in all those who insist not only that those of other faiths are doomed, but that their own more tolerant coreligionists are damned as well.

The weak need certainty, while the strong can afford doubt (and reasonable doubts are the catalyst of all human progress). As with men, so with nations. Failing states and cultures crave beliefs as firm as iron. But iron, struck with sufficient force, shatters. The information revolution has the required force, and to spare.

Wars and Rumors of War

The information wars have already begun. They have little to do with the Pentagon's dreams of cyber-strikes and network paralysis, although these are certainly matters worthy of judicious consideration. The information wars that will shape our time are not about what information is electronically vulnerable, but about what information is culturally permissible. The closest military organizations come to the real challenge is when they attempt, amateurishly, psychological operations campaigns or fumble with "perception management."

Certainly the digital dimension has expanded, somewhat, the range of conventional war—but conventional war is of declining relevance. What matters is the power of information to terrify men of decayed belief. We live in a world in which the West is most willing to fight for economic causes, while the rest of the world squabbles over identity, be it religious or ethnic. Certainly there have been plenty of rehearsals for these conflicts over blood and belief down the millennia, but the global lines have never been so sharply drawn. On one side are the Western and sympathetic states that believe in the freedom of information, while the opposition is composed of those terrified at the freedom information brings. This is not a precursor to a next world war—humankind is too disparate, and material power too lopsided at present. Rather, it portends a long, bitter, intermittent series of struggles on various fronts between those who cling to the hope that they can control their neighbors' beliefs and behaviors, and those states committed to the risks, misbehaviors, and triumphs of free societies. Barring unforeseeable cataclysms, the free societies will win. But the extent of human misery we shall see along the way is incalculable.

Consider a minor player on the world stage who has been hyped by his enemies into international stardom. Osama bin Laden is not waging war against the West's realities. He doesn't know them. He struggles against a riveting, overwhelming, wildly skewed, personal vision of the West, exemplified by an America he has conjured from shreds of information and his own deepest fears. (A startling Freudian note is that all cultures in which women are openly repressed and the males remain psychologically infantile display strong anti-American currents—Western civilization's discontents are minor compared to those crippling social relations elsewhere.) Mr. bin Laden's acolytes know little—often nothing—of the mundane West, but are galvanized by the psychologically rewarding opportunity to hate. Men of few earthly prospects, they imagine a divine mission for themselves. It is the summit of self-gratification.

The remarkable ability of men and women to deny reality is driven home by Osama bin Laden's counterparts in the United States itself: those citizens who, in the Year of Our Lord 2000, want to ban the teaching of evolution, remove "offensive" books from school shelves, limit women's choices, and glorify themselves by consigning their fellow citizens to a medieval version of Hell. It is never enough to "protect" their own children or spouses—those immoralists who do not see the light must be protected from themselves. It is an old and universal story newly supercharged by the threats the literalists of faith detect in the information age—although, like those elsewhere who reject the content, they are usually ready to employ the means of the information revolution to their own ends.

An exemplary case from the technologically distant past is the Iranian revolution of the late 1970s. The faction that ultimately seized control of the state apparatus had as its goal secession from the Western-dominated course of history. Yet even twenty years ago—light years in informational terms—it proved impossible. The most powerful result of the Iranian revolution has been to deny Iran the chance to behave competitively for more than two decades—while killing a great many Iranians along the way. At the risk of redundancy: There is no real choice. You either outperform the global leaders, create a competitive niche, or fall behind. Cultural and economic autonomy is no longer possible.

Recently, in Indonesia, we have seen the inevitable consequences of informational underdevelopment when exacerbated by demagoguery (and by irrational borders). In East Timor, in Aceh, the Moluccas, and elsewhere, the global plague of ideas spurred hateful messages of nationalism and religious fundamentalism that destroyed Indonesia's threadbare hope of being an equitable, secular state. In the absence of trustworthy data and a framework for national understanding, rumors ignited massacres. And now it is too late to preserve the Indonesian state within its postcolonial borders without levels of oppression the rest of the world is likely to find intolerable. Regarding the remarks above to the effect that the European concept of the state—with all its vanities—may prove imperialism's most pernicious legacy, Jakarta's reflexive unwillingness to consider a peaceful shedding of those regions that reject its rule underscores the point.

In mainland China, the Beijing government wages multiple counterinformational campaigns against its own population, from utterly wrongheaded attempts to regulate the internet and limit access to technologies to the suppression of religious sects that likely would have found far fewer adherents in a more informationally adept state. In India, Hindu extremists sense that traditional advantages are undermined by any increase in social and religious freedoms, so they murder Christian converts and missionaries. In Kashmir, religion overlaid with ethnicity draws endless blood on both sides. In Pakistan, a pandering leader banished English-language curricula from the school system a quarter century ago in an early nod to anti-globalization pressures. Since then, Pakistan has gone backward in virtually every sphere, and is less equipped for global competition than it was when Zulfikar ali Bhutto did more than any other man in its history to destroy the country's future.

Overdue Upheavals

The popular struggles, terrorist acts, violent conflicts, and occasional wars ignited by the global information revolution will prove largely impossible to prevent, since few states will be willing to take the risks involved in unclenching antiquated notions of sovereignty in time for their citizens to find a comfortable place in the new global environment. The information revolution can only be locally delayed, not avoided. Unschooled populations will be exposed, haphazardly, to data they cannot digest, resulting in local tumult and transnational acts of desperation.

Yet there is a positive transformation on the horizon, if still a distant one. The era of the common man that Marxism failed so painfully to induce is coming at last, driven by the democratization of information. For all the dangers described above, facts in the hands of men and women everywhere will ultimately displace even the sweetest falsehoods—though the latter will never disappear entirely, given human nature and even the best society's inevitable inequities. The problem is not the ultimate end, but the long, difficult transition faced by the world in our lifetimes.

Still, those of us who believe in the importance of fundamental human rights and decencies have reasons aplenty for optimism. Never before has there been such an irresistible threat to the old, unjust orders. We have entered an age when the individual's ability to comprehend data, assimilate ideas, and synthesize innovations upsets hierarchies that have apportioned unmerited rewards for centuries. This is the age not only of mass culture, but of opportunity for the masses. While much of the West has a lead of a century or two, the effects have begun to reach the remotest outposts of oppression. Already, an Untouchable may prove a far better software writer than a Brahmin; a woman may demand a voice in her own fate (still at her own risk, though); the highly talented outsider trumps the backward insider; victims tell their tales to microphones and video cameras; and people everywhere have a growing awareness, however flawed, of the possibilities that would be their birthright elsewhere. Add greed and fear on the part of those whose traditional privileges are under assault, and the likelihood of violent upheavals and reactions threatens to slow, if not outpace, progress in many lagging countries. Yet many an individual will shine, and in the end it is the genius of those individuals that will bring about the collapse of the last autocratic regimes.

The information revolution is by far the greatest transnational threat of our time. It is also man's hope. I believe, firmly, that societies that embrace informational freedom will triumph. But the victory will not come without costs.

When Devils Walk the Earth

*The Mentality and Roots of Terrorism,
and How to Respond*

This essay was written in October, 2001, for the Center for Emerging Threats and Opportunities, and is published here with the gracious permission of the CETO, and with thanks to the United States Marine Corps.

The Monster's Mind

There are two basic types of terrorist: the practical and the apocalyptic. While there are exceptions to each basic pattern, gray areas in between the two categories, and rare terrorists who evolve from one type into the other (usually from the practical to the apocalyptic), these remain the two most useful classifications in attempts to understand and defeat our enemies who employ terror. Failure to distinguish between the different threats posed by these two very different types of terrorists led to fatal misjudgments, such as the conviction that skyjackers should not be opposed in the air, since any action would only endanger passengers, based upon the assumption that aircraft seized by terrorists were bargaining chips, not weapons. But the actions of the practical terrorist, to whom we have grown accustomed, are calculated to change political circumstances, while for the apocalyptic terrorist, destruction is an end in itself, despite his extravagant statements about strategic objectives. For all his violence, the practical—political—terrorist is a man of hope. The religious, apocalyptic terrorist is a captive of his own rage, disappointments, and fantasies. One may be controlled. The other must be killed.

Lesser Devils

Practical terrorists, with whom we long have struggled, may behave savagely, but they have tangible goals and a logical approach

113

to achieving them. Their logic may be cruel or cynical, but there is a rational (if sometimes extreme or tenuous) relationship between their long-term goals, means, risks, assets, and interim objectives. Ideology can dominate their thinking, but it does not break loose entirely from mundane reality; indeed, their struggle may be for elementary survival under oppressive conditions. While their convictions and techniques make them appear "fanatical" to the layman, their determination is fueled by the intellect and common emotions, not by the spiritual message or transcendent vision of the true fanatic.

Even when championing a particular religious minority, practical terrorists are concerned with rights, status, and apportionment in the here and now, not beyond the grave (the IRA, for example, or the Stern Gang). They make perceived (or real) injustice their cause, not infidelity or apostasy, and may pay scant attention to the religious rituals of those whom they see themselves as defending. While an ideology may substitute for religion in their psychological makeup, as it did for many Communist true believers, their concerns are bellies, wallets, security, land, and authority, not souls. They often bitterly reject the otherworldly promises of organized religion, which they may view as a tool of the established order, even as they develop their own secular liturgies. They may be at once the self-appointed representatives of a religious minority and opponents of that minority's prevailing religious hierarchy (the Molly Maguires in the Pennsylvania anthracite fields in the nineteenth century, or Quebecois separatists in Canada's more recent history).

Even when practical terrorists routinely invoke their religious affiliation, they tend to think in terms of birth and bloodlines (as did virtually all terrorist paramilitaries in the former Yugoslavia, no matter their confession). Critically, they view their own deaths as a misfortune, however necessary or noble, and not as an embrace of the divine. They would rather live than die, and regard death as final, not as a promotion. They approach the theological plane only in the cloudy belief that they will "live on" in the people whose cause they have made their own. They want rewards on earth, and do not expect them in heaven.

The practical terrorist may have ambitious dreams—the overthrow of a state or the institution of a radically new political system—

and may be willing to undergo great hardship and sacrifice in pursuit of those dreams—but he (or she) is rarely suicidal and does not view death and destruction as goals unto themselves. He is conservative in the sense that he wishes to preserve a party organization, or just his small cell, for the day when he imagines he or his fellow conspirators will "take over." Suicide attacks are extreme tools to him, employed only in desperation and against targets of great value or prestige.

The practical terrorist may be convinced of his beliefs and embittered toward society and "the system," but his goals are always the re-creation of the society or state, not its total annihilation. He may be willing to kill thousands, to use torture, and to subject others to his brutal will, but the environment he wishes to inhabit in the bright future he foresees is of this earth, and there are other flesh-and-blood human beings in it. The practical terrorist may attract helpers who enjoy destruction and cruelty for their own sakes, but the overall terrorist organization remains focused upon political goals that the terrorist leadership judges to be attainable.

While some practical terrorists-may be such die-hard believers that they will fight to the death (or undertake desperate suicide missions), others may mature beyond their terrorist backgrounds, prove open to compromise, even become capable of a degree of give-and-take with the very authorities they once single-mindedly demonized (consider how the image of Yasser Arafat has changed with the years). Some are implacable and obsessive, but others will settle for incremental change—or be co-opted into an evolving political system (one thinks of those contemporary European politicians, exemplified by Germany's brilliant foreign minister, Joschka Fischer, who grew from left-wing street-fighter or conspiratorial backgrounds into surprisingly adept and conscientious statesmen). There are many subdivisions of the practical terrorist category, and it is the task of law enforcement and intelligence services to differentiate among them. For some individuals, affiliation with a terrorist group is a thrilling fad they later abandon; for others it is an all-consuming mission from which they can never extract themselves psychologically. Some can be frightened, persuaded, or bought, while others must be killed, and it is a very sloppy, foolish state that neglects to distinguish the transient helper from the hardcore killer.

There usually are lines the practical terrorist will not cross—some groups he wishes to protect, certain tools he will not employ, some self-imposed limitations upon the scale of his actions. It is extremely unlikely that such a terrorist would employ biological or nuclear weapons, although he might make limited use of chemical weapons. A domestic terrorist who employed NBC weapons, for example, would likely be a psychotic or a member of a delusional group with an apocalyptic vision. Germ warfare, especially, is most liable to be waged along apocalyptic, racial, or religious lines. While the practical terrorist may commit certain deeds to create an atmosphere of terror among a target group or audience, the good opinion of at least a portion of the public remains important to him. He may misread public sentiment and deceive himself about his image, his effect, and the ultimate possibility of attaining his goals, but he does not detach himself entirely from the day-to-day world and its concerns, nor does he fully escape the psychology of popular morality. He may commit atrocious acts—setting off car bombs in public places, kidnapping the innocent relations of his chosen enemies, committing assassinations—but the scale of his actions is usually limited, despite the attendant drama. Perfectly willing to demolish police stations or government offices, he does not destroy entire cities, which he would rather rule than wreck. He wants to lead "his people" to power or to independence, not to their deaths.

The practical terrorist's morality may be very different from that of the average American, and he may even be psychologically unbalanced, but he does not disregard the value of human life entirely. He may commit grand gestures in frustration or desperation (or because he possesses a flair for exploiting the media), but he continues to see himself as the representative of an earthly agenda, not as a divine missionary. He tends to see history as a progression which requires his assistance—not as a collapse toward a longed-for Armageddon. Though subject to bouts of depression, he is ultimately the more hopeful and less pessimistic terrorist. He is concerned with his own failures and those of his group, but not convinced that all those who believe otherwise are eternally damned and condemned to annihilation, or that a sinful world must be consumed by fire. In his dark way, he believes in redemption of the masses, in the possibility that they can, through example, education, or force, be convinced that his way is the enlightened way. The practical terrorist always sees more to be captured than destroyed. He wants prizes. Willing and able to dehumanize specific targets, he is often surprisingly sentimental about specific objects, individuals, or those human types or classes whom he idealizes.

The practical terrorist's commitment to his cause may remain relatively constant, but his actions can be inconsistent—now violent, now passive, violent again, then accommodating. He may be capable of an abrupt change in his perception of who constitutes the "enemy" and how that enemy should be opposed. He is deadly, but usually a greater threat to individuals he deems "guilty" than to the masses. Setbacks can be difficult for him to rationalize, and he may undergo periods of despair, which transform his perception of how best to further his cause. He is usually the terrorist of lesser strength, and always the terrorist of lesser menace. Although we may, in our outrage, term him a madman, his mentality often remains recognizably like our own. There is logic to his actions.

The practical terrorist's hellish counterpart, the apocalyptic terrorist, is mentally divorced from our world and its values and from any respect for flesh and blood. The practical terrorist has dreams. The apocalyptic terrorist is lost in a nightmare.

The Original Smart Bombs
The "pure" practical terrorist is an idealist, sometimes very well educated (historically, secular universities have been excellent recruiting grounds for terrorists who want to force improvement upon the world). While it may seem counterintuitive, the apocalyptic, religious terrorist tends to be recruited from the ranks of the fearful and threatened, from among the worried, not the confident; he is a coward in the face of life, if not in the face of death (this is absolutely applicable to the key operatives of the September 11, 2001, plot).

Despite the media-driven image of Islamic terrorists representing hordes of the Faithful, apocalyptic terrorists, such as the members of al Qa'eda, tend to act out of intensely personal disaffection and a sense of alienation from social norms, while the practical terrorist is more apt to feel driven by group grievances (though he, too, is rarely a "successful" member of society before his conversion to terror). The apocalyptic terrorist "wants out," while the practical terrorist wants "back in," although on much-improved terms of his own dictation. (Another aspect of this psychology is that practical terrorists, even when involved in international movements, prefer to focus on the locale of their personal grievances, while apocalyptic terrorists view the greater world as their enemy and are far more likely to transpose blame from their own societies onto other cultures.)

While both types find comfort—a home and brotherhood—in the terrorist organization, the practical terrorist imagines himself as a representative of his people, while the apocalyptic terrorist sees himself as chosen and apart, despite his occasional rhetoric about protecting the masses adhering to his faith. The practical terrorist idealizes his own kind—his people—while the apocalyptic terrorist insists that only his personal ideals have any validity. The practical terrorist is impassioned and imagines that his deeds will help his brethren in the general population, while the apocalyptic terrorist is detached from compassion by his faith and only wants to punish the "sinful," whom he finds ever more numerous as he is progressively hypnotized by the dogma that comforts him.

Except for the most cynical gunmen, practical terrorists believe that mankind can be persuaded (or forced) to regret past errors and make amends, and that reform of the masses is possible (although a certain amount of coercion may be required). But apocalyptic terrorists (such as Osama bin Laden) are merciless. Practical terrorists may see acts of retribution as a tactical means, but apocalyptic terrorists view themselves as tools of a divine and uncompromising retribution. Retribution against unbelievers, heretics, and even their own brethren whose belief is less pure is the real strategic goal of apocalyptic terrorists, even when they do not fully realize it themselves or cannot articulate it. Even among average Americans, there is often a great gulf between what people consciously think they believe and the "slumbering" deeper beliefs that catalytic events awaken—such as the frank thirst for revenge felt by tens of millions of "peaceful" Americans in the wake of the events of September 11. It is considerably less likely that a morally crippled, obsessed, apocalyptic terrorist cocooned in an extreme religious vision will be able to articulate his real goals; we cannot know apocalyptic terrorists by their pronouncements so well as by their deeds, since much of what they say is meant to make their intentions seem more innocent or justified than they are.

Often, apocalyptic terrorists are lying even to themselves. Apocalyptic terrorists are whirling in the throes of a peculiar, malignant madness and barely know what they believe in the depths of their souls—in fact, much of their activity is an attempt to avoid recognition of the darkness within themselves, a struggle to depict themselves as (avenging) angels of light. Centuries ago, we might have said they were possessed by devils. Today, we must at least accept that they are possessed and governed by a devilish vision.

The practical terrorist punishes others to force change. The religious terrorist may speak of changes he desires in this world, but his true goal is simply the punishment of others—in the largest possible numbers—as an offering to the bloodthirsty, vengeful God he has created for himself. This apocalyptic terrorist may identify himself as a Muslim or a Christian, but he is more akin to an Aztec sacrificing long lines of prisoners on an altar of blood (one of the many psychological dimensions yet to be explored in terrorist studies is the atavistic equation of bloodshed with cleansing—an all-too-literal bath of blood).

No change in the world order will ever content the apocalyptic terrorist, since his actual discontents are internal to himself and no alteration in the external environment could sate his appetite for retribution against those he needs to believe are evil and guilty of causing his personal sufferings and disappointments—for such men, suicidal acts have a fulfilling logic, since only their own destruction can bring them lasting peace. Above all, they need other humans to hate while they remain alive; this is the only release for the profound self-hatred underlying the egotism that lets them set themselves up as God's judges—as imitation gods themselves—upon this earth. In theological terms, there is no greater blasphemer in any religion than the killer who appoints himself as God's agent, or assumes a godlike right to judge entire populations for himself, but the divine mission of the apocalyptic terrorist leaves no room for theological niceties. Pretending to defend his religion, he creates a vengeful splinter religion of his own.

The health of any religious community can be gauged by the degree to which it rejects these bloody apostles of terror, and the

Islamic world's acceptance of apocalyptic terrorists as heroes is perhaps the most profound indicator of its spiritual crisis and decay. Make no mistake: The terrorist "martyrs" of September 11, 2001, and Osama bin Laden will be remembered by Islamic historians and by generation after generation of Muslim children as great heroes in the struggle for true religion and justice. No matter what Islamic governments may say to please us, many millions of Muslims around the world felt tremendous pride in the atrocities in New York, Washington, and Pennsylvania. This makes it all the more vital that the United States kill Osama bin Laden, exterminate al Qa'eda, destroy the Taliban, and depose any other governments found to have supported their terrorism. If Osama bin Laden survives to thumb his nose at an "impotent superpower," he will attract hundreds of thousands of supporters and tens of millions more sympathizers. He is already a hero, and he must not be allowed to remain a triumphant one. He is an apocalyptic terrorist of the worst kind, and his superficial agenda (deposing the government of Saudi Arabia, expelling U.S. troops from the Middle East, imposing Sharia law) is nothing compared to his compulsion to slaughter and destroy.

Although his vision is closer to the grimmest passages of Christianity's Book of Revelation than to anything in the Koran, Osama bin Laden has been able to convince countless Muslims that his vision is of the purest and proudest Islamic form. This should be a huge warning flag to the West about the spiritual crisis in the Islamic world. Logic of the sort cherished on campuses and in government bureaucracies does not apply. This battle is being fought within the realms of the emotions and the soul, not of the intellect. We face a situation so perverse that it is as if tens of millions of frustrated Christians decided that Kali, the Hindu goddess of death and destruction, embodied the true teachings of Jesus Christ. We are witnessing the horrific mutation of a great world religion, and the Islamic world likely will prove the greatest breeding ground of apocalyptic terrorists in history.

Small and Vicious Gods

The belief systems of practical terrorists are often modular; some such men can learn, evolve, synthesize, or realign their views. But the apocalyptic terrorist cannot tolerate any debate or dissent—all divergent opinions are a direct threat to his mental house of cards. The apocalyptic terrorist embraces a totality of belief and maintains it with an ironclad resolution attained by only the most extreme—and psychotic—secular terrorists. First identifying himself as a tool of his God, he soon begins to assume his right to godlike powers. The practical terrorist is in conflict with the existing system, but the apocalyptic terrorist sees himself as infinitely superior to it. The practical terrorist looks up at the authority he seeks to replace, but the apocalyptic terrorist looks down on the humankind he despises. Despite enforcing rigorous discipline within the terrorist organization, the practical terrorist nonetheless retains a sense of human imperfection. The religious, apocalyptic terrorist believes that those who are imperfect deserve extermination (in one of terrorism's gray-area anomalies, the "secular" Nazi regime took on an essentially religious vision that embraced state terror—Hitler's attitude toward the Jews was astonishingly similar to Osama bin Laden's view of Jews, Christians, and even secular Muslims; of course, the desire to please God or authority by slaughtering unbelievers has a long tradition in many religions, from medieval Catholicism to contemporary Hindu extremism).

Scared of the Girls
Both types of terrorists draw accomplices and foot soldiers from the uneducated masses, but the leadership in each type of movement tends to have at least a smattering of higher education and may even be highly intelligent and learned in terms of the host society's norms. In both cases, however, their vanity cannot satisfy itself with what the system offers. The terrorist is always an egotist with a (desperate, fragile) sense of unappreciated superiority, aggravated by his inability to establish satisfying social, personal, or vocational relationships. The terrorist is convinced that he is right, but is not much concerned with being just. He wants to "show" the world or even God. At the core of many a terrorist leader is a spoiled brat disappointed by the failures of adulthood.

Perhaps the most routine commonality between the practical and apocalyptic terrorist is the male terrorist's inability to develop and maintain healthy, enduring relationships with women—although the practical terrorist is more apt to idealize members of the opposite sex, who then disappoint him, and to imagine himself re-created as a storybook hero of the sort he believes would appeal to his fantasy woman (Timothy McVeigh), while the apocalyptic terrorist fears, despises, and hates females (Mohammed Atta, whose testament perfectly captured the Islamic fanatic's revulsion toward women).

Practical terrorists may be puritanical, but they are much more likely to accord women admission to and high status in their organizations (from numerous historical left-wing terrorist groups to the Tamil Tigers). Practical terrorists may even show an egalitarian attitude toward the sexes, though by no means always—it very much depends on societal context—while the apocalyptic terrorist usually mistrusts and shuns women (al Qa'eda and other Islamic terrorist organizations are classic examples, although some Christian fringe groups also seem to believe that the word "evil" is derived from the root word "Eve"). There is great cultural variation in the attitudes of terrorists of both kinds toward women, and a few apocalyptic cults have even been led by female prophets, but apocalyptic terrorists generally denigrate or actively humiliate women far more often than they value them, while practical terrorists, at worst, relegate women to the status customary in the society in which they operate.

Nonetheless, the statistical inability of terrorists of both kinds to form an enduring sexual relationship with a beloved partner is an aspect of terrorist psychology that has gone largely unexplored—we are so determined to be "serious" and to be taken seriously by our peers that we may have missed the forest for the trees. A review of historical terror cases makes it startlingly clear: Terrorists rarely have successful dating histories. Sexual fears and humiliation as young adults—and the consequent loneliness and alienation—may be the single greatest unrecognized catalyst in the making of a terrorist (whether Mohammed Atta or Timothy McVeigh). A terrorist's passion for political reform or preserving rain forests, or his compulsion to serve God through colossal destruction, may be more of a final symptom than a root cause.

Terrorists are disturbed, unhappy men. We have done an inadequate job of asking what has made them so unhappy that they seek release in killing their fellow human beings. We look for answers in economic statistics, while ignoring the furious power of the soul.

There have been plentiful exceptions, but the general rule is that the more repressed the society and the more fervent its rejection of reciprocity in sexual relations, the more terrorists it produces; and the greater the gap in social status between men and women in the society, the more likely it is to produce suicidal male terrorists. Societies that dehumanize women dehumanize everyone except those males in authority positions—and the ability to dehumanize his targets is essential to the psychology of the terrorist. While those who will become terrorists may wed to accommodate social norms or familial insistence, the rarest form of human being may be a happily married terrorist.

Avenging Angels

Apocalyptic terrorists are a far more serious matter than even the deadliest practical terrorists, and these religion-robed monsters are at war with the United States and the West today. Jealous of our success and our power, terrified and threatened by the free, unstructured nature of our societies, and incapable of performing competitively in the twenty-first century, they have convinced themselves that our way of life is satanic and that we are the enemies of their religion and their God. Nothing we can do will persuade them otherwise (it is a dangerous peculiarity of the West to imagine that we can "explain everything" satisfactorily to those who hate us—apocalyptic terrorists and their masses of sympathizers don't want explanations, they want revenge).

Muslim apocalyptic terrorists do not understand the reality of our society or our daily lives, and they do not want to understand. They can live among us and see only evil, even as they enjoy a shabby range of pleasures, from video games to prostitutes. Their extreme vision of the world constructs evil even from good and easily rationalizes away the virtues of other societies and civilizations. They need to hate us, and their hatred is the most satisfying element in their lives. Death and destruction delight them. They cannot be reasoned with, appeased, or even intimidated. No human voice can persuade the man who believes that God is speaking in his other ear. Apocalyptic terrorists must be destroyed. There is no alternative to killing the hardcore believers, and it may be necessary to kill thousands of them, if we are to protect the lives of millions of our own citizens.

We still fail to recognize that the atrocities of September 11, 2001, composed the most successful—and dramatic—achievement of the Islamic world against the West in centuries, greater than the Ottoman victory at Gallipoli, the establishment of Arab states, the nationalization of the Suez Canal, or the Iranian Counter-Revolution of 1979. It was a great day in Muslim history, and it will be remembered as such, no matter what tribulations we visit upon the terrorist networks and their state accomplices in retaliation. This was their big win, and let us hope it is the only one.

The Fertile Fields of Terror

But Don't We Have Our Own Fundamentalist Terrorists?

There are certainly domestic terrorists in the United States who claim religious justification for their deeds, such as those who bomb Planned Parenthood clinics, murder doctors who perform abortions, or perpetrate vicious hoaxes. But such men and women usually are practical terrorists, not apocalyptic, and have tangible social goals. They do not seek to destroy entire populations, but to alter specific practices within a society of which they are otherwise hopeful. While the acceleration of societal (and technological) change and the attendant psychological disorientation may spark the rise of domestic apocalyptic cults that seek to jump-start Armageddon, we have been lucky thus far—a tribute to the opportunities offered by our society and to our cultural robustness.

At present, the greatest domestic danger remains the lone psychotic triggered into action by the hate-filled rants of televangelists and other demagogues, by the insidious false communalism of the internet, or simply by a self-constructed vision. Abroad, the globalization of information has been the single most destabilizing factor in foreign cultures, and even here the information revolution has had its dark side, making the propaganda of prejudice and blame available as never before. Accusations that draw only laughter from the rest of us may spur the waiting madman to commit horrendous deeds, and, in the future, we who profit so richly from the free flow of information may find ourselves compelled to a more vigorous censorship of hate speech and the paraphernalia of bigotry. Much of the Islamic world has been poisoned by false, but wonderfully comforting, information, and we do not yet know the degree to which the same thing is happening here. The man of no prospects, in any culture or civilization, is always glad to be told that his failures are not his fault and that there is a target he can blame. Individual and group success disarms hatred more effectively than laws or lectures, and we must hope that our continued success is ever more inclusive of those citizens now relegated to the social fringes, from whose ranks the commandos of domestic terror are drawn.

Some of our domestic cult groups already have veered across the border toward apocalyptic behavior, but most of these bands of believers are *introverted* millenarian movements that seek to inaugurate the "end of days" and the Kingdom of God by suicidal gestures, rather than by mass attacks on outsiders. We must be on guard against small groups who buckle psychologically under the pressures of modern life and take refuge in *extroverted* millenarian movements that lash out in attempts to bring down the heavens upon us all, but, for now at least, the greatest risk from apocalyptic movements comes from abroad—and overwhelmingly from the Islamic world. Christian extremists may yet turn to direct action to bring on the "end of days," as they did five centuries ago (see below), but our society appears to be sufficiently inclusive and promising to content all but a few alienated individuals and small cells with limited goals. Nonetheless, we are playing the odds, with no guarantee that events will not trigger greater domestic threats from those convinced that God requires them to kill.

Consider a few patterns of domestic religious "terrorism" to date, with their American twists and heritage:

The "Reverend" Jim Jones and the grape Kool-Aid mass suicide and murders in Jonestown, Guiana, a generation ago; David Koresh's Branch Davidians; or the odd If-I-kill-myself-God's-spaceship-will-carry-me-away cult are introverted millennial variations of terrorist movements, but are not usually classified under "terrorism" because their acts are directed against their own followers and themselves. They are as close as Americans have come, in our time, to domestic apocalyptic terrorism (even the Unabomber, who made a secular religion of his crusade against technological progress, targeted specific individuals in his attempts to "alert" our society and did not use his abilities to attack undifferentiated citizens in a broad manner). Fortunately, the tendency in contemporary Western cults with Christian roots is to retreat from society, rather than to try actively to reform it—withdrawal from the world long has been a tradition in the American grain, dating to the earliest New England settlements, whose inhabitants sought to build exclusive "cities on a hill" and who sought to divorce themselves from the perceived corruption and very real persecution of the Old World (the benign Shakers or the gentle Brethren of the Ephrata Cloister strike more responsive chords in the American psyche than do bloody cults).

As an aside, one of the reasons Eastern religions have a special resonance with many Christians—although not with Muslims—may be our conditioning over centuries to revere ascetic withdrawals from the world on the part of saints and lesser believers, from Saint Anthony to the Shakers. Such retreats bear recognizable similarities to the Buddhist and Hindu traditions of the renunciation of mortal things. Islam certainly has its ascetics and renunciations, but, as practiced today in the realms of Sharia law (as opposed to those subregions where the far less menacing Sufi traditions dominate belief), it is much more of an applied religion, with a much greater focus on efforts to censor and discipline the world that is—reminiscent of medieval Catholicism. Contrary to recommending that believers "render unto Caesar what is Caesar's," Muslims expect Caesar to render unto their faith, an attitude the Protestant Reformation blessedly deconstructed in the West.

Americans who sincerely believe that a remarriage of government and religion is just what the cosmic doctor ordered should be very careful what they wish for, since states wed to single religions consistently find that the relationship is bad for both the religion and the state—although profitable to demagogues, as in Iran. The practice of religion is always most free where its relationship with government is least adhesive, and, in every society, those who wish to impose one religion's dominance on the state tend to be authoritarian in disposition. Osama bin Laden's vision of a properly run society is much closer to John Calvin's oppressive Geneva than to the brilliance and humanity of Moorish Cordoba or the flowering of Samarkand—before the murder of Ulug Begh by the "mad mullahs" of the day. In fact, the intellectual and spiritual calcification of Islam can be dated precisely to that assassination five and a half centuries ago.

In one of the many ironies of history, two great religions have swapped places over the last half millennium, with Christianity breaking free of medieval intellectual and social repression, while the once effervescent world of Islam has embraced the comforts of shackles and ignorance. Today, at least, the Judeo-Christian world faces forward, while the Islamic world looks backward with longing and wallows in comforting myths.

About Those Myths . . .

Myth is far more powerful than fact, not only in the Islamic world but wherever men and women seek absolution for their individual and collective failures. For all the Muslim world's rhetoric about the damage done by the Crusades, internal Crusades within Europe— against heretics and Jews—took many more lives over the centuries than did pre-Renaissance Europe's small-scale adventures in Palestine. Today, more Muslims live in the greater Washington, D.C., area than the total number of Crusaders who marched east over two centuries, and Washington does not feel under siege from these local residents. The power of the Crusader myth in today's Middle East has far more to do with the perception of collective failure and vulnerability than with reality—after all, the Islamic Ottomans conducted a centuries-long, much more successful crusade against Europe thereafter, and Islamic warriors threatened the marches of Europe well into the nineteenth century. Islamic invaders did far more damage to the Ukraine and Poland than the Crusaders did to Palestine. Those in the Middle East who cite the Crusader conquest of Jerusalem as an act of peerless historical viciousness might do well to remember Islam's conquest of Constantinople and Budapest, and the Ottoman progress to the gates of Vienna. If the streets of Jerusalem ran with blood, so did the streets—and churches—of Constantinople. There is plenty of historical guilt to pass around. We are blessed to live in a civilization that has moved on—but we face threats from a civilization that clings to a cosmetically enhanced past. While well-intentioned Westerners have gone to great lengths to refute Samuel Huntington's thesis of a "clash of civilizations," the man in the street in the Islamic world believes, intuitively, that the clash has been going on for a very long time, and no argument will dissuade him from his delicious belief in Western malevolence. How better to explain his wasted life in a ravaged state?

Until September 11, 2001, the most appalling terrorist act on American soil since British atrocities during our Revolutionary War was the Oklahoma City bombing, which was the deed of a practical terrorist who had deluded himself into believing America was ripe for another revolution that required only a catalytic event. It was about as vicious as an act of practical terrorism ever gets, and the difference in scope and scale (as well as intention) between the attack on one midsized Federal building in Oklahoma and the attacks on the World Trade Center provides a very good measure of the relative dangers of practical versus apocalyptic terrorism. Indeed, we may find that apocalyptic terror is capable of deeds far in excess of those in New York (especially employing weapons of mass destruction), while practical terror always has a ceiling. Admittedly, that ceiling may be much higher in other cultures, especially when speaking of ideology-based, regime-sponsored terror employed against the regime's own population during an era of transition, as in Stalin's Soviet Union, Mao's China, or Pol Pot's Cambodia, but this essay will confine itself to international and anti-state terrorism, in the interests of pertinence and brevity. One concern we should have about practical terrorists, though, is the copycat effect—will they think bigger now that they have seen what apocalyptic terrorists achieved on September 11, 2001?

While a few of the most extreme fundamentalist Christians in America have committed terrorist acts to achieve explicit goals, they tend to be "off-the-reservation" individuals or small groups who interpret doctrine with obsessive rigor and whose parent churches, though sometimes vociferous, do not encourage or support their acts of terror. Despite the cloak of religion, these terrorists have more in common with the Weathermen or the Symbionese Liberation Army than they do with al Qa'eda. They want to change society's rules, not to destroy society. The behavior patterns of these domestic fanatics are, as stated above, those of practical terrorists, even in the way some of them idealize "unborn children" and mothers, while demonizing those women whose behavior they find anathema. Apocalyptic terrorists demonize plenty of their fellow human beings, but idealize none except their own leaders and martyrs to the cause. The idealization of a segment of humanity is a consistent hallmark of the practical terrorist.

Anti-choice terrorists in the United States are not trying to jump-start the Book of Revelation. Whatever we may feel individually about the issue of pro-life versus pro-choice, the extremists who indulge in terrorizing behavior have a practical agenda that hopes to change behaviors and laws. Their greatest similarity to apocalyptic terrorists is that they long to turn back the clock to a past they have idealized, as did the decidedly secular Unabomber. In the past, much terrorism sought to modernize decaying societies; today, terrorism increasingly seeks to restore past strictures on behavior. Much of the terrorism of the nineteenth and twentieth centuries was revolutionary, but, increasingly, both practical and apocalyptic terrorists are reactionary. And the issue of the role of women in society almost invariably plays a role in their agendas. (Women seem to get the worst of it in every religion, and it is likely that only the splintering of Western churches allowed the productive liberation of women in our own societies; wherever a single orthodoxy prevails, women occupy a subordinate position in society. Even in the United States, a geographical plot of the regions that maintain the strongest insistence on "traditional" roles for women consistently highlights those regions that are the least developed economically and culturally, and the most religiously homogeneous.)

Perhaps the closest figure to Osama bin Laden that America has ever produced was John Brown. Millions of people thought he was right, too. And we have to wonder what that cherished American "saint" might have done had he possessed twenty-first-century technology. He too reveled in a "cleansing" bath of blood. Perhaps our saving grace today is merely that successful economies and flowering societies spawn fewer zealots. But should apocalyptic terrorists from the Islamic world ever manage a truly devastating attack upon America, they might find a new John Brown waiting in our wings—with twenty-first-century technology. Certainly, no sane person in the West wants the current conflict with terrorism to become a religious war. But the apocalyptic terrorists and their supporters already consider it to be one. And we in America probably underestimate our own capacity for savagery against another religion, if sufficiently provoked. Abraham Lincoln may be the greatest figure in American history, but John Brown is the most haunting.

Longing for the End of Days

The apocalyptic terrorists of the Islamic world are the most menacing individuals in the world today. And they intend to be. It is difficult for citizens in a successful, secular society to grasp the degree to which these men see themselves as God's avengers. In the aftermath of September 11, 2001, numerous analysts and commentators have attempted to discover coherent goals and logical behavior in the actions of such terrorists. But we lack the vocabulary or knowledge of the human psyche to cleanly describe the motivations, impulses, and visions of such men.

One way to visualize the difference between the more familiar practical terrorists and these apocalyptic terrorists is to describe their archetypes in terms of painting. The exemplary practical terrorist is like a classic representational painter, a Poussin or even a da Vinci: The canvas is coherent at a distance, and, the closer you come to the surface, the more fine detail and granularity you see. But apocalyptic terrorists are like the high impressionists—Cezanne, for example. Their "work" is only coherent when viewed from a certain distance. As you approach the canvas, the forms dissolve into splotches and lose their apparent definition. So, too, the apocalyptic terrorist may seem to have explanations, even justifications, for his attacks. He "wants the U.S. out of all Islamic countries," or reviles the invasive corruption of the West, or desires the establishment of a Palestinian state (on his own strict terms). But, upon closer inspection, all these relatively rational purposes begin to blur and dissolve. It is impossible to content the apocalyptic terrorist. His agenda is against this world, not of it. Viewed closely, his vision is inchoate, intuitive, and destructive without limit. It is reality that has not pleased him, and he wants to destroy reality.

Although he views the world as sinful and corrupt, the apocalyptic terrorist's vision of an afterlife is ecstatic. He is absolutely certain that his deeds will be rewarded in the heaven of his particular god. This model is by no means limited to Islamic terrorists—it enraptures apocalyptic terrorists in every susceptible religion. Our problem is that today the failures and psychological debilities of the Muslim world spawn an increasing number of these deadly visionaries and their sufficiently convinced accomplices.

Aggressive religious cults are a predictable aberration of troubled societies struggling through periods of profound change. Some human beings simply cannot deal with the sudden fracturing of their verities and the inadequacy of their long-held, cherished beliefs. Particularly for the apocalyptic terrorist, belief is all or nothing. If his earlier beliefs—either in a particular form of religion or in a cultural milieu—fail to answer his practical and, above all, psychological needs, he tends to rush to another extreme. The appearance of suicidal Islamic terrorists who, earlier in their lives, seemed well-integrated into society and even fond of Western things is a perfect manifestation of this phenomenon. We fail to recognize the difficulty those from other cultures face in internalizing the extremely complex, synthetic value system that allows Americans to operate in our very challenging, apparently contradictory, supercharged society. An outsider can take pleasure in a pair of Nikes or Hollywood films, even revel in the sexual freedom he finds among some segments of Western societies, only to find that his cultural background has not armored him for the disjunctions of the "American way of life."

Americans are masterful at social improvisation and evolution (obviously with many individual exceptions), but this is not a developed skill in more traditional societies. A single, ill-timed rejection, a number of real or perceived humiliations, a gnawing sense of inadequacy and anomie, a failed university course, a lost job, or a nasty touch of venereal disease all can turn the seemingly Westernized visitor from a traditional society into a rabid hater of all things Western as he turns for emotional comfort to the verities of an idealized version of his root culture (from which he earlier had thought to escape). Others need no direct contact with the West to feel immensely threatened by its implications of moral lawlessness (as perceived by the outsiders) and ruthless competition (which they suspect they cannot outface).

Whether the terrorist has an old immigration stamp in his passport or has never left the alleys of Cairo or Karachi, the unifying factor is the fragility of his "cradle," the inadequacy of cherished

Islamic traditions to cope not only with the postmodern, but even with primitive versions of the modern world. A religio-social society that restricts the flow of information; prefers myth to reality; oppresses women; makes family, clan, or ethnic identity the basis for social and economic relations; subverts the rule of secular law; undervalues scientific and liberal education; discourages independent thought; and believes that ancient religious law should govern all human relations has no hope whatsoever of competing with America and the vibrant, creative states of the West and the Pacific Rim. We are succeeding, the Islamic world is failing, and they hate us for it. The preceding sentence encapsulates the cause of the terrorism of September 11, 2001, and no amount of "rational" analysis or nervous explanation will make this basic truth go away.

The last time a "world" and an all-encompassing way of life failed in the West was during the early years of the Protestant Reformation. (Of note, economic failures alone do not seem to drive people to apocalyptic behaviors. The Irish Potato Famine, the eviction of Highland crofters, the collapse of the Silesian weaving industry, the destruction of the artisan's way of life by mass manufacturing, and the breakdown of coal mining all failed to spawn millenarian movements; apocalyptic behavior is spawned by cultural failure in the broadest sense.) The "great chain of being" worldview that comforted a majority of the European population during the Middle Ages could not withstand the stresses of nascent modernity and, above all, the explosion of information after Gutenberg's development of the movable type printing press in the mid-fifteenth century. Although the theological and social issues took centuries to resolve (and some *still* have not been laid to rest), the fate of the Protestant Reformation was essentially decided in its first dozen years. The subsequent hundred and twenty-odd years of interconfessional warfare was about the boundaries of Protestantism, not really about its existence—although contemporaries saw it otherwise. In that initial "long decade," a way of life developed over centuries, a sequence of beliefs and behaviors that had withstood near-constant feudal warfare, recurrent famines, and the unparalleled slaughter of the Black Death collapsed with astonishing speed north of the Alps. Certainly there long had been fissures in the fabric of society and state, and economic burdens helped trigger the assault on the old, uniform system, but what matters for our discussion is that the deepest verities—issues of salvation, sanctity, and the very nature of worship, as well as elementary questions of how church power is vested and which behaviors find divine favor—were suddenly open to debate not only by learned theologians but also by common men and women (and a great many not-very-learned men of the cloth). As the old, monolithic structure of belief and prescribed behavior broke down—with a speed that would bewilder even today's mentally agile Americans—millions of human beings lost their bearings. Some quickly found refuge in a new mainstream of Protestant churches, while others never let go of, or quickly re-embraced, the Roman church. But many thousands could not content themselves with either the old way or the more temperate of the new ways. And they initiated the greatest outbreak of popular terror the West has ever known, the Peasants' Revolt in the Germanies in the 1520s. Bloodier than any revolutionary movement prior to the Russian Civil War, its impulses were apocalyptic in the extreme.

The Peasants' Revolt, or Peasants' Wars, is misnamed to a degree, since the rebellious leaders were extreme-radical theologians, lesser knights, and some members of a fractious, often impecunious nobility. The peasants and some disaffected townsmen provided the mass, not the minds—although some hallucinatory visionaries did emerge from the lower levels of society. And, as East German historians anxiously pointed out during the Cold War, the outbreak of millenarian terror in the mid-1520s had secular antecedents in the *Bundschuh* movement and disparate local revolts that preceded the Reformation. But it was the crisis of faith and the loss of the certainty of salvation as a reward for traditional behavior (and a new calculus for damnation) that catalyzed disparate local movements with concrete grudges into a horde of impassioned killers chasing redemption with swords, scythes, and torches.

Although the East Germans of the old German Democratic Republic tried to repackage him as a proto-socialist, the revolutionary and theologian Thomas Muentzer may have been the Western figure closest to Osama bin Laden (the practical terrorists of the Counter-Reformation and the Inquisition don't even come close). Muentzer, who led his rebels behind a blood-red cross (alternatively reported as a blood-red sword), left a trail of devastation across the middle of the Germanies that only ceased when a coalition of the nobility and knights brought him to a final, apocalyptic battle that ended with an uncompromising pursuit and massacre of the insurgents, followed by the ingenious torture and executions of their captured leaders.

The suddenness and scale of the rebellion had caught all of the authorities of the day by surprise, and it took time to organize an effective response. In one of the paradoxes of history, the decisive revolutionary in the history of the West, Martin Luther, was terrified by the insurgency's embrace of social chaos and the lack of obedience to traditional authority (which he wrestled with rather successfully himself), as well as by the explicit threat to the security of his own reformed church, which was still struggling for legitimacy. In what many consider the greatest blot upon his life and work, Luther wrote a vitriolic public manifesto justifying the extermination of the rebels by any means necessary. To be fair, Luther always saw himself as a loyal, if misunderstood reformer of a true church, not as a revolutionary, but few men know themselves of their effects. Luther condemned that which he himself had unleashed. (His situation bore at least a superficial similarity to the role of the U.S. in fostering fundamentalist extremism in Afghanistan and Pakistan, the excesses of which now appall us.)

In the meantime, the various ill-disciplined bands of peasants and townsmen, some attracted to charismatic leadership and others simply delighted by the opportunity for revenge and destruction, had sacked castles and towns, tortured, raped, and slaughtered any members of the elite who fell into their hands, devastated churches and iconic art, and reveled in destruction. While there was a great deal of simply "having their own back" in all this for the peasants and the poor of the towns, Muentzer and the other charismatic extremists preached an "end of days" and a sort of purification through destruction that absolved their followers in advance. Muentzer and his familiars read messages in the Heavens, heard God's voice on a private line, and interpreted the Scriptures (especially the Book of Revelation) in a manner that gave their followers license to almost any excess. Their mentality of dragging heaven down to earth through violence, of helping God bring on His Day of Judgment, and of avenging the oppressed through the slaughter of real or imagined oppressors provides the last, five-centuries-old shred of evidence for the campus leftist's argument that "We're really all alike." Indeed, Osama bin Laden is Islam's Thomas Muentzer—a hero to many, a demon to the rest of us. Like John Brown, Muentzer lacked our ultramodern technology of destruction. But had he possessed nuclear, chemical, or biological weapons, he doubtless would have used them. The authorities he attempted to bring down with terror realized that he had to be killed, and they killed him and as many of his followers as they could track down. The soil of Thuringia, northern Franconia, Eastern Hesse, and the foothills of the Harz were soaked with blood. But Central Europe never suffered another apocalyptic uprising of a similar scale. And the chastened followers of Muentzer and his co-believers who survived, though they long nursed grievances, turned inward, forming, among others, the Anabaptist movements from the Rhineland that helped pioneer America.

Dying for God

An obvious counterargument to the suggestion that apocalyptic terrorists are possessed by a suicidal impulse is that Osama bin Laden seems to want to stay alive. But the desire for self-annihilation takes many forms. In the case of the operational leaders of the September 11 attacks, there was, indeed, an impatience with this world and a readiness to embrace a self-justifying excuse for leaving it behind. Although each of those terrorists would have rejected out of hand the suggestion that they were suicidal or that their discontents were primarily of an inward nature, the fact is that few such men willingly recognize their own motives—or have either the wish or the ability to do so. Often motive is more easily identified from without. But men who are at peace with themselves and the world do not destroy themselves and as large a portion of the world as they can take down with them.

As dangerous as the "martyrs" of September 11, 2001, were, those of the Osama bin Laden cast are much more worrisome. With or without weapons of mass destruction, the foot-soldier terrorists rushing to kill themselves in a dramatic, annihilating gesture may create plenty of horror and havoc, but the "long-run suicides," those who judge themselves too important to throw away in a "minor" episode, are more dangerous by far. The do-it-now personalities attack specific targets, but the apocalyptic masters seek to destroy vast systems. (Of note, the demands of practical terrorists sometimes diminish over time, as they gain perspective on what is or is not possible, but the demands of apocalyptic terrorists only increase and grow ever more fantastic.)

Osama bin Laden is willing to die—but he wants a commensurate effect when he goes. He is in no hurry and takes great pleasure from the rising crescendo of destruction he can effect through his underlings. But he is not a survive-at-any-cost figure (unlike bureaucrat-terrorists, such as Saddam or Milosevic). Osama bin Laden will, indeed, die for his beliefs—and he will do so with great willingness if he believes he can extract a cataclysmic price in return for his own life. While it would be inaccurate to say there is nothing at which he would not stop, the things that would give him pause are inconsequential to us—taboos in daily behavior, notions of physical pollution, and the corruption of religious rituals. The totems of belief and reassuring behavior are more important to him than complex theological arguments—no matter how much Islamic commentary he may have memorized to use to support his position. He may know all of the Koran by heart—but that, too, is a ritual function. His theology cannot be penetrated by argument, though it can be bolstered by agreement. In terms of religion, he imagines himself as Allah's humble servant but is, in fact, an extreme egomaniac, "leading God from below." When he imagines his own end, it is less a vision of entering a physical paradise and more a sense of merging with his god. He wants to go out with a very big bang.

This is not to suggest that Osama bin Laden is plotting his own end, or that he is eager to die. Rather, he is *willing* to die, and he finds the notion of transcendence through death enticing rather than forbidding. The world reaches him only in negative senses, and, unless the biology of fear kicks in as he faces his own death, he will not much regret leaving this world behind. The corollary, of course, is that he is never reluctant to sacrifice others to his vision and his will. As of this writing there is a theory making the rounds that Osama is, in fact, a very clever manipulator who has a complex, rational plan to get what he wants. This is probably true—but only reflects the least, most superficial part of his character. There are many varieties of madness, and a Hitler can plan very well under congenial circumstances; so, too, does Osama bin Laden. But he cannot be dealt with as a rational actor, since, under the cunning surface, he is irrational in the extreme. His methods make cruel sense, but his goals are far beyond the demise of a particular regime or the recognition of a Palestinian state. He wants to destroy, at the very least, a civilization he has cast as satanic. He does not want to defeat the West—he wants to annihilate us. If he had the technology today, he would use it.

Evidence and the Believer

One of the most frustrating things for Westerners since September 11, 2001, has been the demands throughout the Islamic world for "proof" that Osama bin Laden was behind the attacks. At the same time, "friendly" Arab governments condone or even quietly support suggestions that "Zionists" directed the attacks, that American Jews were warned before the strikes on the World Trade Center and that 4,000 of them did not show up for work on the fateful day. We cannot believe that anyone could believe such folly and we want to extend proof of the truth. But empirical reality is almost irrelevant within the Islamic world—comforting myths are much more powerful. The mental processes at work are so fundamentally different from our own that we literally cannot comprehend them.

Were we to provide a videotaped confession by Osama bin Laden, Muslims would insist that Hollywood had staged it. Were we to provide multimedia records of Arabs committing the deeds of September 11, the response would be the same. Statistics, facts, evidence, proof—none of this has much weight in the Muslim consciousness. I have personally never quite gotten used to the stunning ability of even educated people between the Nile and the Himalayas to believe with deep conviction and passion that which is patently, provably false.

Another aspect of the Islamic mind is its ability to disaggregate and compartmentalize. One moment, a Pakistani or an Egyptian might tell you that Israel staged the attacks on the World Trade Center and the Pentagon, then, a moment later, tell you what a great hero Osama bin Laden is and that the Muslims who piloted the planes were great heroes. We see an obvious lapse in logic, but our Muslim counterpart sees nothing of the kind. He can comfortably believe both "truths."

Part of the problem is that empirical truth comforts us, since we're a success story. The Joe-Friday facts support our satisfying view of ourselves. But few facts support a positive self-image within the Islamic world. The flight into fantasy has been going on for a very long time—at least since the expulsion of the Moors from Spain in 1492—but the impact of globalization, modernity, and now post-modernity has driven hundreds of millions of Muslims into a fabulous refuge of their own collective construction. Powerful myths may be the only thing the Islamic world is good at building any longer.

What it means for us is that we should not waste too much effort trying to prove that which will never be believed, no matter how much supporting data we offer. We can convince through our deeds alone—and even then only partially. When we kill Osama bin Laden, millions will refuse to believe in his death (even if we should put the corpse on a Middle East tour, complete with on-the-spot DNA sampling). And the talent for overlaying conspiracies on even the most benign Western actions will always override the reality of any good we seek to do or accomplish. (Of course America has its own conspiracy fanatics, but in our society they exist on the margins, while the belief in complex, malevolent Western and "Zionist" conspiracies is integral to middle-of-the-road discourse in the Muslim world.)

We are dealing with a delusional civilization. This is a new problem in history. Certainly the degree of delusion varies from individual to individual, to some extent between social classes, and somewhat between peoples and states. But it means that the American and Western tradition of reasoning with opponents, of convincing doubters, and of marshalling evidence has far less potency—often none—in dealing with the Islamic world.

We may believe with great satisfaction that we have the truth on our side, but myth is on their side, and myth can be more powerful than truth. Some noble or hapless souls may sacrifice their lives in service to the truth. But millions will rush to die for a cherished myth.

Only physical reality, brought home with stunning force, can make much of an impression. Even that will be rationalized away in time. But where the truth cannot make headway, punitive or preventive violence must protect us.

We too have our comforting myths, among them that all the people of the world are really "just like us," that all men are finally subject to reason, and, most perniciously, that violence is a desperate measure that solves nothing. In fact, billions of people are not "like us," surprisingly few men are subject to reason when reason threatens their most precious beliefs, and violence is often the only meaningful solution.

Palestinian Terrorists and the Dark Transformation

We are worried about the Palestinian problem for many of the wrong reasons. Beyond our appalling double standard of criticizing Israel for killing known terrorists and their commanders while tut-tutting at Palestinian suicide bombings that intentionally kill and maim dozens of innocents, we are making the classic American error of pursuing short-term comfort over long-term benefits, pursuing the impossible goal of placating the Islamic world (impossible, at least, without countenancing the destruction of Israel). In theory, the goal of a Palestinian state makes sense and, in reality, its creation appears inevitable, so doubtless we must make the best of it. Our error is to imagine that the creation of that state will bring peace. On the contrary, it will only elevate the struggle to another level. Too many Palestinians are now the enemies of any peace that allows Israel's continued existence, and, beyond the near-Babel of rhetoric, for many militants the ultimate destruction of Israel is a far more captivating goal than the establishment of a rule-of-law Palestinian state that will require them to deal with an unsatisfying daily reality. We do not have to like everything the Israelis do to recognize that our long-term interests and theirs coincide. We will never find a resolute ally on the other side, and this new cockpit of crisis, from the Nile to the Hindu Kush (and perhaps beyond) consumes concessions with an insatiable appetite.

What is immediately relevant to a discussion of terrorism, however, is the metamorphosis that has been underway in the ranks of Palestinian terrorists. Over the past few decades they have evolved from a mostly secular, practical outlook with finite (if sometimes extreme) goals to an increasingly apocalyptic orientation. The shift is still under way, and terrorists of the more secular variety still exist, but fervent Islam increasingly trumps political calculation. A cardinal symptom is the increasing percentage of suicide bombers. Palestinians have long been willing to die for their cause (in many ways an easier alternative to devoting a life of hard work to the construction of a state and its infrastructure), but the terrorist who *might* die in the course of a daring operation is giving way more and more to the terrorist who *intends* to die as a consequence of his action. And if you compare the rhetoric of the 1970s and 1980s to the fevered declarations of contemporary Palestinian terrorists, their supporters, and their advocates, the intensifying embrace of religion is unmistakable.

An analyst with no other knowledge of the situation would assume that this radicalization into apocalyptic religious behavior must be the result of the failure of the secular approach, but the actual situation is the reverse: The Palestinians have made impressive progress toward complete self-government and a state of their own; they have won an astonishing legitimacy in the eyes of the world, including the United States; and, except for the destruction of Israel, their original aims are well on the way to fulfillment. Another analyst might say that the pace has been too slow, that discontents were allowed to boil over. In retrospect, however, Palestinian progress has been relatively swift in historical terms. The source of the radicalization lies elsewhere.

The Palestinians, who are in many respects the most successful, educated, secular, and "Westernized" Arabs since the shattering of Lebanon a generation ago, have been catching the contagion sweeping the Arab world, if more slowly than in more backward regions. Increasingly, Israel is more of a mythologized object than a tangible reality (although for Palestinians the reality admittedly can be pretty harsh), more a demon to be slain than a state to be challenged. The thorough demonization of Israel is now the single biggest obstacle to any peace plan. While there always was a religious and civilizational element to the conflict in Palestine, the change over the past decades has been profound. No matter how generous the terms offered to a future Palestinian state, a substantial, deadly portion of the Palestinian population (to say nothing of Arabs of other nationalities) will never be satisfied, materially or, more importantly, psychologically. The Arab world's spiritual crisis, born of a generalized failure, needs the demon Israel (and the demon America) far more than it needs peace in the West Bank or Gaza. Israel is the great excuse for failure, and it will never be viewed as a mere tolerable neighbor.

The roots of the fervor that transmutes all too easily into an apocalyptic vision lie in the general failure of the Islamic world to compete. What had been a political crisis is now a massive psychological crisis. Some years ago, a popular work of history was entitled *The Madness of Crowds*. We are now dealing with the madness of a civilization. Of course, many readers will dismiss this as hateful or vicious thinking—and I personally wish the reality were otherwise. But the doubters have only to wait. Islam's sense of failure is only going to intensify (because its counterproductive behaviors and values will not change), and the apocalyptic, vengeful impulse will intensify in turn. It is one of the tragedies of the Arab world that a deadly, crippling segment among the Palestinians—who had at least a chance of performing competitively—has been collapsing backward into a medieval vision of religion just as they approach their long-championed secular goals. While it is impossible to predict the pace and scope of this transformation—and it may yet be stymied by Palestinian secularists, who increasingly realize that they, too, are in a battle with religious extremism—we may find ourselves hoping the blander forces of corruption, greed, and selfishness in the Palestinian Authority will somehow trump the fervor of the rising generation of believers. It is not only an unattractive position in which to find ourselves, but an almost hopeless one.

Elsewhere the same phenomenon of transformation from practical to apocalyptic terrorism has taken hold broadly. Where once Islamic terrorists espoused sloppy versions of socialism, communism, Nasserism, Arab nationalism, or many another fuzzy ism, they are now increasingly *Islamic* terrorists. It is a long way down into the darkness from the once-feared terrorists of Black September to the mass murderers of September 11. For all of us who have lived through the last half century, it is astonishing to note that George Habash now looks moderate in comparison to the hypercharged, god-intoxicated terrorists of today.

As the Israelis have already learned, even if they cannot openly acknowledge it, there is no solution to this challenge, only a determination to survive on the most advantageous terms possible. A friend of mine commented, shortly after September 11, that "we're all Israelis now." He was correct, in the sense that our lives are no longer inviolable. But we have far greater power and wealth than does Israel, and better geography, globalization notwithstanding. We have the power to set the terms strategically, and even to fix the terms of most tactical encounters. But before we can do so, we must recognize how the world and terrorism have changed. And then we must have the strength of will to do what must be done.

Fighting Terror:
Dos and Don'ts for a Superpower

1. Be feared.

2. Identify the type of terrorists you face, and know your enemy as well as you possibly can. Although tactics may be similar, strategies for dealing with practical versus apocalyptic terrorists can differ widely. Practical terrorists may have legitimate grievances that deserve consideration, although their methods cannot be tolerated. Apocalyptic terrorists, no matter what their rhetoric, seek your destruction and must be killed to the last man. The apt metaphor is cancer—you cannot hope for success if you only cut out part of the tumor. For the apocalyptic terrorist, evading your efforts can easily be turned into a public triumph. Our bloodiest successes will create far fewer terrorists and sympathizers than our best-intentioned failures.

3. Do not be afraid to be powerful. Cold War–era gambits of proportionate response and dialog may have some utility in dealing with practical terrorists, but they are counterproductive in dealing with apocalyptic terrorists. Our great strengths are wealth and raw power. When we fail to bring those strengths to bear, we contribute to our own defeat. For a superpower to think small—which has been our habit across the last decade, at least—is self-defeating folly. Our responses to terrorist acts should make the world gasp.

4. Speak bluntly. Euphemisms are interpreted as weakness by our enemies and mislead the American people. Speak of killing terrorists and destroying their organizations. Timid

speech leads to timid actions. Explain when necessary, but do not apologize. Expressions of regret are never seen as a mark of decency by terrorists or their supporters, but only as a sign that our will is faltering. Blame the terrorists as the root cause whenever operations have unintended negative consequences. Never go on the rhetorical defensive.

5. Concentrate on winning the propaganda war where it is winnable. Focus on keeping or enhancing the support from allies and well-disposed clients. Do not waste an inordinate amount of effort trying to win unwinnable hearts and minds. Convince hostile populations through victory.

6. Do not be drawn into a public dialog with terrorists—especially not with apocalyptic terrorists. You cannot win. You legitimize the terrorists by addressing them even through a third medium, and their extravagant claims will resound more successfully on their own home ground than anything you can say. Ignore absurd accusations, and never let the enemy's claims slow or sidetrack you. The terrorist wants you to react, and your best means of unbalancing him and his plan is to ignore his accusations.

7. Avoid "planning creep." Within our vast bureaucratic system, too many voices compete for attention and innumerable agendas—often selfish and personal—intrude on any attempt to act decisively. Focus on the basic mission—the destruction of the terrorists—with all the moral, intellectual, and practical rigor you can bring to bear. All other issues, from future nation-building to alliance consensus to humanitarian concerns, are secondary.

8. Maintain resolve. Especially in the Middle East and Central Asia, "experts" and diplomats will always present you with a multitude of good reasons for doing nothing, or for doing too little (or for doing exactly the wrong thing). Fight as hard as you can within the system to prevent diplomats from gaining influence over the strategic campaign. Although their intentions are often good, our diplomats and their obsolete strategic views are the terrorist's unwitting allies—and diplomats are extremely jealous of military success and military authority

in "their" region (where their expertise is never as deep or subtle as they believe it to be). Beyond the problem with our diplomats, the broader forces of bureaucratic entropy are an internal threat. The counterterrorist campaign must be not only resolute but constantly self-rejuvenating—in ideas, techniques, military and interagency combinations, and sheer energy. "Old hands" must be stimulated constantly by new ideas.

9. When in doubt, hit harder than you think necessary. Success will be forgiven. Even the best-intentioned failure will not. When military force is used against terrorist networks, it should be used with such power that it stuns even our allies. We must get over our "cowardice in means." While small-scale raids and other knife-point operations are useful against individual targets, broader operations should be overwhelming. Of course, targeting limitations may inhibit some efforts, but, whenever possible, maximum force should be used in simultaneous operations at the very beginning of a campaign. Do not hesitate to supplement initial target lists with extensive bombing attacks on "nothing" if they can increase the initial psychological impact. Demonstrate power whenever you can. Show, don't tell.

10. Whenever legal conditions permit, kill terrorists on the spot (do not give them a chance to surrender, if you can help it). Contrary to academic wisdom, the surest way to make a martyr of a terrorist is to capture, convict, and imprison him, leading to endless efforts by sympathizers to stage kidnappings, hijackings, and other events intended to liberate the imprisoned terrorist. This is war, not law enforcement.

11. Never listen to those who warn that ferocity on our part reduces us to the level of the terrorist. That is the argument of the campus, not of the battlefield, and it insults America's service members and the American people. Historically we have proven time after time that we can do a tough, dirty job for our country without any damage to our nation's moral fabric (Hiroshima and Nagasaki did not interfere with American democracy, values, or behavior).

12. Spare and protect innocent civilians whenever possible, but do not let the prospect of civilian casualties interfere with ultimate mission accomplishment. This is a fight to protect the American people, and we must proceed, whatever the cost, or the price in American lives may be devastating. In a choice between "us and them," the choice is always "us."

13. Do not allow the terrorists to hide behind religion. Apocalyptic terrorists cite religion as a justification for attacking us; we cannot let them hide behind religious holidays, taboos, strictures, or even sacred terrain. We must establish a consistent reputation for relentless pursuit and destruction of those who kill our citizens. Until we do this, our hesitation will continue to strengthen our enemy's ranks and his resolve.

14. Do not allow third parties to broker a "peace," a truce, or any pause in operations. One of the most difficult challenges in fighting terrorism on a global scale is the drag produced by nervous allies. We must be single-minded. The best thing we can do for our allies in the long term is to be so resolute and so strong that they value their alliance with us all the more. We must recognize the innate strength of our position and stop allowing regional leaders with counterproductive local agendas to subdue or dilute our efforts.

15. Don't flinch. If an operation goes awry and friendly casualties are unexpectedly high, immediately bolster morale and the military's image by striking back swiftly in a manner that inflicts the maximum possible number of casualties on the enemy and his supporters. Hit back as graphically as possible, to impress upon the local and regional players that you weren't badly hurt or deterred in the least.

16. Do not worry about alienating already hostile populations.

17. Whenever possible, humiliate your enemy in the eyes of his own people. Do not try to use reasonable arguments against him. Shame him publicly, any way you can. Create doubt where you cannot excite support. Most apocalyptic terrorists come from cultures of male vanity. Disgrace them at every opportunity. Done successfully, this both degrades them in

the eyes of their followers and supporters and provokes the terrorists to respond, increasing their vulnerability.

18. If the terrorists hide, strike at what they hold dear, using clandestine means and, whenever possible, foreign agents to provoke them to break cover and react. Do not be squeamish. Your enemy is not. Subtlety is not a superpower strength. The raw power to do that which is necessary is our great advantage. We forget that while the world may happily chide or accuse us—or complain of our "inhumanity"—no one can stop us if we maintain our strength of will. Much of the world will complain no matter what we do. Hatred of America is the default position of failed individuals and failing states around the world in every civilization, and there is nothing we can do to change those minds. We refuse to understand how much of humanity will find excuses for evil so long as the evil strikes those who are more successful than the apologists themselves. This is as true of American academics, whose eagerness to declare our military efforts a failure is unflagging, and European clerics, who still cannot forgive America's magnanimity at the end of World War II, as it is of unemployed Egyptians or Pakistanis. The psychologically marginalized are at least as dangerous as the physically deprived.

19. Do not allow the terrorists sanctuary in any country, at any time, under any circumstances. Counterterrorist operations must be relentless. This does not necessarily mean that military operations will be constantly underway—sometimes it will be surveillance efforts, deception plans, or operations by other agencies. But the overall effort must never pause for breath. We must be faster, more resolute, more resourceful—and, ultimately, even more uncompromising than our enemies.

20. Never declare victory. Announce successes and milestones. Never give the terrorists a chance to embarrass you after a public pronouncement that "the war is over."

21. Impress upon the minds of terrorists and potential terrorists everywhere, and upon the populations and governments inclined to support them, that American retaliation will be powerful and uncompromising. You will never deter fanatics,

but you can frighten those who might support, harbor, or attempt to use terrorists for their own ends. Our basic task in the world today is to restore a sense of American power, capability, and resolve. We must be hard, or we will be struck wherever we are soft. It is folly for charity to precede victory. First win, then unclench your fist.

22. Do everything possible to make terrorists and their active supporters live in terror themselves. Turn the tide psychologically and practically. While this will not deter hardcore apocalyptic terrorists, it will dissipate their energies as they try to defend themselves—and fear will deter many less-committed supporters of terror. Do not be distracted by the baggage of the term "assassination." This is a war. The enemy, whether a hijacker or a financier, violates the laws of war by his refusal to wear a uniform and by purposely targeting civilians. He is by definition a war criminal. On our soil, he is either a spy or a saboteur, and not entitled to the protections of the U.S. Constitution. Those who abet terrorists must grow afraid to turn out the lights to go to sleep.

23. Never accept the consensus of the Washington intelligentsia, which looks backward to past failures, not forward to future successes.

24. In dealing with Islamic apocalyptic terrorists, remember that their most cherished symbols are fewer and far more vulnerable than are the West's. Ultimately, no potential target can be regarded as off-limits when the United States is threatened with mass casualties. Worry less about offending foreign sensibilities and more about protecting Americans.

25. Do not look for answers in recent history, which is still unclear and subject to personal emotion. Begin with the study of the classical world—specifically Rome, which is the nearest model to the present-day United States. Mild with subject peoples, to whom they brought the rule of ethical law, the Romans in their rise and at their apogee were implacable with their enemies. The utter destruction of Carthage brought centuries of local peace, while the later empire's attempts to appease barbarians consistently failed.

Stability, America's Enemy

Parameters

Winter 2001–02

The diplomats and decision makers of the United States believe, habitually and uncritically, that stability abroad is our most important strategic objective. They may insist, with fragile sincerity, that democracy and human rights are our international priorities—although our policymakers do not seem to understand the requirements of the first and refuse to meet the requirements of the second. The United States will go to war over economic threats, as in Desert Storm. At present, we are preoccupied with a crusade against terrorism, which is as worthy as it is difficult. But the consistent, pervasive goal of Washington's foreign policy is stability. America's finest values are sacrificed to keep bad governments in place, dysfunctional borders intact, and oppressed human beings well-behaved. In one of the greatest acts of self-betrayal in history, the nation that long was the catalyst of global change and which remains the beneficiary of international upheaval has made stability its diplomatic god.

Our insistence on stability above all stands against the tides of history, and that is always a losing proposition. Nonetheless, our efforts might be understandable were they in our national interest. But they are not. Historically, instability abroad has been to America's advantage, bringing us enhanced prestige and influence, safe-haven-seeking investment, a peerless national currency, and flows of refugees that have proven to be rivers of diamonds (imagine how much poorer our lives would be, in virtually every regard, had our nation not been enriched by refugees from Europe's disturbances in the last century).

Without the instability of the declining eighteenth century, as the old European order decayed, we would not have gained the French assistance decisive to our struggle for independence. Without the instability of the twentieth century, protectionist imperial regimes might have lingered on to stymie our economic expansion. And without the turbulence that seeks to rebalance the world today, much of humanity would continue to rot under the corrupt, oppressive regimes that are falling everywhere, from the Balkans to Southeast Asia. A free world subject to popular decision is impossible without the dismantling of the obsolete governments we rush to defend. In one of history's bitterest ironies, the United States finally became, in the 1990s, the reactionary power leftists painted us during the Cold War.

Before examining in greater detail why instability abroad is often to America's long-term benefit, let us consider the foolish manner in which we have descended from being a nation that championed change and human freedom to one that squanders its wealth, power, and lives in defense of a very bad status quo.

We began well enough, applauding Latin America's struggles to liberate itself from the grip of degenerate European empires (except, of course, in the case of Haiti, whose dark-skinned freedom fighters made our own Southern slaveholders nervous). The Monroe Doctrine was not about stability, but about protecting a new and beneficial instability from reactionary Europe. We did take an enormous bite of Mexican territory, which Mexico had inherited and could not manage, but we did not attempt to destroy or to rule Mexico. At the end of our Civil War, we were even prepared to intervene militarily on Mexico's behalf against European interlopers, had not the "Emperor" Maximilian met a fitting end at Mexican hands.

It all began to go wrong when we found ourselves with an accidental empire. Future historians, with the clarity allowed by centuries, may judge the Spanish-American War to have been America's decisive conflict, a quick fight that changed our nation's destiny and practice fundamentally. Brief, nearly bloodless, and wildly victorious, that war's importance has always been underestimated. Unlike almost all of America's other wars, it was a war that need not have been. Because it did happen, we turned outward, abandoning the convent for the streets, and could not go back. With that war, we became an imperial power, if a benign one, thus denying our heritage as the key anti-imperial power in history.

Domestically, the nation we have today is the result of our Civil War. Internationally, our fate was shaped by the Spanish-American War—more than by any of the wars that followed, despite their greater scope and striking results. Occurring at the peak of unbridled domestic capitalism, the Spanish-American War made of us an extractive power, in which the earnings of fruit companies became more important than support for freedom and democracy. Our bayonets served business, not ideals. This pattern of valuing profit above our pride—or even elementary human decency—holds true in our present relationships with states as diverse as Saudi Arabia and China (during the captivity of a U.S. military aircrew in the spring of 2001, some American businessmen went to Capitol Hill to make China's case, rather than rallying to support our service members; our diplomatic blank check written to Saudi Arabia on behalf of our oil interests has allowed behind-the-scenes Saudi support for terrorists, while Saudi intelligence services stonewall us and Saudi citizens commit unprecedented acts of violence against the United States).

Despite evidence to the contrary throughout the twentieth century, it has remained our conviction that stability abroad is good for business and, thus, for the United States—yet the globalization of America's economic reach was enabled only by the colossal instabilities of collapsing empires. We argued that peace was good for business, no matter what the human cost of an artificial peace imposed with arms, across a century when wars, revolutions, and decade after decade of instability opened markets to American goods, investors, and ideas. Were the maps of today identical to those of a century ago, with the same closed imperial systems in place, our present wealth and power would be impossible. America has always had a genius for picking up the pieces—the problems arise when we insist on putting those pieces back together exactly as they were before. I know of no significant example in history where an attempt to restore the status quo antebellum really worked. The new "old" regime always turns out to be a different beast, despite attempts to fit it with a worn-out saddle. Neither bribes nor bullets (nor clumsy, corrupting aid) can make the clock run backward.

Consider another decisive event roughly contemporary to our war with Spain, the Boxer Rebellion in China. Anxious to prove we were equal to any member of the club of great powers, we joined the punitive expedition to Peking (as it then was spelled) and fought against an indigenous movement which, despite its grim methods, hoped to free its country from outrageous foreign exploitation and humiliation. Of course, that was a time when men with yellow skins were judged by most Americans as incapable of anything but mischief or lassitude, and I do not imagine that we might have switched sides—after all, our own legation was under siege, along with those of other, far more brutal powers. Still, imagine how much less savage the twentieth century might have been in Asia, and how much more peaceable the world today, had the Boxers won. The weakness upon which the European powers insisted frustrated any hope of internal development and left China naked in the face of Japanese aggression a generation later. Even during the greatest struggle in China's history—that against Japanese barbarism—we demonstrated our appetite for an imagined stability, creating for ourselves an image of Chiang Kai-shek that ignored his venality, callousness, cowardice, and impotence.

Our support for Chiang prefigured the behavior of the American diplomats of the eruptive 1990s, men and women who pretended that a functioning government remained wherever a single midlevel bureaucrat had a working phone in the blazing capital city. Stamp our feet in outrage as we will at Chinese intransigence today, we hardly may claim to have been China's benefactor in the past. As the nineteenth century ended and the twentieth began, we chose to collude in defending the existing world order, thereby losing a world of possibilities. Our actions may have been inevitable in the context of the times, but that does not make them wise.

The Great War began to break up the old imperial system that hindered the expansion of American trade, but we did our best to defend the old order to spite ourselves. Apart from President Wilson's handwringing at Versailles, our newly acquired appetite for order trumped any concern we had for human freedom and self-determination. And we paid a rarely acknowledged price for our complicity in propping up the *ancien régime* one more time. Given our preference for micro-causation and our snapshot approach to historical analysis, we may have misunderstood the true cause of the Great Depression. The "irrational exuberance" of the day served as an accelerator, but the historical force that drove so much of the developed world into the Depression was the attempt by the cartel of Great War victors to preserve the imperial trading order, with its restricted markets and an inherent stress on the metropolitan production of every type of industrial good without regard to efficiency. The imperial system, despite a bit of jerry-rigging, no longer answered the world's economic requirements. A brutally simple economic law is that only the expansion of possibilities enables the expansion of wealth, but the goal of Europe's waning empires was to restrict possibilities. Another seeming law is that developed economies cannot exist in equilibrium: When they cease to advance, they retreat. The old preglobalization machine could not go forward anymore. The Depression marked the breakdown of a world economic system that had lingered into decrepitude.

Of note, the nations most immediately affected by the Depression were all trading nations, because those were the states the international system had failed; the more autarchic the state, the less it suffered in the short term, giving rise to the illusion that isolated Russia and sequestered Germany provided viable models for the future. We defended a static world order and ultimately reaped the most destructive war in history (one doesn't need a revisionist bent to recognize the economic logic that drove the monstrous German and Japanese regimes to attack the tottering imperial system that excluded them from dependable access to resources). Even our willingness to wink at the rise of Hitler and Mussolini was symptomatic of a preference for stability above all. Mussolini "made the trains run on time," and Hitler did seem to get the Weimar Republic under control at last. Did the Great Depression and the Second World War occur in the forms in which we experienced them simply because America voted, along with the depleted European victors at the end of the Great War, to stop the clock wherever the clock could not be turned back?

History insists. The thrust of the imperial twilight was toward breaking down antiquated structures, and World War II did just that. The single great beneficiary was the United States. Yet we assumed our resounding success was somehow fragile and provisional; immensely powerful, we exaggerated our weaknesses. The Cold War was the last gasp of the last old empire, the Soviet incarnation of the Russian domain of the czars, overextended—fatally—into Eastern and Central Europe. And the Cold War deformed American strategic thought and our applied values beyond recognition. From the amoral defender of Europe's rotten empires, we descended to an immoral propping up of every soulless dictator who preferred our payments to those offered by Moscow. We utterly rejected our professed values, consistently struggling against genuine national liberation movements because we saw the hand of Moscow wherever a poor man reached out for food or asked for dignity. At our worst in the Middle East, we unreservedly supported—or enthroned—medieval despots who suppressed popular liberalization efforts, thus driving moderate dissidents into the arms of fanatics. From our diplomatic personnel held hostage in Iran a generation ago, to the September 11, 2001, terrorist attack on the United States, we have suffered for our support of repressive, "stable" regimes that radicalized their own impoverished citizens. In the interests of stability, we looked the other way while secret police tortured and shabby armies massacred their own people, from Iran to Guatemala. But the shah always falls.

Would that we could tattoo that on the back of every diplomat's hand: The shah *always* falls. Our age—roughly the period from 1898 through the end of the twenty-first century—is an age of devolution, of breaking down, of the casting off of old forms of government and territorial organization in favor of the popular will. Certainly, the forces of reaction can look very strong—deceptively strong—and the temptation is always to back the devil you know (and who allows you to explore for oil on his territory). But make no mistake—in one essential respect, today's America is on the same side as the most repressive voices in the Islamic world and the hard, old men in Beijing: We are trying to freeze history in place. And it cannot be done. In our ill-considered pursuit of stability (a contradiction in terms), we have raised up devils, from terrorists to dictators, who will not be easily put down.

The Cold War warped our thinking so badly that when the Soviet empire finally collapsed in 1991, we proclaimed a new world order while thoughtlessly doing our best to preserve the old one. Our diplomats and decision makers needed new thinking at least as badly as did the men in Moscow. Look at our track record over the last decade: It is a litany of predetermined failures that would be laughable were it not for the human suffering that resulted.

- When our greatest enemy, the Soviet empire, finally came apart, then–Secretary of State James Baker hurriedly tried to persuade the empire's components to remain together. Blessedly, the newly independent states weren't having any of that nonsense. When the American effort to keep Humpty Dumpty up on his wall failed, we nonetheless continued, unto this day, to support the territorial integrity of a Russian Federation that remains an enfeebled, but cruel empire. No matter how many Chechens may be slaughtered, we content ourselves with a polite wag of the finger, shrug our shoulders, then concede that massacre is an internal matter.

- After a stunning battlefield victory against Iraq, we ensured that Iraq would not suffer a "power vacuum," but would remain a sovereign state within its existing borders—even though Iraq was an unnatural, constructed state, not an organic one, and the price of its continued existence was the slaughter of Shi'ites in the south, the continued suffering of Kurds in the north, and the deprivation of the remainder of Iraq's population to suit the vanity of a criminal dictator. Infatuated, as usual, by the mirage of a restored status quo antebellum, we still face the same enemy we did a decade ago. Another reason for leaving Saddam in place was our fear of offending neighboring Arab monarchs and leaders, who themselves dread deposition. Our reward has been their discreet approval of the worst terrorists in history (no Arab or other Islamic state has made a serious effort to interfere with Osama bin Laden or his confederates; on the contrary, many

are quietly gleeful at American suffering, even while profess-
ing their "deepest sympathies," and elements within Saudi
Arabia and Pakistan have provided funding or other support
for anti-American terrorism).

- In Somalia, we insisted that a collection of incessantly competing tribes was a bona fide state, and we paid for our willful
  illusions in blood and embarrassment (note to Washington:
  Lines on a map do not make a functional state).

- In Haiti, our priority has not been popular well-being, but
  the preservation of a central state apparatus, however incapable, demeaning, and corrupt.

- In the former Yugoslavia—a miniature empire if ever there
  was one—the senior Bush administration and then the Clinton administration attempted to persuade the constituent
  parts of an ever-shrinking "state" that it was in their best
  interests to remain together, citing our own campus theorists
  who reasoned ethnic hatred out of existence and insisted
  that, all in all, the peoples of Yugoslavia got along just fine.
  Of course, the specimen populations paid insufficient heed
  to our professors and slaughtered each other with enthusiasm. Instead of considering the evidence of ethnic incom-
  patibility at this point in history, as displayed in blood before
  our eyes, we sent in our troops in the blithe expectation that
  corpses might be made to shake hands with one another.
  Today we pretend that the Bosnian Federation is more than
  a hate-crippled criminal refuge and that Kosovo will someday be a happy component of Greater Serbia. As of this writing, we are making believe that a Band-Aid or two will fix
  whatever might be wrong with Macedonia. Our quest for stability in the Balkans has led to a false, fragile stability
  dependent on the presence, for decades to come, of foreign
  troops. To our credit, we stopped the killing, though belatedly, but we botched the peace so badly that our most enduring achievement has been to make the Balkans safe for black
  marketeers.

Operation Desert Storm was our only victory of the past decade, and we threw its fruits away. We clutched the false god Stability to our bosoms, and now we are paying for our idol worship. History (for want of a better word) does have a godlike force, and we have stood against it. We have devalued our heritage, behaved as hypocrites, and succored monsters—and there is no sign that we will change our ways. From decomposing Indonesia (the questions are only of the speed of secession and the cost in blood) to the Arabian peninsula, we refuse to imagine the good that change might bring.

How did we come to this? In all other spheres, we have been the most creative, imaginative, innovative, and flexible nation in history. How is it that our diplomats and those who must rely upon them fell in love with the past, when our national triumphs have resulted from embracing the future?

Unfortunately, it can be easily explained. In times of sudden change, men look to what they know. When, after 1898, America abruptly found itself a world power with possessions offshore and across the Pacific, our diplomats relied on the existing model—the European system of collusion and apportionment designed at the Congress of Vienna by Prince Metternich, manipulated artfully in the next generation by Palmerston and his associates, and perfected, tragically, by Bismarck, whose genius led him to design a European security system that only a genius could maintain (and Bismarck's successors were not men of genius). Just on the eve of a new century that would sweep away the old order, we bought into the European system of mutual protection and guarantees (even defeated countries are not allowed to disappear; the lives of rulers, however awful their behavior, are sacrosanct; and states do not interfere in the domestic affairs of other states, etc.).

It was especially easy for our diplomats to accept the "wisdom" of the European way of organizing a strategic regime because, at that time, our diplomatic corps was dominated by the sons of "good" New England and mid-Atlantic families whose ties to and affinities toward the Old World were already out of step with those of their less decorous and more vigorous countrymen. If the Army belonged to those born in Virginia and farther south (and west), then the Department of State belonged to those from Virginia and farther north, and to the aspirants from elsewhere who emulated our Anglophiles and Europhiles most sincerely. Today, in 2001, America's diplomatic wisdom is that of Metternich and Castlereagh, brilliant reactionaries whose intent was to turn back the clock of history, then freeze the hands in place, after the Napoleonic tumult. America's international successes in the twentieth century occurred *despite* our diplomatic corps' values and beliefs.

Surely there is a middle way between supporting every failing state (usually a state that deserves to fail) and hunkering down in a bunker in Kansas while genocide prevails. The greatest immediate difficulty is that any such "middle way" would, in fact, be a number—perhaps a great number—of different ways. The classical age of diplomacy, from Metternich through Bismarck to Kissinger, is finished. In truth, a one-size-fits-all diplomatic framework never really worked, but during the Cold War we expended tremendous efforts to make it function, or at least to pretend it was working. Today, in a world that is systemically, developmentally, economically, and culturally differentiated and differentiating—despite the surface effects of globalization—our diplomacy cannot rely on easy-to-use constructs or unifying ideology (a great triumph of the twentieth century was the destruction of the historical aberration of ideology in the West; today's European "socialists" owe more to trial and error than to Marx, LaSalle, or Liebknecht, and all but the most bigoted Americans are political pragmatists in the clinch).

Our strategic approach must be situational, though shaped in each separate case by our national interests and informed by our core values. Of course, we must recognize the limits of the possible, but our greatest problem as a global power seems to be understanding what is impossible abroad, whether the impossibility is creating enduring ethnic harmony in the Balkans through armed patrols, willing a Somali state into existence through the presence of a few thousand undersupported troops, or trying to control terrorists with blustering threats and the occasional cruise-missile spanking.

The hardest thing is always to think clearly, to slash through the inherited beliefs that no one ever examines, and to defy the wise men who have built careers on exorbitant failures. All people, in every culture, are captive to slogans, but Americans must strive to do a little better. We have made a slogan of democracy abroad, imagining it as a practical means when it is, in fact, the glorious end of a long and difficult road. We speak of human rights, then wink at the mundane evil of Saudi Arabia, the grotesque oppression in China, and any African massacres that don't leak to the press— because, inside our system of diplomacy, human rights are finally regarded as a soft issue. Yet sincere and tenacious support for human rights is always good policy in the long term. The oppressor falls, whether in one year or fifty, and it is easier to do business with a nation whose freedom struggle you have supported than with one whose suffering you ignored or even abetted.

Regarding the business sector, it is the job of Wall Street to maintain short-term vigilance. But Washington must learn to counterbalance that short-term view with a longer-term perspective. Instead of a revolving door, there should be a steel wall between Wall Street and Washington. Diplomatic and military concessions to a repressive regime that allows select U.S.-headquartered corporations economic advantages today may prove a very poor investment for our country's greater interests tomorrow. We need to think across disciplines, to break the dual stranglehold of diplomatic tradition and economic immediacy. Were we only to apply our own professed ideals where it is rational and possible to do so, we would, indeed, find our way to a better, safer world in time. But we must stop trying to arrest the decomposition of empire's legacy. We are in a period of unprecedented and inevitable global change, and we must learn to accommodate and to help shape local changes constructively. But we cannot prevent the future from arriving.

Again, there is no unified field theory of diplomacy at our disposal. This is the hardest thing for Washingtonians to understand. Our responses to the world's dramas must be crafted on a case-by-case basis and founded upon nuanced knowledge of each specific situation. There is no single framework, and the rules change from continent to continent and even from week to week. Our national interest, too, evolves. Only our core values—the rule of law, the rights of the individual, and religious and ethnic tolerance—remain constant.

Democracy is a highly evolved mechanism for maintaining the society we have achieved, but it is not a tool for creating a society worth maintaining. Without good and respected laws, a commit-

ment to essential human rights, and the willingness to honor differences of birth and confession, democracy is just a con game for bullies. Democracy as we know it may also require a certain level of
popular affluence. But democracy alone will not bring affluence.
Weak, new governments, or those transforming themselves, need
training wheels on the bicycle of state, and we try to insist instead
that every government should jump on a Harley. Far from building
trust, democracy may shatter the remaining social bonds of weak or
brutalized societies, dividing survivors into ethnic or religious factions. The overhasty imposition of democracy can lead directly to a
degeneration in the respect for human rights. Where citizens have
not learned to value their collective interests, democracy intensifies
ethnic and religious polarization. Democracy must be earned and
learned. It cannot be decreed from without. In a grim paradox, our
insistence on instant democracy in shattered states (never in strong
states or in those with which we do lucrative business, of course) is
our greatest contribution to global instability. We have become
strategic doctors determined to prescribe the same cure for every
patient we see, before we have bothered to examine the patient's
individual symptoms. Without a thought, we apply the rules of the
Congress of Vienna to Somalia, Bosnia, and the West Bank, then try
to graft on democracy overnight. We might as well attempt to cure
cancer by the application of the best medicine of the eighteenth
century.

Let us examine, briefly, just a small selection of the strategic issues
facing the United States in which the quest for stability may prove
antithetical to American interests.

   The Balkans represent the worst of all worlds: The slaughters
occurred, fatally deepening the local hatreds, before any of the
world's mature governments intervened, and now we are left with
artificial states overlapping with de facto states, each within unsatisfactory boundaries, each with irreconcilable minorities, and each
abundantly armed and criminally funded. "If only" may be pathetic
words, but consider what might have been had the Euro-American
community recognized, early on, that Yugoslavia was a Frankenstein's monster of a state that begged to be dismantled. There would
have been no way to satisfy all, but plebiscites under international

auspices—on which we had the raw power to insist—would have saved countless lives and prevented much, if not all, of the misery that benefited only criminals, bigots, and journalists.

The Russian Federation gets a pass, no matter how awful or simply contrary its behavior, in the interests of stability. Having faced down and defeated the magnificently armed Soviet Union, we have talked ourselves into fearing the weak rump state that survived its ruin. In Washington, a great deal of sanctimonious cant may be heard about the danger of nuclear weapons falling into criminal hands should Russian stability fail, even though the Soviet regime was the most powerful criminal organization in history and those left behind are petty thugs by comparison, incapable of initiating a nuclear war as Moscow suffers through its new "time of troubles." A Russia in which power devolves to outlying regions or from which territories might secede would be a more promising, amenable Russia than the slimmed-down autocracy with which we are currently enamored.

Above all, though, we must demand an accountable Russia. In dealing with Moscow, the best policy is one of calm fearlessness and quiet rigor. We should accept neither lawless behavior nor tyranny in the name of law, when it is within our power to resist it (in this regard, our power lies primarily in blocking or discouraging grants, loans, or access to beneficial financial terms). Our support for human rights should be unwavering. Instead of excusing Russia's misbehaviors, we should deal with Moscow equitably (the one thing we have never tried), rewarding good behavior and punishing bad behavior—making a wide range of linkages explicit to the Kremlin. Never hand out rewards in advance in the hope that good behavior will be forthcoming from Moscow. Yes, Russia is suffering through a period of psychological dislocation that requires patience and understanding, but there is a crucial difference between under-standing and indulgence. We must display the enlightened firmness of a parent dealing with an unruly child: Russia must never be allowed to throw a tantrum and have its way. Finally, even should Moscow aid us in our fight against terrorism, that will not give license to the Kremlin to terrorize its own people.

China's future is unpredictable, whether the analyst sits in Wash-ington or Beijing. One potential course would be a breakdown of central control and a return to fractious regionalism. Should such a scenario come to pass, our instinctive reaction would be to support the failing central power against insurgent or secessionist regions in the interests of stability—especially given the tens of billions of dollars U.S.–based corporations have invested, and continue to invest, in China. But we must struggle against the short-term view. A fractured, squabbling China would be less threatening to U.S. strategic interests in the region and might well emerge as a far more advantageous business partner (or partners). At present, our China policy, which drains American coffers to enrich a minority of American businesses, is captive to lobbyists and demonstrates no strategic vision beyond that of individual corporations. We pay China to become stronger and to prolong internal oppression—and if China weakens, we will prop up the vicious regime that spites us today. The ideal China would be a federalized, populist state, observant of basic human rights, that is economically open and militarily subdued. We are more likely to back a disciplined, tank-patrolled, centralized state that is economically restrictive—in the interests of stability. Faced with the slightest possibility of disorder, we will grunt and digest any number of Tiananmen massacres.

Africa is slowly and agonizingly struggling to undo the deformations colonial regimes left behind. In the heartrending tragedies of West Africa, where stability was the only Western idol (at least we are true to our monotheist heritage), we and the Europeans supported hollow men and hollow regimes for so long that the inevitable collapse has been especially horrific. Yet even now, we will deal with the devil, if the devil will just promise to stop the massacres for the weekend. We must rethink our approach to West Africa fundamentally, and recognize our culpability. "States" such as Sierra Leone and Liberia are now so thoroughly broken that they require international mandates for reorganization under neocolonial regimes. Borders should be redrawn—in other states as well—to reflect tribal and ethnic differences or harmonies. Elective affinities are welcome, but brotherhood cannot be enforced to suit nineteenth-century boundaries. In Africa, separatism is a natural and healthy force, until it is perverted by delay. Much of Africa has to be reduced from imperial-sized states to elemental building blocks before the construction of healthy organizational entities (perhaps called "states," but perhaps not) can begin anew on a more natural and hopeful foundation.

In Central and East Africa, the process has taken a modified form, with African power groupings redrawing boundaries on their own, despite fervent denials that they are doing any such thing. In this region, outsiders simply need to keep their hands off, except when the killing threatens to become too egregious. Wherever possible, Africans need to discover African solutions, with corrective hands applied only when human rights abuses escalate intolerably. (Of course, it would be best if we could stop all human rights abuses, but we cannot. Regrettably, we must ignore Africa's misdemeanors and concentrate on the felonies, at least for now.) Any attempts to enforce the old European-designed borders indefinitely are bound to fail, while exciting ethnic tensions to an even greater degree than wrongheaded meddling did in the former Yugoslavia.

The Middle East defies solution. A functional compromise between Israelis and Palestinians was impossible when the fanatics were merely on one side, and now they compose the decisive elements on both sides. Barring cataclysms, an Israeli born as this essay is written is likely to wade through his or her entire life in an ebb and flow of conflict. Meaning well, and behaving foolishly, we plunged into the Arab-Israeli conflict as an "honest broker," although neither side can accept the compromises required by such brokering, while our baggage as both Israel's primary supporter and the longtime backer of many of the most reprehensible Arab regimes is a debilitating handicap to mediation. We declare that stability in the Middle East is critical, no matter if it is impossible without a Carthaginian peace imposed by one side or the other.

The Israelis and the Palestinians can coexist. They already do. But their coexistence is of a different, dynamic nature that belies the meaning we attach to the term. Their struggle fulfills both sides. The Palestinians will never be satisfied, no matter how much they might regain, and the siege mentality Israelis affect to deplore may be essential to the continued vigor of their state. For both factions, struggle and the self-justification it allows may be the most fulfilling condition.

Americans assume that violent disorder is an unnatural state that must be resolved, but high levels of violence in a society or region may simply maintain a different kind of equilibrium than that to which we are accustomed. At the very least, periods of violence may be lengthy transitions that cannot be artificially fore-shortened. We need not condone violence to recognize that it is not an artificial imposition upon human nature, nor will insisting that violence is unnatural make it so. We know so little about the com-plex origins of violence that our beliefs about it are no more than superstitions. Whether in regard to the violence of the man or the mass, our theories attempt to explain it away rather than to under-stand it. The Middle East may be inhumane, but it is one of the most explicitly human places on earth.

And would a peaceful resolution of the Middle East confronta-tion benefit the United States, after all? Hardcore terrorists would not cease and desist—no peace could ever satisfy them. And wouldn't we lose critical leverage? Israel, no longer dependent upon the United States as its ultimate defender, might prove a wor-risome maverick. The Arab world might come to rely even more heavily upon the United States, but that would be one of history's great booby prizes.

Nor do the repressive, borrowed-time Arab governments in the region really want to see a successful, independent Palestinian state. The Palestinian struggle is a wonderful diversion for deprived Islamic populations elsewhere, but none of the Arab elites truth-fully likes or trusts the Palestinians, who, if they achieved a viable, populist state of their own, would provide an unsettling example to the subjects of neighboring regimes. Arab rulers regard the Pales-tinians as too unpredictable, too obstreperous, too secular, too vig-orous, and much too creative (resembling the Israelis, in fact). As it is, the rest of the Arab world is happy to fight to the last Palestinian, insisting the Palestinians maintain demands unacceptable to Israel. The struggle will go on for a long time to come. The best the United States can do at present is to inhibit the most excessive viola-tions of human rights, while placing responsibility for the conflict on the shoulders of the participants, not on our own. We also must avoid absurd knee-jerk reactions, such as condemning legitimate efforts by Israel to strike guilty individuals, which is a far more humane and incisive policy than Palestinian suicide-bomber attacks on discos and restaurants.

By exciting false hopes of an ill-defined peace, we only inflame passions we cannot quench. Again, we have gotten into the habit of speaking loudly and laying our stick aside. We would do better with fewer press releases and more behind-the-scenes firmness—when engagement is to our advantage. And the occasional show of overwhelming force in the region works wonders.

Islamic terrorism merits separate discussion now. It is not the result of creative instability, but of the atrophy of a civilization exacerbated by generations of Western support for an artificial stability in the Arab and Islamic world. While most Islamic terrorism is culturally reactionary, another aspect of it is an impulse for change perverted by hopelessness. And terrorism is, finally, a brutal annoyance, but not a threat to America's survival, despite the grim events of September 11. Osama bin Laden and his ilk may kill thousands of Americans through flamboyant terrorist acts, but their deeds reflect tormented desperation and fear, not confidence or any positive capability. Terrorists may be able to destroy, but they cannot build, either a skyscraper or a successful state. Destruction is the only thing of which they remain capable, and destruction is their true god. These men seek annihilation, not only ours, but also their own. No entrances are left open to them, only the possibility of a dramatic exit. They are failed men from failed states in a failing civilization. Claiming to represent the oppressed (but enraged by the "liberal" behavior of most Palestinians), fundamentalist terrorists of so hardened a temper would not be contented, but only further inflamed, by any peace settlement that did not inaugurate their version of the Kingdom of God on earth. They are not fighting for a just peace, but for their peace—and even if they attained that peace, they would desire another. They are, in every sense, lost souls, the irredeemable. Their savagery is not a result of the failure of any peace process, but a reaction to their own personal failures and to the failures of their entire way of life.

These lines are written on the thirteenth day of September 2001, two days after the most horrendous terrorist attack in history, and America is seized by a just fury in which even the worst effects of local disasters are exaggerated. But before this essay goes to press, Americans will realize that their lives remain gloriously normal, even as the media delights in hysteria. Despite the thousands of personal tragedies and the practical disruptions that resulted from the seizure of commercial aircraft and the attacks on the

World Trade Center and the Pentagon, the astonishing thing is how little permanent effect the terrorists will have had on daily life in the United States. There will be a scar, but the long-term effects of this grotesque tragedy will ultimately strengthen America. It has reminded us of who we are, and now we are rolling up our sleeves for the task ahead.

Without in any way belittling the tragedy, the fact is that the United States will emerge stronger and more united, with a sobered sense of strategic reality that will serve us well in the decades to come. In the long term, the terrorist immolations in New York, at the Pentagon, and in the Pennsylvania hills will prove to be counter-productive to the terrorists' cause, context, and ambitions. We are a phenomenally strong and resilient nation, while the societies that spawned our enemies are decaying and capable only of lashing out at the innocent.

Afghanistan. If any conflict of the last three decades requires a revised assessment, it is the Soviet engagement in Afghanistan. Blinded by the brinksmanship and the reflexive opposition of the Cold War era, we failed to see that the Russians, in this peculiar instance, were the forces of civilization and progress. I do not defend their tactical behavior, but they did attempt to sustain a relatively enlightened, secular regime against backward, viciously cruel religious extremists—whom we supported, only to reap a monstrous harvest. Our backing of the most socially repressive elements within the Afghan resistance (because they were the "most effective") backfired beyond all calculation. Incredibly, blinded again by the seeming verities of the Cold War, we trusted the advice of Pakistan's Inter-Service Intelligence Agency (ISI), an inherently anti-Western organization that has since supported both the Taliban and Osama bin Laden, as well as lesser terrorists, providing them with weapons, funds, safe havens, and free passage to the rest of the world.

Afghanistan, as we realize all too well in the autumn of 2001, has become the terrorist haven of the world, and we helped to make it so. We were determined that communism would not be allowed to destabilize the region. Now, in one of the bitter returns of history, our military forces in the skies over Afghanistan may face American-made and American-provided surface-to-air missiles. Our folly in Afghanistan should be final proof of the falsity of the dictum that "the enemy of my enemy is my friend." Sometimes, the enemy of your enemy is just practicing for the big game.

Cuba may be a small problem in the geostrategic sense, but it certainly fixes America's attention. The instability likely to embarrass us in Cuba will come after Castro's disappearance, as the island's current regime weakens and dissolves. The Batista-Cubans we have harbored in South Florida, whose political influence has maintained one of the most counterproductive of American policies, will try to reclaim, purchase, and bribe their way into power in the land they or their elders exploited and then fled. The Cubans who stayed in Cuba, for better and worse, do not want their rich relatives back. And were we to be the least bit just, we would recognize that those who stayed behind have earned the right to decide how their island will be governed in the future. For all our ranting about the Castro dictatorship—which may not be admirable, but which is far more liberal and equitable than many of America's client governments (tourists clamor to go to Havana, not Riyadh)—an honest appraisal reveals that the average Cuban, though impoverished by the policies both of his own government and of the United States, enjoys a better quality of life than that of the average resident of many a "free" Caribbean state. If we intervene at some future date to protect the "rights" and the "legitimate property" of the Miami Cubans at the expense of the Cuban people themselves, we will shame ourselves inexcusably. Post-Castro Cuba, on its own, has an unusually good chance of evolving into a model democracy, but it will not do so if we sanction and support the carpetbagging of émigrés who have never found American democracy fully to their tastes.

Devolution threatens a great range of other states, from Pakistan to Italy. The problems of each will be unique. But the common thread will be that attempts to arrest instability and to prolong the lives of decayed, unnatural states, rather than to assist populations through longed-for political reorganizations, will always carry an exorbitant price and, ultimately, will fail.

At present, a portion of the armed forces of the United States is mired in stability operations that simply bide time in the hope that somehow things will come out right, while an even greater portion is focused on avenging the recent terrorist attacks against America.

We may wish all of these endeavors Godspeed, yet it would be a disservice to the men and women in uniform not to ask how we have come to this pass. Self-examination in the strategic sphere has not been an American strength. Perhaps it is time to make it one.

Meanwhile, we deny causes, ignore unpleasant realities, put on our flak jackets, and hope for the best. Certainly we should not replace stability operations with "instability operations" to provoke or accelerate change beyond its local, organic pace. And we must differentiate between unpopular terrorist groups and genuine mass movements: There is a great difference between the vicious Basque terrorists of the ETA and the African National Congress that triumphed over apartheid. All dissident organizations are not equally legitimate.

But we do need to stop providing life-support to terminally ill governments, and we must be open to new, unprecedented solutions, from plebiscites that alter borders to emergent or re-emergent forms of administration in failed states, whether enlightened corporate imperialism or postmodern tribalism. If the corporation can manage more humanely than the dictator, why not give it a chance? If the tribe can govern more effectively than a thieving, oppressive government, why not let the tribe reclaim its own land?

Of late, we have heard all too much about the United States being the world's policeman. We are not, we cannot afford to be, and we couldn't bring it off if we tried—not least because policemen have to be on the beat everywhere, around the clock, and their most successful work is preventive (a concept that democracies, which are reactive in foreign policy, find anathema). Apart from our new and essential crusade against terrorism, which must pursue preemptive measures, our role should be that of a global referee, calling time out when the players hit below the belt or get too rough, and clarifying the rules of the game (no genocide, no ethnic cleansing, no mass rape, no torture, etc.). Instead of trying to stop the game, which was our approach across the past decade, we should try to facilitate it when it is played by legitimate players for legitimate stakes. In the case of terrorists, of course, we need to throw them out of the game permanently.

But what on earth is wrong with people wanting their freedom? Why shouldn't populations want the armed forces of a central government that is essentially an occupying power to leave their territory? Why are yesterday's borders more important than today's lives? Why should we support religiously intolerant regimes that virtually enslave women and persecute nonbelievers to death? How much mass suffering is it worth to keep things geostrategically tidy? How dare we send our soldiers to support bigoted monarchies that forbid our troops to worship as they choose? How stable can any government be that fears a Christmas tree? Why should we pretend that every war criminal is really a democrat waiting for his opportunity to vote? Why should we reflexively support the rich and powerful against the poor they abuse and exploit? Why must we insist that history can be made to run backward?

A new century demands new ideas. The notion that stability is the fundamental strategic virtue is not going to be one of them.

The Black Art of Intelligence

With the Atlantic Ocean separating us, my extended family's generations slipped out of synchronization. Thus, it was my cousin who served in World War II on the German side. A tactical reconnaissance NCO, or *Aufklaerer*—one of the most dangerous jobs in any army—he fought on the Eastern Front throughout the war, yet never was captured or seriously wounded. When we met at last, in the early 1980s, I encountered a vigorous, sinewy, skeptical Hessian farmer. Serving at the time as the intelligence officer in a U.S. Army infantry battalion, I asked my cousin how he had managed to survive on a battleground that consumed millions. Matter-of-factly, he told me he just "knew" where the enemy had been and where danger lay. It startled me, because I already had my own catalog of peculiar experiences, from exercises to real-world analysis, in which I, too, just seemed to know—beyond the logic of intelligence reports and indicators—what was going to happen. I could no more explain my ability to read a situation than could my cousin.

Certainly what I frequently was able to do had no place in the careful processes devised to train intelligence analysts and officers—although formal techniques have their value—nor did I ever make an issue of how I "knew" things. My greatest challenge was convincing superiors who wanted proof that two and two made five. These were good, often brave men whom the intelligence system had failed earlier in their careers in Vietnam and continually in the Cold War. When trusted, I could deliver to an uncanny degree, whether delineating Soviet war plans in Europe, locating a small special operations unit hiding in a vast area, or, when alone in the Caucasus, sensing where I could and could not go. Now much of this was simply common sense, that least valued quality in armies and governments. I also enjoyed the lack of a good education, which put me well ahead of officers whose vision of the world and humankind had been distorted by fine universities. But the similarity of experience between my cousin, who survived the cruelest front of the worst war in history, and my own chocolate-soldier peacetime adventures still strikes me as more than coincidence. Traits do run in families, from physical robustness to mental acumen to artistic talent. Did it matter that my anthracite-mining father, in his prime, could walk into a valley and say, "There's coal over there," and coal would be found where he pointed? Was it relevant that my paternal grandmother could "read" certain illnesses and cure them by the laying on of hands—while repeating incantations from the Scriptures?

These things are true. But are they relevant to anything?

I believe so. I offer these bits of family lore first as a delayed answer to all those who, over the years, have asked me, "But how do you *know* that?" and, second, to tease those already convinced that I've long been "off the reservation." Third, and most importantly, this tale-telling makes an extreme case for a proposition I have argued for years: that intelligence analysis, done well, requires not only rigorous training and much practical experience, but innate talent, a predisposition. One need not have a mystical bent to accept that all men (and women) are not created equal when it comes to the ability to do intelligence work. We accept readily enough that specific talents are required to play major-league sports, for a successful career in the arts, or even to become a great con man. (One of the problems we have with our intelligence services, by the way, is that they are run by minor con men, mere bookies.) We still hear that someone is a "born leader" as we wonder at his or her inexplicable charisma and quick grasp of necessary matters. Yet we assume that anyone with a moderately high IQ can be trained in a few months to grasp an enemy's mentality, character, fears, intentions, hopes, beliefs, vulnerabilities, and individuality—without even speaking his language.

As a result, we have a network of intelligence services that can count bomb craters with great accuracy, but upon which we cannot count to warn us of "illogical" dangers, such as the brilliant, if ultimately counterproductive, strikes of September 11, 2001. As I have written—to the point of whining—it is a paradox of the twenty-first century that, in this age of technological wonders, the threats to our lives, wealth, and order are fundamentally, crudely human. We may diagram bunkers, bombs, and entire armies, but we falter at understanding the human soul. Nor will the human heart fit into our templates. Love, fear, and hatred, not machines, are the stuff of which wars are made, whether we speak of terrorist jihads, campaigns of ethnic cleansing, or conventional offensives (and do not underestimate the deadly power of love, whether felt toward a god, a people, a clan, a flag, or an individual).

During my bleak Washington years as an intelligence officer, no one dared to speak of the forces of love or hatred, or of any other emotion. Nor could they say anything profound about religion or culture. The sexual devils that haunt entire civilizations, as the fear of female sexuality cripples the Islamic world, were beyond the pale of "serious" discussions. Statistics were preferred, whether dependable or not, and intercepts or satellite imagery were quite the thing. Intelligence products were tailored to the available information, when we should have been demanding information to support our genuine intelligence needs. The system was at once superficially prim and intellectually slovenly. Briefings and discussions were as studiously gray as the men and women behind the podium or around the table, and all the human wilderness wherein past civilizations have perished—the furious, wild, destructive, often monstrous power of the human animal itself—was banished as a topic of discussion. More than any other figure, we all resembled T. S. Eliot's prematurely old paragon of timidity, J. Alfred Prufrock, who asks himself eternally, "Dare I eat a peach?" We tried to deal with the torrid world of flesh and blood as if it were made of fitted nuts and bolts. We understood nothing that mattered.

Without such understanding, we are reduced to the retaliatory exercise of power and expressions of regret for preventable losses. There is no lack of bravery in the ranks of our armed forces, but bureaucratic cowardice rules in our intelligence establishment (as well as at the highest levels of military command). Whenever my turn came up to represent the Army Staff at the National Intelligence Council, or NIC, whose meetings were held in the CIA's dull and spotless headquarters, representatives of all the intelligence players would sit around a table, show off their knowledge of trivia, then agree, by the end of the session, on a lowest-common-denominator position. The intelligence produced was not bad—only mediocre. It told you a bit about things, but not enough. There was great pressure on all participants and their organizations not to make a fuss. A dissenter might "take a footnote," but the practice was discouraged. The point, you see, was not to get things right, but to avoid getting them demonstrably wrong—a critical distinction. Boldness, no matter its quality, was not wanted. And insight had to be backed up with hard data—proven beyond a doubt, which is impossible in serious intelligence work. The desired result was to make certain that we could, when faced with catastrophe, all point at one another as having agreed in the errant assessment: "This is what the entire intelligence community believed, based on the best information available." Perhaps we might inscribe that on the graves of our fellow citizens who died because of our inadequacy.

Rare was the man or woman who even cared.

My own form of cowardice was to avoid the NIC sessions whenever I could, while writing what I believed to be true in unclassified journals. Today I stand by all that I wrote ten years ago but do not believe our intelligence community could say the same of a fraction of the drivel it produced. Of course, by the time the over-classified reports and studies are made available to researchers, those who drafted and approved them will be long retired (after many promotions) or dead. But our habit of stamping high classifications on low-quality work to dignify it is yet another subject.

Theoretically, we petty creatures who came together to discuss the strategic future were the best and the brightest; in fact, we were dreary bureaucrats, far less than the sum of our parts. But, then, our intelligence community is, above all, a massive bureaucracy—and bureaucracies discourage risk-taking or excellence that does not match the models of the past. The motto of our vast intelligence establishment is "Play it safe." The mindset may protect careers but does little for our country.

Nor do I underestimate the technological wonders at our disposal, for I have seen what these near-miraculous machines can do, but I know too well that my countrymen overestimate those same seductive devices. It is always safer, bureaucratically, to rely on what the machine tells you, whether or not it is appropriate, than on the fallible human being who begs you to believe him. No one is ever fired for showing the boss satellite photos, but it is a rare man or woman who will back a subordinate based on the analyst's personal experience of foreign people and parts. Trust the machine, and you will prosper, even as your country's needs go unsatisfied.

Understanding, understanding, understanding! Get at the human beings, and the rest falls into line. Understanding your enemy is the most effective weapon of all, but it is a weapon we rarely wield.

We have tried—clumsily, if earnestly—to make intelligence into a science, when it is an art. Certainly, science plays a mighty role within the larger boundaries of the art, from those fabulous collection systems to communications to computer analysis of technical data. Nor will we ever have an intelligence community composed solely of virtuosos—not everyone should be expected to be a soloist or even the first violin. Someone has to raise the curtain, turn the pages, and work on the acoustics in the hall—but, in the world of intelligence, the stagehands have taken over the performance.

The last clarinetist in a quality orchestra has to have a dependable level of competence, or the sound of the entire orchestra suffers. But diplomas alone do not make musicians, and they do not make intelligence analysts. At present, we pretend that anyone with a college degree can play in the intelligence world (in the military, the degree is not even required). Try that at the New York Philharmonic ("Oh, you just graduated from Julliard? Thank God, we've been looking for a replacement for Maestro Masur . . ."). For those logic lovers out there, does it make sense for our premier intelligence organizations to have lower standards than a third-rate orchestra somewhere in the Midwest? Pretending that intelligence analysis is, if not fully quantifiable, at least subject to methodical processes has left us skilled at predicting the arrival time of a tank within range of our weapons, but helpless at seeing into the mind, heart, and soul of the enemy leader who commands, perhaps, five thousand tanks—or five thousand terrorists. We lack a natural sense of pitch, of human harmonies and discords. And we play the same tune over and over again.

As for science, the one thing we have not even tried to do with it is to use it to select potential analysts for their counter-scientific skills, for talents that would augment, even fulfill, the technological array we can bring to bear upon our enemies. But that, of course, would lie in the future, well beyond the numbing tests the military and government now use to guarantee the standardization of mediocrity ("Mark your choice with a number two pencil and erase any errors completely . . ."). I do not think we need a horde of mystics and cabalists in Pentagon cubicles or gathering in covens in the cafeteria at the Defense Intelligence Agency. But we need to try to understand that a good analyst's mind is wired a bit differently—he or she need not go into a trance and speak in tongues but had better have a richer, cannier vision of the world than that possessed by the average Washingtonian bureaucrat. Sometimes, in the phantasmagoria of human hatred and violence, two and two not only make five, but ultimately add up to twenty-seven . . . or to collapsed skyscrapers.

We view analysts as parts of the intelligence machine—and interchangeable parts, at that. But good analysts—the truly good ones—are rare and, sometimes, irreplaceable. That, too, is anathema to a bureaucracy and to a military that still has an industrial-age, draft-era mentality within its personnel system. We must find ways to attract, identify, develop, and retain analysts who have special potential. In far too many intelligence organizations, someone becomes a specialist simply by virtue of assignment or duty position (Brazilian navy desk last week, terrorism expert today). We neglect intelligence—not because it isn't vitally necessary, but because it is very hard to do well (and, in the military, because it's geek stuff—real men don't think). Were we a weaker power, we would pay far more attention to intelligence, since it is a great equalizer. Instead, we rely on strength and wealth to get us through. But poor intelligence forces even a superpower to be reactive, when it should be leading, preventing, and shaping.

Much has been made of September 11, 2001, as an intelligence failure. Well, it was and it wasn't. Not even the finest intelligence organization, with highly developed cadres not only in the analytical field but also in the other vital, difficult field of Human Intelligence, would be able to predict and prevent every event. The world is too complex and too vast, and humanity too ingenious. No intelligence structure will ever be perfect—at least, not in our lifetimes. But we can do a great deal better than we have done up to now.

The status quo is perverse. We will spend tens of billions of dollars on a network of satellites, then pay the young man or woman analyzing the data a salary far below that of a plumber. In my own career, I repeatedly was encouraged to take jobs that had nothing to do with intelligence but which were considered the premier Military Intelligence positions. Friends at the National Security Agency or Central Intelligence Agency routinely found themselves required to leave the analytical fields in which they were skilled and go into management in order to gain the promotions they needed to care for growing families. Analysis was the bottom rung, an entry-level job—and even the best analysts saw their work so neutered as it filtered up through the bureaucracy that the insights of greatest value often disappeared long before the paper or study reached the National Command Authority. No one in the management chain wanted to risk being asked a question by his boss for which there was no documented answer. Intelligence work became a poor cousin of academic research—with all "new" products relying on the wisdom of that which had been published (safely) in the past. It was especially laughable when a general or senior executive would say, "Now, I want you to think out of the box on this." What he meant was that he wanted to hear fresh justifications for his existing beliefs. The only innovations the system valued were those that saved money on office supplies.

Of course, when things go wrong we immediately hear cries from Congress and the pundits for intelligence reform. Now, let me tell you what intelligence reform means to the Hill: more money for the contractors who build the systems whose data we lack the manpower to analyze. There is always a constituency to buy expensive hardware, but there is no enduring constituency for the skilled human beings we sorely lack. In the military sphere, the cost of one F-22 fighter—an utterly unnecessary, irrelevant system—could fund about 2,000 more analysts for five years . . . or train about 2,500 more linguists in the nation's best language programs. (Foreign language ability is another human skill in chronically short supply in our intelligence community, and, personally, I believe analysts should speak the language or languages of their target region.)

Our intelligence machinery does produce wonders upon occasion. But that machinery simply has limits that only human beings can extend. The recent conflict in Afghanistan made this abundantly clear. Despite the hundreds of billions of dollars worth of intelligence surveillance equipment available to us, our bombing remained largely ineffectual until special operations teams hit the ground, drew information from the local combatants, spotted targets with their own eyes, and directed the airstrikes. We could have bombed Afghanistan for a year and had less effect than that produced by a few weeks of bombing guided by skilled human beings on the ground. Similarly, the literally immeasurable amounts of data generated by our technical systems have little meaning—or can actually deceive us—if we do not have skilled analysts with good instincts honed by experience to help us understand what it all means, or, to be more accurate, to tell us what the few pertinent drops in the vast flood of information mean.

Good instincts? That's a quality that never shows up on report cards. Yet, I've known plenty of well-educated, knowledgeable, dedicated, brutally hard-working intelligence officers who were worthless when it came to serious intelligence analysis. They could make the office look good in a bureaucratic environment; they could brief; they could do research—but they could not understand that, sometimes, the world refuses to behave as they were taught it should behave. They plotted out the templates, scratched their heads, and got a kicked-puppy look when the bad guys failed to behave as the Intelligence School at Fort Huachuca said they must.

In one tactical assignment, I had a subordinate officer who was superb in every respect that mattered to the institutional Army— but his instincts actually tipped into the negative column and he got even simple analytical calls whoppingly wrong. (Fortunately, this was in peacetime, at Fort Hood, where nothing much matters.) In the same organization, I had an officer who looked more than a little rough around the edges, who couldn't keep a smirk off his face when the leadership came around barking platitudes, and who had a gut instinct for battlefields, psychology, and plain old human nastiness that no training course could ever instill. He was the one I would have relied on in wartime. Despite my best efforts, guess which one the Army promoted, and which one was passed over and forced out of uniform?

Ultimately, intelligence work comes down to dealing with humanity. After all the calls are intercepted and the missiles counted, the bank accounts monitored and the nerve gas canisters located, we still need to look inside the minds, hearts, and souls of other human beings. And, unlike the mechanical and electronic things of which we are so fond, human beings are not fully predictable or understandable—even to themselves. Contrary to the wisdom of Washington and the academic world, human beings are not rational creatures. Laws, customs, and enlightened self-interest may drive men and women to behave predictably some of the time—in daylight, on a peaceful street—but in the dark night of the soul, or in the stunning midnight of atrocity, the rational man dissolves into the feral, instinctive, vividly mad descendant of Cain.

Perhaps, one day, satellites will be able to locate every single one of our opponents. But I doubt that they will ever be able to see into the human interior to tell us what our nemeses intend, or hope, or fear. What will X do tomorrow? The truth is that X himself does not know for certain. The deed yet undone contains myriad alternatives. A good analyst, enraptured by his work, may actually have a better grasp of what X will do than X does himself. To many, this will sound impossible. But it is only impossible for those who rely upon technology to cope with humanity.

This is hardly a new tug-of-war. Those who insist that all things are knowable and that men and women act rationally have been on one side of the stadium of mankind for centuries, while the opposing bleachers have been filled by those who insist that even the light of reason casts dark shadows, and that man's nature is never fully knowable. In our technologically advanced culture, the power of systems easily seduces the multitude to believe that machines are, or soon will be, omnipotent—an enduring myth. But at the most elementary, unshakable level, we have barely begun to understand the complexities, motivations, and patterns of human behavior. The frightened cling to the tangible, and the worried demand simple answers. But an effective intelligence system must learn to deal with the ineffable and dauntingly complex. As Shakespeare put it four centuries ago, "There are more things in heaven and earth, Horatio, than are dreamt of in your philosophy." Words to live by for the Director of Central Intelligence.

Of course, we will never have an intelligence system composed purely of virtuoso analysts and linguistic geniuses. But with an intelligence budget above thirty billion dollars a year, we certainly can do better than we are doing now. A little more money—just a tiny fraction of the budget lavished on technology—redirected to Human Intelligence operatives, to analysts, and to linguists could make an enormous difference. But personnel policies would have to be reformed at the same time—and in the absence of additional money for analysts, linguists, and Humint specialists, personnel system reform becomes even more important. Once within the system, the basic question is simple to articulate, if difficult to answer: How can we exploit the gifted, instead of rewarding the conformist? We are always readier to embrace the individual who commits himself slavishly to the system as it exists than the one who devotes himself to improving the system—with the inevitable pain change brings. We make far too much of loyalty, and far too little of integrity, despite our wanton use of the latter word.

Talented people are difficult, from start to finish. They require special care and feeding—not consistently, but often unexpectedly. Brilliant analysts may be a chronic annoyance in the otherwise collegial staff meeting; they're often priggishly self-righteous and sometimes obsessive: Arcane in their interests, they are, as the English used to put it, "not the club-able sort." They may occasionally look like model soldiers or fashionistas (not hard, by Washington standards)—but they also may look like they need help dressing themselves. And they don't play golf. My point is that intelligence personnel, above all, cannot be judged by externals—but that is how our system likes to judge people, since it's the easiest way. If only shiny boots indicated intellect, we would have the most brilliant military in history. It's no accident that the one thing we're good at in intelligence is "reading externals," milking the value from surface data, whether targeting information or communications webs. But, in the end, it is the internals that matter.

How might we best go about building a better cadre of intelligence analysts and related personnel? In the long term, we might be able to develop sophisticated testing to identify certain deep traits. But, for now, the required steps are easy to list, but much harder to implement.

First, analysts need to be valued, with the most talented identified, protected, and groomed. This is surprisingly tough, since most of the managers in our intelligence system are bureaucrats who truly cannot tell the difference between compiled information and valuable intelligence—and all managers, in uniform or not, tend to promote in their own image.

Second, especially in the military, supervisors need to recognize that the most-talented young people tend to make more mistakes. They're at least trying things out, instead of waiting cautiously for orders. In the "zero-defects" military our generals and admirals continue to insist doesn't exist—although it shaped their every step—promising young analysts (and other soldiers) see their careers ended for minor infractions by commanders or other bosses afraid that, if unpunished, the incidents might damage their own future prospects. When young, the smartest people often do the dumbest things. Some survive within organizations by luck (almost invariably, because of a far-sighted superior). Most don't make it past the first cut.

Third, analysts have to be rewarded. In the military, this means appropriate promotions—yet in the Army's Military Intelligence branch, the quickest way to the top is to avoid actual intelligence jobs and build a career in management (disingenuously called "leadership"). In the rest of the intelligence community, it means respect but, frankly, it also means money. Intelligence work may sound seductive to a recent college graduate, but to a husband or wife in the mid-thirties, with a mortgage on a townhouse in Springfield, Virginia, and two kids who are going to need college money in no time at all, life as a GS-11 with little prospect of serious advancement doesn't look quite so romantic. In a capitalist society, you don't always get what you pay for—but you rarely get what you don't pay for. If the government wants superior analysts and agents who speak multiple foreign languages and are willing to work overseas for years in particularly unpleasant circumstances, or to serve in that Heart of

Darkness known as the Greater Washington Area, they should be paid at least as well as accountants by midcareer. And they should be defended, not hung out to dry, when they do get things wrong.

We want to do intelligence cleanly, without embarrassment. That's another losing proposition. Clandestine and covert intelligence work, if it is to be successful, often has to engage in practices unthinkable within America's borders. But that is yet another issue that wants discussion at another time. This brief essay is concerned with the art of intelligence analysis—a field in which we insist that our product dare not be offensive to other religions, cultures, minorities, or to either political party, just in case a White House staffer leaks it. The most wrongheaded words a manager in the intelligence world can mouth are, "You can't say that." We live in a world where every unpleasant truth must be spoken, before it becomes far more unpleasant.

I offer no formula for analysis itself, beyond hard work, open eyes, and dedication—without which even a great talent is meaningless. I have always been skeptical of those prescribed by-the-numbers processes taught in our intelligence schools. Past a certain point, they only blind us. And perhaps all that I have written about the need for special abilities is nonsense. Perhaps all that is required is the willingness to see things as they truly are. But that is a rare enough quality by itself.

I am convinced that talent matters profoundly. We never would pretend that we could take people with no gift for music—no matter how great their raw intelligence—and turn them into fine pianists. Is it such a stretch to imagine that an art form whose ultimate task it is to intuit the deep secrets of an enemy's mind—or soul, as I prefer to put it—might also require special talent? Certainly talent isn't everything. No matter how much innate talent he or she might possess, a musician needs training, practice, experience, and time to develop to his or her full potential. A maturation process is always required—even for a Mozart (of course, his talent was fairly mature by age six, so we have to be flexible). But the talent has to be there to begin with, whether we speak of artists or of analysts, and talent is as little understood as love or hope or the aching for God—or the indelible will to violence.

Henry Ford did wonders for the American economy of his day, but his model of the workplace has done terrible and enduring damage to the American government and, especially, to our military. The business of protecting our nation with the best possible intelligence cannot be done with faceless workers who function as interchangeable parts, no matter the current management fad inflicted upon them. We Americans pride ourselves on our individualism. Recognition of the indispensable contribution of talented individuals to our intelligence system is long overdue. Machines may decipher a world of technical data, but only a gifted analyst can read the heart and soul of another human being.

Hidden Unities

Alternative Strategic Divisions

*Prepared for the Center for Emerging Threats and Opportunities
in June 2002 and published here with the generous permission of the
CETO and with thanks to the United States Marine Corps.*

A More Unified World Than We Know

Perhaps the finest painting of a prize fight hangs in the National
Gallery of Art in Washington, D.C. Titled *Both Members of This Club,*
the work is by the American painter George Bellows. The painting
shows two old-fashioned sluggers, identical but for skin color,
pounding each other to a pulp. Both the painting and its title might
serve as a perfect metaphor for the long-enduring and now renewed
violence between Muslim countries and those that are, by heredity,
Christian, Jewish, or Judeo-Christian.

Everybody in the fight is a member of the same club: The grand
and hyper-violent club of monotheist cultures.

The vast territory between Ireland in the west and Afghanistan
in the east, between Scandinavia in the north and the long transition zone of the southern Sahara, is one "club," a single strategic
zone (North America is an adjunct to it, but increasingly separate
from this macro-region). The countless wars within those boundaries all have been family feuds within the dynamic and long-expan-
sive domain of monotheism. Centered historically on the eastern
Mediterranean, this is a single civilization that has mutated, along its
expanded frontiers, into a wide range of cultures that may claim, in
some respects, to be civilizations in their own right. But the distinctive characteristic of this there-is-only-one-god strategic region has
been its aggressiveness, both toward other "members of the club"
and toward other civilizations.

This historical predisposition to conquer and convert shapes the behavior even of those members of this vast community who have turned their backs on active religion, as is the case with the states of northern Europe. Europe's superficial pacifism of the moment lacks only the right provocation, the right historical circumstance, to turn again to violence directed at non-Europeans. One of the worst mistakes today's strategic analysts make is to assume that, since Europe is so piously anti-military and "soft" today, it will remain so tomorrow. This is the same assumption that the Japanese made about the United States six decades ago, and which Osama bin Laden made about America more recently.

Violence toward other cultures is deeply—ineradicably—embedded in the European branches of monotheist civilization. It is only a matter of when the violence will reemerge, what form it will take, and whether that violence will prove antithetical to U.S. values and interests. The Europeans who pretend to the moral high ground today are the heirs of those Europeans who, in 1912, insisted that the continent's nations were too civilized ever to make war on one another again.

The Club Rules

While we may recognize, at least in less controversial historical terms, that both Christianity and Islam have been fierce, messianic, driven faiths, the long sweep of history has obscured the similar nature of the other great monotheist religion, Judaism. Long strategically dormant, Judaism has returned as a strategic factor with a vengeance in the Middle East, where, despite Israel's veneer of secularization, the deeper struggle remains one between two monotheist faiths—which are, by their essential nature, incapable of peaceful coexistence. While Judaism, unlike Islam or Christianity, does not seek to convert its enemies to its faith, it is psychologically programmed for exclusive violence as surely as are its sister religions. One God means one way, and one way means our way.

We tend to view Judaism as a passive faith suddenly converted to defensive violence by the Holocaust, but this is a short-sighted reading of history: All monotheist religions produce cultures that are furiously aggressive and missionary. Even after their societies secularize, the mindset lingers. Only the powerlessness of Jewish communities scattered in the Diaspora tempered their ingrained impulse to conquer and subjugate. Judaism hasn't reimagined itself in Israel; rather, it has rejoined the club from which centuries of powerlessness had excluded it.

Prior to the Roman destruction of the Jewish state, whenever Jewish political entities were not subjugated by intrusive empires, they behaved very aggressively, indeed, toward their neighbors—as Israel has done in our lifetimes (and, of course, as its monotheist, Islamic neighbors do toward Israel, less rationally and far more vindictively). Each of the three great monotheist religions has a history of atrocity, if one goes back far enough. It appears to be only a matter of who held power when.

Today, "Western" cultures, Christian, Judeo-Christian, and Jewish, behave more humanely, as a rule, than do Muslim cultures. But that is, at least partly, because we are so powerful and wealthy we can afford this indulgence. Much of the Islamic world is in the throes of a complex, multilayered, psychologically devastating crisis. And when in crisis, monotheist cultures default to collective violence toward nonbelievers, whether in their midst or abroad.

The United States (and Canada), with its uniquely intermingled society, is in the least danger of turning on its minorities. But any member of a religious or ethnic minority in Europe had best be doing all he or she can to prop up the wealth and social accord of the state and the rule of law. Europe does not, will not, and cannot assimilate immigrant communities from other cultures. While we should not exaggerate the power of current rightward trends in the European political environment (the danger is not short-term, unless a very great provocation occurs, such as a cataclysmic terrorist act), in the long term, European societies may become, at best, cellular and informally segregated. At worst, we may see the rigorous, even violent, exclusion of unassimilated minorities and the establishment of a buffer zone, with puppet regimes that serve Europe's security needs, along the Mediterranean littoral.

Without drawing any premature conclusions, Americans would be foolish not to recognize that Europe is far more volatile than those endless, soporific pronouncements from Brussels would have it.

Crusades Without a God

All cultures generated by only-one-god religions—Christian, Muslim, or Jewish—believe in one path to the truth. The debate—often bloody—is over which path is best, not over the equivalent value of alternate paths. These are all-or-nothing cultures. This "one true path" mentality compels them to inflict their vision of both religious and secular order on others.

Even now, when Europe is "de-religioned," by and large, and the United States would find it inconceivable to launch an overt religious crusade, this our-way-is-the-only-way prejudice subconsciously informs our actions. We still want things our way and cannot really accept that the differing ways of others have full validity; rather, we assume that they are only less developed and must, eventually, learn our way of doing things and come to appreciate that our approach is the only right approach. Our desire to create democracies and market economies abroad, laudable though such systems may be, is an inheritance from nineteenth-century missionaries yearning to convert the "heathen Chinese" or the African tribesman. Our most bellicose armchair strategists make much of supposed Chinese aggressiveness, but, to date, no Chinese government has insisted that the United States or anyone else adopt Chinese behaviors, social views, governmental forms, and business practices: Our way may, indeed, be for the good of all, but the alacrity with which we insist on it is unmistakably intolerant and close-minded missionary behavior. We are programmed to insist.

The all-or-nothing nature of our current, postmodern war against terrorism is masked by diplomatic manners, and that, in turn, obscures the fundamental and fateful division between Judeo-Christian culture and Islamic culture today: The historic break over the role of women in society. This is the one truly irreconcilable difference between "Western" societies and Middle-Eastern Islam. Although it may appear absurd to many a strategist, the current war against terror, and the recent fighting in Afghanistan, is, essentially, a war over women's rights and women's roles. The alteration in women's roles in the West is the most profound advance in human social history—more revolutionary even than the advent of democracy—and the most unsettling change to traditional societies. A male in a traditional Islamic society can more easily accept a monstrous dictator above him than a wife who insists on standing beside him. Although Islam's complaints about the West are couched in terms of sin and corruption, the real fear is of female freedom.

The battle for hegemony between the great monotheist religions—the imposition of social order, when not religious practice—will continue to be the defining struggle of our time. It will wear a variety of disguises. But it is a struggle between stubborn, self-righteous cultures, our own included. Our great advantage is that our own culture evolves constantly and has not closed the door on change; still, we must be fair and note that no cultures except the monotheists are currently attempting to force their values on others beyond their borders, whether we speak of the terrorist's brutal, oppressive version of Islam, or of our own belief in democracy and markets for all. I do not suggest we are wrong in our prejudices, only that we must recognize them as prejudices if we want to understand the hostile reactions our proselytizing elicits from much of the world. We imagine ourselves as a sort of strategic Santa Claus, bearing a sack full of better ways to do things, but much of the world sees a fire-and-brimstone preacher with a Big Mac in one hand and a precision-guided bomb in the other.

A Little More on Europe

In the short through mid term, at least, violence will continue to erupt primarily from the self-destructive, humiliated Muslim territories, but, in the grand historical arc, it would be folly to imagine that today's passive—when not pacifist—Europe will always remain so. Europe has turned inward before and it remained so through much of the Middle Ages, only to look outward with a vengeance during its five-hundred-year colonial phase. And even the introverted Middle Ages produced the Crusades—so startling because they were a sudden, expansionist aberration during a period of strategic introspection. Because Europe is passive today does not mean Europe will be passive against future threats—or even in the face of future opportunities. If we examine history objectively, Europe has been the least consistent, least predictable subregion of the world, full of nasty surprises for everyone else. Europe is history's manic-depressive. Contrary to the popular wisdom, Europe is far less steady and dependable than the United States. While Europeans view themselves as the masters of the arts of civilization, their historical behavior has more closely resembled that of today's soccer hooligans.

The Great, Grim Zone of Monotheism

If we sweep our hand across the map, from the lands of the Celts to the extremes of Central Asia, we will not pass over a single people who have not, at one time or another, behaved with extreme aggression toward their neighbors and, in the European instance, toward the entire world.

In our anger at the savagery of Islamic terrorists and our disgust at the social orders in so many Middle Eastern states, we are best served by the cool-headed recognition that, for all its unacceptable brutality, Middle Eastern Islam is fighting a defensive battle against the overwhelming cultural superiority and practical power of the Judeo-Christian band of states and nations. This recognition does not excuse terrorism, but may help us better understand it. Islamic terrorism is the violence of extreme desperation, symptomatic of the startling failure of Middle Eastern Islamic culture to compete with "the West" on a single productive front. Their failure is not our fault, but it is certainly our problem.

For all their documented violence, the Crusades are a red herring when invoked by Muslims to explain away their contemporary failures. Compared to a thousand years of Muslim attacks against and occupation of Europe's borderlands, from the Iberian Peninsula to the gates of Vienna to the Crimean khanate—and the occupation of Greece, the "cradle" of Western civilization into the nineteenth century—the Crusades amounted to little more than a long weekend during which a loutish collection of European tourists behaved particularly badly. Of course, the role of the Crusades in Islamic myth is far more important than the historical reality, but the critical point, at a time when the word "crusade" is so geopolitically loaded, is that these three monotheist religions have all produced crusader cultures (and Israel's West Bank settlements should be viewed in this context), from Joshua leveling the walls of Jericho, to the early Muslims thrusting up into France, to British missionaries (and soldiers) in Africa, to Osama bin Laden.

Whatever our personal religious convictions, we would do well to recognize that, strategically, the exclusive nature of monotheist religions makes them particularly ferocious, messianic, and . . . prone to crusading, no matter the name with which they cover it over.

Our current war against terror is a civil war on a very grand level, fought against irreconcilable brothers. In Cain and Abel country.

The Bogus Peril in Asia

As this paper proposes below, concern about Asian superpowers and any Asian "will to conquest" beyond regional goals utterly misreads the relevant cultural and social dynamics. The violence of the coming decades will continue to be spawned primarily by monotheist cultures, between themselves and with others. The greatest danger from the *bete noir* of the last decade, China, is not from intercontinental ballistic missiles, but from the possibility that the spiritual vacuum left by the Communist interregnum may open the door to some new, contagious, messianic, monotheist cult. Again, we must lay our personal beliefs aside to recognize that the worst thing that could happen to this world, short of nuclear or natural cataclysm, would be the sudden rise of an aggressive new (or reinterpreted) monotheist religion in China, leading China to turn its back on thousands of years of introversion to become a religious crusader. While this remains, in 2002, only one remote possibility among many, it is the one about which we should worry most profoundly. When Beijing cracks down on Falun Gong, it is clearly an unacceptable violation of human rights. But it is also evidence that the old men in Beijing recognize far more clearly than do we that intense, exclusive belief is transformative.

And all monotheist religions begin their careers with bursts of violent conquest.

A World Divided by Three

For American purposes, the world beyond our home territories—the United States, Canada, and the northern two-thirds of Mexico—can be divided into three strategic zones, each with its distinct character, challenges and opportunities:

- The Monotheist Zone, with its source in the eastern Mediterranean

- The Sino-Vedic Zone, with its bipolar powers, China and India
- The Postcolonial Zone, encompassing sub-Saharan Africa and Latin America

Each of these zones will be described at greater length below. First, let us consider alternative ways to categorize states and their behavior.

Bridges and Barriers, Survivors, Sleepwalkers and Pioneers

There are many valid terms used to classify states, whether as democracies, dictatorships, market economies, theocracies, constitutional monarchies, failed states, and so on. But these are political terms that tell us largely of a state's present condition and little or nothing of its purpose. The focus of this essay is on cultural affinities and functions, and on strategic roles. New, alternative terms will be introduced. They will not describe every state, but our focus is on key or exemplary states. While many more categories might be devised, the following five classifications will be used to describe states of particular interest:

Bridge states connect two civilizations or two cultures within a civilization, allowing the passage of everything from ideas to armies. While their native cultures usually reflect a great deal of fusion, their core identity associates, at varying points in history, with one civilization or culture or another. They may be conquered and converted by a given side, but their geographic location or temperament tends to keep them open to outside influences and to keep caravans, cargo trucks, or new concepts in transit across their territories. They may or may not be originators of new ideas, techniques, or movements, but they always feel their impact. Our era of confrontations and sharply drawn lines is not an especially fertile one for bridge states, yet many of those territories which have served this function historically continue to do so today. Examples of traditional bridge states are the predecessor states that occupied the land composing today's Turkey, golden-age Persia, Poland, and perhaps the most important bridge states in history, sixteenth-century Spain and Portugal (see below).

In the postmodern period, both Mexico and South Africa may evolve into crucial bridge states, with the process already well underway in Mexico; similarly, Brazil could prove to be an unexpected bridge state between the Americas and Africa in the outyears, as could the United States. Today's key bridge states are often smaller in scale (normal during a period of continental or global structural crisis): Singapore and the unofficial "city-states" of Miami—which has emerged as the media and financial capital of much of Latin America—and Hong Kong and Shanghai, with their unacknowledged degrees of practical autonomy. Bangalore and Hyderabad in India may be emerging as crucial "city-states" that function as cultural bridges, although it is too early to judge whether their impact will remain local or expand regionally.

Of note, city-states and cities possessed of informal degrees of independence or particular power always seem to have served as cultural bridges, from ancient Alexandria and Ephesus, down through Venice, Toledo, late-Ottoman Istanbul, Mexico City, and Beirut, although the latter has plunged tragically backward, to modern-day Vancouver. Port cities and littoral countries are, of course, always most exposed to international movements of any kind; conversely, port cities and densely-populated littoral countries are evolutionary by nature and seem to suffer—or benefit from—a sort of cultural dilution that prevents them from generating new and powerful religious, philosophical, or political movements.

The most powerful, as well as the most destructive, ideas tend to germinate and burst forth from inland areas where they can grow in the safety of relative isolation during their fragile infancy. The proximity to the sea, when measured by modern standards, of the lands that generated Judaism, then Christianity and Islam, obscures the relative poverty and isolation in which these violent faiths developed. While the cosmopolitan nature of the Roman Empire enabled the spread of Christianity, it had nothing to do with its creation, which was inherently anti-cosmopolitan, millenarian, and culturally reactionary in its original tenets. Likewise, deserts protected Islam in its infancy, while the relative openness and vast, indefensible borders of surrounding empires enabled its spread.

Bridge countries, at their best, temper the human impulse to exclusivity and devastating violence. In practical terms, there are fewer true bridge countries today than there were a hundred years ago, in the waning decades of colonialism, when imperial forces kept their colonies open, at least to influences from the empire's homelands. Despite a great deal of nonsense spouted about the information age breaking down barriers, many countries are struggling to build their cultural barriers ever higher. They may not succeed in the long run, but a retreat to exclusivity is the trend in many of the least successful or most threatened regions of the world.

Barrier states are those which block either invading armies or invading ideas. There is a natural tendency to associate barrier states with forbidding mountain ranges, deserts, or other physical obstacles, but ideological impenetrability is often a more effective wall of resistance—and it is certainly more dangerous in our time. Barrier states can either keep ideas from their own people, serve as a wall to the transmission of ideas beyond their territory, or both. Some states may serve as both barriers and bridges, simultaneously or at different points in history.

There have been, in fact, a surprising number of dual-function states. For example, Poland, a state crucial to European development—and a barrier state despite its lack of defensible borders—served alternately as a bridge state funneling European ideas eastward and a barrier that decisively thwarted threats to Europe from the east, from the defeat at Liegnitz that nonetheless turned back the Mongols, through the repeated deflections of Turkish and Tartar Islamic threats that climaxed in King Jan Sobieski's rescue of Vienna, to the "Miracle on the Vistula" when a scraped-together Polish army defeated the Bolshevik invasion that aimed through Poland toward sympathetic millions in Germany. Today, Poland again serves as a bridge between Europe and unsettled Russia and Ukraine to the east—and, if the E.U. has its way, it will serve as a barrier against illegal immigration. To a remarkable extent, this country that disappeared from the map for over a century continues to play the role it did in the Europe of five hundred years ago.

Spain, too, served for centuries as a barrier to Muslim expansion northward into Europe, while serving as a bridge that allowed the passage of Muslim scholarship and the revived Greek classics northward, as the forces of Castille, Navarre, and Aragon slowly rolled back the borders of Muslim Spain until, in 1492, the last Moors were expelled (along with Spain's Jews and much of the peninsula's cultural dynamism). Thereafter, Spain played a fateful, eccentric role first of transmitting European culture—and religion—to the New World, while, increasingly, serving as a barrier to later European cultural developments and keeping its empire (as did Portugal) frozen in cultural time. But more of Spain below. . . .

An impressive number of the world's recent conflicts occurred in old barrier states and territories, such as Serbia and Croatia, Georgia and Armenia, Chechnya and Afghanistan. These all are or once served as frontier states between cultures or civilizations, and Samuel Huntington's description of the fault lines between civilizations applies, of course, to the frontiers of faith, above all. To a powerful extent, belief is the decisive factor in creating a civilization's identity, not only in the religious sense but in the broader sense of values and identities.

Religion is culture, and culture is fate.

Certainly, in speaking of modern barrier states, religion is the number one determinant within the monotheist world and on its frontiers. While those frontiers shift with historical reallocations of power, the most notable development is the re-creation of an Arabic Islamic world that is erecting its barriers higher each day. The Arab territories had begun, in the nineteenth century, to open up to western influences, but the process over the last half century has been one of closing doors, of rebuilding the old walls of the Islamic world of a thousand years ago—though without the long-gone dynamism and power. A broad belt of states across North Africa and the Arabian Peninsula into the Levant and eastward to Mesopotamia has turned inward, refusing to accept the demands either of modernity or postmodernity. Even Lebanon, which seemed so promising a generation ago, has gone backward, and "liberal" Arab states, such as Jordan and Morocco, may be living on borrowed time. Egypt, once something of a bridge state, has become a barrier to outside ideas and has chosen repression and a marginal economy over openness and progress.

Of course, this belt of barrier states reaches even farther east, at present, through Iran, unsettled Afghanistan, and into Pakistan, touching distant, undecided Bangladesh. Although, for now, Islam's retreat from the modern world ends there, it is difficult to find many historical examples of so vast a region erecting barriers against the influence and ideas of the rest of the world. Only the Spanish Empire, from Phillip II until the occupation of Spain by Napoleon's armies, came close. And the lesson of the Spanish attempt to hermetically seal a vast empire is that the results are deformed economies and stunted cultures. Latin America is still fighting that hermetic, colonial legacy. It is difficult, given the accelerated pace of global development, to see how Islam's homelands will ever recover from their attempt at cultural secession.

Other barrier states—those which focused on protecting their own people from outside influences—include China and Japan through much of their histories, Russia between the lifting of the Mongol Yoke and the reign of Peter the Great (some would argue beyond him, as well), and the northern states of medieval India, whose complex behavior failed to save them from conquest, but preserved the integral Hindu states of southern, inland India from monotheist expansionism (other than some limited missionary successes). Curiously, France has made halfhearted attempts to become Europe's barrier state against American power and influence, but lacks the will and wherewithal to do so successfully.

Successful barrier states must be willing to kill—and, above all, to kill their own people.

Survivor states, for the purposes of this study, are those which contain a people that has suffered attempted genocide, or that perceives itself as having been so threatened. While the first type deals with reality and the second largely with self-created myth, all survivor states are ferocious when they perceive themselves in danger; expansive where lost historical territory, Lebensraum, or the need for defensible borders are concerned; intolerant to the degree that they view neighboring populations as less fully human than themselves; and obsessed with the notion of a historical mission. While such states are almost always small (Russia offers the only partial, great exception to this rule), they are disproportionately volatile and tend to spark larger conflicts than mere border wars. When survivor states are located next to one another, the situation is impossible to defuse completely and the maintenance of peace requires ceaseless external pressure or outright occupation.

In their do-anything-to-survive obsession, survivor states often will abrogate the rule of law, cut deals with criminals or even terrorists, and commit war crimes themselves—justifying their actions by all that their people have suffered in the past. Some survivor states may be democracies and have thriving economies but most maintain a self-defeating siege mentality disproportionate to real and immediate threats. Wherever there is a survivor state on the map, planners can expect eventual trouble.

Obvious survivor states include Rwanda, Armenia, and Israel, but the list becomes much longer when nascent states and those who have mythologized threats to themselves are added on. Then the list includes Bosnia, Croatia, Serbia, Greece (which behaves as though the Turkish occupation ended last week), Turkey (in a grand and peculiar sense, viewing itself as the battle-hardened remnant of the Ottoman Empire, forged in its own war of liberation against the Levantine Greeks, under Kemal Ataturk's near-messianic leadership), the non-state state of Kosova, and the Palestinian state-to-be. An eventual Kurdish state, perhaps created unintentionally with the fall, through whatever means, of Saddam Hussein, would certainly qualify, as might spinoff, ethnic states from a failed effort to reunite Afghanistan. Paraguay, still suffering from the effects of a disastrous war over a century ago, also displays limited survivor-state characteristics. So might East Timor, if its democracy and economic development fail to take hold. Cambodia has the potential to become a classic survivor state, but here, too, the jury is still out. Chechnya, should it ever gain its independence, undoubtedly would behave as a survivor state. Perhaps the mildest form of survivor behavior is exemplified by South Korea, although its occupation by Japan remains a highly-charged issue. The war-ravaged states of West Africa might also have some potential to emerge as survivor states behaviorally, although this is unlikely, given the odds against internal unity, their poverty, and the bankruptcy of their cultures. Even so, we cannot judge the degree to which a survivor mentality, in some local mutation, may linger in Africa in the wake of its particularly severe colonial experience—this remains a great question mark on that undecided continent.

The volatility of survivor states and the dangers they pose must be obvious to anyone who simply reads the list of names above. But, again, plotting them on the map shows a clear concentration of these dangerous entities in the Monotheist Zone, especially where its internal cultures and the divergent branches of its civilization(s) collide. There is an almost uninterrupted belt of these survivor states stretching from Croatia around the eastern rim of the Mediterranean to Gaza and northeastward to the Caucasus.

Watch this space.

Perhaps the greatest error well-intentioned diplomats and analysts make regarding the Middle East is to assume that the creation of a Palestinian state side by side with Israel might bring peace. The chances of two such embittered, bloodied survivor states getting along peaceably, while differing in religion and culture and forced to live side by side, are close to zero.

Even where an uneasy peace prevails, as between Armenia and Turkey, or between Turkey and Greece, the situation remains fragile and dangerous—even though the rest of the world sees clearly that the mundane cultures and even the cuisines are nearly identical, and that cooperation—"burying the hatchet"—would benefit everyone. The notion that states act rationally in their own self-interest is a liberal fantasy. It would be entirely in the practical self-interest of each of these states to cooperate, however grudgingly, with one another. But they will not do so, and they continue to dream of burying the hatchet in each other's heads.

States may, as noted above, display more than one identity at the same time, as in serving as both bridges and barriers. Likewise, bridge states, such as Turkey, may also interpret themselves as survivor states, and historical barrier states, such as Croatia or Armenia, are classic survivor states (their roles as barriers eventually caught up to them). But the most explosive combination of all is that of survivor state and pioneer state, which will be described below.

Sleepwalker states are those which, either content with or clinging to traditional beliefs and rigid structures of social organization, miss out on one of humankind's social or technical leaps forward. When the future arrives, as it inevitably does, they react with graphic, but ineffectual violence that consistently fails to maintain the existing order, but which excites the aggressor or intruder state to even more ferocious violence in response, creating a crisis of confidence and the collapse of the governing order (a precise description of the war against al Qa'eda and the Taliban in Afghanistan). While sleepwalker states existed at least as long ago as the declining Hittite empire, and include historical examples as diverse as the Aztec empire and the late Mughal states of India, the most instructive state for us, historically, is China, while the obvious current sleepwalker states are—without exception—Islamic. Even Burma/Myanmar has realized it must open itself to outside influences and investments, although it remains uncertain how to proceed.

China, vast and populous, with its own powerful culture, was content for millennia to live within its own world. Border conquests and even the rare fleet sent on a voyage of discovery were only ephemeral events. China's interests remained more exclusively internal than those of any other such power or state in history. Although a few technologies crept in, the arrival of Western gunboats on Chinese rivers awakened a remarkably introverted culture from a very deep slumber. Chinese responses to the appearance of technologically and organizationally superior intruders included, most spectacularly, waves of anti-foreign violence, from the disastrous Opium Wars, through local rebellions, to the messianic fervor of the Boxer Rebellion. Perhaps a longer historical perspective will allow us to see that Chinese Communism, too, was a millenarian phenomenon, messianic without a formal messiah (until Mao's later elevation), and a fervent collective response to the failure of the old order to defend or redeem China—a religion without god. Now, with the decay of Communism to an empty shell, another wave of collective fervor may be in the cards. This may not happen soon—or at all—but the rise of a new, galvanizing, intoxicating religious movement in China would be the scenario most likely to turn China to aggression.

The immediate problem, however, arises from the sleepwalker states of Middle Eastern Islam, extended at least as far as the Indus River in the east. The rise of fundamentalist terrorism against the West and its influences are the Muslim version—on a far grander scale—of the Boxer Rebellion, a movement born not of confidence, but of frustration and inchoate rage. The siege of the foreign lega-tions in Peking (nowadays Beijing) prefigured the terrorist attacks on foreign bases and embassies in the Middle East and Africa. What all millenarian, messianic movements have in common is that, although they speak of inaugurating a golden age, they all desire to recapture the past, to return their societies to an imagined purity rid of foreign influences. And it simply cannot be done.

The windfall of oil wealth, and the subsequent Arab-internal aid, long allowed Muslim countries between North Africa and the Hindu Kush to drowse while much of the rest of the world, espe-cially the West and the dynamos of East Asia, took off, developing new methods of social organization, of wealth distribution, of tech-nological innovation, and, above all, of greater human efficiency. Now these Muslim states, and especially most Arab states, are so far behind developmentally—especially in the realm of human effi-ciency—that it is impossible for this author to see how they could begin to catch up and compete with societies that have raced gener-ations, if not centuries, beyond them. A missionary, monotheist cul-ture spanning continents has been thrust onto the defensive (through its own failures, we must repeat). And these sleepwalker states, as they begin to awaken to their true condition, exhibit some of the worst survivor-state behaviors. We may be witnessing the development of the world's first survivor civilization, in the negative sense of the survivor-state characteristics described above, but with-out their virtues. The states of the Arab Islamic world are already caught in a no-man's-land: They are strong enough to hate, but too weak to reform. It is a prescription for continued failure.

Whether we speak of awakened China in the nineteenth and twentieth centuries, or of Islam today, sleepwalker states awake from their dreams of stasis to sudden disorientation, broad failure, and external influences. Violence is their natural response.

Pioneer states are the natural antagonists of sleepwalker states. Pioneer states lead human social, technical, and organizational progress. In their developing phases and at their apogees, these states or cultures are open to new ideas, experimentation, and change to a degree uncharacteristic of humankind (cultures tend to be conservative and closed, once developed). Pioneer states may arise at any time, but are most apt to appear and triumph during times of upheaval or decay in neighboring states and cultures. Pioneer states can be global or near-global in their reach (the Roman Empire; the Ottoman Empire for about two hundred years, down to the death of Suleiman the Magnificent; the British Empire; and today's United States), or regional in their impact (Israel, Singapore—which is also a bridge state, as noted above—and, perhaps in the out-years, Indonesia, Iran, and Australia/New Zealand, each of which possesses highly eccentric characteristics that could lead to innovative social orders).

In considering history's most influential pioneer states, it is all too easy to see them first as military powers; however, with the exception of the Ottoman Empire, each of the global or near-global players mentioned above maintained peacetime military establishments that, while technologically advanced, superbly trained, and disciplined, were quite small in comparison to their far-ranging responsibilities. The real power of pioneer states is their development of new formulae for maximizing the potential of their populations, their openness to new possibilities, their extraordinary ambition, and their capacity for internal debate among the governing elites (the lack of the latter crippled the Ottoman Empire early on). Of note, when Rome lost its taste for internal dialog and began to rely more heavily on its military for the maintenance of metropolitan order, it began to decay. In their heydays, too, Rome, the British Empire, and even the Ottoman Empire, as well as today's United States, were open to talent from within or without, to new ideas, and to open regimes for determining the status of the individual. In today's America, of course, we can recreate ourselves several times in a lifetime, whether we use as examples Madonna's various career incarnations, actors turned politicians, military retirees turned investment bankers, or the person who gains a college degree and a new profession in midlife. Our picture of the British empire's class system tends to be skewed badly by novels and films, and we forget the relatively humble, or frankly disadvantaged, births of many of the great men of empire, from Robert Clive, conqueror of so much of India, to Benjamin Disraeli, Victorian-era Prime Minister and best-selling novelist, whose family lineage was

Jewish. Certainly, there was snobbery and bigotry aplenty in the British Empire, but, especially on the empire's frontiers, there never was a dearth of self-made men. Even the Ottoman Empire, in its centuries of blazing greatness, employed Jews, Christians, and just about any other talent that could be drawn to the Ottoman standard. The greatest mosques built by the Ottomans in Constantinople, Edirne, and elsewhere were designed by Sinan, born an Armenian Christian. Openness to the greater world—the bane of sleepwalker states—is the oxygen of pioneer states.

The Spanish empire is a great and obvious exception. Although rough men of relatively humble origins, from an Italian sailor to Hernando Cortez, explored and conquered the empire, the repressive, bigoted genius of Philip II closed the door to further innovation and the influences of post-Renaissance culture, and quickly ran down his state bureaucracy until it functioned without creativity or integrity. A man of extreme religious self-righteousness whose character resembled that of Osama bin Laden (Friedrich Schiller's description of Philip II could be applied directly to bin Laden), Philip II personally destroyed the hope of competitive progress in Spain's dominions. While the empire nonetheless lasted four hundred years, Philip II's forcible transformation of Spain from nascent pioneer state (and empire) to one of the great sleepwalker states of history meant that Spain's dominions abroad existed in a near-hermetic time capsule, corrupt, priest-haunted, and decrepit, and that the home country, in the early twentieth century, was less industrialized than Japan. Of course, the tale of Spanish cultural, economic, and military failure is more complex than can be described here, but the salient feature for our purposes is that Philip II and his emulative successors were inflexible—and committed to preserving their order, their empire, and their faith, rather than developing these things. It is, perhaps, no mere coincidence that, after frontier Catholicism, the greatest influence that shaped the Spanish states was the long Moorish occupation of the Peninsula, during which, despite intermittent cultural flowerings, Islamic fundamentalist movements repeatedly crushed attempts at social and spiritual development. Imperial Spain thus had before it two prime examples of how to rule: the ferocity of its embattled faith, multiplied by the fervor of the Counter-Reformation, and the example of its Moorish enemies, in which more liberal, open regimes consistently fell prey to fundamentalist conquerors—who were the great nemeses of the Spanish knights (when the Spanish were not fighting as mercenaries in Moorish pay). A state born in war and expanded through war, and confined within a fundamentalist religion, Spain never learned to value anything more than an uncompromising faith and a merciless sword.

It is also characteristic of pioneer states that, while they make war ferociously when they must, they consistently operate under a code of humane laws, written or customary. For example, our image of the Ottoman Empire is skewed by a sense of its Islamic otherness, and by its long, pathetic decline. But, in its heyday, it was the most open, dynamic, and tolerant of empires. The Jews driven from Spain found a refuge in Constantinople, where their descendents still live quietly. And when the "liberating" Christian armies of the Habsburgs retook Budapest at the end of the seventeenth century, the first thing the soldiers did was to massacre the Jews in the city's thriving ghetto. Islam, once the most tolerant and dynamic monotheist faith, has simply traded places with yesterday's Christians.

Collectible frontiers are a commodity requiring discussion in association with pioneer states. Monotheist civilizations and cultures are inherently expansive, missionary, proselytizing. They require frontiers that can be "collected" into the faith or the ideological fold. A particular reason for Islam's calcification and violent dismay—in addition to its systemic failures—is that it is now blocked in and cannot "collect" any additional territory or populations. While we hear a great deal about Islamic expansion in places such as the Philippines or Indonesia, the fact is that Islam's expansion reached its farthest extent centuries ago and, since then, has been battling either to hold the line or for incremental, local gains. No religion in recorded history expanded more swiftly than did Islam in its first few centuries. It possessed a stunning force, both ideologically and militarily. But, today, Islam's only serious gains are internal—demographic increases which are anything but positive, as they produce ever more unemployed or under-employed young males in societies with insufficient resources to appease them.

Middle Eastern Islam feels enclosed, surrounded, and stunned by the success of Western pioneer states, especially the United States. And Arab governments are forced to divide up shrinking pies among ever more numerous hungry mouths. Despite the frantic calls for jihad, Islam isn't going anywhere beyond its present borders—except in the forms of immigration or terrorism.

European and North American powers also have deep expansionist urges, so obviously manifested during the age of European colonialism. We now see Europe—and the U.S.—as averse to the old-fashioned conquest of others. In fact, we have simply developed new, more successful means for conquest, on the cultural and economic fronts. As I have noted in other writings, military conquest is ultimately expensive—sometimes, as in the Spanish case, to the point of bankrupting the conqueror. Physical occupation simply does not pay in the long run. To their enormous advantage, today's Europeans and Americans have figured out the art of looting without shooting.

It would be a grave mistake not to take the mullahs and Islamic commentators seriously when they insist that Islam and the Judeo-Christian cultures are at war. They recognize more clearly than do we that we are engaged in a new form of conquest, infiltrating their societies with seductive technologies, customs, and behaviors that subvert the standing order. Islamic resistance is violent and vocal, so we foolishly imagine it is powerful. But, the events of September 11, 2001, notwithstanding, Islam's impact on the West in our lifetimes has been negligible, while our impact on the Islamic states has been profound, disruptive, and shaming.

For the United States, much of the world remains a collectible frontier, though in terms of economic advantage, cultural infiltration, and strategic influence, not religious conversion or physical occupation. And our efforts to spread our preferred behaviors do, indeed, amount to a crusade, if a well-intentioned and only intermittently violent one. We fail to see that our entire mindset vis-à-vis the rest of the world is shaped by our religious traditions, every bit as much as are the less-successful prejudices of the Islamic world. Even the atheists among us are the children of Godfrey of Bouillon and Richard the Lionhearted . . . or of St. Francis Xavier and David

Livingstone. Kentucky Fried Chicken, Nikes, and pop stars may not seem much like aggressive missionary gospels to us, but to the most reactionary portions of the Islamic world, they are nothing less.

The media, with exuberant irresponsibility, repeatedly tell us of some young man in Houston converting to Islam, scare-mongering with the suggestion that Islam is taking over the world. In fact, the most rapidly-expanding religion in the world, in terms of converts and geographic spread, is not only Christianity, but specifically evangelical Protestant Christianity, with its injunction to believers to "spread the Good News." While the devout Christians among us may applaud this development, the strategists among us should be on high alert. As a number of articles and even a recent book have suggested, the spread of evangelical Christianity may prove an even greater source of instability and violence in the out-years than the decay of Islamic cultures.

The Three Strategic Zones
North America, from Mexico City to Barrow, Alaska, constitutes a region apart—the home territories of human innovation in our time and the pioneer region containing the ultimate pioneer state, the United States. While some analysts may discount the inclusion of northern Mexico in this zone, it is this writer's belief that, while formal sovereignty and official borders will remain in place between successful states, the coming generations will see more innovation and relative progress on our southern border than on our northern border, and there will be greater integration across both borders. This does not suggest than Canada will lag, only that Canada is already highly developed, with less margin for innovation and development, and that Canada will inevitably follow developments in the United States, complaining all the way. Mexico, with its greater problems, also has greater potential for innovative change and the pursuit of alternative solutions to social dilemmas. Per capita income in Mexico will continue to lag behind incomes to the north, but a richer, symbiotic relationship across our borders will develop than has been the case in the past. Mexico is only now casting off the crippling shell of its colonial legacy.

In any case, the United States will continue, for the foreseeable future, to be the world's leading pioneer state, breaking down ever more barriers, while possessing wealth and power without precedent in history.

The Monotheist Zone

The frontiers of the Monotheist Zone, where Judaism, Christianity, and Islam were born, matured, and continue to dominate the cultural landscape, have shifted back and forth over the centuries. On the eastern, Islamic frontier, the border has been pushed back across northern India toward the Indus River—after centuries of Islamic Mughal rule and the British interval. Although over 130 million Muslims still live in India, Hindu culture dominates today. On the Monotheist Zone's southern border, too, Islam has reached its limit and may begin to recede. In southern Sudan, where the borderlands shift into a syncretic Christianity, tracing east into Ethiopia and west through Nigeria (where Muslims still attempt to push their frontier southward) the most dynamic, if not always the most politically powerful, faith is that of the "African Christ." The hybrid, localized Christianity of black Africa—in the Postcolonial Zone—is unfinished and vivid, with a dynamism lacking in the sub-Saharan extremes of Islam. But this does not yet equal an extension of the Monotheist Zone. African Christianity is very much a work in progress, where the religion evolves almost daily, incorporating local traditions, beliefs, and behaviors. It is not monolithic—and may not even turn out to be monotheist in the traditional sense. African Christianity, despite the advent of African cardinals and recognized churches, may develop into a unique, third-path Christianity, the tenets of which would be dramatically different from those of Catholicism or Protestantism, sub-Saharan Africa's two parent forms of monotheism. In any case, the traditional Monotheist Zone ends where African Christianity begins.

In the northeast, where Russia has spent centuries engaging in missionary conquest, first extending Orthodox Christianity, then Leninist Communism, the expansive phase clearly is over and the best Russians can do is to attempt to hold a slowly shriveling line. Given demographic disparities, it is difficult to see how Moscow will maintain its control over the eastern provinces of the Russian Federation across our new century. The only frontiers on which the Monotheist Zone is not shrinking are the largely postreligious states of Europe (although monotheist mentalities and behaviors persist, and likely will for centuries to come). While recent events make the Islamic states of the Monotheist Zone appear far more powerful and threatening than they in fact are, pundits and analysts insist that Europe has lost its way and its will. Yet Europe retains great wealth and residual power. If we have seen no major wars in Europe since 1945 (although there have been adventures enough beyond Europe, though nothing on the scale of the colonial era), it is because Europeans have not been galvanized by significant threats. We must beware making the same mistake the Japanese made before Pearl Harbor (and that Osama bin Laden made) in judging Americans, who were deemed morally weak and unwilling to fight or sacrifice. Given the right threat, Europe—or key parts of Europe—may prove every bit as ferocious as in past centuries. Certainly it is hard to imagine this today. But it is always difficult to foresee the sudden changes that keep human history so painfully interesting.

While the aging of populations in Europe appears to be leading to states that lack the manpower to defend themselves, with lurid images of masses of immigrants, legal or illegal, swamping Italy, or France or Spain or Germany, it is every bit as possible that demographic threats from beyond could appear sufficiently threatening to trigger the rise of new, exclusive regimes in Europe that, while preserving democratic forms for their citizens, behave brutally on and beyond their borders. Difficult as this may be to imagine, it is far less difficult than imagining the Somme or Verdun was for Europeans in 1900. History doesn't really march—it lurches, staggers, plunges, and smashes.

In the meantime, Muslim states in this zone will continue to struggle with issues of identity and modernity, and few give cause for optimism. The likeliest scenario isn't a single colossal confrontation between Islam and the West, but decades of intermittent terrorism, state breakdown, stalling on reforms, occasional revolutions, lesser wars, and punitive expeditions—and, sometimes, progress.

Most European states remain pioneer states to some degree, open, however reluctantly, to innovation and reform—though certainly not on the scale to which the United States embraces change. But every Muslim country in the Monotheist Zone has behaved as some variety of sleepwalker state—obviously, Saudi Arabia, Egypt, Yemen, and their ilk, but also the Gulf States, where petrodollar lollipops cannot sweeten a failed history forever.

Even Turkey forever disappoints on the development front. Hard-luck Turkey has much of the corruption of nearby Arab states but, fortunately, its self-image is not as utterly disconnected from reality. Among the few strategically crucial states in the Monotheist Zone, Turkey is the single remaining bridge state in the Middle East. The Turks will never be as successful as we might wish, but they will never be as hopeless as their Arab neighbors.

The dark horse, developmentally and strategically, is Iran. Despite sensational headlines and tactical reverses, Iran is decades ahead of other Middle Eastern states that have not yet undergone their experiments with religious rule. The Iranian people have tried theocracy, and it has not worked for them. Like alcoholics who need to hit bottom before they can reform and begin building new lives, Iran has bottomed out and may be the first (hopefully not the only) Muslim-populated state to forge its way to a working compromise with the demands of the modern and postmodern worlds. Despite its flares of extremism, Iran—the population of which is overwhelmingly Persian, Kurdish, and Azeri Turk, with few Arabs—has never practiced a form of Islam as repressive and inhumane as the Saudi variant. Partly this has to do with Shi'ism and Sufi influences (and a lingering flame of Zoroastrianism, which no regime has ever been able to exterminate from the culture), but it also has to do with the Persian confidence that comes from thousands of years of cultural achievement. Iran may prove the first successful market democracy in the Islamic portion of the Monotheist Zone, if events in Iraq do not surprise us. If so, Teheran may have a fight on its hands, again, with its Arab neighbors. In essence, Iran has been a sleepwalker but may develop into Middle Asia's first pioneer state—while its neighbors continue to stumble backward.

Afghanistan long has been a frontier state, and its natural border is farther east, along the Indus River, which has been the natural dividing line between Middle Asia and the Indian subcontinent since Alexander crossed it. While we may wish Afghanistan well and hope for the best, its society is so conservative, so backward and physically shattered, that the best result we can get may be a more peaceful, somewhat more equitable and just state that does not soon revert to overt oppression and terrorism. Certainly efforts expended on Afghanistan are not wasted, since the region desperately needs a success story—but that success story is likeliest to come next door, in Iran (or in Iraq), where a new model of Islamic society may emerge across the next generation. It is only a matter of time before the United States and Iran are again strategic partners, and, while we now rely on the badly-failed state of Pakistan as our urgent proxy, the out-years may see Iran as our partner and local policeman once again. At present, we are needlessly in contention with Iran over the future of Afghanistan and other matters, but that is more a function of the bad will among an aging generation of leaders on both sides than it is a reflection of the future or genuine interests. Like India, Iran has no friends among its neighbors and must come, ultimately, to an accommodation with the United States.

Then comes Israel. Simultaneously a survivor state and a pioneer state—the most dynamic, aggressive combination—Israel is surround on three sides by sleepwalker states. As noted above, should a Palestinian state come into an independent existence, it, too, would perceive itself as a survivor state, virtually guaranteeing continued friction. But the danger is even greater (although, on moral grounds, the Palestinians are ultimately entitled to a state): First, the Palestinians are the most creative and innovative of the Arab peoples, a fact obscured by the public and media-enhanced roles of the old guard of terrorists and corrupt power brokers. In fact, the Palestinians are (relatively) highly educated, comparatively secular, and scattered in their own global diaspora. A Palestinian state that could shake off the corruption and authoritarianism of the Arafat model would attract a great deal of money from Palestinians abroad and a return to the homelands of many highly-skilled workers. This Palestinian state, too, could become something of a pioneer state. But no one in the region—especially the other Arab states—wants that to happen. Second, a Palestinian state with a survivor-state mentality (and especially if it began to become a pioneer state as well) would exert tremendous pressure on Jordan. Given the high proportion of Palestinians among Jordan's population, the Palestinian state might make its next priority "reunion" with Jordan, but a form of reunion that would not include the Hashemite dynasty.

Israel truly is a model pioneer society, even in the most literal sense of having pioneered the land and made it fertile. But it is the social, intellectual, and organizational innovations that finally make it intolerable to the sleepwalker states surrounding it. Monotheist religions are very good haters, yet Israel's best chance for peaceful relations with its neighbors would be if it were a traditional, closed, hierarchical society, rather than the open society it has been since its inception. Even Israel's stunning success would be more tolerable to its neighbors if Israel oppressed its women, censored its media, and mandated religious observance for all.

The only chance for peace in the long term in the ancient, Eastern Mediterranean homelands of the Monotheist Zone would be extraordinary upheavals in the short term that shattered regional hierarchies. It is extremely unlikely that this could occur without a great deal of bloodshed. And Arab Islam may be so trapped in its myths and regressive beliefs that change proves impossible.

The Monotheist Zone will continue to be both a cockpit of violence and an exporter of violence. While we Americans must focus on the troubled situation in the zone's Islamic states, the more interesting and surprising future may come in the zone's European region, which has been the greatest exporter of violence over the past five hundred years. While dire warnings are not (yet) warranted, Europe may remain steelier and more vengeful than we sense, resembling the United States on the eve of December 7, 1941. Major terrorist incidents may be Europe's Pearl Harbor. In the long term, it may be some utterly unforeseen event, rather than the anticipated results of aging populations and the determination to maintain its wealth, that returns Europe to its tradition of violent solutions to practical frustrations.

The Sino-Vedic Zone

In using the term Vedic (of the Vedas, India's ancient holy texts) instead of Hindu, I intentionally have chosen a term with ancient roots. We Americans, with our habit of obsessing on the crisis of the moment, often fail to identify root causes because we make no efforts to place events in a historical context. The Vedic period in India occurred roughly between 1500 and 500 B.C.E. After three thousand years, the same cultural river continues to flow through the subcontinent. Similarly, in China, enduring historical patterns—which Communism did *not* destroy—date to a similar period.

When we view contemporary India as shifty and truculent, or speak worriedly of Chinese missiles, we express immediate concerns but miss the salient factors behind India's noisome behavior and China's quest for arms.

Compared to the wars of conquest fought, endlessly, within the Monotheist Zone and then beyond it by monotheist powers, China and India appear almost miraculous in their lack of aggression toward each other or toward the greater world. While they certainly fought frequent wars internally, within their own cultures, or on disputed borders, these vast countries, during periods of relative unity, had the capacity to amass tremendous wealth and power for state purposes—despite the poverty of their general populations. Yet neither thought it worthwhile to attempt to build an empire far beyond its cultural borders, and their few wars of conquest were limited to pacifying frontiers. While mountain and jungle barriers played their roles, it remains fascinating that China never tried to conquer India, or vice versa. Their most violent encounters were border skirmishes during the Cold War. Until the Communist reformation, when a foreign philosophy formulated in Europe by a monotheist culture was forced upon the Chinese people—China's most aggressive period occurred when Mongol khans ruled old Cathay. India's farthest-reaching foreign adventures occurred when it was ruled by the British. While internal violence in both countries was sometimes ferocious, neither felt compelled to export Confucianism and ancestor worship by the sword or to impose Hinduism on foreign populations through military occupation. Buddhism, the closest thing to a missionary religion this zone produced, stressed nonviolence and teaching by example. It subsumed and incorporated existing gods, rather than "breaking the idols."

Certainly the peoples of Southeast Asia fought wars of aggression against one another, yet these were ethnic, not religious, conflicts. Local "empires," whether Khmer, Vietnamese, Siamese, Burman, Javanese, or any other, all sought security and wealth—power—but not to impose lifestyles or modes of belief. The territories that became Indonesia produced lengthy, bloody dynastic struggles, savage pirates, and bitter resistance to colonial conquest, but the existing cultural conditions were so deeply embedded that even the arrival of Islam turned few into crusaders for the faith. Today, Muslim monotheism may be the cause of, or the excuse for, a good bit of violence in the Indonesian archipelago, but independent Indonesia's foreign wars since independence were fought over disputed territory, not religion. Indonesia has become something of a bellwether country, in which the world will see what modern Islam can make of itself, but, for now, the most impressive thing about this "Muslim" state is how secular it remains.

Indeed, India's worst problems with invaders and border aggressors over the past thousand years consistently have been attacks from the West by monotheist warriors. First Afghan and Central Asian Muslims established empires in Northern India, which were then superseded by the Islamic Mughals, who reigned, ever more feebly, until those other insatiable, self-righteous, and fierce monotheists, the British, arrived. Today, India faces terrorist attacks and subversion in Kashmir from rigorously, intolerantly monotheist Pakistan.

China, in the modern era, also suffered partial conquest and successive humiliations at the hands of monotheist cultures from Europe (and the emperor-worshipping Japanese). The Chinese embrace of Communism has been read in many different ways, but it may also be viewed as an attempt to wield an equally powerful, intolerant "monotheist" belief system against China's harassers.

Having fought the Chinese in Korea and experienced their mischief in Vietnam—while listening to swords rattling over Taiwan—we view the Chinese as aggressive. And the Chinese clearly do intend to control a regional sphere of influence, if they can. But what should astonish us is how narrow, how local, Chinese interests are. Chinese ships are not standing ready off America's coast (or Australia's or Indonesia's coasts, for that matter), and China's brief Cold War flirtation with exporting military elements—primarily advisers—to distant lands has largely withered. The Chinese are certainly glad to export arms, primarily for money, partly for influence. But, contrary to the nightmares of the 1950s, there is no indication that the Chinese have global aspirations—if anything, their desire for hegemony has shrunk markedly since their Communist apogee some decades ago. The Chinese want security and whatever useful authority they can gain over their neighbors, but we have no serious indications of greater aspirations on Beijing's part. While we must remain wary of Chinese threats to our interests and allies, we also must remember that, while we see our own interests on China's borders, the reverse is not true.

The greatest danger of eventual war between India and China will arise if China continues its quest for port facilities on the approaches to the Indian Ocean. Chinese involvement in Burma—in multiple spheres, from business to intelligence-gathering—has belatedly attracted India's attention. China, facing a de facto strategic blockade to the east, where U.S. allies and U.S. ships stand just off its coast, has been seeking alternative routes to the world to even the odds. Beijing sees the path south as the only useful direction in which China can move to extend its influence and lifelines without directly confronting U.S. military power, interests, and allies. While China may, indeed, turn more aggressive than it has been historically—countries and cultures can and do change—for now, at least, China's slow-motion Burmese adventure looks more like an attempt to establish a backup lifeline and to secure its flanks than like the beginning of a quest to dominate India's traditional sphere of influence.

As for Chinese "fifth columns" among the populations of Southeast Asia, the "overseas" Chinese residents are hated in Indonesia, integrated in Thailand (except for the old Kuomintang colonies in the north), distrusted—though valued—in Malaysia, and masters in Singapore—but Singapore, a monument to the genius of the Chinese character once freed of China's grip, certainly wants nothing to do with the regime in Beijing. Despite some nostalgia, the Chinese residents of Southeast Asia recognize that Beijing wishes to use them but does not trust or truly support them. And the Chinese are entirely unwelcome in today's Vietnam.

China's most successful "conquests" consist of long-established business communities with only tenuous political ties to the old homeland. While Chinese culture is one of the strongest on earth, enduring, at times, for centuries in émigré communities, there is a great deal of suspicion among "overseas" Chinese about the Beijing government. Any scenario that includes a Chinese takeover of Southeast Asia, abetted by local Chinese residents, is nonsense.

Indeed, despite the forces of globalization, China may be entering another troubled, introverted period in which domestic challenges, discontents, and requirements take precedence over foreign policy issues so decisively that China's armed forces will receive an ever-smaller percentage of GDP—perhaps even a great deal less in real terms—than they have in the past. China is proud, and frustrated at our presence so near to its borders, but its ambitions—except for trade—are entirely local. Forty years ago, the Chinese strategic presence abroad reached as far as the Congo. Today military advisers have been replaced with cheap exports, and China's Communism amounts to no more than an old whore's insistence on her virginity.

We can have a war with China, if we want one. But we must recognize that both China and India were dealt losing hands historically, despite their contentment within their own borders, and were traumatized by contact with the Monotheist Zone—and, in China's case, by the Japanese, as well, whose imperialism mimicked, in the most brutal fashion possible, the conquests of the Western powers in the past. China and India have been struggling to find their balance again, to adjust to the relatively recent shocks of external power exerted against them, and to absorb the lessons and technologies they must if they are to compete in the twenty-first century. For Americans, the 1989 massacre of Chinese students in Beijing is already ancient history. For the Chinese, the opium wars of the 1840s are yesterday.

Despite its greater poverty and slower progress on the economic front, India has long been absorptive, accepting foreign influences from successive waves of invaders and apostles, then Indianizing them. In a sense, China faces a more difficult time of it psychologically, because it lacks the tradition of openness to foreign ideas and methods and made a dogma of its cultural superiority for centuries—indeed, for millennia. China, despite its impressive gains in power since the Communist victory, still perceives itself as weak, wounded, and threatened. Beijing's most militant statements are little more than the barking of a nervous dog. And now, after the latest series of displays of American military capabilities, the Chinese absolutely do not want to fight the United States. Nor could they afford to, given their economy's desperate reliance on China's trade surplus with the U.S. (and others). The Chinese economy is far more fragile than outsiders credit, essentially an automobile that keeps running with a nearly-empty tank, relying on the driver to keep adding another pint of gas just in time.

If we stand back just slightly, it becomes clear that every major war of conquest in Asia, at least since the strange eruption of the Mongols, was either initiated by or the result of actions by Monotheist Zone powers. From the Muslims sweeping into northern India over half a millennium ago, through the Western colonial phase, to Japan's imitation of Western imperialism, to the Communist takeover of China, every great war that reached across major cultural borders was either begun by Monotheist Zone powers or their actions, or inspired by Western ideologies and practices transplanted to Asia. Even during the Cold War, border fights resulted primarily from the often-arbitrary boundaries imposed by the old colonial powers and left behind for newly independent states to manage. Both modern nationalism and Communism were Western creations. Today, we view Asia as the world's most dangerous powder keg. If it is—and I do not believe that to be the case—it is because we filled it with powder. More importantly, this is a region that, while violent enough in local wars, never generated anything like the wars of conquest that took European empires around the globe—or even anything like the globe-spanning interests that steer U.S. Navy carriers through the waters off Taiwan.

Japan, particularly, is misunderstood—because of the horrific aberration of the Greater East Asia Co-Prosperity Sphere and Japanese wartime atrocities. In the West, we speak glibly of samurai and admire the battle ballets in Kurosawa's films. But traditional Japanese warfare, within Japan, appears to have resembled the ritual, rules-laden battles of pre-Columbian America more closely than it did the fluid, merciless warfare pioneered in monotheist domains. In both China and Japan, ritual, in many spheres, became substance in and of itself, defusing or dissipating aggressive tendencies and preserving social order. Japan went wild because it misread the lessons of Western colonialism, perceiving an absence of rules where the rules were only very complex and profoundly different from those prevailing locally.

When speaking of the "inhumanity of the East," we would do well to recall that China's greatest military classic, Sun Tzu's *Art of War*, is startlingly humane in its admonitions, while the West's dominant work of military theory, Clausewitz's *On War*, constructed a theoretical model of wars of annihilation that soon enough became real. The fundamental difference in temperament between Clausewitz and Sun Tzu is that the Chinese author never forgot his sense of humanity, while Clausewitz saw humanity's foibles as an impediment to ideal war-making. We know of no Chinese general setting out to conquer the world. There never was a far-flung Chinese empire that spanned oceans and foreign continents. No Napoleon. No Hitler. No Philip II. No Umayyad or Abassid caliphs. Not even a Mussolini.

We are reading our own history onto the Chinese.

Yes, But . . .

Of course, we cannot know the future with certainty. Population pressures, crises of various descriptions, unexpected cataclysms . . . many things could turn the Sino-Vedic Zone outward, making would-be conquerors out of history's homebodies. But we must beware relying only upon our most recent experiences for indications of what the future holds. Even our own Indochina wars were fought against indigenous enemies inspired by European philosophical systems—Communism, nationalism, or an amalgam of both. And we went there, they didn't come here.

The Sino-Vedic Zone has long held the greatest concentration of sleepwalker states—in benign form—in history. In the nineteenth and twentieth centuries, those states began to awaken. But the Sino-Vedic Zone's sleepwalker states rarely behaved as violently as those of the Monotheist Zone, and when they did it was to cast off foreign occupations. This zone has not generated any global terrorist threats—except for the participation of the zone's Muslims, to a limited degree, in terrorist schemes that originated elsewhere. And, of course, Islam is as much an import, if an older one, to the region as is Communism. Japanese extremists are imitative and overwhelmingly focused on Japan. Where enduring civil strife exists in this zone, it is consistently either between monotheist and old-religion factions, as in India, or between two imported monotheist faiths, Christianity and Islam, as in the Philippines and Indonesia. Naturally, when we look at Asia, we see the technologies we have "given" them. But, if we are honest about everything else we have exported to them—the colonial experience, monotheism, nationalism, Communism . . . it doesn't look as if the Sino-Vedic Zone has gotten a very good deal.

In classifying the region's states, a sample gives the flavor of the whole. China, of course, has served for thousands of years as a barrier state, blocking foreign influences from its own population and, for many a century, isolating Korea and Japan as well. Today, the rulers in Beijing wish to maintain their old barriers but cannot. The greatest dangers that could appear in China are the rise of a galvanizing, messianic cult religion to replace Communism, or the continued trend in China to perceive itself as a survivor state, harmed in the past and threatened in the present. A virulent explosion of Chinese nationalism, fortified by a new, dynamic religious cult, would be much more worthy of our fear than the shabby, phony Communism preached but no longer really practiced.

India is so complex it defies easy categorization, but in one curious—and hopeful—respect it resembles the United States more than it does any major Asian country: India is absorptive, able to ingest, transmute, and use an endless stream of foreign concepts and ideas. The plague of nationalism, which excited an uncharacteristic, postcolonial xenophobia, damaged this tradition in the twentieth century, but there are hopeful signs that, in the new century, India (or parts of India) may make much greater progress than in the past. India might be categorized as a bridge state, but it is—and always has been—a bridge from the world to itself.

Overwhelmingly, the Sino-Vedic Zone is an area in which the violence attempts to resolve local issues. Except for a still-limited amount of Islamic terrorism, it does not export violence to the rest of the world. That remains the job of the Monotheist Zone, in which militant Islam is the current multinational consortium of aggression.

Australia and New Zealand are, geographically but not culturally, part of the Sino-Vedic Zone. Curiously, these two former colonies of a great monotheist power have altered their hereditary identities and have no interests in conquest or the export of violence (except the violence employed, reluctantly, by peacemakers and peacekeepers). In both cases, plentiful territory and small populations are certainly factors in the nations' contentment, as are the unique colonial experiences of both. But if they are unlikely to wage aggressive wars (New Zealand, at least for now, has no capacity to do so), they also need not fear military aggression from neighboring states— although they will continue to have plentiful problems with neighboring populations, immigrants, and so on, and regional states are glad to look the other way if they can export their own problems to their neighbors. But the searing experience of Japanese aggression, as noted above, was a historical anomaly. Nothing is certain, given humankind's capacity for mischief, but colossal wars in Asia in the twenty-first century are unlikely to develop *within* the Sino-Vedic Zone—and much likelier to develop *between* zones. As I write, India and Pakistan, two border countries at the eastern and western ends of the Monotheist and Sino-Vedic Zones are in danger of a nuclear exchange. Samuel Huntington's thesis regarding the clash of civilizations may have been dead right (no pun intended) in theory, but he drew the lines in the wrong places.

The twenty-first century may (or may not) be a Pacific Century, but it is unlikely to be a Pacific Military Century. The portion of the globe which so focuses the attention of American strategists today may prove to be the least threatening in coming decades. The key variable isn't China's external ambitions, but its internal condition.

The Postcolonial Zone
This zone includes sub-Saharan Africa and Latin America as far north as Cuba and Mexico's southernmost states (Chiapas, Oaxaca, etc.). This is the zone to which U.S. strategists, planners, and analysts pay the least attention, since it appears to offer no serious threats to our security. Yet this is an area of tremendous unrecognized potential. If it is largely poor and frequently appears chaotic (which we automatically ascribe, in whispers, to "backwardness"), it is because the Postcolonial Zone is an area still struggling to find a healthy form after centuries of occupation. It cannot go back, but it is unsure how to go forward. Crises as diverse as the current economic chaos in "developed" Argentina and the recent butchery in Sierra Leone are parts of the same puzzle: How do these countries resolve their internal contradictions and move forward after long

periods of European domination—or even their creation and population by European immigrants? Despite the age of some of its societies, especially in Africa, the Postcolonial Zone remains unshaped clay in the strategic sense. It is humankind's last great laboratory, where alternative futures are under development. And it is the last great collectible frontier.

I term this zone "Postcolonial" simply because, from Peru to Tanzania, its societies are still struggling, sometimes desperately, to make sense of themselves in the aftermath of the age of European colonialism. They have fundamental problems of identity, although for very different reasons in Africa and Latin America. This is where colonialism hit hardest, or created the most profound disruptions to indigenous cultures (when it did not simply annihilate them). While colonialism certainly was active elsewhere, it had less impact: China was humiliated, but never fully occupied, and Chinese culture is so robust it never lost its sense of identity; likewise, India, though occupied, never much doubted its Indian-ness or the quality and value of its traditions. Sino-Vedic Zone populations simply wanted the colonial powers to go. Even Indonesia, with its old, complex, layered culture, changed less under colonial rule than the states of the Postcolonial Zone. Africa and Latin America, however, are still fighting—sometimes literally—to overcome their colonial legacies. There is no end in sight to this struggle, but there are a number of reasons to hope.

The Undecided Future

For sub-Saharan Africa, colonialism was almost entirely a tragedy, crushing fragile societies and creating artificial identities, whether social hierarchies foreign to the indigenous systems or simply the entire notion of Western-style states. Africa continues to suffer recurrent bouts of bloodshed because of the colonial legacy of dysfunctional borders that either force tribes together that do not want to be together, or divide tribes and peoples between multiple states, although they believe they belong together. The European-drawn map of Africa simply doesn't work as designed, and the old colonial powers left those borders intact as a curse; meanwhile, Africa's independent, artificial states are struggling to function the way the Western model insists they should. But Western states—and old states elsewhere—grew organically, over long centuries, and developed their identities slowly. . . or, more correctly put, their identities slowly congealed. At independence, virtually every African state was nothing but a pretense, with unprepared locals occupying the offices just vacated by Europeans, but without a deep grasp of what those offices must do. Understandably, the new rulers concentrated on the outward forms, which they could more easily emulate, and neglected the inner substance of government, with which they had little or no experience. Newly independent Africa never had a chance. Now, painfully, Africans are trying to create chances, against daunting odds. Not every country will survive, and we must expect a great deal of turmoil as this region attempts to fix itself after being massively damaged by external forces.

Certainly, Africa has had—and continues to have—more than its share of horror stories—massacres, man-made famines, pointless wars. But given the brutality of the European colonialists in so many of the states, the lack of preparation of an educated local class suited for government, the foreign nature of the rules of statehood and the practices of the world community, and the real or relative poverty of so much of the continent, perhaps we should be less shocked than we affect to be. While we must not paint pre-colonial Africa in false, romantic colors as an ideal society (wars, slaving, conquest, and massacres are old African traditions—just as they are old human traditions just about everywhere else as well), we will never know how the region might have developed—or failed to develop— left to its own devices. When we see country X's strongman abuse his own subordinates and treat his people callously, he simply is behaving as Europeans did before him when dealing with the native population. This is the way the powerful man believes "real" leaders behave; showing disdain for inferiors is simply the way things are done. This is beginning to change, as the generation of leaders who knew the European governors and bureaucracies firsthand leaves the stage. But the question of identity remains—not the old leftist silliness about what it means to be black and African, but the more meaningful, if less gratifying, question of what it means to be a citizen of a state. Africa's dilemmas have less to do with what color makes of a man than with what states make of their constitutions. To suggest otherwise is nothing but leftist racism and paternalism.

Viewed objectively, the current struggles we see in Africa—the near or complete anarchy in shattered West African states; the inner formlessness and sputtering warfare of Congo; the furious disappointment of Zimbabwe; the ethnic and religious divisions, as well as the crippling corruption, in Nigeria; the recent slaughters in Rwanda and Burundi—amount to a continent trying to find its way out of a swamp into which others led it. Countries of more immediate promise, such as South Africa and Senegal, have plentiful issues of their own to resolve, and no country is fully safe from the temptations of factionalism and selfishness. But just as we may suspect that Africa's internal strife will not end overnight, we also may fairly assume that it will not last forever. The fundamental question, despite the obscurant horrors of AIDS, dictatorship, and violent atrocity, is: What might come out of all this? What might the Africa of the future look like? Or will it be Africas, in the plural, perhaps with social progress and the development of regional power in South Africa and in East Africa, with regressive social and government structures (or the lack thereof) elsewhere? Will we see a rich Africa and a poor one? What will the region's deep cultural differences bring about? Which qualities will prove strongest, blood ties, belief, or allegiance to the state? At present, the trend is for African states to differentiate themselves from one another as regards progress, but the events of a decade are fragile indicators of the long-term future. Will Africa force the world to redefine success, on lower but far broader terms?

The safest bet is, indeed, that Africa's future will not be uniform, that the process of differentiation between successful states and the failed will continue. Perhaps no continent faces so many negative factors, or has so many variables at work. But when Africa begins to wake from its often-nightmarish sleep to look for alternative bonds of community, it will not look north, where it is bounded by implacable, age-old enemies who simply have put on velvet gloves. Nor can it look east, where it faces the most ferocious prejudices. When Africa finally turns its face to the world, it will look across the Atlantic, to the Americas.

The Three Non-Amigos

Latin America, the other half of the Postcolonial Zone, presents three distinct cultures to the world, none of which has integrated deeply with the others. Some countries, such as Peru or Brazil, exhibit two competing cultures within their borders, while others, such as Argentina or Chile, are dominated by a single culture. Bolivia contains two parallel, but weirdly separate cultures (and a number of odd subcultures). A very few countries, most notably Cuba, have moved toward a genuine fusion culture (in this regard, Mexico is promising over the long term). But for most Latin American countries of varied ethnic and cultural composition, integration is often superficial—constitutionally enshrined, but disregarded in practice—and more about socio-political claims than about genuine fusion (most obviously, in Brazil). Latin America remains a region of "soft apartheid."

The three basic cultures of Latin American are:

- Latin (European in origin)
- African
- Indian (indigenous)

None of these cultures are "pure" today. Each has mutated over the centuries (or, in the case of Iberian populations transplanted to Latin American, failed to develop psychologically from a colonial mentality). Today's ethnic Europeans are not only profoundly different from the contemporary populations of their ancestral countries, behind which they lag in terms of social development, but differ widely within the region. African culture, too, incorporated local influences. Perhaps the least changed are the indigenous populations, wherever they have survived in sufficient density to maintain autonomous cultures—as in Bolivia and much of Peru, but even in remote areas of Mexico, Venezuela, or in upper-Amazon Brazil (although eco-tourism likely will destroy the integrity of local tribes in ways that European conquerors failed to do).

Unable to blend constructively over the centuries, each culture has stagnated. While we may admire the music or dance of Brazil or Argentina, with their fusion of influences, sambas and tangos do not build healthy postmodern societies by themselves.

Yet there is more cause for hope today than there ever has been for Latin America. While the current cliché of the triumph of democracy does, indeed, have its positive aspects, the most important factor changing Latin America is the rise of a new generation of leaders, largely educated in the United States, who are not content with the bad habits of centuries. Democracy doesn't make men, men make democracy—although some Washington pundits imagine democracy as some sort of political miracle of loaves and fishes of which men and women are but the passive recipients. The second most important factor is the rise of a global information culture. Though it has yet to affect the lower classes and the underclass to a meaningful degree, it is making a tremendous difference in the awareness, ambitions, and attitudes of the middle classes and skilled members of the working class. The third factor is demographic growth, which is forcing change by itself. Finally, the wild card is the spread (as in Africa) of charismatic Protestant Christianity, which, while empowering to individuals and entire classes, may have the capacity, in the long term, to release uncontrollable social energies. While the world watches Asia, the most innovative and surprising futures—and, potentially, the unexpected dangers—may be brewing up slowly in the Postcolonial Zone of Latin America and sub-Saharan Africa.

This largely ignored region has the greatest capacity for building alternative futures of any portion of the globe.

Equality? In Principle, of Course . . .

Most of Latin America maintains a soft apartheid system in which ethnic Europeans continue to dominate the political, economic, cultural, and social scene. In countries such as Argentina, where the indigenous population was virtually exterminated (quite late, in the nineteenth century, from the southern pampas to Patagonia) and slaves were few, this hardly matters—the population is Latin, primarily ethnic Italian, then Spanish, with a broad monotheist admixture below those two primary groups (from Welsh to Lebanese). Argentina is something of a dream country for leftists to study, since its fundamental structural problem is its class system, with an extravagant, shamelessly corrupt ruling class, a servile middle class (servile at least until now), and a yearning, politically vigorous proletariat that historically has been susceptible to demagogues, from

Rosas through Peron to Menem, the latter a man who could sell you the same bottle of snake oil several times over.

Yet Argentina has proved that leftist, statist solutions do not work, foundering on simple greed. Today's Argentina, with its aspirations to first-world status, has simply been living beyond its means far too long. It is the state equivalent of an individual who grabbed every credit card offer that ever arrived in the mail, then maxed out the cards immediately. Even before its current financial crisis, Argentina had the highest rate of citizens undergoing psychoanalysis in the world, as well as a high suicide rate (just listen to a few good tangos—they're suicide soundtracks). If Argentina were a single human being, we would recognize the personality type immediately: the sort who always looks for the easy way out, the angle, the quick fix, the high-liver who doesn't worry about paying his bills. Today, there is an especially sharp edge to the social divisions in Argentina, with the population divided anew into those few who could hoard dollars offshore and the majority of the population, which relied on its salaries and passbook savings to survive. The fact that a majority of the population is suffering to some degree would make Argentina ripe for another round of authoritarianism, were it not for the fecklessness of the political class and the overall sense of being defeated.

Argentines know they need serious reforms, but they do not want them to interfere with their lifestyles. The country looks played out. Of course, so did Germany in 1932. I do not suggest that the rise of an extreme right-wing movement is on the horizon—another round of empty populism is more likely—but that no one yet knows which path Argentina will follow as it tries to marshal its energies to move forward again. What does a relatively developed (and almost hysterically vain) country do when its leaders have bankrupted it and there are no appealing options left?

The Postcolonial Zone truly is humankind's biggest laboratory.

In Brazil, a country of profound ethnic complexity, national propaganda has long held that society is integrated—yet, with few exceptions, the rich are white, mixed-race citizens are in the middle, the blacks are the poorest of the poor, and the Indians of the interior are regarded as curiosities beyond the pale—as pet Martians valued by space travelers from Europe and North America. Yet, in a disconnect of the sort that isn't supposed to happen, according to development theory, Brazil's popular culture is perhaps the best integrated and most mature in the entire zone: The music is African combined with Portuguese to create a distinctive new form that is as light and flirty as the best Argentine music is brooding and self-dramatizing (although I must confess I prefer the Argentine tangos of Piazzolla—real wrist-slasher, it's-been-raining-for-a-month-and-my-baby's-long-gone stuff). Likewise, Brazilian social mores are unique and, if anything, behaviorally anti-Catholic (whereas, in Mexico, the local hybrid of Catholicism, an admixture of Spanish medievalism and Indian traditions, remains extraordinarily powerful, despite decades of ruthless government attempts to destroy organized religion in the wake of the Mexican Revolution). An academic analyst looking only at the statistics of poverty, exclusion, and inequity, but not knowing the name of the country, would predict that Brazil was over-ripe for a revolution. But national character trumps theory. Brazil, despite intervals of authoritarianism, has been remarkably stable in comparison to many of its neighbors. Brazil is an extremely violent country, but the violence is personal, not collective or purposeful.

In Peru, recent elections constituted a genuine upheaval, with Alejandro Toledo, an ethnic Indian (albeit with a North American wife), elected to the presidency. In the Latin American context, this is a far greater jolt than the election of an American of African ancestry to the Presidency would be in the United States. While I am not espousing Marxist solutions to anything (because they just don't work), analysis of the class system remains the best initial approach to understanding Latin America's persistent problems—and that class system is based primarily upon race, secondarily upon wealth and culture.

There are a few hopeful exceptions: Mexico, where genuine and powerful changes are underway at last, despite deep remaining problems; Chile, where a modern society appears to be solidifying itself, though ultra-conservative elements remain influential; and Cuba, whose government we may despise, but whose genuine integration and limited meritocracy (restricted by political, not social, barriers), provides one of the few inspiring models for a workable fusion of society in Latin America. In the post-Castro years, Cuba has a very good chance at becoming a model democratic, market-economy state, without significant racial divisions—but it will not become a "model" for others (talk of Cuban models—except the sort who walk down a runway—will die with Castro). Social models don't work. Countries do not imitate when it comes to social systems. They may imitate forms of government or economy, but populations grow into their own organic forms of social organization. Attempts to force deep and broad social changes on a population never succeed, no matter how many are killed to clear the way, as the last century proved all too painfully. You can, in a successful, rule-of-law state, force through one reasoned change at a time, as the United States did with court-ordered school integration. But you cannot force human beings of different ethnic, religious, and cultural backgrounds to harmonize until they are ready.

The current turmoil in Venezuela, too, is essentially an ethnically based class struggle, pitting the least successful mixed-race citizens and Indians, led by their savior of the moment, President Hugo Chavez, against a white and pale-mestizo traditional ruling class. Colonial rule is gone, but colonial class distinctions persist to an astonishing degree. While leftist revolutionaries, from Guevara to Allende, had no workable solutions, we must admit that they were correct that Latin American societies were—and remain—brutally unfair. And race continues to trump every other factor, even in (or especially in) countries where the overwhelming majority of the population are non-white. Even in the most promising countries, when any family has a blue-eyed, blond-haired male child, that child will be treated as the family's great hope and may expect social deference.

Except for countries with high levels of ethnic homogeneity, such as Chile, the most hopeful countries in Latin America are the northernmost—Mexico and Cuba—adjacent to the U.S. and subject to its magnetic pull. They are not the richest countries (especially not Cuba), but their emerging social orders are setting them up for future success, whereas we should worry about potential stagnation in Argentina and even Brazil, countries which so often have looked so irresistibly inviting to so many analysts and investors. Whether modern (and postmodern) values can triumph over the *prevailing feudalism* of Latin American society in the coming decades is the primary issue confronting the vast region between Tierra del Fuego and the Rio Grande.

The Last Preserve of Feudalism

I term this region—Africa and Latin America—the Postcolonial Zone because it is that portion of the earth where, even two hundred years after independence (in Latin America's case), the pernicious legacies of colonialism endure most powerfully. We tend to think of colonialism as a formal mechanism, such as the rule of a given territory by a distant state imposed in order to extract benefits from the colony. But colonialism is also a matter of culture and mentality. In this regard, Latin America is still very much a collection of colonies. Two centuries after Bolivar, O'Higgins, and San Martin, the spirit of the *conquistadores* of five centuries ago, their public behavior and social values, persists, from the barrios of Los Angeles to the Rio de la Plata.

An in-depth study of the formation of sixteenth-century Spanish culture and its export is far beyond the scope of this paper (although this is a topic of immediate relevance to understanding today's Latin America), and what follows is only a very short summary of influences and connections that usually go ignored by strategists and theorists of international diplomacy. And all this is predicated upon the conviction, based upon extensive firsthand observation of the world, that you cannot get close to meaningful insights unless you are willing to examine current problems in a deep historical context. Just as a psychologist will ask about a troubled human being's childhood, we must ask about the troubled childhood of nations, if we wish to understand them.

The first thing any student of Latin America must grasp is the origin of today's Latin American male values and the lingering ideal of the strongman, or *caudillo*, with his dual nature of tyrant and dispenser of gifts—even where he is officially gone from the political scene (President Menem of Argentina was nothing more than a modernized "big man," one who ruled with bribes rather than bullets). The real origin of the Latin American strongman, obsessed with public honor and personal authority, goes even beyond the Spain of the early sixteenth century, with its ruthless knights, so mighty of sword arm, but utterly lacking in personal restraint . . . all the way back to the Moorish occupation of Spain. The political strongman, but also the dominant family head in a Brazilian *favela* or a shack across the river from El Paso, the brutal drug lord, and the teenage assassin who kills from greed and vanity, can each be traced to the intolerant Islamic culture of North Africa—which gutted the rich, creative culture of Iberian Islam centuries before the end of the Spanish *reconquista* in 1492 made a formal end of the Muslim presence.

In late-medieval Spain, the two dominant monotheist forces of the age, Islam and Catholicism, did battle. The fanaticism on one side inspired greater fanaticism on the other, inspiring, in turn, yet more fanaticism (the Spanish Inquisition, which we associate with hunting witches, had far more to do with uncovering false conversions among Muslims and Jews, and with maintaining religious militancy). Despite the attempts of revisionist historians to paint late-Moorish Spain as something of a dreamy Atlantis destroyed by nasty Christians, by the closing centuries of the Moorish presence both sides had hardened ideologically. Yes, Christian knights sometimes fought as mercenaries under Muslim banners—not least Rodrigo Diaz, "El Cid," whose nickname has Islamic origins: *al sayyid*, the big man, chief, or lord—and feudal states crossed religious lines for their advantage. But, ultimately, this became a bitter struggle between two aggressive, expansionist faiths. At first, Christianity was on the defensive, then Islam found itself on the ropes—across eight centuries of struggle, a period of turbulence that could not help but shape the Spanish character.

Indeed, both sides learned from one another—with the Christians getting the advantage of the lingering traces of Islamic scholarship and thought left over from the true golden centuries of Muslim Cordoban culture toward the close of the first millennium. But the *conquistadores* who came to the New World, men such as Cortez and Pizarro, were an amalgam of European feudal knights and Islamic warriors, combining, along with their exemplary bravery, the most callous, intolerant, and brutal qualities of both cultures. A true man despised the importance of life, although he generally preferred to illustrate the principle on others. And the centuries of religious warfare in Spain had taught even men for whom religion was a mere formality to regard their enemies as less than human. Slaughtering Aztecs or Incas came naturally to these conquerors, especially when local practices appeared repellent and opaque to Spanish logic. The persistent Latin male values of personal honor requiring the respect of others; physical prowess (or, at least, the ability to enforce physical domination); empowering wealth as the ultimate worldly attainment and the association of land, or at least turf, with wealth; control of females and an emphasis on female "virtue" within the family, but on the "conquest" of females without; the low priority assigned to education; the lack of personal self-restraint; the sudden lurches into piety; and the emphasis on building, through largesse and favors, a web of personal allegiances and obligations, are all fundamentally anti-modern qualities. It is only a slight exaggeration to claim that, behaviorally, Latin males are medieval Muslims crossed with a Spanish Catholic knight of the waning Middle Ages.

Another related contribution to the persistence of feudal social forms, even in the face of liberal constitutions, is the emphasis on the extended family as society's organizing principle in Latin America. This obviously inhibits the development of a meritocracy, but it also tends to consolidate assets in land and foreign accounts, starving societies of investment capital—and of the psychological investment necessary for development and a sense of civic responsibility. Colombia, today, remains very much a feudal society, where no one much wants to fight for the state (we may hope that this will change), but where families will do all they can to maintain their own power. A rich Colombian will readily pay a kidnapper's ransom demands, but will go to great lengths to avoid paying his taxes.

The United States had many advantages in its cultural development, but two are of immediate consequence: The U.S. attracted a wide range of immigrants from different cultures, and, from the beginning, multiple interpretations of religious faith existed—and thrived. Citizens of the thirteen colonies and then the United States had to build cooperative relationships across familial, national-origin, and religious lines. Latin America, on the other hand, suffered from an iron uniformity from the beginning, and family-centered, rather than corporate, behavior became the fundamental organizing principle of both society and politics. We find it unthinkable that a modern politician would provide plum jobs for all of his relatives, but the traditional Latin American politician would find it incomprehensible not to do so. This has begun to change at the top, but, in building a modern society, the local level is decisive.

When you study the political alignments in most of Latin America, the U.S. political system is a guide of little value. Study the factions of fifteenth-century Spain and how allegiances were built—or, better still, the history plays of Shakespeare—all the Henry plays and Richard II, Richard III, and King John. Coalitions are still built upon families, secondarily upon ideologies or laws. Latin America is still very much a medieval society—with skyscrapers, corporate jets, and Mercedes limos.

Like Islam, Latin America skipped the Renaissance.

The Hermetically-Sealed Empire

If you lived in Buenos Aires in the eighteenth century and wished to order a book from Europe—and if the book was not forbidden by church or crown—your position on a great river feeding into the Atlantic Ocean was irrelevant. Because Spain maintained careful control over trade and movement, long employing only a few approved ports (all in the Caribbean) for an entire continent's trade with the world, your order traveled by mule westward over the Andes to Lima, Peru. Then your order sailed north to Panama, crossed the isthmus on another mule, and boarded a ship for Spain. The book then retraced the same route to your hands (I am resisting jokes about the original Amazon.com).

This mercantile lunacy had several effects, none of them good. First, it sealed a continent from external influences, which Spain judged wise, but which meant that ecclesiastical painting in eighteenth-century South America looked like sixteenth-century painting in Europe. Societies were closed, inbred, ordered closely by church and state, and isolated. Lacking exposure to wave after wave of European intellectual and social dynamism (by the end of the seventeenth century, Spain itself had become a backwater, so Latin America was the distant backwater of a backwater), societies followed a different developmental path, preserving social structures, strictures, and patterns of behavior that elsewhere had died away. By the nineteenth century, the duel over a point of honor was outlawed in most European states, but it still occurs in the Latin American world, as far north as Los Angeles—although it is altogether a less formal affair these days.

When the colonial yoke was thrown off by the Spanish colonies in the first decades of the nineteenth century, it made surprisingly little difference. Travel opportunities abroad increased for the upper classes, but internal travel became even more dangerous as rural order broke down. The rich could buy a wider range of products. And taxes, when they could be collected, were stolen locally, instead of in Madrid. But the revolutions, and the near-endless coups and revolutions that followed those revolutions, had something of the nature of wild, bloody parties, a letting-off of steam, after which little changed and long hangovers had to be endured. The true believers fared worst, and Simon Bolivar died of a broken heart.

Globalized information is finally having an impact upon Latin America, waking broad swathes of the population to new possibilities and providing foreign comparisons for local conditions. Perhaps the most profound effect of the information explosion in Latin America is that it works against fatalism, suggesting that things do not have to be the way they are now and always have been. We will not know the results for at least a generation—perhaps longer—but the proliferation of citizens' organizations is one hopeful indicator. And it is harder for any leader to tell great lies and have them believed.

These days, the books arrive much more quickly.

The Mighty Fallen

It is easy to forget that Portugal initiated the age of European colonialism. Not only was tiny Portugal once a great imperial power, but its empire quietly lingered on long after others had faded away. This "Lusitanian Empire" once stretched from Brazil, along the African coast, to Goa in India, and beyond to East Timor. And that empire, though impoverished and threadbare, ended less than three decades ago. It was the longest-lasting European empire. When the last Portuguese troops left Mozambique and Angola, and the Indonesians grabbed East Timor, it marked the end of five hundred years of foreign adventures for Lisbon. As with the influence of eight hundred years of Moorish Islamic occupation on Spain, so Portugal influenced much of the world far more than we realize today. And the empire continues to strike back. Mariza, one of the two greatest fado singers of our time (fado is the haunting, ravishing national style of song in Portugal) is black, with roots in Mozambique, and Cesaria Evora, a Cape Verdean who sings in Portuguese, has become a world-music star. Of course, Brazilian music is sung in Portuguese as well, as is a surprising amount of new music from Africa. Ms. Evora is especially interesting, because her music, from her island home set well off the West African coast, blends African, Brazilian, and Portuguese strains until they are something new and inseparable. Perhaps she is simply a singer among many—but I wonder if she is a cultural harbinger of a reordered world.

There are two important influences we miss in assessing Latin America. The first is the Portuguese influence, which ties that continent-within-a-continent, Brazil, not only to Europe (a fading tie), but also to so much of Africa. Slavery only ended in Brazil a few years after the American Civil War (and de facto slavery lingered much longer). Integration within Brazilian society, though professed, is in many ways less accomplished than it is in the United States. Yet the influence of Africa on Brazilian society is profound, and Brazil, with its historical, cultural, ethnic, and linguistic ties, could function as an important bridge country to Africa in the future. Because of the way we compartmentalize, we overlook the existence of a centuries-old tie between Africa and Latin America.

Nor is that tie limited to Portuguese-speaking countries. Spanish-language countries of the slave belt, from Brazil northward through the Guyanas, Venezuela, and lowland Colombia into Panama, then across so much of the Caribbean, all have cultures that, to greater or lesser degrees, have digested African influences brought by slaves. Even English- and French-speaking islands, from Haiti to Jamaica, bind Africa to the New World—and the New World to Africa. "Afro-American" culture isn't something limited to our own black citizens. It is one way of describing our entire culture.

While there is one important difference between the former Portuguese and Spanish colonies—Portuguese influence crossed the Atlantic in both directions, while Spanish influence was largely a one-way affair, making Brazil's ties to Africa much richer in their potential—the African influence on Latin America, and the search for common ground between these two elements of the Postcolonial Zone could prove a very productive line of inquiry.

Of course, this writer is not the first to notice that Africa's influence upon Latin America could be turned around into Latin

American influence on Africa. As soon as the Portuguese left Angola, Fidel Castro dispatched Cuban troops to assist in the "liberation struggle." We saw it as World Communism on the march. But it was really a canny recognition of natural affinities. Ultimately, the Cubans lacked the resources to hang on in Africa (although the parties they backed won, and ours lost, more often than not). But the United States has almost inexhaustible resources. Should we be clever enough to learn from Castro's failed vision?

Consider the strategic neglect of the entire Postcolonial Zone. Europe sends aid to Africa, but even the French presence is much diminished. There is little current sense of the continent's potential, only of its liabilities. In Latin America, some countries have complex European ties, from the tragicomic Argentine love for things British (despite the Falklands War) to Madrid's attempts to keep a trans-Atlantic political bridge in reasonably good repair. But Latin America has long been a graveyard for European ambitions (and empires), and the neglect with which it is regarded as a strategic factor is curious, amounting to a surrender to the Monroe Doctrine in an expanded form and to U.S. hegemony. The only missing piece is that the U.S. doesn't bother to be much of a hegemon.

Are we looking in the wrong places for strategic advantage? Or at least not looking in enough different places?

Unexpected Opportunities

Certainly, we will need to pay attention to the Islamic world for many years to come. And China is far too great to ignore, whatever behavior we expect from Beijing. But consider just a few ways in which the traditional wisdom—or just plain habit—might be turned on its head. This extended essay finally comes down to three alternative lines of strategic thought:

- We see Europe as safe and benign, assuming it will always remain so. Yet, if attacked or sufficiently threatened, Europe may turn again to the export of violence. The United States need not worry overmuch, but other states sharing the Monotheist Zone with Europe had best be careful—especially Islamic states whose citizens might initiate campaigns of terror against Europe, imagining Europeans to be weak-willed.

- We see Asia as the region of the greatest future potential when, in fact, North America is the area of the greatest continuing potential. Asia, while it may grow wealthier, is less likely to innovate new social and governmental forms. Asian development will be evolutionary, not revolutionary, and some countries may stagnate for decades in a cultural straitjacket, as Japan is in danger of doing. For alternative futures, we must look to areas we have ignored.

- When we look at Africa and, to a lesser degree, Latin America, we see only problems. Given the unfinished nature of these societies, this may be the last human frontier, the zone in which the twenty-first century will see the most dramatic— and perhaps positive—changes. We are foolish if we refuse even to consider the potential in front of us, especially since Africa's and Latin America's natural strategic partner is North America. Ours is the society with cultural ties to both continents, we have done them the least harm, and we provide the most attractive model for the future. We have an appeal as irresistible as our wealth and power are great. Natural affinities are there, right in front of our faces, but our attention is fixed elsewhere. With exclusive, competitive societies in Asia and introverted societies in Europe, our natural sphere of influence lies southward. Africa, especially, may not seem very appealing to American strategic thinkers at present, but that is because we think in short stretches when we think about the future—we run strategic sprints when the greatest power in history is a natural for the marathon. If we truly were adept, the twenty-first century might end with a cultural and economic triangle (and, frankly, a new, benign form of American empire) encompassing North America, Latin America, and much of Africa. Latin America and sub-Saharan Africa may be our last "collectible frontiers." If you want to expand your power and influence, "go where they ain't."

What if the twenty-first century turns out to be an Atlantic, not a Pacific century, based on a huge Afro-Latino-American triangle of strategic power and resources, with aging Fortress Europe looking on?

The future likely will turn out far differently than any of us can imagine, but that does not mean we can afford not to imagine it.

In Conclusion

This is, of course, a brief and superficial overview of the strategic environment. To some, it may appear marginally relevant, at best, given the immediacy of our struggle with terrorism. But that is a struggle we are bound to win, although we likely will suffer painful wounds along the way. I argue, instead, that this is exactly the time to devote at least a fraction of our attention and resources to the out-years, to alternatives, to both threats *and* opportunities.

The twentieth century conditioned us to think about the threats. Thus, we may be missing some of the greatest opportunities in history. Beyond all the speculation here about the effects of different forms of religion, the power of culture, the patterns of history, and issues of wealth and might, we may, without embarrassment, acknowledge that the United States has one distinguishing gift that sets it apart: We are able to see the potential in others. The vast Post-colonial Zone, spanning two continents, is waiting for us to notice its potential.

This is not necessarily an argument for more aid (although, in the case of Africa, effectively targeted, stringently controlled aid might work wonders) or for a flood of investment (a bucket poured well, here and there, might be preferable). And it is certainly not a recommendation for military exploits or political bullying. In the end, I only suggest that those who live in poverty and powerlessness in disordered societies today need not always be poor and weak. How might we make today's victims tomorrow's allies?

Cuba sent arms to Africa, but it also sent doctors. Castro's vision failed, but he *had* a vision, for exactly those continents under discussion here. He saw the hidden unities. Surely, the United States can do better than that old, failed cigar-chomper in Havana. If he could see the potential a quarter century ago, how on earth can we continue to miss it?

God's Real Estate

New York Post

April 13, 2003

One of the greatest blessings enjoyed by the United States is that God hasn't claimed any local real estate. The insistence in so much of the world that one divinity or another cherishes a specific handful of dust remains one of humankind's great curses.

Viewed honestly, the competition between faiths and creeds over sacred ground remains a cancer of the human condition. Whether we speak of millennia of bloody contests for control of Jerusalem or the bloodshed over plans to build a Hindu temple on the site of a razed mosque in Ayodhya, the importance of Karbala in Iraq or the destruction of Sufi shrines by Muslim fundamentalists, competing claims over bits of earth have spawned the world's most enduring and inherently insoluble conflicts.

The amount of suffering human beings are willing to inflict on one another over a corner of dirt is impossible to reconcile with the basic tenets of any of the world's leading religions. Men will fight for their religion, but they will massacre for their religion's totems. And sacred earth is the greatest totem of all, the ultimate idol.

Certainly, some religious groups in the United States value specific pieces of land, from the national shrine of the Virgin in Emmitsburg, Maryland, to the grounds of the Mormon Temple in Salt Lake City. But the roots do not run sufficiently deep to tap history's underground rivers of blood and, still more vitally, the sanctified ground is not contested.

We Americans also benefit from religious diversity so great that no single group can bully the others any longer. Our civilization is young, its potential far from exhausted, and our land is wide. But the ancient homelands of the world's dominant religions have produced successive systems of belief that cannot be reconciled with one another, all competing for validation in close proximity.

While most of us may yearn for peaceful, equitable solutions to enduring religious conflicts, realism demands that we ask whether or not these competitions over bits of earth can ever be brought to an end without catastrophe to one side, the other, or both.

Of course, we all want peace in the Middle East. But is peace a realistic expectation when the claims of each party to the same small portions of earth are as irreducible and divinely sanctioned as the claims of the other? Outsiders ask why a shrine cannot be shared, but the hard core of believers in every great religion equates compromise with blasphemy.

Still worse, the world's competitions over sacred plots of soil profoundly energize believers on all sides. In the endless contest between systems of belief, ruins, temples, and shrines are tangible manifestations of religion, far easier for fanatics to embrace than are otherworldly spirits and admonitions to charity. Men who barely understand the tenets of their faith will die blissfully for a half-acre of wasteland anointed by their god. But they would much rather slaughter the competition for it.

This focus on real estate above all drags God (by any name) out of the heavens and makes of Him little more than a merciless landlord. One cannot help suspecting that, no matter how devout the intention, insisting that God is more richly present in one locale than another reduces the divine to a human scale, making of faith little more than a range war. Fastening God to a plot of earth renders the incomprehensible a finite thing we can touch, but it replaces transcendent beauty with the greed of ownership.

I do not suggest a solution to this problem, since I see none. But we need to define the problem more clearly and honestly than we have yet done, if we Americans are to act wisely and incisively in this tumultuous world. We need to be extremely wary of embroiling ourselves in any conflict that centers on the claims of competing religions to mastery of a particular sliver of earth.

This leads the argument to Israel (although there is no end of other examples, if often on a lesser scale). I am a firm and determined supporter of Israel, out of moral obligation and deep conviction. The people of Israel are fighting for survival against enemies who seek to destroy them, and the prospect of genocide is intolerable. Yet I cannot help feeling that the promised land for every religion represented in the United States lies here in America, not in the ghost-ridden domains of history.

Doubtless, this view will be judged insensitive by many. But isn't it a reduction of the divine to insist that God resides particularly in St. Peter's Basilica, or in any one mosque or temple? We struggle to tie God down like Gulliver. Despite the insistence of dubious texts on the sanctity of one bit of ground or another, one suspects that the true Jerusalem abides within us.

When we see Hindus and Muslims butchering each other over a forsaken acre in India, or listen to the maddened voices on every side in the Middle East, as we witness Nigerian Muslims desecrating churches while Nigerian Christians defile mosques, how can we escape the feeling that we have done a poor job of reverence? We have elevated dust above divinity.

Such conflicts may define much of our new century.

There are many respects in which the United States differs wonderfully from the old worlds we Americans left behind. But is there any more important advantage in continuing to build our unprecedented multi-ethnic, multi-faith society than the inability of zealots in our midst to convince us that God favors one bit of earth over another?

When our congregations outgrow our churches, temples, or mosques, we build anew on a bigger plot, either down the street or miles away in a suburb. Communion in the "little brown church in the vale" has always been a movable feast. This flexibility grants us a tremendous strategic and moral advantage.

Of course, we Americans have strong religious traditions. The vision of a "city on a hill" is part of the fabric of our national being. But that city has never been a physical place, except in the sense of the nation as a whole. The simple fact that God—again, by any name or names—doesn't do real estate in the United States is so great a blessing that one almost suspects that we are—all of us, no matter our faith—truly a chosen people.

In Praise of Attrition

Parameters

Summer 2004

"Who dares to call the child by its true name?"

—Goethe, *Faust*

In our military, the danger of accepting the traditional wisdom has become part of the traditional wisdom. Despite our lip service to creativity and innovation, we rarely pause to question fundamentals. Partly, of course, this is because officers in today's Army or Marine Corps operate at a wartime tempo, with little leisure for reflection. Yet, even more fundamentally, deep prejudices have crept into our military—as well as into the civilian world—that obscure elementary truths.

There is no better example of our unthinking embrace of an error than our rejection of the term "war of attrition." The belief that attrition, as an objective or a result, is inherently negative is simply wrong. A soldier's job is to kill the enemy. All else, however important it may appear at the moment, is secondary. And to kill the enemy is to attrit the enemy. All wars in which bullets—or arrows—fly are wars of attrition.

Of course, the term "war of attrition" conjures the unimaginative slaughter of the Western Front, with massive casualties on both sides. Last year, when journalists wanted to denigrate our military's occupation efforts in Iraq, the term bubbled up again and again. The notion that killing even the enemy is a bad thing in war has been exacerbated by the defense industry's claims, seconded by glib military careerists, that precision weapons and technology in general had irrevocably changed the nature of warfare. But the nature of warfare never changes—only its superficial manifestations.

The U.S. Army also did great harm to its own intellectual and practical grasp of war by trolling for theories, especially in the 1980s. Theories don't win wars. Well-trained, well-led soldiers in well-equipped armies do. And they do so by killing effectively. Yet we heard a great deal of nonsense about "maneuver warfare" as the solution to all our woes, from our numerical disadvantage vis-à-vis the Warsaw Pact to our knowledge that the "active defense" on the old inner-German border was political tomfoolery and a military sham—and, frankly, the best an Army gutted by Vietnam and its long hangover could hope to do.

Maneuver is not a solution unto itself, any more than technology is. It exists in an ever-readjusting balance with fires. Neither fires nor maneuver can be dispensed with. This sounds obvious, but that which is obvious is not always that which is valued or pursued. Those who would be theorists always prefer the arcane to the actual.

Precious few military campaigns have been won by maneuver alone—at least not since the Renaissance and the days of chessboard battles between corporate condottieri. Napoleon's Ulm campaign, the Japanese march on Singapore, and a few others make up the short list of "bloodless" victories.

Even campaigns that appear to be triumphs of maneuver prove, on closer inspection, to have been successful because of a dynamic combination of fire and maneuver. The opening, conventional phase of the Franco-Prussian War, culminating in the grand envelopment at Sedan, is often cited as an example of brilliant maneuver at the operational level—yet the road to Paris was paved with more German than French corpses. It was a bloody war that happened to be fought on the move. Other campaigns whose success was built on audacious maneuvers nonetheless required attrition battles along the way or at their climax, from Moltke's brilliant concentration on multiple axes at Koenigsgraetz (urgent marches to a gory day), to the German blitzkrieg efforts against the Poles, French, and Russians, and on to Operation Desert Storm, in which daring operational maneuvers positioned tactical firepower for a series of short, convincingly sharp engagements. Even the Inchon landing, one of the two or three most daring operations led by an American field commander, failed to bring the Korean War to a conclusion.

More often than not, an overreliance on bold operational maneuvers to win a swift campaign led to disappointment, even disaster. One may argue for centuries about the diversion of a half dozen German divisions from the right flank of the Schlieffen Plan in 1914, but the attempt to win the war in one swift sweep led to more than four years of stalemate on the Western Front. In the same campaign season, Russian attempts at grand maneuver in the vicinity of the Masurian lakes collapsed in the face of counter-maneuvers and sharp encounter battles—a German active defense that drew on Napoleon's "strategy of the central position"—while, in Galicia, aggressive maneuvering proved to be exactly the wrong approach for the Austro-Hungarian military—which was ill-prepared for encounter battles.

There is no substitute for shedding the enemy's blood.

Despite initial maneuver victories against Russia and in the Western Desert, a German overreliance on maneuver as a substitute for adequate firepower ultimately led to the destruction of Nazi armies. Time and again, from Lee's disastrous Gettysburg campaign to the race to the Yalu in Korea, overconfidence in an army's capabilities to continue to assert its power during grand maneuvers has led to stunning reverses. The results were not merely a matter of Clausewitzian culminating points, but of fundamentally flawed strategies.

Operation Iraqi Freedom, one of the most successful military campaigns in history, was intended to be a new kind of war of maneuver, in which aerial weapons would "shock and awe" a humbled opponent into surrender while ground forces did a little light dusting in the house of war. But instead of being decided by maneuvered technologies, the three-week war was fought and won—triumphantly—by soldiers and marines employing both aggressive operational maneuvers *and* devastating tactical firepower.

The point is not that maneuver is the stepbrother of firepower, but that there is no single answer to the battlefield, no formula. The commander's age-old need to balance incisive movements with the application of weaponry is unlikely to change even well beyond our lifetimes. It's not an either-or matter; it's about getting the integration right in each specific case.

Although no two campaigns are identical, the closest we can come to an American superpower model of war would be this:

strategic maneuver, then operational maneuver to deliver fires, then tactical fires to enable further maneuver. Increasingly, strategic fires play a role—although they do not win wars or decide them. Of course, no battlefield is ever quite so simple as this proposition, but any force that loses its elementary focus on killing the enemy swiftly and relentlessly until that enemy surrenders unconditionally cripples itself.

Far from entering an age of maneuver, we have entered a new age of attrition warfare in two kinds: First, the war against religious terrorism is unquestionably a war of attrition—if one of your enemies is left alive or unimprisoned, he will continue trying to kill you and destroy your civilization. Second, Operation Iraqi Freedom, for all its dashing maneuvers, provided a new example of a postmodern war of attrition—one in which the casualties are overwhelmingly on one side.

Nothing says that wars of attrition have to be fair.

It's essential to purge our minds of the clichéd images the term "war of attrition" evokes. Certainly we do not and will not seek wars in which vast casualties are equally distributed between our own forces and the enemy's. But a one-sided war of attrition, enabled by our broad range of superior capabilities, is a strong model for a twenty-first-century American way of war.

No model is consistently applicable. That is—or should be—a given. Wars create exceptions, to the eternal chagrin of military commanders and the consistent embarrassment of theorists. One of our greatest national and military strengths is our adaptability. Unlike many other cultures, we have an almost-primal aversion to wearing the straitjacket of theory, and our independence of mind serves us very well indeed. But the theorists are always there, like devils whispering in our ears, telling us that airpower will win this war, or that satellite "intelligence" obviates the need for human effort, or that a mortal enemy will be persuaded to surrender by a sound-and-light show.

Precision weapons unquestionably have value, but they are expensive and do not cause adequate destruction to impress a hardened enemy. The first time a guided bomb hits the deputy's desk, it will get his chief's attention, but if precision weaponry fails both to annihilate the enemy's leadership and to somehow convince the army and population it has been defeated, it leaves the job to the soldier once again. Those who live in the technological clouds simply do not grasp the importance of graphic, extensive destruction in convincing an opponent of his defeat.

Focus on killing the enemy. With fires. With maneuver. With sticks and stones and polyunsaturated fats. In a disciplined military, aggressive leaders and troops can always be restrained. But it's difficult to persuade leaders schooled in caution that their mission is not to keep an entire corps' tanks on line, but to rip the enemy's heart out. We have made great progress from the ballet of Desert Storm—"spoiled" only by then–Major General Barry McCaffrey's insistence on breaking out of the chorus line and kicking the enemy instead of thin air—to the close-with-the-enemy spirit of last year's race to Baghdad.

In the bitter years after Vietnam, when our national leaders succumbed to the myth that the American people would not tolerate casualties, elements within our military—although certainly not everyone—grew morally and practically timid. By the mid-1990s, the U.S. Army's informal motto appeared to be "We won't fight, and you can't make us."

There were obvious reasons for this. Our military—especially the Army and Marine Corps—felt betrayed by our national leadership over Vietnam. Then President Reagan evacuated Beirut shortly after the bombing of our Marine barracks on the city's outskirts—beginning a long series of bipartisan retreats in the face of terror that ultimately led to 9/11. We hit a low point in Mogadishu, when Army Rangers, Special Operations elements, and line troops delivered a devastating blow against General Aideed's irregulars—only to have President Clinton declare defeat by pulling out. One may argue about the rationale for our presence in Somalia and about the dangers of mission creep, but once we're in a fight, we need to win it—and remain on the battlefield long enough to convince our enemies they've lost on every count.

Things began to change less than two weeks into our campaign in Afghanistan. At first, there was caution—would the new president run as soon as we suffered casualties? Then, as it dawned on our commanders that the administration would stand behind our forces, we saw one of the most innovative campaigns in military history unfold with stunning speed.

Our military, and especially our Army, has come a long way. But we're still in recovery—almost through our Cold War hangover, but still too vulnerable to the nonsense concocted by desk-bound theoreticians. Evaluating lessons learned in Iraq, a recent draft study for a major joint command spoke of the need for "discourses" between commanders at various levels and their staffs.

Trust me. We don't need discourses. We need plain talk, honest answers, and the will to close with the enemy and kill him. And to keep on killing him until it is unmistakably clear to the entire world who won. When military officers start speaking in academic gobbledygook, it means they have nothing to contribute to the effectiveness of our forces. They badly need an assignment to Fallujah.

Consider our enemies in the War on Terror. Men who believe, literally, that they are on a mission from God to destroy your civilization and who regard death as a promotion are not impressed by elegant maneuvers. You must find them, no matter how long it takes, and then kill them. If they surrender, you must accord them their rights under the laws of war and international conventions. But, as we have learned so painfully from all the mindless, left-wing nonsense spouted about the prisoners at Guantanamo, you are much better off killing them before they have a chance to surrender.

We have heard no end of blather about network-centric warfare, to the great profit of defense contractors. If you want to see a superb—and cheap—example of "net-war," look at al Qa'eda. The mere possession of technology does not ensure that it will be used effectively. And effectiveness is what matters.

It isn't a question of whether or not we *want* to fight a war of attrition against religion-fueled terrorists. We're *in* a war of attrition with them. We have no realistic choice. Indeed, our enemies are, in some respects, better suited to both global and local wars of maneuver than we are. They have a world in which to hide, and the world is full of targets for them. They do not heed laws or boundaries. They make and observe no treaties. They do not expect the approval of the United Nations Security Council. They do not face election cycles. And their weapons are largely provided by our own societies.

We have the technical capabilities to deploy globally, but, for now, we are forced to watch as Pakistani forces fumble efforts to surround and destroy concentrations of terrorists; we cannot enter any country (except, temporarily, Iraq) without the permission of its government. We have many tools—military, diplomatic, economic, cultural, law enforcement, and so on—but we have less freedom of maneuver than our enemies.

But we do have superior killing power, once our enemies have been located. Ultimately, the key advantage of a superpower is super power. Faced with implacable enemies who would kill every man, woman, and child in our country and call the killing good (the ultimate war of attrition), we must be willing to use that power wisely, but remorselessly.

We are, militarily and nationally, in a transition phase. Even after 9/11, we do not fully appreciate the cruelty and determination of our enemies. We will learn our lesson, painfully, because the terrorists will not quit. The only solution is to kill them and keep on killing them: a war of attrition. But a war of attrition fought on our terms, not theirs.

Of course, we shall hear no end of fatuous arguments to the effect that we can't kill our way out of the problem. Well, until a better methodology is discovered, killing every terrorist we can find is a good interim solution. The truth is that even if you can't kill yourself out of the problem, you can make the problem a great deal smaller by effective targeting.

And we shall hear that killing terrorists only creates more terrorists. This is sophomoric nonsense. The surest way to swell the ranks of terror is to follow the approach we did in the decade before 9/11 and do nothing of substance. Success breeds success. Everybody loves a winner. The clichés exist because they're true. Al Qa'eda and related terrorist groups metastasized because they were viewed in the Muslim world as standing up to the West successfully and handing the Great Satan America embarrassing defeats with impunity. Some fanatics will flock to the standard of terror no matter what we do. But it's far easier for Islamic societies to purge themselves of terrorists if the terrorists are on the losing end of the global struggle than if they're allowed to become triumphant heroes to every jobless, unstable teenager in the Middle East and beyond.

Far worse than fighting such a war of attrition aggressively is to pretend you're not in one while your enemy keeps on killing you.

Even the occupation of Iraq is a war of attrition. We're doing remarkably well, given the restrictions under which our forces operate. But no grand maneuvers, no gestures of humanity, no offers of conciliation, and no compromises will persuade the terrorists to halt their efforts to disrupt the development of a democratic, rule-of-law Iraq. On the contrary, anything less than relentless pursuit, with both preemptive and retaliatory action, only encourages the terrorists and remaining Ba'athist gangsters.

With hardcore terrorists, it's not about PSYOP or jobs or deploying dental teams. It's about killing them. Even regarding the general population, which benefits from our reconstruction and development efforts, the best thing we can do for them is to kill terrorists and insurgents. Until the people of Iraq are secure, they are not truly free. The terrorists know that. We pretend otherwise.

This will be a long war, stretching beyond many of our lifetimes. And it will be a long war of attrition. We must ensure that the casualties are always disproportionately on the other side.

Curiously, although our military avoids a "body count" in Iraq—body counts have at least as bad a name as wars of attrition—the media insist on one. Sad to say, the body count cherished by the media is the number of our own troops dead and wounded. With our overcaution, we have allowed the media to create a perception that the losses are consistently on our side. By avoiding an enemy body count, we create an impression of our own defeat.

In a war of attrition, numbers matter.

Regarding the other postmodern form of wars of attrition—the high-velocity conventional operations in which maneuver and firepower, speed and violent systemic shock combine to devastate an opposing force—the Army and Marine Corps need to embrace it, instead of allowing the technical services, the Air Force and Navy, to define the future of war (which the Air Force, especially, is defining wrongly). We will not live to see a magical suite of technologies achieve meaningful victories at no cost in human life. We need to oppose that massive lie at every opportunity. The twenty-first century's opening decades, at least, will be dominated by the up-gunned Cain-and-Abel warfare we have seen from Manhattan to

Bali, from Afghanistan's Shamali Plain to Nasiriyeh, from Fallujah to Madrid.

The problem is that the Department of Defense combines two fundamentally different breeds of military services. In the Air Force and the Navy, people support machines. In the Army and Marine Corps, machines support people. Although expensive technologies can have great utility—and Air Force and Navy assets made notable contributions to the Army-Marine victory in Operation Iraqi Freedom—the technical services have a profoundly diminished utility in the extended range of operations we are required to perform, from urban raids to extended occupations, from foot patrols in remote environments to peacemaking.

The Navy is struggling hard with these issues, but the Air Force is the strongest opponent of admitting that we face wars of attrition, since it has invested overwhelmingly in precision weapons designed to win a war by "deconstructing" the enemy's command networks. But the only way you can decisively cripple the command networks of terrorist organizations is by killing terrorists. Even in Operation Iraqi Freedom, airpower made an invaluable contribution, but attacking military and governmental infrastructure targets proved no substitute for destroying enemy forces. When, in midwar, the focus of the air effort shifted from trying to persuade Saddam Hussein to wave a white handkerchief (which he had no incentive to do) to destroying Iraqi military equipment and killing enemy troops, the utility of airpower soared.

It cannot be repeated often enough: Whatever else you aim to do in wartime, never lose your focus on killing the enemy.

A number of the problems we have faced in the aftermath of Operation Iraqi Freedom arose because we tried to moderate the amount of destruction we inflicted on the Iraqi military. The only result was the rise of an Iraqi *Dolchstosslegende*, the notion that they weren't really defeated, but betrayed. Combined with insufficient numbers of Coalition troops to blanket the country—especially the Sunni triangle—in the weeks immediately following the toppling of the regime, crucial portions of the population never really felt America's power.

It is not enough to materially defeat your enemy. You must convince your enemy that he has been defeated. You cannot do that by bombing empty buildings. You must be willing to kill in the short term to save lives and foster peace in the long term.

This essay does not suppose that warfare is simple: "Just go out and kill 'em." Of course, incisive attacks on command networks and control capabilities, well-considered psychological operations, and humane treatment of civilians and prisoners matter profoundly, along with many other complex factors. But at a time when huckster contractors and "experts" who never served in uniform prophesize bloodless wars and sterile victories through technology, it's essential that those who actually must fight our nation's wars not succumb to the facile theories or shimmering vocabulary of those who wish to explain war to our soldiers from comfortable offices.

It is not a matter of whether attrition is good or bad. It's necessary. Only the shedding of their blood defeats resolute enemies. Especially in our struggle with God-obsessed terrorists—the most implacable enemies our nation has ever faced—there is no economical solution. Unquestionably, our long-term strategy must include a wide range of efforts to do what we, as outsiders, can to address the environmental conditions in which terrorism arises and thrives (often disappointingly little—it's a self-help world). But, for now, all we can do is to impress our enemies, our allies, and all the populations in between that we are winning and will continue to win.

The only way to do that is through killing.

The fifth edition of the *Shorter Oxford English Dictionary* defines to "attrit" as to "wear down in quality or quantity by military attrition." That sounds like the next several years, at least, of the War on Terror. The same dictionary defines "attrition" as "the gradual wearing down of an enemy's forces in sustained warfare." Indeed, that is exactly what we shall have to do against religious terrorists. There is no magic maneuver waiting to be plotted on a map. While sharp tactical movements that bring firepower to bear will bring us important successes along the way, this war is going to be a long, hard slog.

The new trenches are ideological and civilizational, involving the most fundamental differences human beings can have—those over the intentions of God and the roles of men and women. In the short term, we shall have to wear down the enemy's forces; in the longer term, we shall have to wear down the appeal of his beliefs. Our military wars of attrition in the twenty-first century will be only one aspect of a vast metaphysical war of attrition, in which the differences between the sides are so profound they prohibit compromise.

As a result of our recent wars and lesser operations, we have the best-trained, best-led, best-equipped, and most experienced ground forces in the world in our Army and Marine Corps. Potential competitors and even most of our traditional allies have only the knowledge of the classroom and the training range, while we have experience of war and related operations unparalleled in our time. We have the most impressive military establishment, overall, in military history.

Now if only we could steel ourselves to think clearly and speak plainly: There is no shame in calling reality by its proper name. We are fighting, and will fight, wars of attrition. And we are going to win them.

Atlantis, the Ideological Superpower

New Glory

2005

"But, proceeded the Empress, how are you sure that God cannot be known? The several opinions you mortals have of God, answered they, are sufficient witnesses thereof."
—Margaret Cavendish, Duchess of Newcastle

The Muslim fanatics yearning to destroy our civilization sincerely hope to build a better world. Based upon mad and heartless interpretations of the Koran, the utterances of Mohammed, and centuries of arcane Islamic law, their vision of a reordered, globe-spanning society of the faithful is repugnant to us, but to our enemies it is the answer to God's will and human need. Desiring the best for humankind—and certain that they know what the "best" should be—these terrorist chieftains are only the latest incarnation of the monsters who appear in every culture determined to purify us of our sins and weaknesses through an unsparing application of cleansing fire.

September 11 was meant to do us good.

Nothing is more dangerous than human attempts to perfect the world. And there is nothing more common than human discontent with the conditions of this world. While the unhappiness of those whose fates are miserable offers little reason for astonishment, the impatience of the more privileged with their earthly circumstances renders humanity not only the most unstable species, but the deadliest. The common man or woman prays for improvement to his or her lot. But zealots and intellectuals demand nothing less than perfection. That quest for perfection leads to the GULag and Auschwitz.

The myth of a utopia, of a golden age lost or yet to be attained, upon the earth or in an exclusive heaven, haunts history, from the days of myth through our own time. Nor is there any likelihood that the dream of a "better elsewhere" will be extinguished before the end of humankind. Did any generation ever pass without nostalgia for the "good, old days?" How much more powerful the human longing to rediscover Eden, the paradise without flaw or frailty, in which our mightiest myths claim we were safe.

Through horrid years and halcyon days alike, human beings have insisted either on looking backward to a handsomely imagined Camelot or a reimagined caliphate or on staring ahead in the hope that life's travails will end in a paradise beyond the grave. We seem uniquely unfitted for the here and the now. No comfort or accomplishment long contents us, and no beauty sates. We humans have an explosive capacity to convince ourselves that life must have been, must be, or will be better elsewhere. It is astonishing that we have come as far as we have done, that our entire race was not done in by reverie.

Sex and violence are so riveting because they offer the only instances of unqualified immediacy in our lives (and sex does not always do so, as any veteran of its conflicts can attest). The mind or soul is inconstant, ever flittering. The most successful human beings—the happiest—appear to be those who can most fully inhabit the moment, embracing reality, if not always celebrating it. The malcontents, passive or violently active, are those who live in a "someday me," who find no satisfaction in the present or their likeliest tomorrow, who wish away the world as it exists.

Benign dreams of utopias, of perfect worlds or a paradise hereafter, take a range of forms, from the honest believer's confidence in immortality down to the National Public Radio listener's dreams of a cottage in Provence, from gated retirement communities to the insistence of life-worn hippies that Atlantis is merely veiled from the human eye, and from communes that founder because someone eventually has to do the dishes to all-inclusive Caribbean resorts. We bribe ourselves with fantasies as we drive to work each day. If those common daydreams hinder us from appreciating the moment, they rarely do us harm (although it might not do to raise one's belief in Atlantis during a job interview).

Other forms of the passion for utopias turn monstrous. Whether attempts to inaugurate the kingdom of god on earth, or efforts to create a godless paradise, they invariably end in cruelty and death. When we are fortunate, the suffering is not long and the deaths are few. But history is stained crimson by utopias gone mad and littered with the bones of wayward Edens. Among Christians, the admonition of Jesus Christ that his kingdom was not of this earth has been ignored almost as routinely as his warning about our fervor for earthly wealth. Among Muslims, injunctions to charity and mercy are discarded in favor of rigor and oppression. The promised land is usually drenched in blood.

The trend worsened in the modern age, as humankind rejected God for baser superstitions, from nationalism to the class struggle. Now antimodern rebels are resurrecting the cruelest forms of religion from the past and the postmodern world threatens to become grimmer still. As the industrial era reached its apogee in the twentieth century, schemes to purify the world, to create perfect orders, whether in the name of a god-emperor, racial purity, the workers of the world, or a cultural revolution, killed more human beings through war and organized massacre than the worst preceding centuries of plague, famine, and war had managed to do. In an age of weapons of mass destruction religious fanatics returned from history's grave may wreak still greater havoc—and they will insist that their god looks down approvingly, that their deeds are blessed.

All utopian schemes ultimately founder on human complexity. The intellectual's response, whether Marxist or Islamist, is to kill and torment men and women until they behave simply. The industrial age convinced intellectuals that humanity could be reduced to an assembly line, a new twist on the ideal society. The cost of their failure was hundreds of millions of corpses, from Germany to Cambodia.

Once again, Anglo-American exceptionalism served us well. We never were seduced by madcap theories hatched by European intellectuals prescribing how societies should run. Among the healthiest of the common traits of Americans has been our resistance to the schemes for social engineering that plagued the rest of the world.

The anglophone tradition certainly had its utopian thinkers, although the most distinguished cases involved intellectual exercises their own authors might have stamped "Unfit for human consumption."

From the shades of Avalon and Arthurian legend (much influenced by French high-medieval notions of chivalry), down to the Puritans, the fantasy certainly existed that a better world had once been at hand—or might be spanked into existence. From Wat Tyler's Rebellion through the great religious revivals of the eighteenth and nineteenth centuries, Britain never lacked for those who hoped to change the world.

The remarkable thing is that the passion of the zealots never took, at least not enduringly. Even Cromwell's dreary rule resulted more from a struggle over the practical forms of government than from the faith militant (the mistake of historians long has been to consider the Cromwellian interlude and the Restoration separately, instead of recognizing how they interacted in the classic Hegelian manner to yield the synthesis that began with William and Mary). The Puritan attempt to regulate the English people too strictly hardly lasted a decade. Too heavy a hand laid on our daily lives, whether in Britain or America, incited insurmountable resistance. When faced with those of too severe a rectitude, we always reply with Nell Gwynn or Madonna.

Elsewhere, the tyranny of monks or mullahs, from Spain to Saudi Arabia, lasted decades and even centuries. Hanging a handful of supposed witches in New England still fills us with horror and disgust. Elsewhere, torture and execution pleased the masses. In the Middle East, public torments delight crowds to this day. Saudi Arabia constitutes an attempt to create a divinely sanctioned utopia on earth. Predictably, it has become a pit of corruption and extravagant hypocrisy.

Creative, absorptive, and adaptive—never rigid or static—America's heritage has saved us again and again. Our Constitution assumes that men and women are *not* perfectible, and it doesn't raise the bar forbiddingly high. The American Revolution, while it changed the world and certainly seemed a revolution to successive English governments, was never about creating a utopia. As with the comparatively few other successful and enduring political revolutions, ours was about improving social and economic conditions, not about altering them fundamentally. We did not take up arms to establish a millenarian commune but to restore what the Founding Fathers viewed as the inalienable political rights of Englishmen to parliamentary representation and consensual taxation. Our struggle was not about the destruction of all existing governmental and social forms. Had England allowed its North American colonies to become full-fledged members of its body politic, no revolution would have occurred. The English rejected us before we rejected them. We became Americans because we wanted to be English, with the full rights of Englishmen, and were refused. Our revolution moved us far beyond its initial goals, but were we to be more accurate in our language, we would speak of the "American Evolution."

Even the sects that fled to our shores in the earliest years of settlement, each hoping to construct the New Jerusalem amid the forest of a new Eden, proved unable to sustain their severity. When the men of God asked too much of human frailty for too long, their flocks moved on—or removed them. Faith never lacked, but it was saved—usually in time—from madness by English individualism and a yeoman's skepticism (so different from the skepticism of continental intellectuals, then or now). The men and women of the Massachusetts Bay Colony turned out to be from Missouri.

And those English intellectuals who scribbled about perfect societies? One of the most valuable early lessons I received in the cruelty of intellectuals came when I read Thomas More's *Utopia* in my early teens—after purchasing my own copy under the influence of one of the twentieth century's greatest disinformation successes, the film of Robert Bolt's play, *A Man for All Seasons*. I was mortified by what I read. Even then, I realized that More's disciplined world—a harshly limiting place—was not one for the human beings I knew. And it certainly wasn't for me. I began to view Henry VIII more sympathetically.

Predictably, More's work appeared in an age of confusion, when the old order was breaking apart and men were forced to question verities that had endured for centuries. It is always so. Periods of social disintegration and crises of belief, of the evident failure of the old ways, always produce dreams of utopia. We see the pattern repeated as Islamic terrorists nudge their god to hurry up and return the world to a divinely prescribed order—and, not least, to make the rest of us behave.

The "moral behavior" issue is always there. A routine priority is the control of the female. Few millenarian prophets have been women. They are almost invariably embittered men who view women as the handmaidens of the devil in need of chastisement and close management, lamentable necessities to be used sparingly and with distaste. The antifemale rage of Islamic terrorists may be extreme, but it is not unique. Susannah is *always* in trouble with the elders. Few male witches burn. Muslim fanatics mortify themselves with online pornography, then rail against the degeneracy of the West. Whether religious or secular, prophets of a paradise on earth always seek to suppress human desires (and the competitive loyalties they create).

Of course, English-speaking tradition has not been entirely immune to this phenomenon. Even Francis Bacon's *New Atlantis* from 1627 has a cold, Puritan wind running through its pages. His imaginary paradise of "Bensalem" is described proudly by its residents as "the virgin of the world." Published after the Restoration had begun, Henry Neville's *The Isle of Pines* ends with the morals police of his own cobbled-together Atlantis hurling a black man off a cliff for lascivious behavior. Preachers from John Knox through John Wesley on down to the Welsh fire-and-brimstone preachers of early twentieth century chapels and the televangelists of twenty-first-century America have never stopped inveighing against the sins of the flesh. And those of us reared in the English-speaking tradition ignore them when they press a mite too hard. In America, humanity itself always wins in the end.

Elsewhere, it's different. Failing cultures take even the maddest promises of utopia seriously—whether the lies have been told in the name of Karl Marx or Allah.

It has been observed repeatedly that Communism was a religion without god. Of course, the Stalins and Maos were happy to stand in for vanquished deities and be worshipped themselves. Communism in its various forms and mutations never lacked for liturgy (or prudery). It suggests that, for many human beings, the idea of a god may not be as important as the promise of a utopia. In the Communist interlude—blessedly behind us—the golden age was always just around the corner, waiting for one more enemy, internal or external, to be defeated. The promise of that New Atlantis, hatched by a grubby, failed son of the Rhineland who read too much and lived too little, excused the sacrifice or outright murder of hundreds of millions of human beings. For its part, the German cult of National Socialism was deficient compared to the dark genius of Communism. The Nazis could only find enemies outside of the "pure" German race. The genius of Communism (like that of Islamic fundamentalism today) was its ability to find enemies anywhere and everywhere.

Was Marx indispensible to the mass horrors of the twentieth century? Probably not. If the Lenins, Trotskys, and Stalins had not found a useful tool in Communism, another socialist design of European origin would have served as well. The GULag had deep roots in continental European history. Communism wasn't a seed, but merely a fertilizer for murderous sprouts that had been nurtured since the late Middle Ages. The monopoly church of the crusading believed no toll in human suffering was too high to "perfect" God's children. We all can cite a few of the heresies that were suppressed with horrific bloodshed—the Cathars and Hussites, for example—but there were *hundreds* of heretical movements, many no more than efforts at church reform, that the Papacy suppressed with fire and sword. Early Protestants were no more tolerant, if less capable of mass suppression. The Age of Reformation, from 1517 to 1648, saw the sanctioned slaughter of more Europeans by Europeans than any other period prior to the twentieth century—all in the name of purifying societies, of pleasing God, of bringing about His perfect Kingdom. The inquisitions and witch hunts, the massacre of St. Bartholomew's Day, and the broad moral collapse of the Thirty Years' War were all the result of dreams of establishing an earthly order that would better please God.

The notion of human perfectibility is lethal. Europe embraced it, as did many of Europe's colonial-era victims later on. For the Islamic world, it was there from the start.

There's always another enemy. Whether they center on the salvation of the flesh or of the soul, the appetite of utopian schemes for human flesh is insatiable. America's New Jerusalem is so generous in spirit and deed because it has never been imprisoned within a theoretical framework. We have an ergonomic utopia, designed and redesigned by countless users. Above all, our muddling paradise accepts human variety and imperfection. Hester Prynne is vindicated, the elders of Susannah's church are exposed (didn't Jimmy Swaggart read the Bible?). Utopias tried elsewhere have all been based upon texts, either upon the inhuman designs of intellectuals or on inhumane readings of sacred books. They all insisted on human perfectibility. And they all failed.

The inquisition will always uncover heretics. People's courts will always discover doctrinal imperfections in the prisoner. Few Muslims will ever be pure enough to satisfy Islamic extremists. And the old men of every faith and political doctrine will always find the young worrisomely immoral.

If any proof is wanting that men and women make of religion what they will, it certainly lies in the Christian extremist's perversion of Christ's message of human fallibility and redemption, of forgiveness, and of love. Islam doesn't even bother to pardon human weakness, but reaches right for the whip. In his canny memoir, *Tristes Tropiques*, the anthropologist Claude Levi-Strauss termed Islam a "barracks religion." The epithet perfectly suits the Muslim insistence on submission (the literal meaning of "Islam"), on social discipline, on the spit and polish of forms, on the division of humanity into a male officer corps and female enlisted ranks that so cripples Islam today.

Those who inaugurate systems, religious or secular, to perfect humankind invariably find themselves frustrated by the hopeless, glorious intractability of men and women. First the unbelievers, or the heretics, or the capitalists have to go. Then the poets go, along with the dubious books. And the "rich" peasant landholders and the adulterers have to go. Then the comrades whose revolutionary zeal appears in danger of faltering and the fellow believers whose faith may be too weak have to go, too. The soundtrack for history's utopias consists of cell doors slamming and the shrieks of the dying, of bullets fired into the back of heads and the weeping of the survivors.

If Osama bin Laden's most idealistic followers managed to eliminate America and Israel overnight, Europe wouldn't escape their attention. Even now Allah's butchers murder those Muslims whose faith seems heretical, deviant, or simply insufficient. To build an earthly paradise according to the blueprints of the preachers or the intellectuals, you have to kill the teachers, the scientists, the doctors . . . the insubordinate workers, the youthful sinners . . . and after the slaughter the Party's five-year plan is no closer to fulfillment, the world remains a repulsively sinful place, an insult to the god that human killers have yoked to their discontents.

If bloodshed purified the earth, we would all be walking angels.

In contrast to the American Revolution, the French Revolution sought to alter everything within its grasp, from the elimination of traditional hierarchies to the price of bread, from defeating the grip of organized religion to changing the names of the months. Robespierre, Danton, St. Just, Marat, and their ilk sought to purify their world with blood and soon drowned in it themselves. The revolution failed, although it did not lack consequences. Its myth has been far more enduring than its accomplishments.

The French Revolution was radical in both its techniques and its aims, an uproar, a great spasm. Seized by intellectuals, it swiftly lost touch with every reality but the guillotine. Generals were executed for losing battles no general could have won. Ambitions promptly exceeded capabilities. The citizen disappeared into the mob. And, inevitably, enemies were discovered not only beyond French borders among scheming aristocrats and Prussian regiments, but within the revolutionary cadres. In the sudden absence of common values and codified law, the patriotic speech of one resounded as treason in the ears of another. This was a revolution that, literally, talked itself to death, the fate of its strongest voices prefiguring the ends of the Bukharins and Trotskys of another revolutionary era.

The people unleashed cannot endure disorder very long. They soon crave a messiah with parental authority. The French found one in Napoleon, who set Europe on the march toward the mass wars of the future. In popular emotions Napoleon stood for a truant God. Yet there was a difference between the little Corsican, who was interested in his own glory, and the prophets or *mahdis* who claim to act for the glory of their deity. Bloody handed though he was, Napoleon wanted to rule the earth, not destroy it. The true messianic temperament views the destruction of earthly forms as the short path to paradise. The secular leader, even at his worst, is drawn to the things of this world, while the religious firebrand is repulsed by them. The man who believes he acts for his god is the more dangerous of the two, but the charismatic leader, whether religious or secular, is humankind's bane.

We should be grateful for dull presidents.

Although the religious zealot is not merely willing, but impatient to sacrifice his life for his cause, Americans should be wary of impassioned mass movements of any variety, anywhere in the world. If we examine the ease with which the French or Russians or Chinese or Cambodians leapt to a quasi-religious fanaticism even in the absence of god, we find a collective need within populations deprived of traditional structures to believe in something greater than themselves, in a unifying cause, in some justification for their sufferings and sacrifices. Human beings are hardwired for faith. They require it, almost as commonly as they require oxygen. It may take many forms, most of them benign, from identification with a football team to a quiet, luminous faith in the divine. But when the great chain of being is broken, when the heavens appear to be falling and traditions cannot be relied upon for protection or the least certainty, men and women flock to the nearest messiah, whether he appears in religious robes or in a uniform fit for an operetta. They kneel to the man who validates their existence and offers them a purpose. Hitler gave German identity a powerful meaning, absurd as its foundations may have been. He was the perfect idol for his time and place, replacing a sense of injustice with one of pride. Osama bin Laden, like many another self-raised prophet before him, revives the threatened identity of the faithful. He does not simply tell them their faith is valid, he demonstrates its power through acts of revenge against iconic enemies. And few things satisfy humankind as profoundly as seeing the mighty suffer.

Osama bin Laden wasn't an accident. His coming was inevitable. The disarray of Middle Eastern Islam demanded that he appear. We will be fortunate if he isn't merely John the Baptist to a coming terrorist Messiah—or a series of prophets—and we must kill him to demonstrate our greater power. There will be practical results, but those are of lesser consequence. Loath though we would be to admit it, we need to demonstrate that our "god" is more powerful than his. Contrary to the wisdom of the faculty lounge, dead martyrs are far less of a menace than living killers. Others will arise in the wake of dead terrorist leaders, but that is a result not of our actions, but of the disastrous state of Middle Eastern civilization. We will have to keep on killing them until they are decisively discouraged or destroyed. There is no immediate alternative.

All religions have produced fanatics in unstable times. Osama bin Laden and his comrades are products of the crisis within their faith. The times made the men. And they are likely to go on making them. The arch terrorists who claim to represent pure Islam are often nihilistic in their actions, but they provide certainty—clear, incontestable answers—to those who have come to doubt themselves and the power of their creed. They offer a fascist utopia on earth and a well-regulated paradise hereafter. Above all, they remove doubt from the minds of the weak and give purpose to souls adrift and in disarray.

The American assumption is that men need something to live for. The brilliant insight of the master terrorists is that once they have been sufficiently humiliated men will as readily embrace a reason to die. The perfect apocalyptic terrorist—the suicide bomber or the hijacker who does not intend to survive—is the young man or woman for whom life is not only disappointing, but intolerable, the failure who craves an end. The terrorist chiefs give their human tools a deluxe version of their desire.

Suicide "martyrs," when they appear in significant numbers, are symptoms of a society terrified of life. Today the spiritual wounds and material humiliations of Middle Eastern Islam cut so deep that the longing for a shortcut to paradise has infected many thousands, perhaps millions. Those who will become suicide bombers tomorrow are already the walking dead. It may be too late for any action of ours to resurrect them. In their hearts, they have already left this earth behind, with all its dreads and shames. It is an experience so profoundly un-American that we simply cannot comprehend it.

After 9/11, the War on Terror, the liberation of Afghanistan, and the shattering of Saddam Hussein's Iraq, we still refuse to recognize our enemies.

Above all, they are *believers*. Miserable in the here and now, like so many who went before them, they seek a better world than this earth offers them. Their utopia lies beyond the grave. They are the ultimate revolutionaries, willing to destroy all of the earth for a promised garden in paradise. They represent the age-old human quest for Utopia, for Paradise regained, for the pastures of Heaven.

Our grimmest mission in the twenty-first century will be to kill these dreamers.

The Goddess of the
Southern Seas

New Glory

2005

Whenever the State Department issues a travel warning for any location in Southeast Asia, I know exactly what I'll find when I get there: Australians drinking beer around the pool. And that is what I found when I reached Solo.

After literally wading through Jakarta during the flood of 2002, I flew down to Yogyakarta, Java's cultural capital, where the women I encountered made it clear that they think Muslim fundamentalists are nuts. Our embassy, intimidated by a handful of demonstrators trudging about with placards, had declared the city of Solo, just up the road from Yogya, as much too dangerous for travelers, since Solo was the home of Abu Bakar Ba'asyir's extremist religious school and the headquarters for the Mujahidin Council of Indonesia. Reading the warning, one might have expected roadblocks and daylight kidnappings, followed by torture and death.

Of course, there was nothing of the sort. Solo is a pleasant, drowsy, frayed city where Australians, Americans, or anyone else may drink a poolside beer with impunity. Although Ba'asyir certainly had been involved with terrorism (as of this writing, he's under indictment for the second time), he was not about to make a mess in his own backyard. On the single occasion when a handful of students from his ratty little school got carried away and invaded a few cheap hotels in the wake of the first U.S. strikes on the Taliban, Ba'asyir called them off immediately. Like most grand advocates of terror, he does not care to put himself at risk. The local citizenry regard him as a nuisance.

Although it has nothing to do with Ba'asyir, there is, indeed, a large "fundamentalist" Muhammadiye University at the edge of the city, the sort of institution that terrifies our State Department. The university has nothing to do with terror and has not produced a single violent actor. On the contrary, men and women study together on a handsome, up-to-date campus where computers are as much in evidence as the Koran. The girls dress demurely and the boys are polite. All are wonderfully curious about the United States. More than anything else, the campus resembles an American Bible college, except that the Indonesian-Muslim students are more interested in science. Our diplomats won't go near it.

Instead of conjuring bogeymen from nothing, our credentialed representatives in Indonesia should miss no opportunity to interact with such students or to visit the campuses of the various Muhammadiye universities as volunteer lecturers. But our diplomats and their underlings cling to capital cities, pleading crushing workloads, rancid with self-importance.

Still, there was far more to Solo than sunburned Aussies and hospitable young Muslims. The city does have a reputation for being particularly devout (Solo's citizens had been ardent Communists in the Sukarno years, but one religion serves as well as another). Its residents consider themselves impeccable Muslims and they certainly don't have a local nightlife to rival Jakarta's libertinage. But the local folks do have a quirk or two that drives the Saudi financiers of bigotry mad.

The grandest annual event for Solo's Muslims occurs when the *susuhunan*, or sultan, opens the grounds of the *kraton*, his palace park, for a communal celebration. As many as thirty thousand people crowd inside the walls. Their purpose? To join the sultan—a fervent Muslim himself—in paying the city's respects to the Goddess of the Southern Seas.

Trust me: She's not in the Koran. And polytheism is the gravest offense in "pure" Islam.

Indonesia is the world's most populous Muslim country, with two hundred million of the faithful composing more than 90 percent of the inhabitants of the state's seventeen thousand islands, great and small. But the most striking thing about Islam in Indonesia is its variety—or perhaps its commonsensical good health. Among two hundred million Muslims, you can always find a few perverted believers, and anti-Americanism *is* a global fashion statement (in Indonesia, it quickly devolves into a request for aid in gaining a U.S. visa). But Islam in Indonesia ranges from the Arabian rigor of Aceh at the extreme western tip of Sumatra (devastated by the 2004 tsunami) to the surreal beliefs of the Bugis on Sulawesi—or the ceremony in Solo in honor of the Goddess of the Southern Seas.

That goddess is an old Javanese deity, a traditional protector of the island's people. Animism and folk spirits continue to play a role in rural Islam—and immigrants bring country beliefs to the city. If questioned, believers deny it at first—then they pray to a tree when things look bleak. Nor is it only a matter of lingering folk beliefs. Both Hinduism and Buddhism prevailed far longer on the islands that became Indonesia than Islam has yet done (Bali remains Hindu, while Sulawesi and other islands have significant Christian populations). On Java and the outer islands, Islam itself was heavily influenced by "saints" and teachers from the last bright twilight of Sufism in the sixteenth and seventeenth centuries, before that strain of Islam became the champion of ignorance.

This matters. Because nearly all of the forms of Islam at play in Indonesia are inherently more humane than any at work in the Middle East, where the health inspired by competitive belief systems has long been squandered in spiritual dissipation. Islam *will* evolve. But it is most apt to do so on its frontiers, from Michigan to the Straits of Malacca, where it does not suffer the inbreeding that has crippled the faith of the Arabs.

With Washington's genius for missing opportunities, we warned our citizens away from Indonesia after 9/11, gutting the country's tourist industry and further limiting contact with Americans. (Before a skull spiked on a beer bottle persuaded me that I should retrace my steps, a native Christian up-country on Sulawesi asked me, at the height of a pagan ceremony, "But are there Christians in America, sir?").

When not bullying the Jakarta government over one thing or another, we abandon our policy to a few mining interests and businessmen whose shenanigans would not be tolerated in our own country. And we write off the world's largest population of Muslims at a time when the faith of the Prophet has reached a decisive cross-roads.

That isn't a policy. It's indolence.

The United States responded with alacrity and generosity to the tsunami that struck the Indonesian island of Sumatra on December 26, 2004. Whether our efforts will accelerate a return to the healthy relations between Washington and Jakarta remains to be seen (one hopes that Indonesia, vibrant and vital, will at least hold our attention for a time), but the greatest stumbling block impeding constructive relations is the refusal on the part of the United States to understand how Javanese culture, especially, works.

The core issue dividing us has been the role of Indonesian military officers in the human rights violations in East Timor and elsewhere in the 1990s—before the old regime fell and the country became a democracy. Without question, the United States should seek to advance the cause of human rights and support justice for all. But if we mean to make a difference, rather than simply engage in counterproductive fits of public self-righteousness, we must heed the rules under which other societies function.

Public confrontation doesn't work with Indonesians. By issuing statements and holding press conferences, self-appointed human rights advocates may gain opportunities to preen, but they will not get to the guilty. Working with Indonesians, you must accept that the greatest progress is made behind closed doors. Insisting that Jakarta do things the American way is a prescription for failure, not least because we put the Indonesian government—which now must answer to a proud electorate—in the position of either appearing to cave in to American pressure or standing up to Washington. Even when Indonesia's leaders want to cooperate our public condemnations force them into a combative stance. With slovenly good intentions we have managed to rally the people around abusers they otherwise would have disdained. We made the implementation of justice harder than it would have been had we pursued human rights violators more quietly and less fitfully.

It bewilders me that we insist on punishing now democratic Indonesia for deeds committed under a vanquished dictator. By that standard we should still be avoiding military contact with Germany.

Indonesia not only has seen multiple democratic turnovers of power in less than a decade, but its various population groups have rejected Islamic extremism at the polls. Meanwhile, both our government and human rights organizations make a whipping boy of a state determined to become a robust, rule-of-law democracy while ignoring the vastly worse abuses in states such as Saudi Arabia, Zimbabwe, Cuba, or even Russia. Such disgraceful selectivity does not deter the world's torturers.

Human rights should not be used as a partisan political issue. The same standards must be applied universally (although the means to attain those standards will vary). This means that those on the left must be willing to condemn Fidel Castro or Robert Mugabe, while those on the right must stop making excuses for the degenerate House of Saud.

Certainly we should pursue justice against human rights abusers everywhere, nor should we ever relent in our pursuit of them. But if we seek meaningful results and not merely self-gratification or cheap applause, we must study how best to achieve justice in societies whose norms differ profoundly from our own. Had we simply treated Indonesia's successive governments with respect and cultural sensitivity we would have advanced the essential cause of human rights much further than we have done through insults, slights, and acrimony.

Washington needs to make a new start with Indonesia, a country that already has made its own fresh start through courage and common sense. It's we who are prisoners of the past, not the Indonesians. Our posturing and proclamations have done enormous and unnecessary damage. We have undercut our own influence through our vanity and ignorance. If we wish to influence the greatly improved human rights situation in that sprawling country, we need to engage Indonesia on its own cultural terms, not as if it were a recalcitrant colony. The future of Islam is in play in that most populous Muslim country. And all we do is blow raspberries from the bleachers.

Indonesia matters not only because of its potential to serve as a crucible for the Islam of the future, but because of its incomparable location. A growing proportion of the oil leaving the Middle East and the trade entering the Indian Ocean passes through shipping chokepoints adjacent to Indonesia. The country's value as a strategic partner climbs still higher when Indonesia is considered as part of a greater whole, the subworld of the Indian Ocean littoral, stretching from South Africa northward along the old Swahili Coast, curving past the Arab heartlands and Iran, hastening by Pakistan, embracing the timeless prospects and frustrations of India as well as the wrenching failure of Bangladesh, lapping the eccentric successes to the east of the Bay of Bengal, and rounding Singapore to stretch across Indonesia to Australia. No portion of the globe has so great a remaining potential for development. It will be at least as important as a strategic entity in the twenty-first century as it was in the sixteenth.

India, the centerpiece of the Indian Ocean arena, will continue to progress and disappoint. Its high-tech city-states have begun to define an alternative model of development, in which entrepreneurial locales break with the subcontinent's bureaucratic lethargy and even Hinduism's dreadful cruelty to create islands of success in a sea of failure. India's peculiar strength is that two hundred million of its billion inhabitants are perfectly willing to dismiss the fates of the other eight hundred million in order to provide for their own well-being. The hardest knack for an outsider to acquire in India is the typical bourgeois's ability not to see the misery around him. It's a heartlessness with its own peculiar strength, allowing a personal ruthlessness paralleled elsewhere only by savage regimes.

India is moving forward, awkwardly and fitfully, but unmistakably. And the simple fact that the world's largest democracy continues to survive should impress us all. India is one of the few countries cobbled together by an imperial power that appears likely to maintain its territorial integrity (with the possible exception of a portion of Kashmir). There never was a unified India, not even under the Mughals, until Britain created a central administration. And India has had more obstacles to overcome than countries even more destitute and riven. The caste system is the very opposite of a meritocracy, an insidious means of resource allocation designed thousands of years ago to guarantee that the priestly and warrior castes would have first claim on power, goods, and foodstuffs in times of turmoil or famine. The message that the gods have decreed that specific classes of individuals must suffer willingly if they want a better deal in a life to come isn't exclusive to India, but nowhere else has it been so meanly perfected. While the caste system is just beginning to weaken among the educated classes (a work visa for the United States jumps a marriage partner several rungs up the caste queue), it continues to suppress talent to a degree that cripples the country and dehumanizes the society. The most lunatic myth ever propagated in the West is that there is some sort of humane "wisdom of the East."

The government of India has launched no end of programs to ameliorate the harsh effects of caste; though worthwhile, their effect over the years has been discouragingly slight. And the curse of caste is exacerbated by the exuberant corruption in India's government and business community (two faces of the same dominant society-within-a-society). On top of both these plagues, the timing of India's hour of independence could not have been worse. The new state arrived just at the hour when socialism appeared to be humankind's destiny, and for almost half a century India pursued economic policies for which the word "idiotic" may be too gentle. The combination of protectionism, government-stamped monopolies, anti-business policies, nationalization, and swollen state payrolls created an environment in which corruption not only thrived, but was necessary if the economy wasn't to come to a dead halt.

The stirring rhetoric of the Left has been responsible for boundless human misery. The words are lovely, the promises seductive, and the reality miserable. The first four decades after India's 1947 independence should be studied in every business school and political science department as the perfect case study in how to destroy the potential of a talented population.

And India's population *is* talented. Nowhere else in the world is there such a reservoir of reasonably well-educated (often superbly educated) citizens who remain either underemployed or unemployed. Perversely, the venal politicians in New Delhi welcome the export of their number one product, human capital, to the United States, since it both generates revenue and alleviates societal pressures back home—it's the educated, not the ignorant, who make political trouble. A gift for the U.S., the flight of India's best and brightest is the surest sign of the society's disabilities.

For all this, there are hopeful indicators. A new generation of Indian leaders has begun to cast off the straitjacket of socialist policies in the economy, while the country's youth are aggressive, hardworking, hardheaded realists. The success of cities such as Bangalore and Hyderabad, trailed anxiously by Madras/Chennai, New Delhi, and a few other urban areas, signposts one path to development. Yet it is only one path, and India needs multiple routes forward. Not everyone can be employed writing software or answering telephoned complaints. This is a land of massive human potential— as well as of strategic possibilities—that deserves an even richer engagement on the part of Washington than our recent rapprochement. For all its deficiencies, India is a great potential ally and partner of the United States, and we should patiently nurture a relationship that benefits both sides by seeking common ground (even when we must briefly swallow our pride).

Meanwhile, India needs new visionaries, figures who can persuade a misused (when not simply ignored) population to embrace systemic changes against which demagogues have warned them for generations. Calcutta, India's most seductive city, offers a classic example of what went wrong. Despite its horrid reputation, Calcutta has a resilience and style that I, for one, find inspiring. The people just won't—can't—give up. Shabby poets (isn't every Bengali a poet?) meet in coffeehouses whose walls have mottled to various shades of brown, discussing literature as if it were life's one essential; the women are as proud as they are elegant; and the corpses one occasionally jogs over during a morning run are gathered up with reasonable efficiency. The people have sudden smiles whose beauty I have only seen rivaled in Africa, although the city teems with human detritus.

The "city of dreadful night" has a population that treasures education and will sacrifice for it. It's wrenching to visit Calcutta's central library, housed in a decaying British building, where university students defy the heat to study sweat-blackened computer manuals that were out of date a decade ago. There is no money to buy newer texts and the young do their best with the crumbs that Communist city governments have left them.

Calcutta's tragedy was that its government meant well. Enchanted by the promises of Marx, Lenin, and homegrown crackpots, elected Communists chose policies that gave to the poor directly—and swiftly bankrupted an already-impoverished city. Education was slighted in favor of make-work jobs and direct handouts (the states and cities that gave precedence to education are India's relative success stories today). Yet the Bengali tradition of learning persisted. Then, in the late 1980s, the city fathers made a mistake that cripples the city's prospect unto this day.

They banned computers. From municipal offices, from businesses, from any site where their legislative powers reached. The Communists argued that computers were a capitalist plot to deprive the workers of jobs, to eliminate the human factor. As a result, Bangalore became a boomtown, while Calcutta moldered. Today the hapless rulers of Calcutta realize their folly and have been trying to make up lost ground for several years, praising computers and creating dusty business parks. But time lost in the race for prosperity can rarely be regained in such a cutthroat environment. Hyderabad, Madras/Chennai, New Delhi, Bombay/Mumbai, and other cities offer better living conditions, a more adept work force, and, above all, the critical mass of businesses, educational institutions, and services that entice new investors to follow the pioneers to proven ground.

Like so many other states that gained their independence before socialist economics were exposed as a merciless fraud, India still must wait for those aging politicians, professors, and opinion leaders who were infected by socialist mumbo-jumbo to die off. From Africa to Latin America, the generational transition between the old believers and the new pragmatists may inaugurate the greatest positive change in the developing world since the independence years. The worst thing we could wish for developing states would be good health for those whose crackpot philosophies ruined them.

India is at the beginning of a wave of change that will last for generations and alter not only the subcontinent but all of its strategic tributaries. We need to get to the party early on.

Our long-term need to cultivate a strategic partnership with India is hampered at present by the requirement to work with Pakistan against the region's terrorists. But it is unlikely that Pakistan will become a just and prosperous state within our lifetimes. Cooperation will always be welcome, but our future lies with India, to the degree that we must choose. Our goal in the realms of Islam between Fez and Islamabad will be to limit the menace the region poses, but our goal in India would be to encourage the population's extraordinary potential. While India suffers from the self-destructive pride of the poor cousin—and its military ambitions need to be tempered—Washington and New Delhi are equally to blame for past acrimony. We need to work hard, and even occasionally swallow our pride, to bury the lunatic nonsense of the Non-Aligned Movement, in which alliances between failures in the southern hemisphere pretended to rival the coalitions of the successful in the northern hemisphere. The age of empty rhetoric is dying. We need to help states such as India give birth to a new age of realism—and to recognize that lavish pronouncements are no substitute for earnest efforts.

The stakes are incalculably high. The strategic arena of the Indian Ocean includes over two billion souls, from those "Asian tigers" now missing a tooth or two to the postmodern empire South Africa is building. As I saw for myself from Burma/Myanmar to Africa, China long ago began to look south in search of influence, secure oil-supply routes, and a naval outlet that challenges America's global reach. Despite our own naval and air presence in the Indian Ocean and our recent adventures on land just to the north (Iraq is part of the same strategic calculus), we have not built up the close relationships essential to hegemony, leaving a tempting strategic vacuum for regional powers and ambitious states beyond.

This is a great danger to us, to the region, and to world peace. The hard lesson of the past five hundred years is that the Indian Ocean needs a decided hegemon, whether Portuguese, British, or, however reluctantly, American. We need not be so overt or dictatorial as were the colonial powers, but if we do not increase our de facto control of the sea lanes and international airspace, we will only encourage the Chinese to meddle and the Indians to exceed their strategic resources—perhaps at great cost. We must have tacit mastery of the sea and sky, along with the ability to project power ashore when it proves necessary. The Indian Ocean may well become the crucial strategic cockpit of the twenty-first century.

In a sense, it already is. The oil leaving the Persian Gulf traverses Indian Ocean waters, whether on the short route to the Suez Canal or following the ancient trade routes southward along the African coast or southeast to the satisfy the ever-increasing appetites of Asia.

No network of pipelines could replace those sea lanes. Interdict them and the world grows silent and dark.

Imagine if Islamic terrorists possessed sufficient nuclear weapons to interrupt traffic through the Suez Canal—which they would not hesitate to do, since economic damage to existing regimes furthers their purposes, and such an attack would wound the West as well. Suddenly the sea lanes off the coast of East Africa would regain an importance they lost at the premiere of *Aida*, which celebrated the age-old dream of a navigable passage between the Mediterranean and Red Seas. Whether repairs to the canal took months or years, the power that controlled the Indian Ocean sea lanes would control the world.

It had better be us.

Oil supplies, growing commercial possibilities, potential strategic partnerships—and the enduring struggle between the West and Islam. The Indian Ocean is a laboratory of human possibilities, many of them encouraging and profound. But even in the shorter term, we must recognize what the Portuguese saw half a millennium ago: Naval control of its sea-lanes and choke points commands the Middle East's sources of wealth. Then it was the spice trade; today it's the oil trade. Tomorrow it may be primarily the movement of human capital (a thankfully more benign echo of the slave trade that cursed those waters for centuries). But the Indian Ocean is at once a theater for the taking and a realm of opportunity. By nurturing alliances—and keeping our tempers—with the states beyond the Arab fringe of the ocean's littoral, we can acquire a strategic insurance policy for the long term, in case Arab experiments with governmental and societal evolution disappoint us. Should things go well, we may be glad to facilitate the Middle East's integration with the world. But should affairs go badly, we will need to contain the region.

The Arabs remain the nagging strategic problem. Turkey may go sour, or stumble forward. Pakistan could fragment, or muddle through. If only a crisis can be postponed for a sufficient length of time, friendless Iran, Islam's stepchild, is apt to look westward again for strategic adoption. But Arab progress, if it comes, will be fitful and frustrating, slow and costly. We have no choice but to engage—

yet our involvement is little more than a catalyst. The Arabs need to desire positive change sufficiently to bring it into being for themselves. We cannot afford to turn away—our enemies would only pursue us. But we need to recognize that the Middle East is already an area of diminishing strategic returns on our investments. If we are unlucky, those returns may turn entirely negative.

Nonetheless, our obsessive, exclusive focus on the problems of the Middle East blinds us to the grand opportunities elsewhere— almost entirely in the "greater" Southern Hemisphere. Much is made of China, whether by defense contractors who intend to frighten us into extravagant purchases of arms, or by businessmen who would sell America down the river (or up the Yangtze) for a summer house in the Hamptons. But China's market will never provide as much strategic benefit to us as our market provides to Beijing. As is so often the case, a mafia of American corporations holds our policy hostage. The profit of a few costs us strategic freedom of action and dangerous trade deficits.

With our government prevented from attempting to level the playing field of trade, China is, in its very different way, as much a region of diminishing returns on our investments of strategic capital as is the Middle East. Nor will Japan suddenly become a field of opportunity. We need to build constructive relationships with all of the powers of East Asia—to the extent we are able to do so without foolish compromises—but we also must realize that the much-touted "Pacific century" offers us far less than we have been promised.

Look southward. Toward Africa, that perennially insulted continent. Toward Latin America, our limping twin. And toward the Indian Ocean and its powers in waiting.

Late in the last century, leaders from the developing world insisted on a new world order that would hand them for free what they did not deign to earn. Fortunately for all concerned, the handouts never arrived. As a result, a new sense of realism, of almost American pragmatism, is breaking out in unexpected places. There will be a "new world order," along with a shift of strategic competition, a growth in wealth, and a long-overdue opening to neglected human resources. It will happen in the "expanded" Southern Hemisphere.

We are that entire hemisphere's natural partner, but we have some convincing to do.

The Shape of Wars to Come

Armed Forces Journal

May 2005

Beyond the ever-growing range of operations short of combat, there are three types of warfare that the future will force us to master: strategic raids, punitive expeditions, and general wars waged on expanded terms. No category is pure. One form may lead to or include another. Yet there are demands, purposes, and dilemmas specific to each, some peculiar to our position as the world's dominant power. We can no longer think in the theoretician's abstract terms about war but must address the specific issues that face America's armed forces.

Our military is fated to serve as an expeditionary force for an empire based not upon traditional conquests, but on values and ideas. We will take the fight to our enemies—men whose values are irreconcilable with our own and who substitute often-primitive beliefs for ideas of freedom and justice. At times, our opponents will be feudal bands equipped with postmodern technologies; on other occasions, we may confront traditional states. The core issues are who we will send to the fight, how long we will stay, and what we will hope to achieve. None of the possible answers are as clear-cut as they might appear to conventional thinkers.

Strategic Raids

The necessity for a much-enhanced ability to conduct strategic raids goes well beyond the present struggle with terrorism. From eliminating or capturing our mortal enemies to enforcing nuclear security, the capability to dispatch a small but potent force anywhere in the world on short notice isn't a luxury or an add-on capability. This is a fundamental requirement for postmodern security. Having established a precedent for strategic preemption, we need to reassert it whenever the necessity appears.

Strategic raids may be diplomatically risky at times, but our position in the world demands that we be prepared to violate traditional concepts of sovereignty in order to prevent avoidable tragedies—or simply to stop a small threat before it becomes a great one. The crucial requirement isn't global approval, but success. We can afford occasional hard feelings, but we cannot afford to fail. The destruction of a terrorist base will be forgiven as soon as the news cycle shifts, but every "Desert One" has consequences far beyond the immediate embarrassment. Success is forgiven, but failure has lasting penalties.

Strategic raids will come in many designs, with widely varying force packages. Some may be conducted with standoff weapons alone. But we cannot afford puny, token, and ineffective strikes, such as we saw in the Clinton years. Every failure strengthens the enemy's confidence and resolve. Whether small or complex, single-service or joint, strategic raids must be decisive. Every service will have a contribution to make—if not in one raid, then in another— but all will need to revitalize their thinking and pursue practical capabilities to enable us to act with stunning swiftness and irresistible force. This has implications for everything from strategic transport and communications to body armor and ammunition weight, but above all, it requires a far more capable and appropriate intelligence capability than our current system provides.

Punitive Expeditions

We may need to invent a more politically correct name, but the need to think in terms of twenty-first-century equivalents to classic punitive expeditions seems incontestable. Not every country or culture can be redeemed, reformed, and remodeled. In the age of terror and other nonstate threats, we may find it increasingly necessary to enter a territory to conduct operations more extensive and of greater duration than raids, but without the intent to remain any longer than necessary to accomplish the mission. Should we need to deploy to Somalia to destroy terrorist bases, for example, we would be foolish to imagine that a static presence thereafter would be of any benefit to us. Knowing how and when to leave is every bit as important, and often more difficult, than determining how to attack in the first place.

Tomorrow's punitive expeditions may occur in vast jungle expanses—or in the metastasizing cities of the developing world. But we must achieve greater mobility for the entire force engaged— instead of building semipermanent bases, we need to think in terms of a frontier cavalry, forever on the move and bound only to the mission, not to the terrain. Designing the force package appropriate to each effort will require far more imagination than we currently display and the annihilation of traditional concepts of each service's limited roles. Far too many of the impediments to our effectiveness are self-imposed—failures of vision, rather than a lack of physical capabilities.

Postmodern punitive expeditions won't involve burning homes and killing the cattle, but may include the destruction of an infrastructure upon which our enemy relies. Punitive expeditions have to punish. We have gotten too far away from the psychology of war, imagining that we must handle even enemies gently. But ferocity in the short term usually proves most humane in the longer term. Enemies, immediate or potential, must harbor no doubts about our resolve. This will require a major shift in our thinking, but reality will force it upon us.

Postmodern General War

Postmodern general wars may range from our recent three-week campaign in Iraq to an extended conflict with an upstart state or alliance in the out-years. They involve a vision of a more extended— sometimes enduring—commitment of forces than punitive expeditions. Yet both operations have a common requirement: To be effective, we must discard the nonsensical maxim that "if you break it, you own it." Many countries in which we may have to operate are already broken. We would be foolish to impose upon ourselves the obligation to repair them. Even if we could afford it, we often could not accomplish it.

First, the war must be fought and won, of course. We can do that, although the price will vary. The greater danger lies in our thoughtless assumption that the U.S. military must always stay until war's damage is repaired and every last bedroom repainted. At times, as in Afghanistan and Iraq, there will be sound strategic reasons for remaining on the scene or even for staging a full-scale occupation. But we must learn to tell the difference between a society or culture that can be prodded back into shape and one that is genuinely hopeless. The purpose of fighting a war is to win it, not necessarily to indulge ourselves in political and social interior decorating. Assuring an enemy that war will have no lasting penalties only makes war more likely.

The Army We Need

Although we must beware of asymmetrical technologies and innovative thinking in the enemy's camp, the odds are that we will continue to get the machinery of war right. We have made such a deep, long-term capital investment in systems (some far more useful than others) that alarms about any country, including China, racing from behind to challenge us head-on at high noon have more to do with defense-industry marketing and service-staff fantasies than with real possibilities. The one worrisome deficit we already face—and which is unlikely to be alleviated in the future—is in our ground forces. Reviled as expensive and inefficient, land forces continue to be the fundamental requirement for warfare.

We can compensate for every other deficiency because of our redundant systems, but there is no quick and good fix for an abrupt need for more flesh and blood, trained and in uniform. Budget limitations always demand tradeoffs, but the greatest single vulnerability within our armed forces is our austere troop strength. A catastrophic battlefield loss, either to weapons of mass destruction or to an innovative technology, could not be repaired using a World War II-draft model. The skills required for today's infantryman to be effective are an order of magnitude greater than those essential to the rifleman of sixty-plus years ago.

As our defense secretary notoriously (and inappropriately) remarked, "You go to war with the Army you've got." But we may not have the Army we need for future wars or the Marine Corps that global commitments will demand. The time to expand the force is now, not after additional years of Defense Department sleight of hand, deception, and self-delusion.

This is not intended to slight the contributions of either our Navy or our Air Force. Both are peerless, in every sense of the word. But those services face no significant threats and enjoy an indisputable window of superiority that will last for decades. The worst dangers, most frequent challenges, and most consuming missions face our ground forces. And the Army and Marines are just too small. The issue isn't efficiency, but effectiveness and residual capability. We must distinguish between that which we are accustomed to having and that which we truly need.

Cold War divisions of the budget pie were not written in fire by a divine finger. The exigencies of wartime have forced some temporary reallocations of funds, but we need to consider our country's genuine twenty-first-century military needs, rather than succumbing to force of habit. There is always a lobby for another weapons system, but none for the common soldier. We need to rethink our budgeting process from top to bottom, to rid ourselves of inherited prejudices in favor of innovative solutions.

Above all, we need to think, to stop comforting ourselves with slogans when we need creative thought about making war (in a recent, otherwise useful discussion with Air Force generals, I heard the words "air dominance" so often I thought I was listening to the chanting of Buddhist monks).

Of course, we cannot predict the contours of future wars with precision. We need to maintain a flexible force with wide-ranging capabilities. But we have downplayed the human factor for far too long. A basic rule of this high-tech century is that our security challenges are fundamentally—sometimes appallingly—human. And it still takes human beings, whether analysts, agents, or Airborne Rangers, to solve war's human problems.

In the technical services, the Navy and the Air Force, we need to examine our obsession with downsizing numbers, whether of personnel or systems, while claiming that greater efficiency makes it possible to maintain a smaller military establishment. No matter how capable a combat system may be, at some point, less is just less. Efficiency studies collapse on the battlefield, just as the notion of sending "just enough" troops proved a massive error when we occupied Iraq. Postmodern weapons offer us marvelous capabilities, but one is rarely as good as a hundred, no matter the qualitative difference. Numbers have a power all their own—when your magazine is empty, an enemy armed with a kitchen knife can kill you.

The Navy has already begun, albeit haltingly, to discuss the possible need for more, but smaller, ships. For its part, the Air Force must strive to think beyond its current dogma and ask if a mix of high-tech and mid-tech aircraft might not be more desirable than a severely shrunken fleet of planes so expensive the service dreads losing a single one.

Self-Imposed Restrictions

The other great requirement for effectiveness in waging full-scale warfare in this new century is to free ourselves of self-imposed restrictions on everything from concepts of "legal" targeting to our dread of shedding even our enemy's blood. At a time when alternative powers, from terrorist bands to Chinese military thinkers, are constantly broadening their definitions of warfare, we have narrowed our concept of war so severely that we may be astonished (as we were on September 11, 2001) by the breadth of our enemy's vision and his readiness to reject our narrow rules.

Warfare is not a moral endeavor, and unilateral restrictions will not make it one. The purpose of waging war is to win. All else is secondary. The greatest "combat multiplier" we could have in this new age would be simply an unbreakable will to win, no matter the cost, on the part of our nation's leaders.

Whether we speak of strategic raids, punitive expeditions, or postmodern general wars, only victory is moral. There is no virtue in failure.

The Ultimate Weapon

Armed Forces Journal

August 2005

For decades our military has fielded weapons that deliver unprecedented capabilities. Commanders control tools that their predecessors could hardly have imagined. If wars were won on technical specifications, it would be impossible for us to lose.

But wars are won by human beings, not machines. Technological wonders may assist us, but they cannot substitute for courage and strength of will. Indeed the centerpiece precision weapons that theorists insisted had "changed the nature of war" proved to be self-defeating and morally corrosive when far too much was expected of them. We began to plan our wars around our weapons, rather than fielding weapons to suit our wars. A tactical enabler, technology turned out to be a strategic tyrant.

The price of precision has been dangerously shrunken arsenals, fantasies of bloodless war, and combat without the graphic destruction and casualties essential to convince an enemy of his defeat. Without precise intelligence—which we rarely possess—precision weapons make very expensive holes in the wrong walls and only encourage further enemy resistance.

Despite claims of revolutionary effects, precision weapons are simply linear extrapolations of weapons of the past. The roots of precision-strike capabilities lie in the massive numbers of bombs, aircraft, and lives it took to destroy targets in Nazi Germany. Naturally we wanted to do what we had to do more cheaply in terms of lives and aircraft. But the critical distinction weapons developers failed to make—as they fell in love with technology for its own sake—is that precision weapons are about efficiency, while warfare demands effectiveness.

A single aircraft with a single bomb may destroy a bridge or bunker that would have required repeated missions and cost dozens of aircraft even a generation ago. But in our quest for tidy solutions to the bloody dilemmas of war we forgot that, while reducing our own pain is desirable, reducing our enemy's suffering is not.

Precision weapons are splendid for striking a terrorist hideout, if you can find one, but they have only collateral value in winning wars. That value turns negative rapidly, if unrealistic expectations are raised. Promising too much—as the advocates of techno-war invariably do—results in a popular sense of failure even when we perform well above historical norms.

Breakthrough Weapon

But the worst sin of the precision-weapons advocates has been their neglect of the enemy's psychology. A determined opponent must suffer, often terribly. If he does not, he has no incentive to surrender. We are trying to fistfight with feathers.

We analyze war as engineers and attempt to wage it as diplomats. Our enemies, present and potential, think about war as strategists and fight like savages. The asymmetry is not in our favor.

For all of our undeniable, sometimes-valuable technological triumphs, it took our impoverished enemies to develop that breakthrough weapon of our time, the suicide bomber. Cheap, disposable, bloodcurdling, and dauntingly precise, the suicide bomber's perfect guidance system and practical utility negates our expensive advantages at the tactical level—with strategic effect. Explosives, an old car, one willing martyr, and good human intelligence (an outlay of a few hundred dollars, if you steal the car) amount to a weapon that's effective *and* efficient. Terrifying, too.

The suicide bomber is impossible to deter and difficult to interdict. Our expensive aircraft burn fuel above Iraq as generals huddle with lawyers and politicians refuse to accept war's reality. Meanwhile, our enemy is teaching us what warfare means when the nonsense is stripped away: It is about imposing your will on the enemy, any way you can and without hesitation or scruples.

We approach war in terror of lawsuits and criminal charges. Our enemies are enthusiastic killers. Who has the psychological advantage?

Among the many sound reasons for opposing the F/A-22 fighter or the Virginia-class submarine is the fact that such systems, for all their technical qualities, are linear developments of the last century's weapons. Buying them locks us into obsolescent modalities of warfare. We become prisoners of our very expensive purchases.

Advertisements may claim that this or that platform is "revolutionary," but it's difficult to find a single system under development for any service that breaks with inherited concepts of how we should equip, organize, and fight.

The closest thing we have to a revolutionary system at present is the unmanned aerial vehicle (UAV). In the long term, UAV technology may help us achieve remarkable successes in specific forms of conflict, such as combating terrorism, though UAVs will not win general wars.

The most useful UAV capabilities for the peculiar forms of militarized police work our age demands would be "bloodhound" technologies that target a single individual—a high-value target—or a series of individuals who fit a hostile profile, whether terrorists or enemy soldiers. Tomorrow's UAVs should do the work of bounty hunters. We cannot predict with confidence which line of research might prove the most effective in developing tomorrow's hunter-killer UAVs, but various recognition technologies will take us far beyond current limitations.

Future UAVs will be able to loiter, go to ground, hide indefinitely, calculate, and patiently hunt their quarry. Target identifiers may be any combination of visual recognition, scent identification, behavioral profiling, association patterns, or hypercomplex programs that still lie beyond the horizon. The UAV that "foxhunts" is inevitable, and it will be a great aid when it comes.

But the war-winning technology of this century will be far more comprehensive in its effects and vastly more terrifying in its capabilities than the most lethal UAV. The bad news is that our enemies are apt to develop that wonder-weapon first, since it contradicts every illusion we have come to cherish about war.

The military equipment we currently own shackles our imaginations. We can't see beyond our trillions of dollars of hardware. Unencumbered by our wealth of possessions, our enemies are free to dream.

Ideal Weapon

The twenty-first-century weapon of genius will be far darker than nuclear bombs or even engineered viruses. It will cut to the soul of warfare, focusing on war's fundamental purpose. Potential state enemies, such as China, are far more likely to pursue it than we are. And none of the weapons we have under development will have the least effect against it.

What is the purpose of going to war? To convince the enemy to submit to your will. What would the ideal weapon do? Reach past every physical defense to control the enemy's behavior.

The weapons of tomorrow will be behavior-control technologies that penetrate titanium and bone to target the human brain and nervous system. And they're closer than anyone thinks.

Certainly a well-aimed bullet, or even a spear, makes a very effective behavior-control weapon under the right circumstances. *All* weapons aim at convincing the enemy to surrender. But imagine a weapon that could reach into the sky and, instead of shooting down an aircraft, fatally disorient the pilot or even take control of his decision-making ability. Imagine a weapon that could persuade a targeted individual of an attacker's good intentions, render a squad unable to think, paralyze an aircraft carrier's entire crew, or strip the will to fight from a field army—or a nation.

We wrack our brains about how to build more effective aircraft, more survivable ships, and safer personnel carriers. But our present and potential enemies know they cannot compete within such conventional parameters. Even now, terrorists concentrate on reaching past the military metal to the consciousness of the masses: They already view the media as a behavior-shaping weapon. Tomorrow's grander enemies may focus on directly disabling the human brains serving the "unsinkable" ship and on crippling the minds that move combat vehicles forward.

We have become so enchanted with technology that we have lost sight of the purpose of any war. Possessing less, our enemies must think harder. Terrorists and developing-world colonels alike understand that war is a contest of wills in which any rule may be broken, while we fight as if afraid of committing a foul. Despite our recent experiences, we suffer from an imagination deficit when it comes to warfare.

Behavior-control weapons aren't even a new concept. The Soviets were interested in them before their empire's collapse. The extent to which the Russians continue to pursue such technologies today remains unclear, but it would be surprising if the Chinese (or even the Indians) were not deeply interested in developing capabilities that allowed them to leap past our physical superiority.

Given our research-and-development infrastructure, we would have the best chance of developing a suite of behavior-control technologies, but remain the least likely to investigate such revolutionary capabilities. The reasons range from our mammoth investment (sunk costs) in equipping our forces for war through the defense industry's fear that such weapons might derail profitable programs to ethical concerns.

We are suffocating under the weight of the force we currently have and suffering from a mindset that demands ever-better versions of the weapons with which we're comfortable. We need to pause and consider that, should an enemy develop behavior-control weapons, the only reliable deterrent would be even more capable weapons of our own. If we find ourselves defenseless, we may, literally, never know what hit us. We could possess the finest traditional military in history, yet find ourselves enslaved.

Drugs and Music
There are so many potential approaches to behavior-control weapons that it's impossible to forecast which type will appear first, but the advent of such tools is a question of when, not if. These will be the ultimate weapons of war, able to pierce the chaos and cost of battle to literally change an enemy's mind.

In one of the hideous paradoxes of which history is so fond, we may see our dream of bloodless war come true at last—but in place of gore we could see thousands (or millions) of human beings with permanently impaired mental faculties. The irreparable destruction of decision-making powers or even consciousness could result in the casualties of the future being veterans with severely diminished mental capacities—perhaps unable to perform routine functions—or even large segments of the population reduced to a status of "living dead." At best, we might hope for Orwellian weapons that would merely make us do our master's bidding without a thought.

Imagine a battlefield on which, in the space of moments, we were confronted with thousands of American troops reduced to an infantile state from which there would be no possibility of recovery. What if an enemy then threatened to turn such a weapon on our civilian population?

Were we even to consider developing such weapons ourselves, our line of research would pursue the ability to inflict temporary effects that created windows of opportunity, while avoiding permanent "inhumane" damage. Our enemies would not have such scruples. From the perspective of a power facing war with the United States, the more terrifying the results of a weapon's use, the likelier it would be to collapse the will of our government and population. In the language of an earlier age of danger, we would pursue "low-yield" solutions, while our enemies would strive for the largest yields attainable.

Strategic behavior-control weapons may be generations away; however, given the pace and nonlinearity of technological change, we simply cannot know. But the initial tactical systems probably will be difficult to calibrate for "nonscarring" impacts. More sophisticated, better-focused behavior-control weapons might appear eventually, but the first such weapons fielded may be indiscriminate and devastating to the victims—again, better suited to the temperament of our enemies than to our own.

There is also a possibility that the first power to possess a strategic behavior-control capability will achieve such global control that there would be no need to further develop the weapon. Far from seeing universal democracy in the future, behavior-control weapons in the wrong hands could result in universal slavery.

If this sounds like the stuff of science fiction, consider a few developments that point toward behavior-control weapons.

Last spring, a scientific study concluded that a compound derived from studying the brain could inspire unwarranted trust in the person who inhaled it, disarming innate suspicions. Corporate America doubtless leapt to attention, dreaming of how such a formula might be employed against the American consumer, but the military implication was obvious and, presumably, ignored. What if an aerosol deployed on the battlefield could erase an enemy's hostility and create friendly feelings toward the opponent? What if the new chemical warfare transformed a combatant's attitude from "Kill 'em all!" to "Hey, peace, dude!"? What if such a weapon could be applied to an entire city? By an enemy bent on savagery, not on taking prisoners?

In truth, behavior-control weapons have existed for generations, although the military exploits them halfheartedly. Packaged-content broadcast and communications means, from radio through television to the internet, all successfully alter human behavior, persuading us to watch this, read that, and above all, buy the advertised product. What is a good television commercial if not an exercise in behavior control? Internet offers modify our behavior. And you're likelier to get a speeding ticket while listening to a heavy metal radio station than while tuning in to a Chopin nocturne.

Broadcast sound, then sound and image compounded, have proved to be such extraordinarily successful behavior-modification tools that businesses around the world spend billions of dollars on advertising each year. If commercials didn't work, they would have disappeared. But we *do* buy what we are told to buy.

What if a future broadcast weapon could exploit tomorrow's research into the finest nuances of brain function and compact a lifetime's worth of persuasive sensory effects into a burst transmission "shot" at a bomber's crew? What if we could move beyond the need for pictures and noise to excite associative responses, and work directly upon the electrical or chemical reactions within the brain?

We've known since the interwar years that sonic effects can shape the behavior of crowds. At Nazi rallies, subsonic bass tones were used to unsettle the audience and prepare it for a frenzied response to Hitler. Music has been a part of war and politics for centuries. Sonic weapons that combine extreme intensity with the artful manipulation of cognition may achieve far more than rap music blared at today's terrorist prisoners can do. The light shows of 1960s

San Francisco may prove to be the grandparents of tomorrow's sensory manipulation systems, while the CIA's pre-hippie-era experimentation with LSD may simply have been too far ahead of its time.

How do you induce euphoric passivity in a tank crew? "Better living through chemistry," as a pop phrase of the 1960s had it. As we worry over the last century's weapons of mass destruction, are we about to enter a new age of chemical warfare?

The Will to Win

Whether the initial wave of behavior-control weapons involves sonic tools, chemicals, microwaves, hyperbroadcasts, or means still hiding beyond research horizons, we would be foolish not to consider the potential for such asymmetrical means to wreak havoc upon our approach to warfare—and even upon our homeland.

The possibilities sketched here are superficial and perhaps wrong in detail. But behavior-control weapons are so obviously the logical culmination of warfare that blithe disregard for an entire field of research guarantees disaster.

As this series of columns has stressed, we must regain a visceral grasp of what war means. It isn't merely about target sets, or arriving on the objective, or about exit strategies. War is about persuading the enemy to obey you, to do what you want him to do, even though it may be anathema to all his values.

For now, though, warfare remains about killing the enemy and smashing his environment with sufficient force and resolve to make further resistance psychologically and physically impossible. There may be small wars, but there are no soft wars. Nothing matters more than the will to win.

In the future we may see a true revolution in military affairs whose effects dwarf the overhyped gimmicks of our time. We or our enemies may achieve bloodless war, after all. But if anyone does so, the result is apt to be more horrible—more inhumane on the most fundamental level—than anything military planners now imagine.

Warfare is about changing the enemy's mind. The weapons of tomorrow will do it directly.

Occupation 101

Armed Forces Journal

September 2005

Few matters in military affairs lend themselves to checklists. One is preventive maintenance. Another is preflight checks. A third is the occupation of a defeated state.

Had we planned to botch the occupation of Iraq, we hardly could have done worse than the administration did without a plan. Despite inadequate support and abysmal civilian leadership, our troops saved us from disaster.

Now the Iraqis are beginning to pull some of the weight. But had the Office of the Secretary of Defense (OSD) adhered to common sense and tasked the military to develop a full-scale occupation plan, we would have saved many American and Iraqi lives, the situation in postwar Iraq would have been far more tractable, and international terrorists would not have gained momentum.

The civilians atop the Pentagon were ideologues determined to have their war. Nothing was going to stop them. Some were true believers, convinced that Saddam Hussein's overthrow would lead to the Age of Aquarius in Baghdad, but the critical realization that forbade serious occupation planning was that the projected costs in troops, resources, and funding would have caused Congress to think twice.

The situation was worsened by the conviction among civilian appointees who never had served in the military that they understood twenty-first-century warfare better than the generals. For the ideologues in OSD, military officers were second-raters, at best, and our troops were merely the janitors of policy. No senior official had a family member at risk. War had no visceral reality for them. It was simply a continuation of policy through other means—a loathsome European dictum that never applied to America.

Ridding Iraq and the world of Saddam was a noble thing. But the willful ineptitude with which OSD did it remains inexcusable.

Done is done, as the ideologues realized all along. We are in Iraq, winning is vital, and it's too late to correct the mistakes that didn't have to be made. We'll be compensating until the day the last American soldier leaves Mesopotamia. But we'll need to do better next time.

And there will be a next time.

Our military doesn't want the occupation mission. But no one else can do it. No other organization has the resources, skills, or sense of responsibility. From the Philippines through Germany and Japan, the Army in particular has conducted successful occupations. And the Army will need to do it in the future, assisted by the other services.

If the Army doesn't emerge from its experience in Iraq with a sound doctrine for future occupations, the blame won't fall on civilians next time, but on the generals who ducked their responsibilities to our soldiers and our nation. We cannot pretend we will never do this again—any more than we can wish away war itself.

The Rules

1. Plan and prepare for the worst case. This is the iron rule of military planning. If you go in loaded for bear, you can handle the squirrels. Plan for every contingency imaginable, then plan for the unimaginable. This is the sort of common sense taught at every staff college. Good intentions and crossed fingers are no substitute. As former Army Chief of Staff Gen. Gordon Sullivan put it, "Hope is not a method." Any senior commander prevented from doing detailed planning should resign. Publicly. Otherwise, the blood of his soldiers and the shame of the nation will be on his head and hands.

2. Impose the rule of law immediately. This means martial law in the first hours, days, and weeks of an occupation, although we may employ less menacing terminology. The rigorous enforcement of basic laws is every bit as much to the benefit of the subject population as it is to us. When the political order collapses, hurling the economy and society into crisis, the defeated crave certainty and security. Rhetoric about democracy can come later. In the awful confusion of war's aftermath, the average citizen needs to be reassured that his family, his home, and the streets are safe—that criminals and renegades will not be allowed to prey upon him or his loved ones.

Psychologically, the defeated population is reduced to a childish state. They don't want unregulated freedom. They need clear, parental rules. They need to know that crime will be punished and good behavior rewarded. The situation is identical to that faced by a teacher on the first day of class: If order isn't established from the opening bell, it's hard to impose it later in the term.

When U.S. forces arrive in a given country, they're granted a period when the population is disoriented, malleable, and responsive. Squandering that window is a tragic error, and the occupation may never fully recover.

When our troops arrived in Baghdad without orders to impose the rule of law, we lost our credibility with many Iraqis. Some expected punishment, but few expected us to tolerate a looting and arson spree by criminal elements. By allowing looters free rein, we alienated law-abiding citizens. And we embarrassed ourselves in the eyes of the world.

The rule of law is essential for all else we hope to achieve. Without it, you not only will not have order in the streets, but you will never establish a true market economy where corruption is under control. You certainly cannot build a just democracy. We like to speak in stirring terms about our noble intentions, but men and women need to feel safe when they walk the streets or shut their doors at night. Attempting to put "freedom and democracy" before the rule of law is a prescription for anarchy and violence.

There's no way in which we could have made every Iraqi love us. But had we brought the rule of law from the first hours of occupation, most would have respected us.

3. Send enough troops from the start. There is no such thing as "occupation-lite." Presence matters. The defeated population needs to see our troops on every corner. Visible troops create an image of power that declarations from headquarters cannot rival. The people need to feel overwhelmed, to sense the occupier's omnipresence and, by extension, omnipotence. Out of sight is out of mind.

If troops are deployed in sufficient numbers at the start of an occupation, it may be possible to draw them down in a matter of months. But stingy deployments that attempt to hold down the political costs at home guarantee that the enemy will not experience an enduring sense of defeat. A lack of occupation troops inspires resistance—and we find ourselves deploying additional forces to support a troubled effort.

Numbers matter. In an occupation, no technology, ideology, or amount of financial generosity can substitute for adequate troop strength. In a thoroughly broken society, such as Iraq, only large numbers of occupation troops provide a sound foundation for the rebirth of civil order. Wherever we cannot be, latent enemies emerge. The primary tool of a successful occupation is the *visible* soldier.

4. Don't turn an occupation into a looting orgy for American contractors. Lavishing inappropriate contracts on American firms to "rebuild" Iraq not only squandered tens of billions of taxpayer dollars, but actually worked against us on the ground. We created false expectations for Iraqis, making promises we couldn't begin to keep. Again and again, civilian contractors failed to complete their missions. Some fled. The administration's ideological obsession with outsourcing impeded military operations as well. While the policy's defenders may point to local successes, the overall effort remains an expensive shambles.

We didn't send in American firms to rebuild Germany and Japan. We made the locals do the work themselves. They knew their countries better than we could know them. In Iraq, we tried to impose American standards and practices, and more often than not we found ourselves in a stalemate in which the old systems stopped running and the made-in-America systems couldn't be brought online. Even our most successful projects will need American support for years to come.

The focus should have been on enabling Iraqis to help themselves, to fix the systems they had (no matter how decayed). They knew how to do that much. If we wished to be more generous, we needed to take our time and do a thorough, on-the-ground assessment. Instead we created a wish list and stuck the American taxpayer with the bill.

How do you do it right? It isn't hard, if you don't treat war as an opportunity to enrich well-entrenched firms. Operating under emergency wartime provisions, military contracting officers should trail the leading brigades, empowered to write agreements and disburse funds to local authority figures to undertake needed repairs. Even if the locals are barely competent, this is the only strategy that advances our overall goals.

Consider what you achieve when you hire Sheikh Ali to fix the water system. First, he's going to pad the payroll with everyone in his tribe. That's just what we want the sheikh to do.

For any occupation to succeed, you must get young men off the streets. Unemployed young men form the pool in which the resistance fishes. Corruption must be battled in every other instance, but when a local contractor hires five young men to do the job of one, it's a good investment—just make sure those five men show up, stay at work, and get paid, that the money isn't pocketed. Not only do you employ the most dangerous demographic, men with jobs can take care of their families and keep their pride. Humiliate a man through unemployment and you make an enemy.

The other crucial aspect of this approach is that it gives influential locals a stake in the occupation. Never underestimate the power of greed. If opinion makers profit from your presence, they are far more likely to support (or at least tolerate) your programs.

5. Devolve responsibility, retain authority. This relates to the previous rule. If you hire Haji Mustapha's construction firm to unclog the neighborhood drains, you have an out when the people complain that the work is unsatisfactory. Just open your books and direct them to the haji (then threaten to kick the haji off the gravy train). Maintain a monopoly of power, but put responsibility for the infrastructure on local shoulders.

This applies at the national level, as well. As soon as possible, give natives real responsibility for nonessential portfolios. When feasible, allow them the illusion of power over key departments. If they perform to reasonable standards, you can increase their authority. But it's crucial to get Uncle Sam off as many blame-lines as possible. Lay down rigorous guidelines, but put indigenous politicians and bureaucrats to work.

Does any veteran of Fortress Baghdad believe that Iraqis could have done any worse than the young, utterly inexperienced and incompetent political hacks the administration sent to the Green Zone to rebuild a major state and its economy?

6. You can't govern from a distance or without risk. Under the Coalition Provisional Authority, the Green Zone might as well have been in Lincoln, Nebraska. By governing from a hermetic fortress, you never gain a tactile feel for the local reality (even if you think you do). Every bit as bad, you create the impression that you're afraid. And frightened occupiers are rarely successful occupiers.

You must be willing to take judicious risks, and you must smell the country's dust every single day. This is one more reason why the military, with its ability to defend itself and its discipline, has to control an occupation's decisive initial phases. Any deployed government civilians must be willing to bear a measure of risk. During my stay in Iraq last year—strictly among Iraqis—the Green Zone was regarded as a laughingstock and an impediment to progress.

7. When it's time to fight, fight ruthlessly. You cannot begin an occupation gently. As badly as you may want to be loved, it's essential to be feared. At the first sign of an insurgency, terrorist activity or violent criminality, you must respond with a ferocity that shocks your would-be opponents, their sympathizers, and, yes, the media. Bad press in the short term comes to nothing, if you succeed in the longer term. But calibrating an occupation to please the media guarantees a higher toll in bloodshed down the road. Crush resistance immediately, without restraint or compromise. The toll in casualties and human rights will be far lower in the end than if you try to win over implacable enemies.

Our occupation of Iraq—which wasn't supposed to be an occupation—will stand as a textbook case of how to squander opportunities, lives, and taxpayer dollars. Although Iraq may prove a reasonable success, the cost did not have to be so painfully high.

A crucial lesson is that amateurs should not interfere with the practical details of military planning. Although civilian authorities will always decide where and when we go to war, the how should be left to those who have devoted their lives to uniformed service. When that rule is broken, our troops are forced to redeem failed policies with their blood.

Survival Strategy

Middle Eastern Islam, Darwin, and Terrorism

Armed Forces Journal

February 2006

As the Christmas holiday approached, it was time to talk about terrorism. I spent part of a December afternoon in a sterile conference room symbolic of strategic thought in Washington ("Avoid the virus of originality!"). Following a discussion of Middle Eastern Islam's power to generate suicide bombers, a miffed senior official challenged the notion that religion had anything whatsoever to do with the phenomenon.

As sincere as it was wrong, his view of the world was typical of our intelligence and policy communities. The official insisted that faith wasn't really a motivating factor because his agency's compilation of data on suicide bombers revealed that most had either personal grievances—perhaps a relative killed, abused, or imprisoned—or simply a sense of humiliation. Mistaking the trigger for the entire gun, he clung to the last century's rationalist view of the world. The official just could not make the leap of faith required to accept religion as a strategic factor.

He was standing in a downpour, insisting it wasn't the rain that was making him wet. Suicide bombers had worldly grievances, and that was that. The promise of paradise made no difference. It was typical mirror-imaging, all about the usual suspect factors dear to the academic world and Washington think tanks. The official refused to reflect on the obvious: A wide variety of populations around the world have grievances, from Chinese peasants to the minority population of New Orleans, from indigenous populations in Latin America to the Africans tormented by Zimbabwe's Robert Mugabe. Yet neither the Irish Republican Army nor Sudan's Christian tribes, not Falun Gong or Corsican separatists produced suicide bombers. While the world beyond the Muslim heartlands has generated terrorists aplenty, the phenomenon of suicide bombing remains overwhelmingly Islamic and Middle Eastern.

Religion isn't only a matter of personal faith, but of social and psychological context as well. While we struggle to deny it, the religious environment of today's Middle East is acutely conducive to violent self-sacrifice, to willing death in violent jihad. Tumbling backward from its bitter confrontation with the modern world, Middle Eastern Islam's culture makes paradise a given for the believer who sacrifices his life in the struggle against the infidel, the Crusader, the Jew, or the apostate. (On the other hand, Western atheist suicide bombers are in notably short supply.) The suicide bomber need not even appear to have been especially religious as remembered by his acquaintances: The Middle Eastern Muslim's belief in paradise after death is as casual and pervasive as was the medieval European's faith in the existence of a hell with horned devils. The reward of paradise is assumed.

Suicide bomber X or Y certainly may feel that his people have been shamed or that his sister has been embarrassed, and that he must respond violently to the antagonist in question. Yet while plenty of other cultures generate hyperviolent behavior under stress, none but Middle Eastern Islam has given rise to the cult of the suicide bomber. The promise of paradise, with its literal treats, is undeniably a crucial determinant, whether at the subconscious or conscious level. The culture of contemporary Middle Eastern Islam makes death an appealing option.

Still, after the Koran and the hadiths have been studied and analyzed, after allowances have been made for the mesmerizing personas of terrorist chieftains and all the practical catalysts for action have been calculated, the question remains: Why has the cult of the suicide bomber developed so swiftly today, and why is it rooted in the Middle East and not elsewhere (when from Indonesia to Kosovo, Muslims behave violently but not suicidally)?

The answer is timely, given the current fuss about intelligent design versus the theory of evolution in our own country: Suppose that Darwin was right conceptually, but failed to grasp that religion is a highly evolved survival strategy for human collectives?

Faith as a Strategic Factor
Once a human collective expands beyond the family, clan, and tribe, decisive unity demands a higher organizing principle sufficiently powerful to entice the individual to sacrifice himself for the common good of a group whose identity is no longer defined by blood ties. A man or woman will die for the child of his or her flesh, but how can the broader collective inspire one stranger to volunteer his life to guarantee the survival of a stranger whose only tie is one of abstract identity?

No organizing principle, not even nationalism (a secular, debased religion), has proven so reliable and galvanizing as religious faith. Religion not only unites, it unites exclusively. Throughout history, religious wars have proved the cruelest in their execution and the most difficult to end satisfactorily (toss in racial differences and you have a formula for permanent struggle). The paradox is that, in pursuit of a "more godly" way of life, human beings have justified the slaughter of millions of other human beings through the centuries.

Even in adversity or miserable defeat, religious identity has allowed human collectives to survive when linear analysis would foretell their inevitable disintegration. Without their powerful monotheism and the conviction that they are chosen by their god, would any Jews survive today as practitioners of their faith? Even in the Diaspora and in the course of two millennia of pogroms that culminated in a massive, organized genocide, Jews withstood the worst that humankind could direct at them. Their survival and ultimate triumph cannot be explained by the safe, academic (and politically correct) factors beloved of our analysts. Faith provided the unity—even in geographical separation and during immense suffering—to preserve the genetic collective.

Could anything but a powerful new faith have united the backward tribes of Arabia into the conquering armies that exploded out of the desert thirteen centuries ago to conquer so much of the world in Allah's name? From the beginning of the sixteenth century into the early twentieth, European conquerors justified themselves—not always cynically—in terms of the apostolic spread of their redemptive faith. Religious fervor fueled phenomenal courage not only among missionaries, but among the Victorian era's "martyr officers," from Gordon in Khartoum to Conolly in Bukhara. In Rome's centuries of decline, her legions were held together more by the cult of Mithras (and their own self-interest) than by allegiance to any caesar.

And faiths are never more ferocious than when they're cornered. The responses of the human collective to an external threat can be delayed by various practical factors, from physical weakness to internecine struggles, but when the empire of faith strikes back, it does so ruthlessly. The crusades were, indeed, barbaric acts of aggression, rampaging from the Iberian Peninsula to the banks of the Jordan (and the conquest of the New World may be viewed as the last and grandest Christian crusade). But the crusades did not occur in a strategic vacuum: They were Europe's response to the Islamic jihad that had taken Muslim warriors to the Marne and dispossessed Christianity of all of its birthright cities—not only Jerusalem, but Alexandria, the cradle of Christian thought and doctrine, Antioch, Damascus, Philadelphia, Ephesus, and so on.

It's often been noted that the first crusade achieved an astonishing military upset by not only reaching the Holy Land but conquering Jerusalem (where the crusaders indulged in a stunning massacre not only of Muslims and Jews, but of eastern-rite Christians, too). The issue raised less frequently is: How were the fragmented European powers—deadly rivals—able to unite long enough to conquer so many of the wealthiest cities of the then-dominant Islamic world? Could any factor other than faith have excited and sustained such unity? Greed might have been satisfied closer to home. Even beyond the historian's observation that the pope sought to exploit crusading ventures as a means to staunch the endemic bloodletting in Europe itself or Marxist arguments about surplus population, and allowing that there was plenty of disunity and calculation among the crusaders and their various backers during their two centuries in the Levant, the phenomenon of the crusades cannot be explained without the fuel of faith.

However false they judge the tenets of religion to be, even nonbelievers recognize the power of faith to shape (or misshape) individual lives. Cynics may snort at the notion of harp-wielding, nightgowned angels with feathered wings, declaring religion nothing but a con to keep the workers and peasants in line, but they cannot deny the psychological comfort provided by the promise—true or false—of a better life beyond the mortal flesh. Religious conviction is a mighty force in the life of a man or woman of faith, and no scientist would argue against the empirical data to that point. Why is it, then, that we are so anxious to avoid recognizing the far greater impact of religious beliefs shared by an embattled human collective?

Threatened faiths lash out. They have done so from first-century Palestine through the Albigensian crusades, from Stalinist purges (Marxism was the degenerate religion of Europe's twentieth-century intellectuals) through intercommunal bloodlettings in post-independence Africa and on to the vicious backlash from defeated Islam today.

Even religious wars within faiths reek of biological survival strategies. The oppressive dominance of Latinate Christianity summoned the north-European Reformation as a response (along with no end of massacres over the contents of the communion cup). The inextinguishable rivalry between Shi'a Islam, with its Persian heart, and the Sunni schools of the Arabs is also about group competition for survival and alpha status. While overarching faiths compete strategically, subordinate branches of any religion function as local survival strategies for their adherents. Despite all the aberrations that can be cited, the development and tenacity of organized religion is evolution at its purest and fiercest.

Beyond blood, nothing binds human beings together more powerfully than a shared religious creed. No heart is mightier or crueler than the one beating in the breast of the holy warrior. And no other factor provides so rich an excuse for mass murder as stern faith.

The Analytical Mismatch

The executive who argued that faith wasn't a consequential factor in the making of suicide bombers was an archetype: The well-educated Westerner who, even if he or she engages in perfunctory attendance at church or temple, has been thoroughly secularized in matters of education, intellect, and the parameters of permissible thought. Secular, analytical thought in the West today is every bit as closed-minded as the worldview of the inquisitors who forced Galileo to recant. Its true believers have simply exchanged one set of rigid doctrines for another.

Without the personal experience of transformative faith, it's nearly impossible for analysts to comprehend the power of religious belief as a decisive motivating factor. One of the most dangerous asymmetries we face is the mismatch between our just-the-facts-ma'am analysts and the visionary ferocity of our enemies.

Merely recognizing the problem isn't enough. Overwhelmingly, analysts active in the intelligence community or in Washington think tanks (to say nothing of those bizarre mental prisons, university campuses) face a terrible challenge in adjusting to the intellectual demands posed by Islamist terrorism. Approaching the problem with a maximum of integrity would mean discarding virtually every theory they have been taught. Understanding the rhapsodic violence of Abu Musab al Zarqawi or even the seductive rhetoric of Osama bin Laden requires us to jettison the crippling heritage of the Enlightenment and much of the rationalist tradition.

Whenever I brief that we are at war with devils, heads nod dully, passing off the terminology as aimed at a theatrical effect. But it isn't. The devils are real. The Western intellect simply cannot bear to see them.

What Will it Take?

Religion is, to say the least, a volatile topic. Even those national leaders willing to come to grips with the need for a tough response to Islamist terror take great pains to assure the world that ours is not a religious war and that the Muslim faith is as peaceful as a newborn sheep in a meadow full of wildflowers. Islam is, of course, an umbrella faith, covering forward-looking movements as well as reactionary, violence-prone sects. But we nonetheless must come to grips with the extent to which Middle Eastern Islam itself has become the problem—not only the cause of structural failure, but an impetus for confessional violence (defensive violence, in the Darwinian context, since it seeks to preserve the threatened community—although it's savagely aggressive from our perspective).

We shy away from a fundamental question of our time: What if Islam is the problem?

Some months ago, an Army general made headlines through his politically incorrect remarks about Islam and Christianity. A devout religious believer, he spoke in a church, in uniform. My personal response to the media's self-righteous, self-important horror was twofold: Yeah, the guy displayed poor judgment by letting loose at a religious event with his fruit salad on his chest. But I also recognized that, as a believer himself, that general was vastly better equipped to grasp the nature of our enemies than our legions of think-tank experts and timid analysts. Put bluntly, it takes one to know one.

If we are serious about understanding our present—and future—enemies, we will have to rid ourselves of both the plague of political correctness (a bipartisan disease so insidious its victims may not recognize the infection debilitating them) and the failed cult of rationalism as the only permissible analytical tool for understanding human affairs. We will need to shift our focus from the individual to the collective and ask forbidden questions, from inquiring about the deeper nature of humankind (which appears to have little to do with our obsession with the individual) to the biological purpose of religion.

The latter issue demands that we set aside our personal beliefs—a very tall order—and attempt to grasp three things: why human beings appear to be hardwired for faith; the circumstances under which faiths inevitably turn violent; and the functions of religion in a Darwinian system of human ecology.

The answers we are likely to get will satisfy neither secular commissars nor their religious counterparts, neither scientists schooled to the last century's reductionist thinking nor those who insist on teaching our children that the bogeyman made the dinosaurs. We are at the dawn of a new and deadly age in which entire civilizations are threatened by the dominance of others. They are going to default to collective survival strategies that will transform their individual members into nonautonomous parts of a whole. We are going to find that, after all, we may not be masters of our individual wills, that far greater forces are at work than those the modern age insisted determined the contours of our lives. Those greater forces may be god or biology—or a combination of the two—but they are going to have a strategic impact that dwarfs the rational factors on which our faltering thinking still relies.

Applied to human affairs, rationalist thought too easily becomes just another superstition. Even the unbelievers among us are engaged in religious war.

Blood Borders

How a Better Middle East Would Look

Armed Forces Journal

June 2006

International borders are never completely just. But the degree of injustice they inflict upon those whom frontiers force together or separate makes an enormous difference—often the difference between freedom and oppression, tolerance and atrocity, the rule of law and terrorism, or even peace and war.

The most arbitrary and distorted borders in the world are in Africa and the Middle East. Drawn by self-interested Europeans (who have had sufficient trouble defining their own frontiers), Africa's borders continue to provoke the deaths of millions of local inhabitants. But the unjust borders in the Middle East—to borrow from Churchill—generate more trouble than can be consumed locally.

While the Middle East has far more problems than dysfunctional borders alone—from cultural stagnation through scandalous inequality to deadly religious extremism—the greatest taboo in striving to understand the region's comprehensive failure isn't Islam but the awful-but-sacrosanct international boundaries worshipped by our own diplomats.

Of course, no adjustment of borders, however draconian, could make every minority in the Middle East happy. In some instances, ethnic and religious groups live intermingled and have intermarried. Elsewhere, reunions based on blood or belief might not prove quite as joyous as their current proponents expect. The boundaries projected in the maps accompanying this article redress the wrongs suffered by the most significant "cheated" population groups, such as the Kurds, Baluch, and Arab Shi'a, but still fail to account adequately for Middle Eastern Christians, Bahais, Ismailis, Naqshbandis, and many other smaller minorities. And one haunting wrong can never be redressed with a reward of territory: the genocide perpetrated against the Armenians by the dying Ottoman Empire.

Yet for all the injustices the borders reimagined here leave unaddressed, without such major boundary revisions, we shall never see a more peaceful Middle East.

Even those who abhor the topic of altering borders would be well served to engage in an exercise that attempts to conceive a fairer, if still imperfect, amendment of national boundaries between the Bosporus and the Indus. Accepting that international statecraft has never developed effective tools—short of war—for readjusting faulty borders, a mental effort to grasp the Middle East's "organic" frontiers nonetheless helps us understand the extent of the difficulties we face and will continue to face. We are dealing with colossal, man-made deformities that will not stop generating hatred and violence until they are corrected.

As for those who refuse to "think the unthinkable," declaring that boundaries must not change and that's that, it pays to remember that boundaries have never stopped changing through the centuries. Borders have never been static, and many frontiers, from Congo through Kosovo to the Caucasus, are changing even now (as ambassadors and special representatives avert their eyes to study the shine on their wingtips).

Oh, and one other dirty little secret from 5,000 years of history: Ethnic cleansing works.

Begin with the border issue most sensitive to American readers: For Israel to have any hope of living in reasonable peace with its neighbors, it will have to return to its pre-1967 borders—with essential local adjustments for legitimate security concerns. But the issue of the territories surrounding Jerusalem, a city stained with thousands of years of blood, may prove intractable beyond our lifetimes. Where all parties have turned their gods into real-estate tycoons, literal turf battles have a tenacity unrivaled by mere greed for oil wealth or ethnic squabbles. So let us set aside this single overstudied issue and turn to those that are studiously ignored.

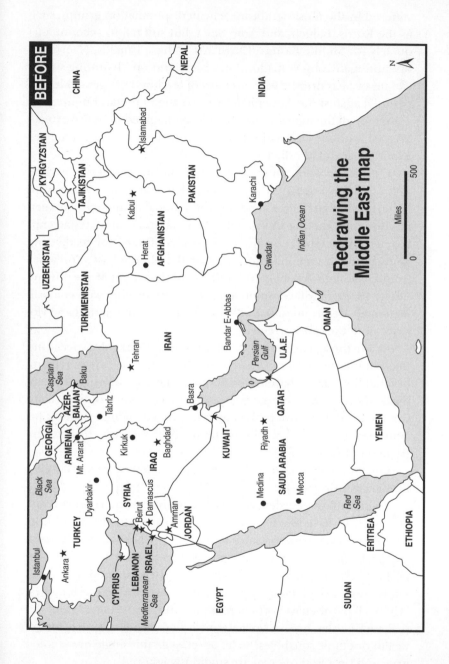

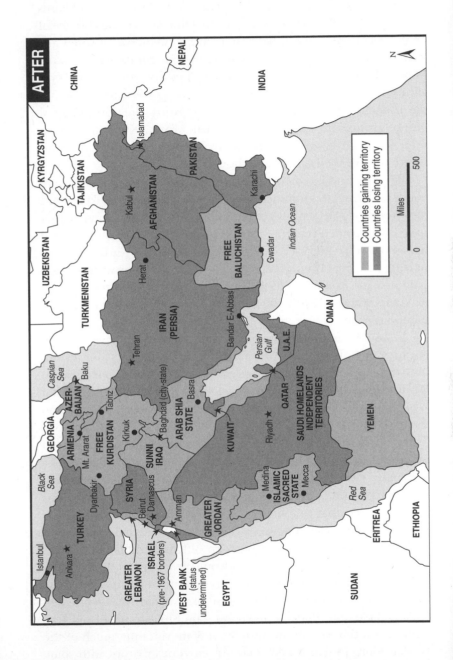

The most glaring injustice in the notoriously unjust lands between the Balkan Mountains and the Himalayas is the absence of an independent Kurdish state. There are between twenty-seven million and thirty-six million Kurds living in contiguous regions in the Middle East (the figures are imprecise because no state has ever allowed an honest census). Greater than the population of present-day Iraq, even the lower figure makes the Kurds the world's largest ethnic group without a state of its own. Worse, Kurds have been oppressed by every government controlling the hills and mountains where they've lived since Xenophon's day.

The U.S. and its coalition partners missed a glorious chance to begin to correct this injustice after Baghdad's fall. A Frankenstein's monster of a state sewn together from ill-fitting parts, Iraq should have been divided into three smaller states immediately. We failed from cowardice and lack of vision, bullying Iraq's Kurds into supporting the new Iraqi government—which they do wistfully as a quid pro quo for our goodwill. But were a free plebiscite to be held, make no mistake: Nearly 100 percent of Iraq's Kurds would vote for independence.

As would the long-suffering Kurds of Turkey, who have endured decades of violent military oppression and a decades-long demotion to "mountain Turks" in an effort to eradicate their identity. While the Kurdish plight at Ankara's hands has eased somewhat over the past decade, the repression recently intensified again and the eastern fifth of Turkey should be viewed as occupied territory. As for the Kurds of Syria and Iran, they, too, would rush to join an independent Kurdistan if they could. The refusal by the world's legitimate democracies to champion Kurdish independence is a human-rights sin of omission far worse than the clumsy, minor sins of commission that routinely excite our media. And by the way: A Free Kurdistan, stretching from Diyarbakir through Tabriz, would be the most pro-Western state between Bulgaria and Japan.

A just alignment in the region would leave Iraq's three Sunni-majority provinces as a truncated state that might eventually choose to unify with a Syria that loses its littoral to a Mediterranean-oriented Greater Lebanon: Phoenicia reborn. The Shi'a south of old Iraq would form the basis of an Arab Shi'a State rimming much of the Persian Gulf. Jordan would retain its current territory, with some southward expansion at Saudi expense. For its part, the unnatural state of Saudi Arabia would suffer as great a dismantling as Pakistan.

A root cause of the broad stagnation in the Muslim world is the Saudi royal family's treatment of Mecca and Medina as its fiefdom. With Islam's holiest shrines under the police-state control of one of the world's most bigoted and oppressive regimes—a regime that commands vast, unearned oil wealth—the Saudis have been able to project their Wahhabi vision of a disciplinarian, intolerant faith far beyond their borders. The rise of the Saudis to wealth and, consequently, influence has been the worst thing to happen to the Muslim world as a whole since the time of the Prophet and the worst thing to happen to Arabs since the Ottoman (if not the Mongol) conquest.

While non-Muslims could not effect a change in the control of Islam's holy cities, imagine how much healthier the Muslim world might become were Mecca and Medina ruled by a rotating council representative of the world's major Muslim schools and movements in an Islamic Sacred State—a sort of Muslim super-Vatican—where the future of a great faith might be debated rather than merely decreed. True justice—which we might not like—would also give Saudi Arabia's coastal oil fields to the Shi'a Arabs who populate that subregion, while a southeastern quadrant would go to Yemen. Confined to a rump Saudi Homelands Independent Territory around Riyadh, the house of Saud would be capable of far less mischief toward Islam and the world.

Iran, a state with madcap boundaries, would lose a great deal of territory to Unified Azerbaijan, Free Kurdistan, the Arab Shi'a State, and Free Baluchistan but would gain the provinces around Herat in today's Afghanistan—a region with a historical and linguistic affinity for Persia. Iran would, in effect, become an ethnic Persian state again, with the most difficult question being whether or not it should keep the port of Bandar Abbas or surrender it to the Arab Shi'a State.

What Afghanistan would lose to Persia in the west, it would gain in the east, as Pakistan's Northwest Frontier tribes would be reunited with their Afghan brethren (the point of this exercise is not to draw maps as we would like them but as local populations would prefer them). Pakistan, another unnatural state, would also lose its Baluch territory to Free Baluchistan. The remaining "natural" Pakistan would lie entirely east of the Indus, except for a westward spur near Karachi.

The city-states of the United Arab Emirates would have a mixed fate—as they probably will in reality. Some might be incorporated in the Arab Shi'a State ringing much of the Persian Gulf (a state more likely to evolve as a counterbalance to, rather than an ally of, Persian Iran). Since all puritanical cultures are hypocritical, Dubai, of necessity, would be allowed to retain its playground status for rich debauchees. Kuwait would remain within its current borders, as would Oman.

In each case, this hypothetical redrawing of boundaries reflects ethnic affinities and religious communalism—in some cases, both. Of course, if we could wave a magic wand and amend the borders under discussion, we would certainly prefer to do so selectively. Yet studying the revised map, in contrast to the map illustrating today's boundaries, offers some sense of the great wrongs that borders drawn by Frenchmen and Englishmen in the twentieth century did to a region struggling to emerge from the humiliations and defeats of the nineteenth century.

Correcting borders to reflect the will of the people may be impossible. For now. But given time—and the inevitable attendant bloodshed—new and natural borders will emerge. Babylon has fallen more than once.

Meanwhile our men and women in uniform will continue to fight for security from terrorism, for the prospect of democracy, and for access to oil supplies in a region that is destined to fight itself. The current human divisions and forced unions between Ankara and Karachi, taken together with the region's self-inflicted woes, form as perfect a breeding ground for religious extremism, a culture of blame, and the recruitment of terrorists as anyone could design. Where men and women look ruefully at their borders, they look enthusiastically for enemies.

From the world's oversupply of terrorists to its paucity of energy supplies, the current deformations of the Middle East promise a worsening, not an improving, situation. In a region where only the worst aspects of nationalism ever took hold and where the most debased aspects of religion threaten to dominate a disappointed faith, the U.S., its allies, and, above all, our armed forces can look for crises without end. While Iraq may provide a counterexample of hope—if we do not quit its soil prematurely—the rest of this vast region offers worsening problems on almost every front.

If the borders of the greater Middle East cannot be amended to reflect the natural ties of blood and faith, we may take it as an article of faith that a portion of the bloodshed in the region will continue to be our own.

Who Wins, Who Loses

Winners
Afghanistan
Arab Shi'a State
Armenia
Azerbaijan
Free Baluchistan
Free Kurdistan
Iran
Islamic Sacred State
Jordan
Lebanon
Yemen

Losers
Afghanistan
Iran
Iraq
Israel
Kuwait
Pakistan
Qatar
Saudi Arabia
Syria
Turkey
United Arab Emirates

Why Clausewitz Had It Backward

Armed Forces Journal

July 2006

Even those who have never read a line written by Carl von Clausewitz, the Prussian military philosopher, accept as truth his dictum that "War is simply a continuation of policy with other means." Yet that statement was only superficially true for the European world in which Clausewitz lived, fought, and wrote, and it never applied to the American people, for whom war signified a failure of policy.

To characterize the conduct of other civilizations and states—from the bygone Hittite and Assyrian empires to today's Islamic heartlands, China, or Russia—Clausewitz's nouns would have to be reversed: "Policy is simply a continuation of war with other means."

Conflict, not peace, is the natural state of human collectives. We need not celebrate the fact but we must recognize it. If peace were the default condition of humankind, wouldn't history look profoundly different? Thousands of years of relentless slaughter cannot be written off as the fault of a few delinquents. Human beings aggregated by affinities of blood, belief, or culture are inherently competitive, not cooperative, and the competition is viscerally—and easily—perceived as a matter of life and death. Pious declarations to the contrary do not change the reality.

Our blindness to this fundamental and enduring principle—that all of a state's nonmilitary actions seek to achieve the ends of warfare through alternative means—leaves us strategically crippled, needlessly vulnerable, and wastefully ineffective. Only our wealth, size, and raw power redeem our strategic incompetence sufficiently to allow us to bumble forward. We continue to regard warfare as something profoundly different from all other official endeavors, as an international breakdown and a last resort (occasional military adventurism notwithstanding), but similar attitudes exist only in a core of other English-speaking countries. Elsewhere, the competition between governments, cultures, civilizations, and religions is viewed as comprehensive and unceasing, and it is waged—instinctively or consciously—with all the available elements of power.

We, not our antagonists, are the odd player out.

Regarding peace as the natural state of man, Americans not only defy history but also donate free victories to competitors and enemies. Although capable of fighting ferociously when aroused, we deny that such conduct comes naturally to us, insisting that Sergeant York merely rose to the occasion. Heritage lasts, and ours was shaped initially by visions of a "peaceable kingdom," a "New Jerusalem," a "shining city on a hill." Our earliest immigrant ancestors fled Europe's wars and strife, determined to change not only their real-estate holdings, but also human nature. This continent was to become a new Eden, and each eruption of organized violence, from King Phillip's War to Operation Iraqi Freedom, has been regarded by us as an anomaly.

Pressed hard enough, we make war brilliantly, but we never cease insisting that we are, by nature, peacemakers. This dualistic character has been addressed by a succession of scholars, but, to my knowledge, not one of them has suggested that warfare might be the human baseline: We do not rise to the occasion of war, but occasionally rise above war—remarkably often, in the exceptional American case.

Yet it may be our predilection for prolonging even the most wretched peace that ultimately makes our wars so bloody. After a century of Euro-American conflicts, it requires little effort to make the case that the quickest way to inspire a shooting war may be to cling to the dream of peace in our time. Denying human bloodlust only permits it free rein while the "virtuous" look away. Idealistic American communists abetted Stalin's crimes, while conservatives insisted that Hitler wasn't our problem. Our domestic leftists insisted that cutting off all support for South Vietnam was the moral and humane thing to do—then, without so much as muttering "Oops!" they looked away from the massacres, tortures, and mass incarcerations that swept Vietnam, Laos, and Cambodia after 1975. The massacre at Srebrenica can't be blamed on Serb militias alone—Europe's pacifists were the enablers. Darfur screams, while we stop up our ears.

The war college motto "In peace, prepare for war" takes us farther along the commonsense highway than platitudes to the effect that "War doesn't change anything" (perhaps the least defensible claim ever made by a human being). But the truly crucial step is to realize that warfare never ceases but only shifts from one medium to others, playing now on the battlefield, later in the economic sphere, then in the cultural arena, and, always, in the pulpit. It isn't Gandhi or Bonhoeffer who looks prophetic, but Trotsky. Every economy is a war economy. And every successful businessman understands this intuitively, even if he has never thought or expressed it clearly. In this new age of wars of faith, the ecumenical obsession of the West is the religious equivalent of Neville Chamberlain's appeasement— just as Islamist crusaders are the equivalent of the prime minister's German interlocutors.

Along with our nibbling at Clausewitz, we also snack on a few crumbs from Sun Tzu, repeating, without any real comprehension, that "to win without fighting is the highest form of victory." Our assumption is that the maxim has a pacific, if not pacifist, sense: victory without bloodshed! Hurrah, hurrah! Such an interpretation is profoundly wrong. Sun Tzu's primary emphasis in that passage isn't on avoiding battle—that's secondary—but on winning by alternative means. The distinction is critical. Sun Tzu would have found Western peacekeeping operations incomprehensible: avoiding battle and losing.

Let's put the wisdom of the amalgam of authors we now know only as "Sun Tzu" in a more accurate perspective: If you can spare your own army by destroying your enemy through hunger, thirst, plague, exhaustion, poverty, mutiny, assassination, subterfuge, lies, or terror, let the enemy suffer and die while you profit from his agony, preserving your forces for battle against the next enemy, who might not be such a patsy. Sun Tzu would have regarded weapons of mass destruction as marvelous, practical tools—as long as only his side possessed them. Sun Tzu is Machiavelli without the conscience.

Even in our religious practice, we gloss over the merciless wars of the Old Testament, although Yahweh waged total war against Pharaoh's Egypt with a succession of plagues (including germ warfare, balancing out the proto-nuclear effects achieved against Sodom and Gomorrah).

The message we refuse to learn is that aggression is necessary and ineradicable. The only hope of minimizing military aggression is to channel the impulse into other, less destructive channels. If we routinely fight with other elements of national power, accepting that we are endlessly at war with our competitors, we are apt to face far fewer military contests.

The conundrum is that our military strength makes our policymakers lazy. Neglectful of other instruments and means of national power, they inevitably find themselves forced to resort to military solutions.

The Chinese understand perfectly that policy is an extension of war beyond the crudities of the battlefield, and they act upon the insight skillfully. The Russians grasp it, too, if less coherently. Muddling Lenin, Trotsky, bitter resentment, and inherited paranoia, the Kremlin acts upon the perception clumsily (as with the depth-of-winter gas shutoffs to Ukraine and then Georgia). The French have acted as if engaged in comprehensive warfare with all other parties for four centuries, failing only because their means were never commensurate with their exaggerated ambitions.

Now our Islamist opponents, with their model of robust jihad, have made operational the idea of multidimensional struggle. They will do anything, in any sphere, to wound us as deeply as they can. In response, we debate the legality of tapping their phones.

This inversion of Clausewitz isn't merely a matter of wordplay but highlights the need for a fundamental shift in our national outlook. We need not announce to the world that we believe we're engaged in an endless war of all against all, but we must learn to act more resolutely in our own interests, to view our foreign endeavors in all policy-related spheres as aspects of an overarching strategy.

The world may not be a zero-sum game (although our antagonists view it as such), but when the winnings are tallied, we want to leave the table with full pockets.

This doesn't mean that we should pursue a statist, minutely planned approach to international activities. But we do need a sense that we have a national purpose that transcends the inherited boundaries of statecraft and that our purpose is to remain dominant. At present, our formal national strategy is as narrow and unimaginative as it is insincere. It is, literally, nothing but words. Instead of working together for the common good, the various branches of our government (to say nothing of our business community) continue to undercut one another's efforts. Citing improved cooperation between departments isn't enough, given how abysmal it has been in the past. Our government needs to function as a team—something it has not done since the Second World War.

We do not need a comprehensive plan, only a comprehensive sense of mission.

We do, however, need to face the coldly cutthroat nature of the world in which we live, in which our ancestors lived, and in which our descendants will continue to live. While awaiting the New Jerusalem, we need to recognize that the old one was blood soaked (and the present one isn't much better). There is nothing human collectives do more effectively than making war. If we want to prevent or limit wars, this means we must obtain the results of a successful war through other means.

To repeat a worn-but-wise phrase (this one attributed to Trotsky), "You may not be interested in war, but war is interested in you."

One of the most pathetic manifestations of our willed naiveté is our insistence on describing foreign states as our "friends." Nations (and entire civilizations) do not have friends. They have allies, and those allies can change over time—just as yesterday's enemies can become today's allies. The British fought us twice (and not gently), after which we spent a century wondering whether we would have to fight again. Now Britain is our closest military ally. During the Civil War, our most important diplomatic ally was imperial Russia; we later fought alongside Russia in its Soviet incarnation during World War II; and, in the wonk-Woodstock atmosphere of the early 1990s, American policy makers insisted that the United States and the new, "democratic" Russia would be best pals forever. In the intervals between and after these brief periods of alliance and fellow feeling, we feared the global spread of Bolshevism, then dreaded a Soviet-launched nuclear holocaust, and now must contend with Moscow's breathtaking lack of scruples, its revived paranoia, its appetite for blackmail, its affection for despotic regimes, its distaste for political freedom, its disregard of human rights—and its dangerous clumsiness in the international china shop (no pun intended). Is Russia now, or has it ever been, our "friend"?

Whatever one thinks of the decision to depose Saddam Hussein, the venomous pro-Ba'athist actions and anti-American rhetoric from longstanding European allies whose minor commercial interests were threatened should have brought us to our senses. While some allies are more dependable than others (because of common interests and shared values) and allies of varied worth can be desirable if the quid pro quos are not forbiddingly painful, we nonetheless must view the world as constantly in competition with us in every form of endeavor related to national power, wealth, and influence. After all, the purpose of any alliance is to take advantage of the ally—if possible, to get the ally to sacrifice and suffer in your place.

This does not mean that we should endeavor to bankrupt or weaken every country on earth, but that we must recognize when it is in our interest to undercut the capabilities and confidence of a rival—even if that rival is a nominal ally.

The Beijing government understands this with such clarity that one can only admire the intellectual integrity of Chinese strategic thinking. Confronted with integrated, well-designed challenges from China in the economic, financial, diplomatic, and—least important for now—military spheres, our response, to the extent that we may claim one, has been piecemeal, intermittent, inept, and weak. The Chinese have brilliantly managed to harness the greed of influential elements within our own business community to prevent the implementation of policies by Washington that might reduce China's artificial trade advantages and limit our own self-inflicted vulnerabilities. By allowing a relative handful of American corporations to grow rich, the Chinese have paralyzed our government's ability to defend our workers, our industries, and our economy. We have reached the point where lobbying veers into treason. The Chinese view our relationship as a war conducted through nonmilitary means. Under such advantageous economic conditions, they are perfectly happy to refrain from shooting.

Defense contractors, as well as desperate generals and admirals, warn of a military confrontation with China. But why on earth would China want one when Beijing is gaining all it needs through far less painful means? Certainly countries have a way of blundering into war—but China would much prefer to avoid a violent conflict with the U.S. Why fight us, when we make a gift of all that Beijing seeks through our tolerance for rigged exchange rates, our acceptance of the dumping of manufactured products, our refusal to live up to our rhetoric about human rights, our rejection of serious policies to protect our intellectual property and copyrights—and our outright gifts of technology?

This is the Sun Tzu that we cite so glibly yet fail to understand.

The Islamist threat is even fiercer—far fiercer—than China when it comes to exploiting policy as a continuation of war with other means. Saudi Arabia, for example, has engaged in a merciless religious war against the West for more than three decades, yet it has not only done so while convincing our national leaders, Republican and Democrat, that we're "friends," but has managed to gain the protection of America's military on the cheap, even as it refuses meaningful cooperation with our forces. To preserve the profits of a handful of multinational oil companies, we protect a repellent, throwback regime that willfully created Osama bin Laden and his ilk. In country after country, I personally witnessed how Saudi money is used to spread anti-Western hatred (and to divide local societies), while America's taxpayers fund a military prostituted to the defense of the degenerate house of Saud.

We're not even mercenaries: Mercenaries at least get paid.

As for the Islamist terrorists, they've adopted a nonstate variant of the "total war" concept developed by Chinese military theorists. No front or sphere is off-limits. We are to be attacked wherever and however it is possible to do so. Indeed, a key lesson we should fear that the terrorists took away from 9/11 isn't that Americans can be killed by the thousands, but that killing Americans by the thousands costs our economy trillions.

We debate the legitimacy of propaganda broadcasts (by other names, of course), while our terrorist enemies run rampant on the internet; govern the content of our own television, radio, and print news through their calculated actions; preach apocalyptic hatred around the world (even in our own country); and exploit our own laws to paralyze us. In response, we send a female political-campaign worker from Texas on a brief tour of the Middle East to "turn the situation around." We not only lack a strategy—we lack a sense of reality.

Wishful thinking can't win wars, and it won't preserve peace. If only we could overcome our bias against honest thinking, we might find that accepting the thousands of years of evidence that government policies are a continuation of war with other means would result in the more effective use of those "other means" and, consequently, a less frequent requirement to go to war.

In one sense, the old American conviction that the advent of war confirms the failure of policy is true: We have to send our military to solve problems because we didn't use the other tools of policy boldly or adeptly. Our antagonists, from Beijing to Baqubah, recognize that victory will require the uncompromising use of every available resource. We default to guns. Certainly terrorists do not shrink from violence, but they view violence as a means, not a solution. The target of the suicide bomb isn't really flesh and blood—it's the video camera, that powerful, postmodern "other means" of securing a military advantage without possessing a military.

By refusing to instill a warlike spirit in other fields of our national policy, we only make "real war" inevitable.

Return of the Tribes

The Weekly Standard

September 4, 2006

Globalization is real, but its power to improve the lot of humankind has been madly oversold. Globalization enthralls and binds together a new aristocracy—the golden crust on the human loaf—but the remaining billions, who lack the culture and confidence to benefit from "one world," have begun to erect barricades against the internationalization of their affairs. And, from Peshawar to Paris, those manning the barricades increasingly turn violent over perceived threats to their accustomed patterns of life. If globalization represents a liberal worldview, renewed localism is a manifestation of reactionary fears, resurgent faiths, and the iron grip of tradition.

Except in the commercial sphere, bet on the localists to prevail. When the topic of resistance to globalization arises, an educated American is apt to think of a French farmer-activist trashing a McDonald's, anarchist mummers shattering windows during World Bank powwows, or just the organic farmer with a stall at the local market. But the swelling resistance to globalization is far more powerful and considerably more complex than a few squads of dropouts aiming rocks at the police in Seattle or Berlin. We are witnessing the return of the tribes—a global phenomenon, but the antithesis of globalization as described in pop bestsellers. The twin tribal identities, ethnic and religious brotherhood, are once again armed and dangerous.

A generation ago, it was unacceptable to use the word tribes. Yet the tribes themselves won through, insisting on their own identity—

whether Xhosa or Zulu, Tikriti or Barzani, or, writ large, French or German. In political terms, globalization peaked between the earnest efforts of the United Nations in the early 1960s and the electoral defeat of the European constitution in 2005 (the French and Dutch votes weren't a rebuff, but an assassination). In Europe, which was to have led the way in transcending nationalism, the European Union will stumble on indefinitely, even making progress in limited spheres, but its philosophical basis is gone. East European laborers and West European farmers alike will continue to exploit the E.U.'s easing of borders and transfers of wealth, but no one believes any longer in a European super-identity destined to supplant one's self-identification as a Dane or Basque. Far from softening, national and other local identities are hardening again, reverting to ever-narrower blood-and-language relationships that Europe's dreamers assumed would fade away.

Who now sees himself as fundamentally Belgian, rather than as a Fleming or Walloon? Catalans deny that they are Spaniards, and the Welsh imagine a national grandeur for themselves. In the last decade, the ineradicable local identities within the former Yugoslavia split apart in a bloodbath, while a mortified Europe looked away for as long as it could. The Yugoslav disaster was written off as an echo from the past—anyway, Serbs, Croats, Bosnians, and Kosovars were "not our kind"—but the Balkan wars instead signaled a much broader popular discontent with pseudo-identities concocted by political elites. The collapse of Yugoslavia hinted at the future of Europe: not necessarily the bloodshed, but the tenacity of historical identity.

Even as they grabbed from one another in Brussels, European elites insisted that continental unification was desirable and inevitable. Until the people said no.

Now, in 2006, we see one European state after another enacting protectionist measures to prevent foreign ownership of vital industries (such as yogurt making). France paused, as hundreds of thousands of its best and brightest protested the creation of new jobs for the less privileged in a spectacular defense of the *ancien régime*. And a new German chancellor has called for saving the European project by destroying it—or at least by hewing down the massive bureaucracy in Brussels that alienated the continent. The future of Europe lies not in a cosmopolitan version of the empire of Charlemagne, but in a postmodern version of the feudal fragmentation that succeeded the Frankish empire. Brussels may be the new medieval Rome, its bureaucratic papacy able to pronounce in limited spheres, but there is ever less fear of excommunication.

Elsewhere, the devolution of identity from the state to the clan or cult is more radical, more anxious, and more volatile. In Iraq, religious, ethnic, and tribal identities dictate the composition of the struggling national government—as they do in Lebanon, Canada, Nigeria, and dozens of other countries (we shall not soon see a Baptist prime minister of Israel—or a Muslim Bundeskanzler, despite those who warn of Eurabia). Even in the United States, with our integrative genius, racial, religious, and ethnic identity politics continue to prosper; we are fortunate that we have no single dominant tribe (minorities might disagree). Still, the success of the United States in breaking down ancient loyalties is remarkable—and anomalous.

While the current American bugbear is Hispanic immigration, most Latinos establish worthy lives in the American grain, just as the Irish and Italians, Slavs and Jews, did before them. American Indians may still think in tribal terms (especially when casino profits are involved), and there is no apparent end to the splinter identities Americans pursue in their social and religious lives, but not even imperial Rome came remotely so close to forging a genuinely new, inclusive identity.

Our peculiar success blinds us to failures abroad. Not only have other states and cultures failed to integrate *Einwanderer* or to agree upon composite identities, they do not desire to do so. The issue of who and what a Frenchman or German is appeared to idealists to have been resolved a century ago. It wasn't. Now newly forged (in both senses of the word) identities in the developing world are dissolving in fits of rage.

European-drawn borders have failed; European models of statehood and statecraft have failed; and, in global terms, European civilization has failed. Unable to see beyond those models, the United States fails to exert influence commensurate with its power, except in the field of popular culture (even Islamist terrorists like a good action flick). With the end of the colonial vision and the swift crack-up of postcolonial dreams—not least, of a socialist paradise—there is a worldwide vacuum of purpose that the glittering trinkets of globalization cannot fill. From the fearmongering of our own media to the sermons of Muqtada al Sadr, the real global commonality is the dread of change. Whether in Tehran or Texas, the established orders have gone into a defensive crouch. Men dream of change, but cling to what they know.

Far from teaching the workers of the world to love one another (or at least to enjoy a Starbucks together), the economic and informational effect of globalization has been to remind people how satisfying it is to hate. Whether threatened in their jobs, their moral code, or their religion, human beings dislocated by change don't want explanations. They want someone to blame.

The New Global Aristocracy

There is, indeed, a globalizing class, and hundreds of millions of human beings share the consumer tastes that announce their membership: Prada handbags for the striving women of Tokyo and Manhattan; the poverty-born music of Cesaria Evora for well-off fans from Frankfurt to San Francisco; the Mercedes sedan and the credit card; voyeuristic leftism for professors in Ann Arbor, Buenos Aires, and Vienna; computers for the literate and solvent from Budapest to Bangalore; wine from the region of the week for London suburbanites or Shanghai's *nouveaux riches*; media conglomerates that eschew patriotism; and, for the platinum specks on that golden crust of humanity, private jets and $30,000-per-week vacation rentals when they weary of their own three or four homes.

Such people may well be more at home with foreigners of their own cultural stratum than with their less fortunate countrymen. For the upper tier of these new aristocrats of globalization, place of residence and citizenship are matters of convenience, taste, and tax codes. This is a nobility with no sense of responsibility to the serfs, and its members are shielded as never before from life's inconveniences. For the billions remaining, globalization and its consort, the information revolution, merely open a window into an exclusive shop they are not allowed to enter. A secondhand Pittsburgh Steelers shirt on a Congolese beggar isn't globalization, but only the hind end of global trade.

The new awareness of the wealth of others is hardly pacifying. On the contrary, it excites the conviction (which local demagogues are delighted to exacerbate) that *they* can only be so rich because they stole what was *ours*. The uneven ability to digest the feast of information suddenly available even in the globe's backwaters doesn't bring humanity together (even if Saudi clerics and American bureaucrats visit the same online porn sites). Rather, it disorients those whose lives previously had been ordered, and creates a sense simultaneously of being cheated of previously unimagined possibilities while having one's essential verities challenged. Feeling helpless and besieged, the victim of globalization turns to the comfort of explanatory, fundamentalist religion or a xenophobia that assures him that, for all his material wants, he is nonetheless superior to others.

The confident may welcome freedom, but the rest want rules. The conviction that a new man freed of archaic identities and primitive loyalties can be created by human contrivance is an old illusion. Rome believed that the new identity it offered not only to its citizens, but also to its remote subjects, must be irresistible. Yet imperial Rome faced no end of revolts from subject tribes, from Britain to Gaul to Palestine. In the end, human collectives with stronger, undiluted identities conquered the empire. From the brief, bloody egalitarianism of the French revolution through socialist visions that promised us the brotherhood of man and an end to war (a conviction especially strong in 1913) to the grisly attempt to create Homo Sovieticus and export him to the world, there has been no shortage of visions of globalization. Even the most powerful attempts to unite humanity failed: the monotheist campaigns to impose one god.

One God, One Way, One World

Monotheism replaced Rome's law codes with the law of God. The first near success of globalization was the bewildering survival and spread of Christianity, the transitional faith between the exclusive tribal monotheism of Judaism and the universal aspirations of Islam. Beginning as a cult uncertain of the legitimacy of proselytizing among those of different inheritances, Christianity quickly developed a taste for salesmanship, adapting its message from one of local destiny to one of universal possibility. Furthermore, its message to the poor (a constituency contemporary globalization ignores) had as exemplary an appeal among the less fortunate of the bygone Mediterranean world as it does today in sub-Saharan Africa. Christianity was an outsider's religion co-opted by rulers, while Islam meant to rule—and include—all social classes from the years of its foundation.

Globalization really got moving with the advent of Islam. Open to converts from its earliest days, Islam moved rapidly, in just a few centuries, from voluntary through coerced to forced conversions. While the latter were never universally demanded, they were frequent (as were forced conversions to Christianity elsewhere). The immediate and enduring conflict between Christianity and Islam involved different visions of globalization, a competition of quality, design, and power (think of it as Toyota vs. Ford in a battle for souls). Those Christian and Muslim visions continue to experience drastic mutations in the battle for new and local loyalties, having now reached every habitable continent. Their success has blinded us to their weakness; neither religion has been able to subdue their old antiglobalist nemesis: magic.

When we speak of religion—that greatest of all strategic factors—our vocabulary is so limited that we conflate radically different impulses, needs, and practices. When breaking down African populations for statistical purposes, for example, demographers are apt to present us with a portrait of country X as 45 percent Christian, 30 percent Muslim, and 25 percent animist/native religion. Such figures are wildly deceptive (as honest missionaries will admit).

African Christians or Muslims rarely abandon tribal practices altogether, shopping daily between belief systems for the best results. Sometimes, the pastor's counsel helps; other times it's the shaman who delivers. The Anglican priest in South Africa decries witchcraft but fails to see that his otherworldly belief system offers no adequate substitute for solving certain types of daily problems. Quite simply, Big Religion and local cults are inherently different commodities. From Brazil to Borneo, local Christians don't see imported and traditional belief systems as mutually exclusive any more than a kitchen fortunate enough to have a refrigerator should therefore be denied a stove.

There's an enormous difference between Big Religions—Islam, Christianity, Hinduism, and the others—and the local cults that endure long beyond their predicted disappearance. This distinction is critical, not only in itself, but also because it is emblematic of the obstacles that local identities present to globalization as we imagine it.

Big Religion interests itself in a world beyond this world, while the emphasis of local faiths has always been on magic (bending aspects of the natural world to the will of the practitioner of hermetic knowledge). Magic affects daily life in the here and now, and its force and appeal can be far more potent than our rationalist worldview accepts: What we cannot explain, we mock. (An advantage Christianity enjoys among the poor of the developing world is the image of Jesus, the Conjure Man, turning water into wine and walking on water—he's a more promising shaman than Mohammed.)

Another aspect of identity that we, the inheritors of proselytizing world religions, fail to grasp is that local cults are exclusive. They not only do not seek new members, but can't imagine integrating outsiders (the politicized tribal beliefs of the Asante in Ghana are a limited exception, since they were devised to confirm the subjugation of neighboring tribes). Cult beliefs are bound to the local soil, the trees, the waters. Tribal religions are about place and person, an identity bound to a specific environment. While slaves did take voodoo practices with them to the new world, the rituals immediately began to mutate under the stress of transplantation. Tribal religions form an invisible defensive wall, as local practices do today, from the Andes to the Caucasus. Even ancestor worship, one of the commonest localist practices, supposes the intervention of the dead in the affairs of living men and women. Built on bones, local religions are cumulative, rather than anticipatory. While both Big Religions and local belief systems proffer creation myths, universal faiths are far more concerned with an end-of-times apocalypse (in the Hindu faith, recurring apocalypses), while local cults rarely see beyond the next harvest. The great faiths lift the native's heart on one day of the week, while local beliefs guide him through the other six.

What we lump together under the term "religion" is better divided into the distinct categories of religion and magic. The reason that so many local cults, from Arizona to Ghana, persist under Christianity or Islam, and why they remain a source of endless frustration to Wahhabi and evangelical missionaries alike, is that they answer different needs. Big Religion is about immortal life. Magic is about acquiring a mate, avoiding snakebite or traffic accidents, gaining wealth. African tribes, as well as the indigenous populations of the Western Hemisphere, can accept a global faith with full sincerity, while seeing no reason to abandon old practices that work.

Even as they change their names, the old gods live, and our attempts to export Western ideas and behaviors are destined to end in similar mutations. Our personal bias may be in favor of the frustrated missionaries who try to dissuade the Christians of up-country Sulawesi from holding elaborate, bankrupting funerals with mass animal sacrifices (death remains far more important than birth or baptism), but the reassuring counter is that in the Indonesian city of Solo, where Abu Bakar Ba'asyir established his famed "terrorist school," the devoutly Muslim population drives Saudi missionaries mad by holding a massive annual ceremony honoring the old Javanese Goddess of the Southern Seas. Likewise, Javanese and Sumatran Muslims go on the hajj with great enthusiasm (on government-organized tours) but continue to revere the spirits of local trees, Sufi saints, and the occasional rock. In Senegal, I found local Muslims irate at the condescending attitudes of Saudi emissaries who condemned their practices as contrary to Islam. With their long-established Muslim brotherhoods and their beloved *marabouts*, the Senegalese responded, "We were Islamic scholars when the Saudis were living in tents."

From West Africa to Indonesia, an unnoted defense against Islamist extremism is the loyalty Muslims have to the local versions of their faith. No one much likes to be told that he and his ancestors have gotten it all wrong for the last five centuries. Foolish Westerners who insist that Islam is a unified religion of believers plotting as one to subjugate the West refuse to see that the fiercest enemy of Salafist fundamentalism is the affection Muslims have for their local ways.

Islamist terrorists are all about globalization, while the hope for peace lies in the grip of local custom.

Uninterested in political correctness, a Muslim from Côte d'Ivoire remarked to me, "You can change the African's dress, you can educate him and change his table manners, but you cannot change the African inside him." He might have said the same of the Russian, the German, or the Chinese. By refusing to acknowledge, much less to attempt to understand, the indestructible differences between human collectives, the twentieth-century intelligentsia smoothed the path to genocide in Rwanda, Bosnia, and Sudan, as well as to the age of globalized terror. Denied differences only fester; ignored long enough, the infection kills.

Our insistence that human beings will grow ever more alike defies the historical evidence, as well as practical and spiritual needs. Paradoxically, we make a great fuss of celebrating diversity, yet claim that human values are converging. We, too, have our superstitions and taboos.

Magic vs. Jihad

The spread of Islam into Europe and Africa struck very different, but equally potent, barriers in the north and south. In Europe, it could not overcome a rival monotheist faith with its own universalist vision. In West Africa, Islam stopped roughly five centuries ago when it left the deserts and grasslands to enter the African forest, that potent domain of magic.

It should excite far more interest than it has that a warrior faith with an unparalleled record of conquest and conversion dead-ended when it reached the realms of illiterate tribes that had not mastered the wheel: In the forests of sub-Saharan Africa, Islam could not conquer, could not convert, and could not convince. On their own turf, local beliefs proved more powerful than a faith that had swept over "civilized" continents.

Forests are the abodes of magic. Look to forested areas for resistance to innovation. Even European fairy tales insist on the forest's mystery. Islam, with its abhorrence of magic, had nothing to offer African forest tribes to replace the beliefs that enveloped them. In northern Europe, too, monotheism faced its greatest difficulty in penetrating forested expanses, and the persistence of essentially pagan folk beliefs in the forested mountains of eastern Europe can startle a visitor today.

The forest, with its magic, is the opponent of globalization. Unlike the monotheist faiths with their propulsive desert origins, it only menaces those who insist on entering it. Now the worrisome question is whether the vast urban slums of the developing world are the world's new forests—impenetrable, exclusive, and deadly. From Sadr City to Brazil's *favelas*, slum dwellers are converting the great monotheist religions back into local cults, complete with various forms of human sacrifice. Far from monolithic, both the Muslim and Christian faiths are splintering, with radical strains emerging that reject the globalization of God and insist that His love is narrow, specific, and highly conditional. The great faiths are becoming tribal religions again.

The Limits of Globalization

After approximately a century of Christian expansion inward from its coasts, Africa remains a jumble of faiths: Muslim in the north of states such as Nigeria, Ghana, Côte d'Ivoire, Sudan, or Kenya, while Christian in the south—and persistently fond of local beliefs throughout. Christian televangelists (the real advance guard of globalization) rail against traditional practices in Ghana, while, at the continent's other extreme, on remote islands off the coast of Mozambique, the population remains strictly Muslim by day but brings out the drums and incantations at night.

The attitude of missionaries, Christian or Muslim, is that such beliefs and practices are a combination of bad habits, naive superstitions, and general ignorance. But the conviction has grown in me as I travel that the missionaries themselves are—willfully—ignorant of systems they cannot respect and so refuse to understand. Religions are like businesses in the sense that they must provide products that work with sufficient regularity to keep customers coming back. Results matter. The psychological comfort and beyond-the-grave promises of Christianity and Islam function transcendently but leave immediate needs unanswered.

In developed societies, civil, commercial, and social institutions fill the gap; elsewhere, magic must. Magic endures because local populations experience sufficient evidence of its power. This is hard for Westerners to accept, but, whether training African militaries or running an aid program in Peru, those who ignore the role of magic in the lives of others will always fall short in their results: When Global Man goes home, the shaman returns.

We laugh at this "mumbo jumbo" from the safety of our own parochial worlds, but the hold of magic remains so tenacious that it continues to inspire human sacrifice in up-country Ghana and self-mutilation from New Mexico to Sulawesi. One way to read the grave discontents of the Middle East is that Sunni Islam, especially, anni-hilated magic, but, unlike Western civilization, failed to substitute other means to satisfy human needs. There is a huge void in the contemporary human experience in the Islamic heartlands: no reassuring magic, no triumphant progress. Islam in the Sunni-Arab world—the incubator of global terror—is all ritual and no results, while even modern, Western Christianity imbues its rituals with sat-isfying mysticism, from the experience of being "born again" to the transubstantiation of bread and wine into body and blood.

What if magic—ritual transactions that address spiritual, psycho-logical, and practical needs—is a strategic factor that we've missed entirely? We would not wish to send our troops anywhere without good maps of the local terrain, but we make no serious effort to map the spiritual world of our enemies or potential allies. Even if magic and local beliefs are merely a worthless travesty of faith, our convic-tions are irrelevant: What matters is what the other man believes.

The power of local beliefs and traditions will continue to frus-trate dreams of a globalized, homogenized society beyond our life-times. If we can recognize and exploit the power of local customs, we may find them the most potent tools we have for containing the religious counterrevolution of our Islamist enemies. If, on the other hand, we continue to deny that local traditions, beliefs, and habits constitute a power to be reckoned with, we will lose potential allies and many a well-meant assistance project will falter as soon as we remove our hand.

As for the potential for violence from insulted local beliefs, con-sider this statement: "They can preach holy war, and that is ever the most deadly kind, for it recks nothing of consequences." This doesn't refer to mad mullahs and postmodern suicide bombers. It's a quotation from a historical novel by Rosemary Sutcliff, *The Eagle of the Ninth*. Published half a century ago for adolescents, it describes a Druid revolt against the Romans in Britain.

Globalization isn't new, but the power of local beliefs, rooted in native earth, is far older. And those local beliefs may prove to be the more powerful, just as they have so often done in the past. From Islamist terrorists fighting to perpetuate the enslavement of women to the Armenian obsession with the soil of Karabakh—from the French rejection of "Anglo-Saxon" economic models to the resistance of African Muslims to Islamist imperialism—the most complex forces at work in the world today, with the greatest potential for both violence and resistance to violence, may be the antiglobal impulses of local societies.

From Liège to Lagos, the tribes are back.

Lessons from Lebanon

The New Model Terrorist Army

Armed Forces Journal

October 2006

Much has been written about Israel's strategic errors in this summer's conflict with Hezbollah, from the embrace of the long-since-discredited notion that a war can be won with air power alone to the fateful indecisiveness of political and military leaders whose plans had gone awry. Israel lost the media war and squandered combat opportunities because of a dread of friendly casualties. Wretched though it was to watch, all of that simply reprised the postmodern Western Way of War, which begins with absurd expectations and ends with a whimper, not a bang.

In short, nothing new. *Im Osten nichts Neues.*

Far more interesting and instructive were the battlefield developments that went largely unremarked—not least because of the paucity of reporters with military experience on the scene. If the conflict in Lebanon and northern Israel merely replayed earlier American and European errors at the strategic level, the tactical fighting proved to be a laboratory of the future.

Hezbollah fielded an impressively innovative military force incisively tailored to meet a specific foe on particular terrain. While it could not match Israel's overall technology, professionalism, or number of troops, that didn't matter. Hezbollah fought with alternative means for asymmetrical goals. On its own terms, it succeeded, adding a new model terrorist army to the already-daunting range of twenty-first-century asymmetrical threats: the army without a state.

At the mention of stateless military organizations, historians flash back to Renaissance-era companies of mercenaries or the armies for rent during the Thirty Years' War, but Hezbollah's ground forces were of a different order: They were not for sale and, while they did not serve a state, they served a multifaceted organization with a unifying vision. Hezbollah's frontline fighters were the new version of the holy warriors of the Mahdi in the Sudan, the Scottish Covenanters, or the Bohemian Hussites. Such forces have taken anywhere from decades to a century to defeat.

What Hezbollah Did

Force tailoring. Hezbollah is the antithesis of the U.S. armed forces, which must be ready for any form of military activities anywhere in the world. Hezbollah faced a known enemy on predetermined terrain. In consequence, the well-funded terror organization was able to organize, equip, train, and deploy a force specifically tailored to stand against the Israel Defense Forces (IDF). Hezbollah wasn't interested in building a versatile force—it put all of its energies and thought into fighting a single enemy in a specific manner.

With decades of experience in low-intensity conflict with the IDF, Hezbollah understood its enemy's strengths and vulnerabilities. The IDF's ground forces remain structured for swift, conventional thrusts toward Damascus or Cairo. So Hezbollah leaders didn't attempt to build traditional brigades or battalions equipped with armored vehicles—the classic Arab error. Instead they concentrated on stockpiling the most sophisticated defensive weapons they could acquire, such as the Kornet, a lethal late-generation Russian antitank missile, as well as a range of rockets, from long-range, Iranian-made weapons to man-portable, point-and-shoot Katyushas. Thanks to the Katyushas, an Arab military force was able to create a substantial number of Israeli refugees for the first time since 1948.

Clear, realistic goals. Hezbollah had no intention of invading Israel and occupying territory—it recognized its limitations. Instead, it assigned its frontline forces the achievable mission of holding out in towns, villages, and small cities that had been turned into virtual fortresses. Attuned to the Israeli fear of friendly casualties—as well as Israel's reluctance to inflict high numbers of civilian casualties among its enemies—Hezbollah structured its defenses to make it forbiddingly expensive for the IDF to seize, sanitize, and hold urbanized terrain.

To be perceived as the victor, Israel had to shatter Hezbollah and drive it from southern Lebanon. But to be declared the winner by regional populations, Hezbollah only had to frustrate the IDF and survive. In the event, Hezbollah turned out to be the first Arab army with a credible claim to having defeated Israel's armed forces.

The ascendancy of the defense. Historically, the military advantage has shifted between attackers and defenders based upon various factors, from new technologies to innovative tactics or asymmetric organizational skills. At the outset of the 1973 Yom Kippur War, the Egyptian operational offensive relied on a tactical defense with Sagger antitank missiles to defeat Israeli armor. After suffering startling initial losses, Israeli ground forces commanders quickly devised tactics for overcoming the Sagger threat: The missiles were difficult to steer, crews were vulnerable to airburst artillery, and, above all, the terrain in the Sinai made it impossible for Egyptian formations to hide from aerial observation and strikes after Israel took control of the skies.

Three decades later in Lebanon, Hezbollah recognized that it had several important advantages that favored the defense. First, late-generation fire-and-forget missiles were faster, more accurate, and easier to wield. Second, the broken, mountainous terrain of southern Lebanon, with its towns and villages crowded within supporting distance of one another, strongly favored a prepared defense. Third, Hezbollah's tactical defense was also a strategic defense, and the terrorist army had years to prepare fixed bunkers and connecting passages. Designed by Iranian engineers, the most formidable of the bunkers proved impervious to Israeli precision weapons—and Hezbollah also took care to embed its defenses amid civilian populations, preventing the Israelis from applying devastating area fires. (I personally witnessed the IDF's carefully controlled use of artillery as calls for fire were answered with a single round or a pair of rounds—in several days at different points along the front, I never heard a battery fire full, repeated volleys.)

Defense in depth. IDF spokespeople repeatedly claimed to have broken through Hezbollah's defenses—only to have Israeli troops encounter additional ambushes, mines, and bunkers. Hezbollah designed its defenses to kill tanks if the IDF tried armored thrusts along traditional movement corridors—but also prepared to take on infantry and engineers. Hezbollah made no attempt to construct a Maginot Line; instead, it built weblike defenses that could absorb penetrations and continue to fight, harass, and hold. By the cease-fire, fighting continued at several points immediately adjacent to the border. The small city of Bint Jbeil, population 20,000, which IDF leaders prematurely and repeatedly claimed to have cleared, never fell completely to the Israelis.

Hezbollah also fielded more trained fighters and auxiliaries than Israeli intelligence predicted, allowing them to cover secondary and tertiary avenues of approach. Repeatedly, Israeli forces blundered into ambushes, as in the battle of Wadi Saluki, when eight Merkava tanks tried to negotiate a path through a steep gorge. In another wadi (ravine) fight, an officer unaccountably ordered a tank platoon into a narrow passage between steep banks—without infantry support to secure the high ground. When an ambush crippled the tanks, a para-recon platoon was inserted to rescue the crews. Over-confident and careless, the paratroopers bunched up. A short-range rocket landed in the middle of the platoon, killing nine IDF soldiers and gravely wounding four more. The mission then became a rescue of the para-recon platoon.

Modular units and mission-type orders. Hezbollah had a more developed, robust chain of command than the IDF expected. It also displayed impressive flexibility, relying on the ability of cellular units to combine rapidly for specific operations or, when cut off, to operate independently after falling in on prepositioned stockpiles of weapons and ammunition. A Hezbollah antitank hunter-killer team had more autonomy than an IDF squad or platoon—and could operate for much longer periods without support from a higher echelon. Although Hezbollah used redundant communications, from cell phones through land lines to messengers, each front-line team of fighters was a machine that would go of itself. Hezbollah's combat cells were a hybrid of guerrillas and regular troops—a form of opponent that U.S. forces are apt to encounter with increasing frequency.

Low-level commanders operated under mission-type orders—not the looser sort meant by the U.S. military but the more restrictive form employed by the Bundeswehr (and, earlier, by the Wehrmacht), in which a tactical leader could not alter his mission but called the in-sector plays to accomplish that mission. It's impossible to gauge how much initiative local Hezbollah commanders exercised, but it appears that some were more creative and adventurous than others—typical of any military. Hezbollah's frontline units proved resilient, however—and they had to be killed. Few surrendered.

Innovative use of weapons. When the IDF failed to take the bait and led with infantry and engineers rather than tank formations, Hezbollah used its arsenal of antitank missiles against dismounted infantrymen—to deadly effect. Accustomed to fighting the ill-equipped and anarchic Palestinian groups in the West Bank and Gaza, dismounted IDF troops assumed that the masonry buildings of southern Lebanon provided adequate cover. When infantrymen bunched inside, Hezbollah hit the houses with double-charge–double-penetrator AT missiles that punched through reinforced walls to kill everyone in the targeted room. The missiles were also used against IDF troops in the open—evidence both of the extent of Hezbollah's stockpiles and a willingness to invent solutions on the spot.

Notoriously, Hezbollah also achieved strategic effects with tactical weapons—the Katyusha rockets it rained down on northern Israel. Armed with excellent strategic targeting data, the Israeli Air Force succeeded in hitting nearly all of Hezbollah's long-range (and more easily detected) rockets on the first night of the war: eighteen out of twenty Iranian-built Zilzal 2 and 3 launchers, as well as virtually all Fajr 4 and 5 weapons, were destroyed, ensuring the safety of Tel Aviv and Jerusalem.

But the terrorist army had stockpiled at least 14,000 short- and mid-range rockets in calibers ranging from less than 100mm through 122mm and 220mm, up to 302mm. Designed seven decades ago as area-suppression and psychological weapons to support tactical assaults against entrenched defenders, the rockets gained a new lease on life as terror weapons with strategic resonance in this summer's conflict. The higher-caliber rockets were used to strike deep into Israel, repeatedly hitting and closing down the vital port city of Haifa and landing halfway down the coast to Tel Aviv (as well as straying into the West Bank). Notoriously inaccurate, the rockets nonetheless achieved multiple strategic goals when employed by a force that had no qualms about inflicting civilian casualties—indeed, killing civilians and terrorizing Israel was a key Hezbollah objective. By midwar, driving through the cities and settlements of northern Israel was eerily reminiscent of science fiction films from the 1950s in which nuclear war or alien invasions turned cities into ghost towns. Arabs and other Muslims found it grimly satisfying that this time Israelis, too, were refugees or driven to huddle underground as the bombs fell.

Israel had no adequate answer to the problem. Its air force achieved an impressive target-identification-to-kill time of less than five minutes—a task eased by the small size of the operational sandbox—but the technique only worked against larger-caliber weapons delivered by formal launchers. The man-pack Katyushas that rained down on Israel day after day proved too elusive for technical collection means. Nor were most of the rockets very powerful, as I can attest from watching them strike. But delivered in sufficient numbers, they did the job. Israel's total casualties remained low (117 soldiers killed and 41 civilians dead), but a new sense of vulnerability stunned the population.

As an Israeli general commented during the last week of the conflict, "Hezbollah prepared for exactly the war we're fighting."

And when the fighting stopped, IDF forces on the scene were bewildered by the numbers of Hezbollah fighters who emerged alive from forward bunkers. For the first time, an Arab army had stood up to the IDF and held much of its ground—the attacking Israelis took the sea but feared the islands, punching into the countryside and approaching the Litani River but unwilling to do more than conduct in-and-out raids on the bunker network in the area's urbanizing terrain; viewed from high ground along the border, the villages and towns in southern Lebanon reach out to one another with tentacles of new construction.

Fear casualties, lose wars. Perhaps Hezbollah's greatest tactical advantage, however, was simply the commitment of its troops. Hezbollah didn't seek to waste its cadres, but it didn't fear losses. Although only the most fanatical sought death, the average Hezbollah soldier was less afraid of dying than his Israeli counterpart. And more Hezbollah fighters did die—although the number was probably closer to 500 than to the 800 some Israelis claimed. Military loss ratios were thus about five Hezbollah fighters to one IDF soldier. It was a ratio Hezbollah was perfectly willing to accept—and hardly a surprising result, given the IDF's overwhelming strength in technology and troops. At some points of decision, the IDF's advantage was as much as ten to one, yet the Israelis remained hesitant to close with the enemy in urban combat.

Effective intelligence. This was the truly unexpected asymmetry. Despite a longstanding reputation for effective work, Israel's intelligence services failed terribly this time (with echoes of 1973). Although capable of identifying key fixed or substantial mobile targets—such as large-signature rocket launchers—Israeli intelligence proved poor at finding operational command sites; underestimated the amount of weaponry available to Hezbollah; missed some late-generation weapons entirely; had no idea how deep, complex, and well-constructed Hezbollah's frontline bunker system had become; and failed to predict Hezbollah's tactical tenacity. Despite decades of contact, Israel did not know its enemy—nor did it accurately read the psychology of the Lebanese people.

Hezbollah, on the other hand, understood Israel's strengths and weaknesses acutely. Although the Hezbollah leader, Hassan Nasrallah, admitted that he did not expect so extensive a military response to the kidnapping of two Israeli soldiers, his organization had sized up the IDF's military capabilities, tactics, personalities, and decision cycle with impressive skill. On paper, the IDF was clearly superior. In practice, its intelligence preparation of the battlefield made Hezbollah surprisingly effective. The terrorist organization also appeared to grasp the political dynamics within Israel far better than Israel read the political complexities of Lebanon.

Israel fought as a limping stepchild of Clausewitz. Hezbollah fought as Sun Tzu's fanatical son.

The War's Peculiar Prophets

Perhaps the oddest thing about the cellular antitank defense Hezbollah employed is that it had been proposed three decades earlier—for NATO, by off-the-reservation European generals. The prophetic books for Hezbollah-style warfare were impractical, military-utopian tomes written at a time of decreasing European defense budgets and the ascendancy of quantitative analysis—and, ironically, in the shadow of the antitank missile's success in the Yom Kippur War.

Senior officers such as Emil Spannochi of Austria (*Verteidigung ohne Selbstzerstoerung*, "Defense Without Self-Destruction"), Franz Uhle-Wettler of Germany (*Gefechtsfeld Mitteleuropa*, "Battlefield Central Europe"), and Guy Brossolet of France (*Essai sur la non-bataille*, loosely, "The Non-Battle War") suggested that an effective and economical method of defeating massed Warsaw Pact armor would be to field large numbers of small cells equipped with antitank weapons to wage a territorial defense in depth.

The prophets called the European battlefield's dynamics utterly wrong. Relying on faulty math that assumed X number of kills for each team, they failed to take into account the psychological effects of masses of armor on small, isolated groups of European reservists—or even active-duty troops. Although the techniques they recommended varied somewhat in their details, all assumed that soldiers would wait patiently for Soviet tanks to come into range, coolly and accurately discharge their weapons in the required number of volleys, and then safely escape to fight again. The theories also assumed that the right number of antitank teams could be concentrated at precisely the right points along exactly the right avenues of approach to pick off passive Warsaw Pact armored vehicles that would present themselves as cardboard ducks in a shooting gallery. It was utter nonsense in the European context.

But it was exactly right for Hezbollah, an organization that had the two crucial ingredients that were missing in Central Europe and NATO: a relatively small piece of restrictive terrain to defend—and fighters willing to die on the spot to kill their enemies. And the IDF, for all its strength, had nothing approaching the number of Warsaw Pact tanks. Furthermore, the Israelis had a distinctly non-Soviet attitude toward friendly casualties.

It's a bizarre quirk of history that European military thinkers in quest of defense on the cheap unwittingly predicted the tactics of a twenty-first-century terrorist army. And the predictions don't end with the examples above: In a collection of articles edited by Carl Friedrich von Weizsaecker in 1984 (*Die Praxis der defensiven Verteidigung—The Practice of Defensive Defense*), the entry by Alexander Acker is titled "Einsatz von Raketenartillcric im Verteigigungsnetz," or "The Employment of Rocket-Artillery in a Defensive Network," although the author didn't quite foresee the use of tactical rockets as strategic terror weapons. Another pertinent essay from the same book dealt with the social and political consequences of alternative concepts of defense—an issue Hezbollah managed to turn into a weapon in and of itself as it lured the IDF to strike civilian targets.

While it wouldn't do to assume that Hezbollah's doctrine designers had read the European texts, it's not beyond the realm of plausibility, given the terrorist organization's extensive ties to northern Europe. But that's a question for historians with time on their hands. What matters is that, however it managed to conceive its battlefield doctrine, Hezbollah developed effective forms of defense and elastic organizational structures superbly suited to its strategic goals. If we can overcome our vanity and set aside, for one moment, our disgust with terrorist organizations, we might recognize that no formal military establishment in our time has done a better job than Hezbollah of preparing for the war it would fight—against a superior enemy. If David didn't kill Goliath this time, he certainly gave the big guy a headache.

Future developments will determine whether Hezbollah won an enduring strategic victory or achieved only the brief illusion of one. Today's champions can turn out to be tomorrow's losers—and the political complexity in Lebanon and the greater Middle East is such that no one can predict with confidence whether Hezbollah will become ever stronger and more influential, or if its moment of triumph was just that—a moment, soon to be eclipsed by greater forces. We do not know what the future holds for Hezbollah, but for now, we would do well to study the prototype it created of an effective twenty-first-century terrorist army.

The "Eurabia" Myth

New York Post

November 26, 2006

A rash of pop prophets tell us that Muslims in Europe are reproducing so fast and European societies are so weak and listless that, before you know it, the continent will become "Eurabia," with all those topless gals on the Riviera wearing veils.

Well, maybe not.

The notion that continental Europeans, who are world-champion haters, will let the impoverished Muslim immigrants they confine to ghettos take over their societies and extend the caliphate from the Amalfi Coast to Amsterdam has it exactly wrong.

The endangered species isn't the "peace loving" European lolling in his or her welfare state, but the continent's Muslim immigrants—and their multigeneration descendents—who were foolish enough to imagine that Europeans would share their toys.

In fact, Muslims are hardly welcome to pick up the trash on Europe's playgrounds.

Don't let Europe's current round of playing pacifist dress-up fool you: This is the continent that perfected genocide and ethnic cleansing, the happy-go-lucky slice of humanity that brought us such recent hits as the Holocaust and Srebrenica.

The historical patterns are clear: When Europeans feel sufficiently threatened—even when the threat's concocted nonsense—they don't just react, they overreact with stunning ferocity. One of their more humane (and frequently employed) techniques has been ethnic cleansing.

And Europeans won't even need to rewrite "The Protocols of the Elders of Zion" with an Islamist theme—real Muslim zealots provide Europe's bigots with all the propaganda they need. Al Qa'eda and its wannabe fans are the worst thing that could have happened to Europe's Muslims. Europe hasn't broken free of its historical addictions—we're going to see Europe's history reprised on meth.

The year 1492 wasn't just big for Columbus. It's also when Spain expelled its culturally magnificent Jewish community en masse—to be followed shortly by the Moors, Muslims who had been on the Iberian Peninsula for more than 800 years.

Jews got the boot elsewhere in Europe, too—if they weren't just killed on the spot. When Shakespeare wrote *The Merchant of Venice*, it's a safe bet he'd never met a Jew. The Chosen People were long gone from Jolly Olde England.

From the French expulsion of the Huguenots right down to the last century's massive ethnic cleansings, Europeans have never been shy about showing "foreigners and subversives" the door.

And Europe's Muslims don't even have roots, by historical standards. For the Europeans, they're just the detritus of colonial history. When Europeans feel sufficiently provoked and threatened—a few serious terrorist attacks could do it—Europe's Muslims will be lucky just to be deported.

Sound impossible? Have the Europeans become too soft for that sort of thing? Has narcotic socialism destroyed their ability to hate? Is their atheism a prelude to total surrender to faith-intoxicated Muslim jihadis?

The answer to all of the above questions is a booming, "No!" The Europeans have enjoyed a comfy ride for the last sixty years—but the very fact that they don't want it to stop increases their rage and sense of being besieged by Muslim minorities they've long refused to assimilate (and which no longer want to assimilate).

We don't need to gloss over the many Muslim acts of barbarism down the centuries to recognize that the Europeans are just better at the extermination process. From the massacre of all Muslims and Jews (and quite a few Eastern Christians) when the Crusaders reached Jerusalem in 1099 to the massacre of all the Jews in Buda (not yet attached to Pest across the Danube) when the "liberating"

Habsburg armies retook the citadel at the end of the seventeenth century, Europeans have just been better organized for genocide.

It's the difference between the messy Turkish execution of the Armenian genocide and the industrial efficiency of the Holocaust. Hey, when you love your work, you get good at it.

Far from enjoying the prospect of taking over Europe by having babies, Europe's Muslims are living on borrowed time. When a third of French voters have demonstrated their willingness to vote for Jean-Marie Le Pen's National Front—a party that makes the Ku Klux Klan seem like Human Rights Watch—all predictions of Europe going gently into that good night are surreal.

I have no difficulty imagining a scenario in which U.S. Navy ships are at anchor and U.S. Marines have gone ashore at Brest, Bremerhaven, or Bari to guarantee the safe evacuation of Europe's Muslims. After all, we were the only ones to do anything about the slaughter of Muslims in the Balkans. And even though we botched it, our effort in Iraq was meant to give the Middle East's Muslims a last chance to escape their self-inflicted misery.

And we're lucky. The United States attracts the quality. American Muslims have a higher income level than our national average. We hear about the handful of rabble-rousers, but more of our fellow Americans who happen to be Muslims are doctors, professors, and entrepreneurs.

And the American dream is still alive and well, thanks: Even the newest taxi driver stumbling over his English grammar knows he can truly become an American.

But European Muslims can't become French or Dutch or Italian or German. Even if they qualify for a passport, they remain second-class citizens. On a good day. And they're supposed to take over the continent that's exported more death than any other?

All the copycat predictions of a Muslim takeover of Europe not only ignore history and Europe's ineradicable viciousness, but do a serious disservice by exacerbating fear and hatred. And when it comes to hatred, trust me: The Europeans don't need our help.

The jobless and hopeless kids in the suburbs may burn a couple of cars, but we'll always have Paris.

Dream Warriors

Armed Forces Journal, online edition

May/June 2007

"Dreams have a vise-like grip on the people of Islam. We never grasped that it was more useful to let our Muslims dream than to build them schools, hospitals and factories."

"You're confusing dreams with hope, aren't you?" asked Donadieu.

"Possibly. But I sense that the dream is vaster and more mysterious than hope."

—Jean Larteguy, *Les Praetorians*, 1961

In his best-selling novel about the French botch-up in Algeria, the former soldier and daring journalist Jean Larteguy prefigured many of the problems that English-speaking nations face today in the Middle East. While there are profound differences between Algeria and Iraq, not least the fact that Iraq has not been settled by over a million American colonists and that today's Muslim warriors are waging reactionary, not revolutionary, warfare, many of the ruminations of the officers facing Arab militants in *The Praetorians* are uncannily familiar to those of U.S. Army and Marine officers today.

The most telling insight in the novel lies in the exchange above (amended from the clunky translation published forty-five years ago): The French have been focusing on statistics and infrastructure—and losing. A veteran officer who's gotten to know the indigenous Algerians recognizes the futility of applying European analytical models to Arabs, but the vast bureaucratic machines of the army and the state plod on, obsessed with their own internal issues and rivalries.

With our armor-plated prejudice in favor of empiricism ("Just the facts, ma'am!"), we're blind to our own irrationality and susceptibility to delusions. Faced with combatively nonempirical cultures, such as those of the Middle East and North Africa, we're baffled: How can our opponents continue to deny proven facts? Our stock response is to insist, yet again, that Arabs, Persians, Afghans, and Pakistanis really want the same things we want, but haven't realized it yet and need to be convinced.

Yet it's our approach to life, although stunningly successful in other spheres, that's out of step with history and humankind when it comes to sorting out the causes for which men (and women) will fight and die—even pursuing death with fanatic enthusiasm. The glimpses we can't avoid of the mentalities of other cultures are so disconcerting to us that, just as Arabs default to blaming the West for all of their ills, we default to our dogmatic insistence that the historical evidence that men fight hardest for God, bloodlines, and collective dreams is wrong and that extremist insurgents, terrorists, and suicide bombers are really fighting because they don't have high-speed internet access.

Until we are willing to confront the mentality—the soul—of our enemies honestly, we can't and won't defeat them.

We seek a logical understanding of mass violence, but war and civil strife rarely explode because of rational grievances. Complaints about oppression, poverty, or injustice may serve as superficial catalysts, but few wars can be traced to objective decision-making by the dispassionate leaders of cool-headed populations. War is an act of passion, not of policy—Clausewitz wrote of a specific period in European history, but largely misread even his own era: Napoleon was a protean, intuitive figure, not a product of the Age of Reason. For the Little Emperor, war was far more than a tool of policy—it was a glorious endeavor in and of itself, a human apotheosis, intensified by that murderous Corsican's surreal visions of universal empire (a caliphate with quiche).

In this new age of atavism and wars spawned by the most elementary human impulses—religious fervor and ethnic supremacy—we need to come to grips with the true roots of mass violence, that ecstatic phenomenon that serves the human aggregate as the equivalent of the individual's sexual passion and release. Whether we speak of the intoxicated crowds that poured into Europe's streets in August 1914, of the orgiastic joy felt by the perpetrators of pogroms, or the coital rhythms of chanting mobs, the mass consumes the

individual. And that mass operates according to a biological impera-
tive we refuse to understand, since an honest evaluation of the murderous transfiguration of human beings absorbed into an aggregate
would destroy so many of our cherished myths about humankind.

The human being is a killer, and the human collective is a killing
machine. The purpose of civilization is to civilize the hunter and
maximize his latent abilities to contribute in other spheres—ultimately strengthening the power of the collective in other ways and
making it as robust behind the phalanx as at the tip of the spear.
Now we face an age in which entire civilizations are in advanced
states of decay and breakdown—shutting down alternative human
courses and releasing the killer again. It's far easier than we wish to
believe to turn a potential neurosurgeon into a mass murderer—or
to excite the dullard mass into a mob. Mundane successes placate
the killer within us, but never extinguish him.

Civilization bribes us to be good; if we are not good, civilization
reveals its steely side. But once a civilization has gone into collapse,
a foreign power's imposition of bits of infrastructure will not arrest
the process. The civilization may have to die before it can be
reborn—at the very least, it requires a deeper transfiguration than
any external power can impose (Cyrus didn't release the Jews from
their Babylonian captivity because he was generous, but because he
recognized that he couldn't change or integrate them, just as the
European colonial powers ultimately abandoned their empires
from an unstated sense of hopelessness). American exceptionalism
aside, human identity is intractable.

By regulating, organizing, and channeling violence, successful
civilizations allow the majority of their members to contribute to
the general welfare while a minority provides security. Except in
times of dire emergency, the superior organizational capabilities of
civilized societies allow them to devote a much smaller percentage
of their human capital to defense than primitive societies can do.
Thus, the most successful civilization in history, that specific to the
United States, has less than one percent of its population under
arms, yet spans the globe with its military and corollary forms of
power. Certainly, size matters—the civilization's size, as well as that
of the military—but you will not find a warrior tribe anywhere in

history that triumphed with under one percent of its members dedicated to warfare.

We just don't want to know what human beings, their societies, and their civilizations are really like.

Wars of Fantasy and Nostalgia

People fight for different things. Americans pledge to protect and defend the Constitution of the United States. We fight for national security and a sometimes nebulous, but ever powerful, vision of freedom. Arabs fight for faith, family, and turf—but not for constitutions. And not only do people fight for different things in different civilizations, even within their cultures they fight for different things at different times: Arab nationalism fifty years ago, fundamentalist Islam today. This second point is vital to our misunderstanding of the conflicts engaging us around the world.

From international statecraft to military counterinsurgency operations, the United States and our core allies still interpret insurrections, rebellions, and terrorism in terms of revolutionary struggle—the organizing principle, at least superficially, of so many twentieth-century insurgencies. But we've undergone a profound global shift (most advanced in the Middle East) from wars of ideology and revolutionary liberation, to reactionary violence either demanding a return to a reimagined golden age, or determined to enforce the implementation of a millenarian kingdom of heaven on earth, or both. As in the quote from Larteguy above, our enemies are fighting for dreams, and not the mundane more-bread dreams of Che Guevara, Leon Trotsky, or even Gamal Abdel Nasser, but for faith-driven fantasies and nostalgia for lost greatness.

Certainly all warfare has a more-power-for-us component, but it's remarkable how frustrated religious visions and nostalgia for a distant past reimagined as a golden age can inspire suicidal struggles on the part of entire populations. This longing for a resurrected utopia that never really existed is so powerful that it even infiltrated avowedly secular mass movements—the Nazi philosophy, such as it was, collapsed into neo-Nordic mumbo-jumbo and third-liter-of-beer notions of a glorious German yesteryear somewhere between Valhalla and *Die Meistersinger von Nuernberg*. In societies regulated by religion, the propensity to believe in Eden betrayed and waiting for redemption is incomparably more powerful. If suicide bombers plague us today, suicidal struggles by rebellious groups empowered by metaphysical visions have plagued civilizations since the murky dawn of history.

Today's insurgents and terrorists aren't fighting for freedom, but for voluntary subjugation to a stern, even punitive regime. Freedom is terrifying. Most human beings welcome just a little more freedom in their daily lives, but are ill-equipped to bear the responsibilities that American-style freedom thrusts upon them. Adults secretly crave rules as surely as do misbehaving children (and every mob quickly produces a leader with a commanding voice). Anarchy in the streets isn't a rebellion against rules, but a protest at their absence: Give an anarchist the right demagogue to follow, and you'll turn him into a storm trooper marching in lockstep.

This phenomenon varies in intensity from society to society and from civilization to civilization, but it manifests itself particularly strongly in today's Middle East. Iraqis may not want Saddam Hussein and the Mukhabarat, but they do require structure to a degree that Americans would find intolerable. Left without rules we would find insufferably strict, Arabs become lost and angry outside their womblike families. Conditioned by their religious culture to life by the checklist, they require a distinctly non-Western degree of regimentation to function as a society.

Instead of simply decrying the fact that our fiercest enemies "want to return to the seventh century," we should attempt to understand why that's their fervent, professed desire—and why the rallying cry appeals to such an astonishing range of people. Not least, they imagine Islam's "golden age" as a time of good order similar to medieval Europe's "great chain of being," when everyone supposedly knew his place and found contentment in it.

Of course, even members of al Qa'eda or the Taliban would find it unpleasant to return entirely to the turbulent aftermath that followed the Prophet's death, or, for that matter, to the mythologized era of the Caliph Harun al Rashid a few centuries later: The cell phone and the dentist would soon be missed.

Yet even such an assessment is too literal, too Western. The bin Ladens and al Zawahiris aren't interested in the perfect replication of the distant past, but in the galvanizing vision of a better, godlier world for which a fairy-story past serves as an inspiration and affirmation. The airbrushed past is just a catalyst for the dream—and, as Larteguy's Frenchman suggests, a mighty dream will mobilize far more potential martyrs than a new sewage system.

In Iraq, we tried to share our own dream, one that's worked remarkably well for us. But our efforts may be as hopeless as an attempt to convince a friend obsessed with a destructive lover to decide, on a rational basis, to choose a less menacing partner: Reason is an ineffective weapon against passion, whether in love or war. Many in the Middle East, perhaps even a majority, have fallen madly in love with fantasies that can only be sustained through a culture of blaming others for all that goes wrong, by embracing self-contradictory conspiracy theories, and by rejecting—in a rage—the contours of more successful civilizations. Like that lovesick friend of ours, humans don't want sober advice, but affirmation that their folly is wisdom.

We're left with a war not of ideas, but of competing visions: On one hand, the congenial disorder, bounded by humane laws, that has allowed us to rise to such heights of power and influence, and, on the other, the reality-shunning fantasies of grandeur resurrected and militant sanctity that blind the people of the Middle East to their own practical self-interest.

After their basic physical needs are satisfied, what invisible needs drive human actions? Certainly it's not the Western admonition to be reasonable. Whether the fantasy is of eternal salvation or of a vanquished national glory revived, human beings will rush to their deaths to sustain their irrational, but satisfying, beliefs.

The Great Reaction

Over the last few centuries, men and women gave their lives for man-wrought utopian visions. But all the invented ideologies not only failed to work, they ultimately failed to satisfy. Now the great reaction has set in, the retrograde shift to defensive intolerance. Even in our own incomparably successful society, both extremes of the political spectrum are no longer occupied by progressives, revolutionaries, or reformers, but by ferocious reactionaries who dream either of a return to a godlier age that never existed as they imagine it, or who fantasize about a neo-agrarian society that has no more chance of coming to pass than al Qa'eda has of reestablishing the caliphate.

From the Taliban to the People for the Ethical Treatment of Animals (PETA), and from the foreign extremists haunting Iraq to the opponents of women's rights in North America, our age is characterized by self-righteous fanatics who—terrified of freedom—believe it their duty to impose their rigid social norms on the rest of humanity. Their rigid visions are unanimously about turning back the clock to a "simpler" age that supposedly didn't suffer from the ills afflicting our own, Eden without the serpents. (It's piquant to note that Hitler, a strict vegetarian and animal-lover, would have backed PETA to the hilt.)

Yet humans are humans. There never was a perfect golden age, and Atlantis remains a dated pop song, not an archaeological site awaiting lucky scuba divers. Nonetheless, the longing for the "lost" golden age or the perfect future is endemic to the human condition—like the poor, fantasies will always be with us for those who cannot accept the challenges of the here and now. The difference today is that both the tumultuous pace and the universal awareness of change are more threatening than they ever have been in the past: Our enemies are fighting either to stop the clock, to turn back the hands, or to make the clock irrelevant by achieving timeless perfection. The one thing they all dislike is American-style progress.

Human beings have always been frightened by change. Today most of humanity is terrified. And tens of millions, if not more, will fight for dreams that promise them an escape from the reality plaguing them with a sense of inadequacy and failure.

We seek to improve the reality of the Middle East, but the people of the Middle East just want to escape reality.

Understanding This Enemy

If we are to avoid the fate of that fictional French officer who, faced with comprehensive failure, belatedly recognized that a people's dreams are more inspiring than the arrival of traffic lights, we have to challenge our own illusions about both our enemies in particular and humanity in general. In some respects, our own behavior patterns have been disturbingly similar to those of the Middle East—just as our opposite numbers reject empirical data in favor of comforting fantasies, we, too, flee from reality when it makes us uncomfortable: The liberal fantasies that "all men want peace," that "war doesn't solve anything," and that's it's in the natural order for societies and civilizations to get along just fine all defy the historical and contemporary evidence.

Just because we don't like the truth doesn't mean that we can declare it false.

We may heartily desire it otherwise, but far too many human beings enjoy killing and abusing others; perhaps a majority of humanity is convinced that its path should be imposed upon all others; and the impulse to wage collective violence, whether in spontaneous massacres or in wars, is irrefutably embedded in the mass psyche—to which the individual is tethered in ways that we refuse to acknowledge or investigate.

When faced with the facts of the human experience, the "enlightened" citizen closes his mind and starts calling the messenger nasty names. But if war is not part of our makeup, why have there been so many wars? Can we really blame a tiny numbers of individuals who suffered unhappy childhoods? Isn't it time that we seriously investigated the ugly phenomena of mass behavior and the collective organism that devours the individual's conscience in times of stress and disorder? A mob is not a collection of individuals, but an organism with its own biological and psychological dynamics. If we continue to see humanity only as a collection of individuals, we will never understand war or insurgencies or terror—or even the popularity of American Idol.

As reality forced our military—or at least the Army and Marines—to confront the changed security environment since 1991, the services entered a painful learning process. In the beginning, there was well-intentioned "cultural understanding," the essential purpose of which was to avoid offending a terrorist's value system. Since then, we've moved on to seeking a more tactically useful grasp of our enemy's culture, the sort of insight that allows us to operate more effectively. But tactical successes, although vital, lead nowhere if our strategic analysis is wrong: We study the individual and extrapolate to the mass, when the correct approach is to seek to understand the mass, then use that knowledge to control individuals. We've got it exactly backward.

Veterans of Iraq and Afghanistan, as well as special-operations forces in general, viscerally grasp that the asymmetries we face today go deeper than mismatches in organizations and weaponry. The problem is that thinking officers have yet to discipline their knowledge into words, into articulate insights and appropriate doctrine. Paradoxically, one of the greatest obstacles we have to understanding our enemies is that our officer corps is too well educated in the formal sense. Officers with master's degrees in international relations and Ph.D.s in government have become prisoners of the outdated theories they encountered in graduate school (alchemy in the age of particle physics).

Perhaps the best piece of advice you can give to an officer with advanced degrees is, "When the reality confronting you contradicts the theory you learned at Harvard or Stanford, believe the reality." This sounds like common sense, but it's routine to encounter dutiful officers struggling to fit a confounding and deadly reality into the cookie-cutter formulas their professors insisted would turn human lead into strategic gold. Postgraduate education, if its teachings are in error, can cripple a talented officer and leave him a menace to his subordinates—or to the entire force, if he rises high enough.

The military can't look to the academic world for answers—the campus is as out of touch with reality as an al Qa'eda cabal in a cave fantasizing about the revival of the caliphate. Academics will defend their obsolete theses to the last infantryman in the streets of Baghdad. Our military leaders, at all levels, must scrutinize their own experiences in the field and do their best to see the facts clearly, to discard the Vaseline-coated lenses their educations convinced them to wear. You can't understand today's conflicts from Cambridge or Ann Arbor. Military men and women have the experience to achieve a fresh, more accurate understanding of human motivation and the roots of conflict. It's their duty to reject the intellectual alchemy of liberal-arts faculties and the circular logic of think tanks.

The professors will tell you that it's all about deprivation and demographics, mistaken American policies and, yes, the need to build those schools, hospitals, and factories. Nothing wrong with a clinic here and a co-ed classroom there, but the real problem is that our opponents refuse to accept the empirical reality we insist is the global standard. If we continue to misunderstand the psychological and spiritual environments in which we operate, the clinics will continue to be bombed and the classrooms will remain empty, their teachers assassinated.

We need to spend at least as much time asking ourselves what our enemies want as we do telling them what we think they should want. Unless we accept the power of the enemy's dreams and deal with those dreams as a motive-shaping reality, we'll get it every bit as wrong as the French did in Algeria.

Learning to Lose

The American Interest

July/August 2007

Hamlet thinks too much. Chewing every side of the argument to mush, he lacks the courage to swallow hard and kill an assassin at prayer—a philosophical "war crime." The archetypal academic, theory-poisoned and indecisive, Hamlet should have stayed at the university in Wittenberg, where his ability to prattle without resolution surely would have gained him early tenure. Mistaking himself for a man of action, he remains self-obsessed throughout the play, taking less interest in the rest of the world than the most narcissistic blogger. To put it mildly, his perception of others is faint, as Ophelia, Polonius, and a platoon of others might testify. Hamlet loves players, because real human beings perplex him (not least his mama, who seems too meaty a woman to have given birth to such a scrap). The unmanly prince dithers, stalking himself, until his belated action— inevitably, too complex in its conception—leaves the stage covered with bodies, including his own.

Henry V, by contrast, was a real king who won battles because he wasn't afraid to get close to the enemy and kill him. Both Shakespeare's titan and the historical figure triumphed militarily over bowel-draining odds, yet neither propounded a high-flown theory of warfare. Both Henrys believed in the doctrine of kingship, but doctrine guides action, while theory inhibits decisiveness. Henry led from the front and checked up on his troops in the dead of night, unlike the slothful chain of command responsible for the Abu Ghraib debacle. In contrast to that of Hamlet, Henry's violence was prompt and always had a point. King Harry could make a decision. His leadership inspired and he never lost sight of his essential requirement: to win, at any cost. First he won militarily, *then* he negotiated from a position of strength.

How easy it is to imagine Hamlet scheming for a higher chair within an Ivy League faculty. If Henry V showed up in the quad, the first graduate assistant to spot him would speed-dial the campus police.

What do Shakespeare's polar-opposite characters have to do with the education of the officer corps of the U.S. Armed Forces— apart from the fact that Shakespeare has to do with nearly everything? Only this: Our military needs Henrys, yet for half a century it's been hellbent and determined to turn out Hamlets with stars on their shoulders.

Setting aside practical training, a task at which the U.S. military is incomparable, an officer's formal education after commissioning comes in two varieties (one is tempted to write "comedy and tragedy"): In-house courses conducted by the services, for the services; and advanced civilian education for officers selected for specialized roles, for those identified as likeliest to rise in rank, and, not least, for those who don't really want to be soldiers and scheme to cajole a free education out of the bureaucracy. (A fourth category is composed of officers who gain a master's degree or the equivalent on their own, in their scarce free time and at far more expense to their personal lives than to the taxpayer, but no officer who saves the government tens of thousands of dollars can be taken seriously.)

The in-house courses, of which there are many, do a competent job of preparing officers for their previous rank. The most effective of the courses through which all officers must pass is the Basic Course (for simplicity's sake, we'll use the nomenclature common to the Army and Marines, since service terminology can vary). The students are lieutenants fresh from a service academy, from the Reserve Officers' Training Program on a civilian campus, or from Officer Candidate School, which commissions soldiers harvested from the enlisted ranks. The Basic Course, followed by a block of specialized training, welcomes the young officer into the service and provides a grounding in his or her branch (Infantry, Military

Intelligence, Ordnance, and so forth). It functions as a transition stage before the young officer is thrust into the never-enough-time atmosphere of a battalion.

Along with the follow-on specialized course, the Basic Course gives the second lieutenant a professional vocabulary and a sufficient sense of what he or she will have to do "in the field" to allow the officer to get started in a first assignment—where the real education of any officer begins.

At the conclusion of their apprenticeships, captains attend the Advanced Course, where the system begins to fray. With at least two assignments behind them, student officers arrive with a disruptive knowledge of how things actually work. They are then instructed by a faculty not always selected from the military's strongest performers on how their branch's doctrine insists they should have done what they did successfully but incorrectly. Some Advanced Course programs are better than others, but few officers learn much of use from them. Their greatest value comes from giving the officer a bit of time with his or her family in a not-quite-serious environment, and in bringing peers together so they can sniff each other—an important matter for those who inevitably will need to rely on one another in future assignments.

The next educational gate is Command and General Staff College (C&GSC) for majors and captains on the promotion list. Once selective, the Army program is now inclusive—and healthier for it. C&GSC's purpose is, as the name suggests, to prepare officers for higher command and staff positions. Once again, the student is asked to forget what he or she has learned in practice in order to master obsolete or obsolescent doctrine approved by a hierarchy of committees, few of whose members have the recent wartime experience common to the students. While elective courses can have real value, major end-of-term exercises in the past have been so far divorced from military reality that only the most careerist students pretended to respect them. As with the Advanced Course, the real value of C&GSC is the gathering in of the tribes, the opportunity for peers—this time from all of their service's branches, as well as from sister services and foreign militaries—to get a sense of each other, to learn from each other, and to build relationships that can have profound effects in future years.

The last formal phase of in-house officer education is the War College, where largely civilian faculties instruct colonels and lieutenant colonels on the countless theories academics have devised for avoiding war. Failed theories of international relations form the core curriculum, augmented by courses on how to lose wars politely, and lectures from government functionaries who never rose quite high enough to discount such ego-boosting appearances.

The value of the officer's year at the War College depends overwhelmingly on whether he or she is interested in learning. This is a year for those who recently relinquished command—an all-consuming endeavor—to read. The best thing that has happened to the various service war colleges in recent years has been the assignment of new war veterans and more creative officers as seminar leaders, but the tenured academics will surely wait them out.

At all levels above the Basic Course, veterans are challenging faculties composed of academics, aging military retirees, and administrators who would rather lose a war than attract uncomfortable attention by exploring controversial subjects (one war college journal has been forbidden from mentioning religion when discussing our current conflicts, which means interpreting Islamist terror as a virgin birth). A few innovators have infiltrated the system and hopeful signs have increased, but one suspects that the force of tradition and the bureaucratic might of the institutions will continue to prevent the military education system from being all that it could be.

As any officer above the rank of second lieutenant knows, our military's real education occurs in units and on their staffs, where doctrinal manuals are only consulted to ensure that a piece of paper has been paragraphed properly before being transmitted to higher headquarters.

Although the reality can be opaque to outsiders, the U.S. military is remarkably supple once it escapes the classroom—considering the institution's behemoth size and complexity. Frankly, we can continue to prosper under the current mediocre system of in-house military education as long as practical training, from infantry patrolling to flying combat aircraft, is superbly conducted. Talent, commitment, and field experience carry us through. Yet we could do far better. The problem is that, to construct an incisively useful military education system for the twenty-first century, we would need to discard most of the current system and start afresh. That would mean taking on hallowed traditions (the Army's C&GSC has its roots in the nineteenth century) and gutting deeply rooted bureaucracies. Iraq is easier.

What might a more effective in-service education look like? That depends on what we really need it to do.

At present, captains and above are taught dubious schoolhouse solutions to problems they have already faced and resolved under fire. The war colleges offer the potential to raise an officer's perspective to the strategic level, but faculties are trapped in dysfunctional twentieth-century theories of international relations and conflict (often in jealous emulation of their civilian campus peers). Unless he draws a strong, uniformed seminar leader, the officer may, indeed, learn a great deal at the war college: most of it wrong.

If you queried commanders in Iraq, Afghanistan, or elsewhere as to what additional skills would be of the greatest benefit to the officers under their command, you initially might get muddled answers. Their subordinate officers are already very good at the applied combat and support skills at which the U.S. military excels. You would have to calm them down a bit and press them, perhaps even leading the witness. Given time to think it over, thoughtful line-unit commanders probably would agree that nothing would give their officers a greater additional advantage than better language skills.

Anyone who has witnessed a lieutenant, captain, or lieutenant colonel interacting with Iraqis through an interpreter immediately grasps the problem: Even with the best hired help, information is filtered and nuances disappear. The officer may be as good as any combat leader in the world when it comes to combat, but he's crippled in his ability to read the signals that may be leading to a fight. As signals intelligence operators used to put it, he's condemned to "reading externals," making judgments based upon outward manifestations, as opposed to deciphering the immediate human message.

While not every infantry officer can be trained as a fluent Arabic, Pashto, or Farsi speaker, nor should he be, the inability to communicate and understand, to activate the magic that comes to those who master the opponent's language, leaves us in the role of eternal outsiders. The widespread dismissal of the importance of language skills for officers in command positions is simply astonishing given the nature of the conflicts we have faced in recent years and will likely face for decades to come. You will find hundreds of senior officers who have been immersed in theories of civil-military relations or (obsolete) deterrence models for each one who can construct a sentence in Arabic or Farsi (or Chinese, for that matter). But nothing could be more irrelevant to today's and tomorrow's enemies than Western theories of statecraft, while the language skills and cultural grasp that foster adroit (and swift) evaluations of the multidimensional conflict environment comprise, in military jargon, a major "combat multiplier."

Wars are won by officers who know the smell of the streets, not by those who swoon over the odor of political science texts. Under the press of tradition and inertia, we continue to train officers according to dreary patterns established decades or even centuries ago. Yet we have been selective (and often penny wise, pound foolish) about the educational traditions we chose to preserve: U.S. Army officers on the eve of the Civil War were far more likely to be able to read professional texts in at least one foreign language than their counterparts today. Our military education system for senior officers, especially, concentrates more energies on teaching them about Washington than on exposing them to the world beyond our shores; thus they rise through the system better prepared to fight for additional funding on Capitol Hill than to fight our enemies abroad.

If we could reform the in-house military education system to make it relevant to the requirements of the twenty-first century, it would first require a great sweeping away of the current system's deadwood. Military *leaders* need to set aside emotion and the force of habit to ask themselves honestly which current courses and institutions are a waste of time. If the issues are "staffed," the bureaucracies will always justify themselves. We need military-education reformers in uniform. Unfortunately, we're likeliest to get more sheep in wolves' clothing—the best description of today's general officers I can offer.

To get a sense of the current misplaced priorities, let us return for a moment to the issue of language skills. At present, language training goes overwhelmingly to enlisted personnel on the unspoken assumption that officers don't have time for that sort of triviality. And even the enlisted personnel who receive language training are almost always from the Military Intelligence Branch. Certainly, MI needs all the linguists it can get. But so do infantry companies—and platoons. Yet the few officers who do receive serious language training of sufficient length to allow conversational fluency are Foreign Area Officers (FAOs) destined for strategic or embassy assignments. While FAOs make an enormous contribution to our military, there are never enough of them to go around—and certainly not enough to beef up ground patrols in Baghdad or the badlands on Afghanistan's border with Pakistan.

The current military leadership—children of the Cold War still—simply cannot bring itself to take foreign language skills for line officers seriously. In a recent dinner conversation, a certain Army Chief of Staff agreed that, yeah, developing language skills is important—right, got it, sure. But it isn't a "wartime priority." Well, first, this struggle we are now in is going to be a very long one, and second, war is the *only* time when you really can change a military. In peacetime, the bureaucrats always win.

There are many other twenty-first-century skills that officers require, some of which are being learned the hard way. But the reluctance to send officers for language and cultural studies programs of serious length in lieu of other time-wasting military-education programs (such as the Advanced Course or C&GSC) reflects institutional prejudice at its most hidebound and destructive. Consider how many American soldiers and Marines may have died in Iraq because their leaders didn't understand what the locals said or scrawled on a wall. Imagine how much more effective our forces might be if language skills were rewarded with increased promotion-board advantages (the crucial link in making any reform stick).

Of course, military officers needn't master every last tribal language, and could not do so in any case. We live at a time when the key languages officers should study are finite in number: Arabic, Farsi, Urdu, Chinese, Swahili, Spanish, African French, Portuguese, Turkish, Russian, and a few others. And as all those who ever mastered a single foreign language know, the ability to live in another tongue opens new mental horizons transferable to still other cultural environments. Foreign language skills, taken seriously, teach us not only how to communicate, but how to think like the other side, how to see differently, and, sometimes, even how to feel differently. But instead of studying the world and how it communicates, we continue to teach officers how they should have formatted that staff report in their assignment before last.

The current status of in-house military education is suboptimal but bearable because even if it doesn't much help officers, it doesn't ruin them either. The graver problem is our habit of sending talented officers to "top" civilian universities, where their critical-thinking faculties are destroyed and their common sense is retarded. Can it be coincidental, after all, that across the half-century during which the cult of higher civilian education for officers prospered, we have gone from winning wars to losing them?

The basic question regarding university and postgraduate education for military officers is, "How much is enough?" Certainly, every officer should have a four-year degree, without which he or she would not be sufficiently attuned to the broader frequencies of American society. For many officers, a master's degree or the equivalent makes sense, as well. But a Ph.D. is deadly (if not to the officer receiving it, then to his subordinates). I know of not a single troop-leading general—not one—whom I believe is a more effective combat commander because he holds a doctorate. On the contrary, too much formal education clouds a senior officer's judgment, inhibits his instincts, and slows his decision making. I have watched with dismay the process of unlearning necessary for the too-cerebral officer to become the visceral killer any battlefield demands. For the better sort, war does eventually knock the Hamlet out of them, but at what interim price? Even Schopenhauer, hardly an illiterate, warned that an excess of theoretical knowledge obscures reality.

Certainly we need *intelligent* generals. But we should fear *intellectual* generals. America won its wars largely by avoiding the soldier-butchering theories of warfare concocted by French and German staff officers with too much time on their hands. Pragmatism is at the heart of America's cultural and economic success, and it long remained the key to our military success. When we began to theorize, we began to lose. In the military context, theory is a killer.

Theory kills both actively and passively. The horrific massacres perpetrated in the name of political theory in the twentieth century should be revelatory to officers with intellectual pretensions, but the lure of theory is simply irresistible to certain breeds of officers. Having pursued an active profession for decades, when suddenly exposed to the theoretical world they become enchanted with its novelty—like the new girlfriend who clouds the devoted husband's judgment. Ill-equipped to navigate the murky waters of theory, they jettison their common sense and the lessons of experience to doggy-paddle behind professors who couldn't swim in real world currents without dragging down every lifeguard in sight. You should never let any full-time university professor near any form of practical responsibility, and you should never let a rising officer near a professor.

My own experiences with officers who pursued doctoral degrees have ranged from the ludicrous to the horrifying. One lieutenant colonel, upon receiving his doctorate, took to smoking a bent-stem pipe and wearing a cardigan. I would've had him shot. Another, more recent experience with an officer who let his education pervert his judgment involved a discussion about how an Army doctrinal manual had gone so terribly wrong. A lieutenant colonel responded to an observation of mine by puffing himself up and beginning, "Speaking as a social scientist—"

"You're not a social scientist," I told him. "You're a soldier."

He looked startled. "Well, I'm a social scientist *and* a soldier."

"No. You can't be both. Which is it?"

To a lay reader, this conversation may strike no chords, but soldiering is a vocation akin to a religious calling. One may have other skills, but no soldier—no *real* soldier—would ever define himself first as a social scientist or as anything else. All else is secondary to the calling, and when the calling fades, it is the soldier's last duty to shed his uniform before shaming it.

The conversation got worse. The "social scientist" had published a book based on his academic work on campus. Having addressed mid-twentieth-century counterinsurgency operations, he was determined to apply "his" solutions to radically different twenty-first-century conflicts. In the best academic tradition, he had no intention of letting the facts interfere. Unfortunately, this officer had been tasked to write Army doctrine. The draft manual he produced was utterly out of touch with reality. Its irrelevance was the topic of our meeting.

Confronted with the utter nonsense the manual propounded, the officer was challenged to defend his winning-hearts-and-minds, don't-shoot, negotiate-with-the-sheikh-and-don't-hurt-his-feelings approach to defeating insurgents (one is compelled to add that the officer and his associates also honored the academic tradition of writing very badly). Pressed, the officer admitted, in front of several of his peers, that the most effective technique employed by the unit with which he had served in Iraq wasn't handing out soccer balls, but strapping dead insurgents across the front of their tanks and driving around for the locals to get a good look—after which the relatives had to come to the military base to ask for the bodies.

"Well, why isn't that in the manual, if that's what worked?" I asked.

It was a rhetorical question. The manual in question wasn't about defeating insurgents, but about political correctness.

The officer isn't a bad man nor even the worst sort of careerist— on the contrary, he's quite talented. But he was determined to defend his thesis to the end, no matter if we lost the struggle in Iraq. He couldn't see that his airy theorizing was going to get soldiers killed for nothing. He had compartmentalized the techniques that actually worked for him and his peers in Iraq from those which he knew the military and political establishment wanted to hear. No conscious decision was involved: This is what the campus had done to him.

The military's adulation of dead theorists at the expense of current experience would be laughable were it not costing the lives of our soldiers and Marines while failing to accomplish the missions assigned to our forces. Even the most talented general with a doctorate must go through the process of unlearning to rid himself of the last century's intellectual baggage, finally enabling himself to see "*das Ding an sich,*" reality itself.

In speaking with officers during their classroom courses, I warn them that, when confronted with a reality that contradicts the theories they have studied at Harvard's John F. Kennedy School of Government, they should believe the reality. Most think I'm just making a joke, but I'm not. That officer who wrote dishonest doctrine to protect his dissertation's reputation had lost all perspective on his profession and his duty. In yet another hallowed academic tradition, he was determined to cram the vast complexity of the world into a neat theoretical briefcase.

Perhaps the most perverted romance of recent decades (Lord knows, that's quite a standard) is the love affair between the military and civilian academics. I challenge any reader to cite a single example of a social science professor's work contributing to any military victory. On the contrary, we have produced generations of officers so diseased with theory that some no longer possess the mental health to grasp the reality unfolding before them. It has been heartbreaking to watch our timid military leadership tie itself into knots in Iraq as it tried to wage the sort of conflict academics assured them was necessary. And then, for ill measure, the academics they revere solemnly warned the public that the generals they had castrated were an unruly threat to the republic. We had, simultaneously, generals who lacked the guts to tell the president the truth and stay-at-home academics who insinuated that coups were just around the corner. The contrast between cowering generals and crowing professors was surreal. And our troops died from the blindness, incompetence, and cowardice of leaders who knew everything except how to make war.

Worse, they didn't even know they were in a war. Many still don't. But the academics who seduced them with fairy-tale theories will prosper from writing texts explaining the failure of the generals.

Imagine how much better it would be to train an officer in a useful language and then launch him into a foreign country for a year to perfect his fluency, instead of sending him to Yale or Princeton. Not one of the generals and admirals who won our nation's wars had doctorates, but they often had extensive experience of the world beyond our shores.

A young George Marshall spent months inspecting Russo-Japanese War battlefields on the Asian mainland, while a not-yet-vinegary Joe Stillwell literally walked across China. Douglas MacArthur had long years of service in the Philippines before the first Japanese aircraft appeared over Luzon. Would they have served our country so well if their time had been spent on a campus instead of getting Asian dust on their boots?

Again, it's a question of the right level of education. A master's degree is useful because it broadens horizons, but a doctorate usually narrows them. Moreover, one should always be suspicious of a line officer willing to spend so much time away from troops. If he wants to spend his life pondering the modern astrology we term "social science," let him take off his uniform. Officers don't need to study elaborate theories of conflict resolution (none of which work, anyway). They need to know how to fight and win wars. They need to have the guts to do what it takes. Above all, they need integrity, which is a hallmark of good military units, but certainly not of the contemporary American campus.

Should we really send our future generals to Princeton, instead of shipping them off to Pakistan for six months or a year? If we are going to use tax dollars to send officers to graduate school, we should at least refuse ever to send them for degrees in political science or sociology. With special exceptions for officers destined for technical assignments, future leaders should study history, languages, and foreign cultures (a bit of anthropology, but light on the postmodernist mumbo-jumbo). In current practice, a master's degree in marketing counts as much for promotion purposes as does a degree in Middle Eastern studies. It's about the merit badge, not the merit.

The natural charge against the arguments advanced here is "anti-intellectualism." And the accusers would be exactly right. Our military should prize intelligence and broad learning, but should abhor intellectual posturing. At present, intellectual posturing trumps practical intelligence. Personally, I value the officer who painstakingly builds a library of cherished books, but fear the officer who revels in academic credentials. The most admirable general officer I've known—a brilliant man and a ferocious battlefield leader who also writes with unfashionable clarity—mocks the master's degree the Army forced him to get as worthless. He's a member of a dying breed.

Reading to aid thinking is a habit usually acquired early on. One of my favorite memories is of sitting in a cavernous classroom as an instructor droned on at Officer Candidate School and thinking myself awfully smart as I read a German translation of Solzhenitsyn under my desk—only to be humbled when I realized that the officer to my right was reading Tacitus in Latin, while the officer to my left was reading medieval poetry in French.

The issue of the future of military education, either within the services or on civilian campuses, comes down to what we expect of our military. If we want our generals and admirals to continue to lose wars while fearing to tell the president the truth, by all means continue with the present system. If, however, we imagine that we might want senior leaders who understand the real and dangerous world beyond our shores, who realize that wars are not won with good table manners, and who believe it their duty to tell the truth to our country's elected leaders, then it's time to stop trying to turn first-rate officers into third-rate academics.

What kind of men do we want to lead our military? Do we want generals who understand the importance of "a little touch of Harry in the night," or Hamlets who spend the night contemplating what they aren't going to do in the morning? Do we want battlefield leaders who inspire their men to "imitate the action of the tiger," as Henry V does before the walls of Harfleur, or do we prefer generals who wring their hands in the face of deadly enemies and ask, "To be, or not to be?" Now *that* is the question.

Better than Genocide

Ethnic Cleansing in Human Affairs

National Review

August 13, 2007

Ethnic cleansing is evil. It can never be condoned. Yet our repugnance at the act leaves us with a dilemma: What are we supposed to do in cases where ethnic cleansing may be impossible to prevent—cases in which well-intentioned efforts to interrupt ethnic cleansing actually make a conflict deadlier?

One problem we face is a muddle in terminology, employing "ethnic cleansing" and "genocide" interchangeably; in fact, there is a profound difference between these two human habits. Genocide is the attempt to *exterminate* a minority. Ethnic cleansing seeks to *expel* a minority. At its less serious end, ethnic cleansing may aim only at the separation of populations deemed incompatible by at least one side, with psychological, legalistic, or financial machinations brought to bear to achieve the desired end. At the other extreme, ethnic cleansing can involve deadly violence and widespread abuse. In the worst cases, ethnic cleansing efforts may harden into genocide.

It must never become the policy of the United States to abet ethnic cleansing. Yet our all-or-nothing reaction when confronted with this common human phenomenon has proven to be consistently ineffective, from the Balkans to Iraq. Until we make an honest attempt to understand the age-old human impulse to rid a troubled society of those who are different in ethnicity or religion, we will continue to fail in our efforts to pacify and repair war-ravaged territories. If our conflicts over the past decade and a half offer any lesson, it's that the rest of the world refuses to conform to our ideal-ized notions of how human beings are designed to behave. We never stop insisting that the peoples of the former Yugoslavia, the tribes of Somalia, the ethnic groups of Afghanistan, and, most painfully, the religious and ethnic factions of Iraq must learn to live in harmony. Those we hope to convince ignore us.

If ethnic cleansing can be prevented and the society rejuve-nated, that's an admirable accomplishment. But not all enraged passions can be calmed, no matter how vociferously we insist other-wise. Once ignited, some human infernos must burn themselves out; and you had best position any firebreaks correctly. To date, our reactions to situations in which ethnic cleansing cannot be arrested have been inept; in Iraq, for example, well-intentioned attempts to stymie neighborhood ethnic cleansing efforts may have led to the targets' being murdered as opposed to merely forcibly removed. We struggle to keep families in their homes; in response, the families are massacred in those homes. We pretend that embedded hatreds are transient misunderstandings, but we're not the victims who pay the price for our fantasies.

As uncomfortable as it may be to face the facts, ethnic cleansing has been a deeply ingrained response of human collectives since the dawn of history, and it's preferable to uncompromising genocide.

A Long History

Why do human collectives feel compelled to expel neighbors with whom they may have lived in relative peace for generations or even centuries? It's a difficult question. The Western model of studying the individual and then extrapolating our findings to the society pre-vents us from understanding mass behavior, which is far more com-plex (and murky) than the sum of individual actions. In much of the world—not least, in the Middle East—a more incisive approach is to examine the mass first, then extrapolate to the individual. We're astonished when foreign actors we know as affable individuals are swept up in mob behavior, but the mob may be their natural ele-ment and the reasonable character we encountered on a personal level a fragile aberration: Even in our own society, the mass remains more powerful than the man.

A related obstacle to understanding the insidious appeal of ethnic cleansing is that our leaders and opinion makers interact disproportionately with foreign urban residents who have a higher
education level, a greater English-language ability, and a more cosmopolitan outlook than the rest of their society. As a result, we're
instructed that a given society doesn't support ethnic cleansing,
since there are mixed marriages in Sarajevo or Baghdad or Weimar
Germany. But the impulse to expel those who are visibly or behaviorally different—or who are merely accused of being different—is
deeply rooted in the human soil. The man in the mansion may tell
you one thing, but the unemployed citizen out on the street may
bring to bear a very different psychology—along with an inchoate
desire for vengeance inseparable from the human condition.

In the Old Testament, you can search fruitlessly through book
after book for an example of disparate populations living happily
side by side as equals. Ethnic cleansing and genocide appear early
and continuously; and it is the differences between the various
nationalities and tribes, not the commonalities, that are stressed in
the foundational text of our civilization. We read not of a multicultural, tolerant society, but of a chosen people charged to conquer.
Tribal genocides erupted throughout history when competition for
scarce resources intensified; genocide is fundamentally Darwinian,
as one group seeks to annihilate another for its own safety or other
perceived benefits. Above the tribal level, though, full-scale genocides have been relatively rare; the more common practice, even in
the case of the ever-cited Mongols, was selective mass-murder to
instill fear—the slaughter of a city's population to persuade other
cities not to resist.

The Romans knew how to punish convincingly but had little
taste for outright genocide. Their preference was for forms of ethnic cleansing that resettled troublesome tribes or dispersed rebellious populations—such as the Jews, following the rebellions of the
first century A.D. (The Greeks, whose "civilized" behavior was a
myth, had been more apt to slaughter rivals, whether in the poetry
of Homer or the reportage of Thucydides.) From the Babylonian
captivity down to Stalin's practice of uprooting restive groups (such
as the Chechens), ethnic cleansing as a tool of statecraft has a long,

if hardly proud, tradition, with genocide reserved as the fail-safe answer.

Further confounding our preconceptions, state-organized programs of ethnic cleansing, for all their heartlessness, look relatively humane compared with the countless outbreaks of ethnic or religious cleansing inspired by roving demagogues, *agents provocateurs*, or simply rumors. While state genocide is the most potent form, state-backed ethnic cleansing tends to be less lethal than popular pogroms, since the state seeks to solve a perceived problem, while the mob wants blood (the horrific genocide perpetrated against the Armenians fatally combined state policy and popular bigotry in a muddle of genocide and ethnic cleansing). Once the people of a troubled society get it into their heads that their neighbors who look or sound or worship differently are enemies bent on subversion, outbursts of extraordinary savagery are the norm.

In this context, ethnic cleansing might be the least horrific of the alternatives. Which atrocity was worse, the French massacre of Protestant Huguenots in the sixteenth century, or Louis XIV's expulsion of them in the seventeenth (a process that harmed the French economy, while benefiting German-speaking states)? The Spanish expulsions of the Jews and then the Moors were a vast human tragedy that ravaged Iberian civilization—but weren't those forced exiles preferable to Hitler's attempt to exterminate European Jewry? Even at the extremes of man-wrought evil, there are gradations of cruelty.

The historical evidence is troubling, since it suggests that ethnic cleansing can lead to peace. For example, the German presence amid Slavic populations in northeastern Europe lasted for eight oppressive centuries before all ethnic Germans were expelled in the wake of the Nazi collapse; after almost a millennium of torment, the region now enjoys an unprecedented level of peace and social justice. Certainly other factors influenced this new calm—but the subtraction of Baltic, Ukrainian, Pomeranian, Silesian, and Sudeten Germans from the social and political equations appears to have been decisive.

In the wake of World War I, Greece and the Turkish rump of the Ottoman Empire exchanged millions of ethnic Turks and Greeks, under miserable conditions. The ethnic cleansing was harsh on both sides and the suffering of these hereditary enemies was immense. Yet despite their history of violent antagonism, Greeks and Turks have remained at peace for more than eight decades since those mass expulsions, with the conflict over Cyprus confined to that unhappy island.

Meanwhile, trouble spots in which populations remain intermingled continue to erupt in violence, from West Africa through the Middle East to the subcontinent and Southeast Asia (where anti-Chinese pogroms are almost as predictable as the monsoon season).

Nor can we Americans claim perfect innocence when it comes to ethnic cleansing. Our treatment of Native Americans remains, along with slavery and its consequences, one of the two great stains upon our history. And our present situation goes unexamined: On one hand, the unprecedented degree of ethnic and religious integration we have achieved (largely in the last half-century) blinds us to the depth and operative power of hatreds elsewhere in the world; on the other, our own society has devised innovative, relatively benign forms of achieving ethnic separation. The "gentrification" of neighborhoods in cities such as Washington, D.C., is a soft form of ethnic cleansing by checkbook and mortgage.

There is also an enduring self-segregation of various groups within our society. Many individuals prefer the familiarity and sense of security delivered by a collective identity, by the codes and symbols of belonging, whether displayed in a barrio or in the economic segregation of a suburban gated community. Even in our remarkable multiethnic, multiconfessional society, there are still race riots—in the course of which interlopers whose skin is the wrong color end up beaten beyond recognition or dead.

Human collectives are still, essentially, warrior bands protective of their turf (even in those gated communities—just attend a homeowners' association meeting). Group competition is powerfully embedded in our psyches. Successful societies channel such impulses constructively, but struggling societies and those that have already succumbed to anarchy revert to narrow (and safe) identities—race, tribe, faith, cult—and respond to perceived threats with assertive group behavior: The individual is lost once the group is awakened. We can deny it as often as we like, but the historical pattern is timeless and enduring: When the majority feels threatened, it lashes out at minorities in its midst. When a minority's ethnicity and religion both differ from the mainstream of a traditional society, that minority is living on borrowed time. The span of imagined safety may last for centuries, but then, one day, the zealots appear on the street corner, whether in brown shirts or wearing Islamist robes.

The Practical Implications

It cannot be stressed too often or too forcefully that ethnic cleansing is a crime against humanity that cannot be excused. The purpose of this essay is to try to understand it—not to condone it—and to consider the implications for our military and diplomatic missions abroad.

Given that we would prefer to prevent any ethnic cleansing, what do we do when it cannot be prevented, when the hatred is too intense and the process has already gone too far? While there will never be a universal answer, given the complexity of each specific case, it can be argued as a case study that ethnic separation at an earlier stage might have prevented the massacre at Srebrenica (of course, no such separations will ever be fully just). Indeed, U.S. diplomats gave tacit approval to the Croatian cleansing of Serbs during the endgame in Croatia and Bosnia. Later, in Kosovo, we sought to persuade Serbs not to drive ethnic Albanians from their homes, but, as soon as victory was delivered to the Kosovars, they set about ethnically cleansing Serbs with high-testosterone vigor. The dynamic in play was such that none of our pleas, lectures, or scoldings were going to alter the hardened attitudes prevailing in either camp. What if the only hope for peace in the territory some still pretend is a unified Kosovo is ethnic separation and partition?

Meanwhile, in Iraq, ethnic-cleansing efforts have been savage. They still fall short of genocide: Confessional murders to date have aimed at intimidation and expulsion, at punishment and advantage, not at annihilation. What if the best hope for social peace is the establishment of exclusive Shi'a or Sunni (or Kurdish) neighborhoods—or towns and cities and provinces? We aren't alarmed by the existence of various ethnic quarters in Singapore or, for that matter, Brooklyn, and we accept that Saudi Arabia would not welcome an influx of Christian settlers to Riyadh. What if the last chance for Iraq to survive as a unified state is for its citizens to live in religiously or ethnically separate communities? What if efforts to prevent ethnic cleansing in Baghdad, for example, not only are doomed to fail, but exacerbate the ultimate intensity of the violence? Would we really prefer that a family die in its home, rather than be driven from it? Our principles are noble, but it's shabby to expect Iraqis to die for them.

There are no easy answers to these questions. But it should be absolutely clear by now that ethnic cleansing is an issue we will face again and again in the decades ahead, and it may not always be possible or even helpful to stop its march. We must face the unsettling question as to whether it's always desirable to force a halt to such purges, instead of acting to ameliorate the suffering of those displaced.

Idealists will continue to insist that Arabs and Jews, Sunnis and Shi'as, Kurds and Turks, Tajiks and Pashtuns, Sudanese blacks and Arabs, or Nigerian Muslims and Christians can all get along. Would that it were so. But to decline to study the possibility that they might refuse to get along, that the individuals we think we know may be consumed by mass passions that reasonable arguments won't tame, is folly. The old military maxim applies: You may hope for the best, but you prepare for the worst.

There is nothing welcome about ethnic or religious cleansing. But if we do not recognize its insistent reemergence in human affairs, and the fact that—in contrast to full-scale genocide—it remains the lesser evil, we will continue to act ineffectually as the innocent suffer.

12 Myths of
Twenty-First-Century War

The American Legion Magazine

November 2007

We're in trouble. We're in danger of losing more wars. Our troops haven't forgotten how to fight. We've never had better men and women in uniform. But our leaders and many of our fellow Americans no longer grasp what war means or what it takes to win.

Thanks to those who have served in uniform, we've lived in such safety and comfort for so long that for many Americans sacrifice means little more than skipping a second trip to the buffet table.

Two trends over the past four decades contributed to our national ignorance of the cost, and necessity, of victory. First, the most privileged Americans used the Vietnam War as an excuse to break their tradition of uniformed service. Ivy League universities once produced heroes. Now they resist Reserve Officer Training Corps representation on their campuses.

Yet our leading universities still produce a disproportionate number of U.S. political leaders. The men and women destined to lead us in wartime dismiss military service as a waste of their time and talents. Delighted to pose for campaign photos with our troops, elected officials in private disdain the military. Only one serious presidential aspirant in either party is a veteran, while another presidential hopeful pays as much for a single haircut as I took home in a month as an Army private.

Second, we've stripped in-depth U.S. history classes out of our schools. Since the 1960s, one history course after another has been cut, while the content of those remaining focuses on social issues and our alleged misdeeds. Dumbed-down textbooks minimize the wars that kept us free. As a result, ignorance of the terrible price our troops had to pay for freedom in the past creates absurd expectations about our present conflicts. When the media offer flawed or biased analyses, the public lacks the knowledge to make informed judgments.

This combination of national leadership with no military expertise and a population that hasn't been taught the cost of freedom leaves us with a government that does whatever seems expedient and a citizenry that believes whatever's comfortable. Thus, myths about war thrive.

Myth No. 1: War doesn't change anything. This campus slogan contradicts all of human history. Over thousands of years, war has been the last resort—and all too frequently the first resort—of tribes, religions, dynasties, empires, states, and demagogues driven by grievance, greed, or a heartless quest for glory. No one believes that war is a good thing, but it is sometimes necessary. We need not agree in our politics or on the manner in which a given war is prosecuted, but we can't pretend that if only we laid down our arms all others would do the same.

Wars, in fact, often change everything. Who would argue that the American Revolution, our Civil War, or World War II changed nothing? Would the world be better today if we had been pacifists in the face of Nazi Germany and imperial Japan?

Certainly not all of the changes warfare has wrought through the centuries have been positive. Even a just war may generate undesirable results, such as Soviet tyranny over half of Europe after 1945. But of one thing we may be certain: a U.S. defeat in any war is a defeat not only for freedom, but for civilization. Our enemies believe that war can change the world. And they won't be deterred by bumper stickers.

Myth No. 2: Victory is impossible today. Victory is always possible, if our nation is willing to do what it takes to win. But victory is, indeed, impossible if U.S. troops are placed under impossible restrictions, if their leaders refuse to act boldly, if every target must be approved by lawyers, and if the American people are disheartened by a constant barrage of negativity from the media. We don't need generals who pop up behind microphones to apologize for every mistake our soldiers make. We need generals who win.

And you can't win if you won't fight. We're at the start of a violent struggle that will ebb and flow for decades, yet our current generation of leaders, in and out of uniform, worries about hurting the enemy's feelings.

One of the tragedies of our involvement in Iraq is that while we did a great thing by removing Saddam Hussein, we tried to do it on the cheap. It's an iron law of warfare that those unwilling to pay the butcher's bill up front will pay it with compound interest in the end. We not only didn't want to pay that bill, but our leaders imagined that we could make friends with our enemies even before they were fully defeated. Killing a few hundred violent actors like Muqtada al Sadr in 2003 would have prevented thousands of subsequent American deaths and tens of thousands of Iraqi deaths. We started something our national leadership lacked the guts to finish.

Despite our missteps, victory looked a great deal less likely in the early months of 1942 than it does against our enemies today. Should we have surrendered after the fall of the Philippines? Today's opinion makers and elected officials have lost their grip on what it takes to win. In the timeless words of Nathan Bedford Forrest, "War means fighting, and fighting means killing."

And in the words of Gen. Douglas MacArthur, "It is fatal to enter any war without the will to win it."

Myth No. 3: Insurgencies can never be defeated. Historically, fewer than one in twenty major insurgencies succeeded. Virtually no minor ones survived. In the mid-twentieth century, insurgencies scored more wins than previously had been the case, but that was because the European colonial powers against which they rebelled had already decided to rid themselves of their imperial possessions. Even so, more insurgencies were defeated than not, from the Philippines to Kenya to Greece. In the entire eighteenth century, our war of independence was the only insurgency that defeated a major foreign power and drove it out for good.

The insurgencies we face today are, in fact, more lethal than the insurrections of the past century. We now face an international terrorist insurgency as well as local rebellions, all motivated by religious passion or ethnicity or a fatal compound of both. The good news is that in over three thousand years of recorded history, insurgencies motivated by faith and blood overwhelmingly failed. The bad news is that they had to be put down with remorseless bloodshed.

Myth No. 4: There's no military solution; only negotiations can solve our problems. In most cases, the reverse is true. Negotiations solve nothing until a military decision has been reached and one side recognizes a peace agreement as its only hope of survival. It would be a welcome development if negotiations fixed the problems we face in Iraq, but we're the only side interested in a negotiated solution. Every other faction—the terrorists, Sunni insurgents, Shi'a militias, Iran, and Syria—is convinced it can win.

The only negotiations that produce lasting results are those conducted from positions of indisputable strength.

Myth No. 5: When we fight back, we only provoke our enemies. When dealing with bullies, either in the schoolyard or in a global war, the opposite is true: If you don't fight back, you encourage your enemy to behave more viciously.

Passive resistance only works when directed against rule-of-law states, such as the core English-speaking nations. It doesn't work where silent protest is answered with a bayonet in the belly or a one-way trip to a political prison. We've allowed far too many myths about the "innate goodness of humanity" to creep up on us. Certainly, many humans would rather be good than bad. But if we're unwilling to fight the fraction of humanity that's evil, armed, and determined to subjugate the rest, we'll face even grimmer conflicts.

Myth No. 6: Killing terrorists only turns them into martyrs. It's an anomaly of today's Western world that privileged individuals feel more sympathy for dictators, mass murderers, and terrorists—consider the irrational protests against Guantanamo—than they do for their victims. We were told, over and over, that killing Osama bin Laden or Abu Musab al Zarqawi, hanging Saddam Hussein, or targeting the Taliban's Mullah Omar would only unite their followers. Well, we haven't yet gotten Osama or Omar, but Zarqawi's dead and forgotten by his own movement, whose members never invoke that butcher's memory. And no one is fighting to avenge Saddam. The harsh truth is that when faced with true fanatics, killing them is the only way to end their influence. Imprisoned, they galvanize protests, kidnappings, bombings, and attacks that seek to free them. Want to make a terrorist a martyr? Just lock him up. Attempts to try such monsters in a court of law turn into mockeries that only provide public platforms for their hate speech, which the global media is delighted to broadcast. Dead, they're dead. And killing them is the ultimate proof that they lack divine protection. Dead terrorists don't kill.

Myth No. 7: If we fight as fiercely as our enemies, we're no better than them. Did the bombing campaign against Germany turn us into Nazis? Did dropping atomic bombs on Japan to end the war and save hundreds of thousands of American lives, as well as millions of Japanese lives, turn us into the beasts who conducted the Bataan Death March?

The greatest immorality is for the United States to lose a war. While we seek to be as humane as the path to victory permits, we cannot shrink from doing what it takes to win. At present, the media and influential elements of our society are obsessed with the small immoralities that are inevitable in wartime. Soldiers are human, and no matter how rigorous their training, a miniscule fraction of our troops will do vicious things and must be punished as a consequence. Not everyone in uniform will turn out to be a saint, and not every chain of command will do its job with equal effectiveness. But obsessing on tragic incidents—of which there have been remarkably few in Iraq or Afghanistan—obscures the greater moral issue: the need to defeat enemies who revel in butchering the innocent, who celebrate atrocities, and who claim their god wants blood.

Myth No. 8: The United States is more hated today than ever before. Those who served in Europe during the Cold War remember enormous, often-violent protests against U.S. policy that dwarfed today's let's-have-fun-on-a-Sunday-afternoon rallies. Older readers recall the huge ban-the-bomb, procommunist demonstrations of the 1950s and the vast seas of demonstrators filling the streets of Paris, Rome, and Berlin to protest our commitment to Vietnam. Imagine if we'd had 24/7 news coverage of those rallies. I well remember serving in Germany in the wake of our withdrawal from Saigon, when U.S. soldiers were despised by the locals—who nonetheless were willing to take our money—and terrorists tried to assassinate U.S. generals.

The fashionable anti-Americanism of the chattering classes hasn't stopped the world from seeking one big green card. As I've traveled around the globe since 9/11, I've found that below the government-spokesman/professional-radical level, the United States remains the great dream for university graduates from Berlin to Bangalore to Bogota.

On the domestic front, we hear ludicrous claims that our country has never been so divided. Well, that leaves out our Civil War. Our historical amnesia also erases the violent protests of the late 1960s and early 1970s, the mass confrontations, rioting, and deaths. Is today's America really more fractured than it was in 1968?

Myth No. 9: Our invasion of Iraq created our terrorist problems. This claim rearranges the order of events, as if the attacks of 9/11 happened after Baghdad fell. Our terrorist problems have been created by the catastrophic failure of Middle Eastern civilization to compete on any front and were exacerbated by the determination of successive U.S. administrations, Democrat and Republican, to pretend that Islamist terrorism was a brief aberration. Refusing to respond to attacks, from the bombings in Beirut to Khobar Towers, from the first attack on the Twin Towers to the near sinking of the USS *Cole*, we allowed our enemies to believe that we were weak and cowardly. Their unchallenged successes served as a powerful recruiting tool.

Did our mistakes on the ground in Iraq radicalize some new recruits for terror? Yes. But imagine how many more recruits there might have been and the damage they might have inflicted on our homeland had we not responded militarily in Afghanistan and then carried the fight to Iraq. Now Iraq is al Qa'eda's Vietnam, not ours.

Myth No. 10: If we just leave, the Iraqis will patch up their differences on their own. The point may come at which we have to accept that Iraqis are so determined to destroy their own future that there's nothing more we can do. But we're not there yet, and leaving immediately would guarantee not just one massacre but a series of slaughters and the delivery of a massive victory to the forces of terrorism. We must be open-minded about practical measures, from changes in strategy to troop reductions, if that's what the developing situation warrants. But it's grossly irresponsible to claim that our presence is the primary cause of the violence in Iraq—an allegation that ignores history.

Myth No. 11: It's all Israel's fault. Or the popular Washington corollary: "The Saudis are our friends." Israel is the Muslim world's excuse for failure, not a reason for it. Even if we didn't support Israel, Islamist extremists would blame us for countless other imagined wrongs, since they fear our freedoms and our culture even more than they do our military. All men and women of conscience must recognize the core difference between Israel and its neighbors: Israel genuinely wants to live in peace, while its genocidal neighbors want Israel erased from the map.

As for the mad belief that the Saudis are our friends, it endures only because the Saudis have spent so much money on both sides of the aisle in Washington. Saudi money continues to subsidize anti-Western extremism, to divide fragile societies, and encourage hatred between Muslims and all others. Saudi extremism has done far more damage to the Middle East than Israel ever did. The Saudis are our enemies.

Myth No. 12: The Middle East's problems are all America's fault. Muslim extremists would like everyone to believe this, but it just isn't true. The collapse of once-great Middle Eastern civilizations has been underway for more than five centuries, and the region became a backwater before the United States became a country. For the first century and a half of our national existence, our relations with the people of the Middle East were largely beneficent and protective, notwithstanding our conflict with the Barbary Pirates in North Africa. But Islamic civilization was on a downward trajectory that could not be arrested. Its social and economic structures, its values, its neglect of education, its lack of scientific curiosity, the indolence of its ruling classes, and its inability to produce a single modern state that served its people all guaranteed that, as the West's progress accelerated, the Middle East would fall ever further behind. The Middle East has itself to blame for its problems.

None of us knows what our strategic future holds, but we have no excuse for not knowing our own past. We need to challenge inaccurate assertions about our policies, about our past, and about war itself. And we need to work within our community and state education systems to return balanced, comprehensive history programs to our schools. The unprecedented wealth and power of the United States allow us to afford many things denied to human beings throughout history. But we, the people, cannot afford ignorance.

Dishonest Doctrine

Armed Forces Journal

December 2007

A year after its publication, the Army and Marine Corps counterinsurgency manual remains deeply disturbing, both for the practical dangers it creates and for the dishonest approach employed to craft it.

The most immediate indication of the manual's limitations has been Army Gen. David Petraeus's approach to counterinsurgency in Iraq. The manual envisions COIN operations by that Age of Aquarius troubadour, Donovan, wearing his love like heaven as he proceeds to lead terrorists, insurgents, and militiamen to a jamboree at Atlantis. Although the finalized document did, ultimately, allow that deadly force might sometimes be required, it preached—beware doctrine that preaches—understanding, engagement, and chat. It was a politically correct document for a politically correct age.

Entrusted with the mission of turning Iraq around, Petraeus turned out to be a marvelously focused and methodical killer, able to set aside the dysfunctional aspects of the doctrine he had signed off on. Given the responsibility of command, he recognized that, when all the frills are stripped away, counterinsurgency warfare is about killing those who need killing, helping those who need help—and knowing the difference between the two (we spent our first four years in Iraq striking out on all three counts). Although Petraeus has, indeed, concentrated many assets on helping those who need help, he grasped that, without providing durable security—which requires killing those who need killing—none of the reconstruction or reconciliation was going to stick. On the ground, Petraeus has supplied the missing kinetic half of the manual.

The troubling aspect of all this for the Army's intellectual integrity comes from the neo-Stalinist approach to history a number of the manual's authors internalized during their pursuit of doctorates on "the best" American campuses. Instead of seeking to analyze the requirements of counterinsurgency warfare rigorously before proceeding to draw impartial conclusions based on a broad array of historical evidence, they took the academic's path of first setting up their thesis, then citing only examples that supported it.

To wit, the most over-cited bit of nonsense from the manual is the claim that counterinsurgency warfare is only 20 percent military and 80 percent political. No analysis of this indefensible proposition occurred. It was quoted because it suited the preformulated argument. Well, the source of that line was Gen. Chang Ting-chen, one of Mao's less distinguished subordinates. Had the authors bothered to look at Mao's writings, they would have read that "political power grows out of the barrel of a gun," that "whoever wants to seize and retain state power must have a strong army," and that "only with guns can the whole world be transformed."

Sorry, but Mao didn't believe that round-table discussions were a substitute for killing his enemies, party purges, mass executions, and the Cultural Revolution. Mao believed in force. In our COIN manual, he's presented as a flower child.

Anyone looking objectively at the situation in Iraq could hardly claim that it's only 20 percent military and 80 percent diplomatic. Even the State Department doesn't really believe that one—or they would've kept a tighter leash on their private security contractors.

Wishful thinking doesn't defeat insurgencies. Without the will to establish and maintain security for the population, nothing else works.

The manual's worth revisiting a bit longer to underscore the dishonesty of the selective use of history. Citing a narrow range of past insurgencies—all ideological, all comparatively recent—the authors carefully ignored parallel or earlier examples that would've undercut their position. For example, the British experience in Malaya is cited ad nauseam (although it's portrayed as far less bloody than it was in fact), but the same decade saw a very different and even more successful British campaign against the Mau Mau insurgency in Kenya. After realizing (a bit ploddingly) that the Mau Mau could not be controlled by colonial police forces, the British took a tough-minded three-track approach: concentration camps for more than one hundred thousand Kenyans; hanging courts that sent more than one thousand Mau Mau activists and sympathizers to the gallows; and relentless military pursuits that tracked down the hardcore insurgents and killed them. It worked. A few years later, British rule ended in Kenya—but only because Britain had decided to give up its empire. And the thousands of British citizens who remained behind in Kenya weren't massacred.

However, citing the British experience in Kenya wouldn't have been politically correct—no matter that it worked after gentler methods had failed. The COIN manual's authors weren't concerned with winning but with defending their dissertations.

Does It Matter?

An apocryphal anecdote from World War II has a German staff officer expressing his frustration that American commanders don't know their own doctrine. Recently, a retired officer and friend argued that doctrine really only matters for us in terms of the atmospherics, the outlook, that it shapes. Well, if that's so, the dishonest atmosphere propagated by that COIN manual is profoundly troubling as a warning of problems to come.

The Army and Marine Corps in Iraq have already moved beyond the manual's grossest limitations, and the document will be rewritten in a few years, so we may be able to shrug off its core contention that the best reply to a terrorist is a big, wet kiss. We had better be concerned, though, about the implications for the next round of doctrine-writing on other military subjects. Can we afford to have future drafting teams employ the same dishonest techniques, allowing the use only of historical examples that support predetermined theses? Must our manuals be politically correct? Don't we care about the truth, about winning, about giving our soldiers and Marines doctrinal tools that keep them alive while helping them kill their enemies?

The formulation of doctrine isn't about persuasion. It's about evidence. If a doctrinal proposition cannot withstand the force of countervailing examples, it's a bad idea. Historical examples and vignettes have a valid, useful place in doctrine: They can serve to illustrate why a commander made a decision or how a particular technique worked in the field. Inevitably, some selectivity comes into play, because no manual can contain all of humankind's military history. But the examples employed must serve honest ends, and they must be counterbalanced, when appropriate. In short, it's fine to cite Malaya as an example of one variety of COIN operation, but it's unacceptable to imply that all counterinsurgency situations will mimic Malaya. You've got to cite Mau Mau, too.

And what about the Moros, the Islamist fanatics in the Philippines who only succumbed to U.S. Army Gatling guns? The bloodiness of that campaign didn't suit the authors of the manual, so the details of one of our own most challenging and ultimately most successful counterinsurgency efforts were glossed over—the facts would've undercut the manual's argument.

Education, clearly, is not synonymous with intellectual integrity. Doctrine should be written by successful battlefield commanders, not by doctors of philosophy playing soldier.

Mythmaking and Monkey Business

From ancient Greece through the contemporary Middle East, leaders and peoples have rewritten history to suit themselves. Historians all too often contributed to the disinformation, whether it was Edward Gibbon, whose lack of firsthand experience with Islam left him intoxicated with Mohammed and his ghazis, or the ludicrous Paul Kennedy, who, on the eve of the Soviet Union's collapse, published a ballyhooed book arguing that it was the United States that was about to go under. We in the West have molested the historical facts to create national myths from Belgrade to Moscow and on to Edinburgh. We've twisted the facts to advance political agendas, claiming either that colonialism was an unalloyed evil or that the future belonged to militant socialism or that Iraq is worse than Vietnam (a proposition that fifty thousand dead Americans would challenge, if they could).

Robust societies can afford a good bit of such monkey business, but selective mythmaking can lead fragile societies to disaster. And no military can afford to indulge in the selective use of history. Soldiers must seek the truth.

Intellectual integrity is ultimately more important to the doctrine writer than intellect itself. The formulation of doctrine has to be an act of selfless service, not the construction of a personal monument. If our military is unwilling to face the most troubling evidence history offers, it would be better served by swearing off the use of history entirely.

Of course, not all doctrine writers are intellectually corrupt. But a final difficulty we have with the use of historical examples to illustrate or underscore doctrine is that most of us have so few of them in our mental catalog. The study of history isn't a matter of a year or two on a campus to get a piece of paper and a personnel-file notation. For an officer, the immersion in history in the broadest sense must be a lifelong pursuit. Beware the officer who reads just a little and falls in love with a single book (say, *Seven Pillars of Wisdom*). He'll cite that book as if quoting from the Gospels, and he'll insist on its relevance even when the problem facing him is of a profoundly different nature.

We'd be better off having our military doctrine written by officers with no historical knowledge than by those with just a few narrow areas of interest: A little knowledge truly is a dangerous thing.

Of course, the best situation would be to have doctrine drafted by veterans who possess a broad sense of history—and who have no personal theories to validate at the expense of our men and women in uniform. But there ain't enough of that commodity to go around.

It's hard to have much hope, given the deplorable state of history studies at every educational level. Wars have been banished from the K-12 curriculum, while universities, determined to discard the West's intellectual advantages, insist on taking as selective an approach to history as any band of Islamist terrorists (to say nothing of their similar interpretations of the past).

But our military can't afford to make excuses. We have to get our doctrine right—both because it helps us fight effectively and because it explains to civilian decision makers what it is that soldiers do. If doctrine creates false expectations, those decision makers will make flawed choices—and those in uniform will pay the price.

Better no doctrine than bad doctrine. Better no history than bad history. The saving grace of our military—historically—has been pragmatism. Unlike European generals, we never sent our soldiers to die for a theory (at least, not until Operation Iraqi Freedom). If our own history has a lesson for those responsible for military doctrine, it's that the only admissible criterion is that the doctrine has to work.

War's Irrational Motivators

Armed Forces Journal

August 2008

The fundamental dictum guiding our diplomats and analysts has been that states and human collectives act in their own rational self-interest. This is utterly wrong, leading us to convoluted analyses that seek to justify our assumption, while guaranteeing diplomatic failure: It's difficult to defeat an enemy or even negotiate with a partner whose motivation you refuse to understand.

The fantasy claiming that states will act in their own rational self-interest is a product of late eighteenth- and nineteenth-century European self-delusion. Babble about enlightened self-interest made no sense when applied to a Promethean figure such as Napoleon—or to Britain's or the Iberian population's resistance to Napoleonic power. Accommodation, not confrontation, would have been the rational choice. The renowned nineteenth-century Austrian diplomat Prince Klemens Metternich was the exception, not the rule, and popular revolutions soon would shake the continent as states consistently failed to act in their own enlightened or rational self-interest. (We mistakenly equate reactionary politics with rational politics). The Prussian wars of aggression later in the nineteenth century masqueraded as Realpolitik but were, in fact, outbursts of nationalist fervor. Then came World War I, perhaps the most irrational major conflict in history.

Yet the myth of rational self-interest as the motivating factor in the behavior of states and peoples persisted. Mussolini launched wars of pride and Hitler indulged in grudge-fight wars of passion—of the

Axis Powers, only Japan showed a glimmer of rational self-interest, although it expressed it in irrational acts. Nonetheless, the comforting delusion that human beings and their governments could, in the end, be counted upon to behave logically persisted. Nuclear arsenals expanded until they were capable of destroying life on earth many times over; their use has been prevented by fear, not reason.

The great decisions of our personal lives, too, are the products of emotion, not rational analysis. (How many of us calmly choose a spouse according to a checklist?) Even academic disciplines increasingly accept the existence of irrationality in individual and collective decision making. The great holdouts against the obvious are in the field of international relations, on campus, in think tanks, and in our State Department—although Pentagon and CIA analysts also contort themselves to fit acts of religious fervor or blood passion into a logical framework. From suicide bombers to the nationalist bumptiousness of today's Russia, analysts strive to construct rational models to explain emotion-driven behavior.

Emotional Self-Interest

Instead of clinging to the failed model of rational self-interest as an analytical tool, substitute "emotional self-interest." It's akin to switching on a light. If, instead of fabricating logical sequences of calculation where none exist, we accept that individuals, peoples, and states act in ways that are emotionally satisfying, no end of knotty analytical problems dissolve. Whether we look at why we vote for the candidates we do, why a terrorist straps on a suicide belt, why Hutus massacred one million Tutsis with cold steel, or why states blunder into war, assessing the degree of emotional satisfaction gained from the act is as enlightening as seeking logic in such deeds is frustrating.

Consider a range of historical examples—chosen from many, many more—that snap into focus if we accept that emotion trumps reason in human affairs:

The Crusades. Since abandoning religious belief as beneath contempt, academic historians have struggled unconvincingly to explain why, over two centuries, hundreds of thousands of European dukes, knights, retainers, laborers, peasants, priests, mendicants, and not a few women left their homes to march east to free the Holy Land through force of arms without so much as reliable maps to guide them. Yes, younger sons were superfluous. But kings went, too. Yes, Europe had surplus labor. But why not let your neighbor risk his life? Yes, there was a chance of glory and wealth. But that was for the very few, not the masses, and even after riches proved illusory for most and tens of thousands perished miserably long before nearing the Holy Land, tens of thousands more knelt and took the cross.

Meta-Darwinism may one day offer a convincing explanation for this phenomenon, but for now the obvious answer is that a contagious, ecstatic vision of a divinely sanctioned mission, reinforced by the promise of eternal salvation, led vast columns of Europeans to brave hunger, thirst, plagues, betrayal, pirates, slavery, and battles against daunting odds in their determination to reach an envisioned Jerusalem of which they possessed not so much as a crude sketch. Few Crusaders survived to claim success of any kind, yet the emotional fervor believers felt was satisfying enough to justify unimaginable suffering. No Marxist explanation of the Crusades works. Emotional self-interest shaped by religious belief was the organizing factor.

The Holocaust. Fast forward to another historical enigma, in which Europe's German-speaking populations (abetted by others) systematically rooted out their Jewish minorities and did their best to exterminate them. In terms of rational self-interest, this was madness: Per capita, Jews made a disproportionate contribution to the modernization of Germany and Austria, leading developments in science, medicine, education, the arts, banking, and industrialization. German Jews, especially, saw themselves as every bit as patriotically German as any other citizen of the Reich (and proved it by winning an impressive number of awards for valor in World War I). The average German lost nothing because of his Jewish fellow citizens and gained a great deal. Yes, some Ostpreussische Junker had mortgaged their estates, while Christian academics sometimes felt envious of the success of their Jewish colleagues. But no explanation couched in terms of rational self-interest begins to offer a convincing explanation for the passion, energy, and commitment of resources in wartime that the German people applied to the destruction of European Jewry.

Instead, look at this monstrous frenzy in terms of the emotional satisfaction it provided. In "the Germanies," anti-Semitism enjoyed a popular appeal dating back to the Crusades and beyond—not only because Jews were different, but also because human beings need a malign force to blame for their self-wrought difficulties (or for acts of nature, such as epidemics). The factual innocence of the Jews was irrelevant. The cathartic satisfaction of taking revenge on a caricatured, dehumanized enemy, in nodding approvingly as thugs smashed shop windows and bellowed "Juden raus!" was enormous: Was anything pleasanter to a good German in 1938 than seeing a middle-class Jewish family reduced to a huddle of overcoats and suitcases? There was no German silent majority opposed to the Holocaust. If the German majority was silent, it was because they had no objections to what was happening and quite liked the whole business.

Enlightened self-interest? A dead end analytically. Emotional self-interest? There you have it. The satisfaction Germans derived from tormenting and murdering their Jewish neighbors was so great it drove them to act in a manner directly opposed to their rational self-interest.

At a minimum, analysts should supplement their standard queries as to which material or practical advantages a foreign power or hostile entity gains from a specific course of action with the question of what level of emotional satisfaction the opponent gains from the act itself. The attacks of September 11, 2001, did not deliver rational benefits to the realms of Sunni Islam, but the emotional high even Middle Eastern moderates felt in their immediate aftermath was unprecedented in recent generations.

Arab states, Palestinians, and Israel. According to rational-self-interest models of statecraft, Arab states and Palestinian leaders should have come to terms with reality and made peace with Israel after their defeat in 1967 or, at the latest, after the follow-up war in 1973. Yet only Egypt pursued a limited peace. For all of the other actors—as well as for many individual Egyptians—the emotional cost of making the best possible peace with Israel was unacceptably high. Although some heads of state reasoned that continuing their hostility through other means was necessary to ensure their personal survival, Arab populations, including the Palestinians, had far more to gain in practical terms through peace, trade, the reduction of military budgets, etc.

Pride trumped profit and progress. Telling themselves that, one day, the "Palestinian homelands" would be free once more—in fact, they were never free—Arab states and Palestinians alike continued to impoverish themselves for an odds-against-it dream. When Washington's emissaries touch down in the West Bank or Damascus with their carefully reasoned briefs as to who would gain what on a practical level, they're deaf and blind to the driving force behind the region's intractability: emotion.

Post-Soviet Russia. The collapse of the USSR resulted in a tremendous outburst of goodwill toward the new Russia. Indeed, it's hard to find another instance of the international community bringing such positive emotions to bear so swiftly on a recently threatening state that had oppressed hundreds of millions. Virtually everyone wanted to cooperate with, do business with, and invest in Russia. Western expectations soared extravagantly. Russia could write its own ticket.

Russia did. Unable to surmount its traditional paranoia, suspicious of the best intentions, humiliated by the loss of empire, and spiteful by character, Russia attempted to bully its former possessions, supplying arms to separatist groups and irredentist factions while invading one of its internal states—Chechnya—in a disastrous bloodbath. Instead of the rule of law, power brokers ruled. Business contracts were abrogated without regard to legality, starry-eyed foreign friends were rebuffed, and, by the time Vladimir Putin succeeded Boris Yeltsin as president, Russia had thrown away its chances for mutually beneficial cooperation with most of its former possessions and with all of its former satellites. Instead, the Kremlin re-embraced rogue regimes.

Rather than patiently developing a seductive energy strategy, in successive fits of pique, the Kremlin cut natural gas supplies to Ukraine and Georgia in the dead of winter, alerting Europe to the long-term dangers of an over-reliance on Russian gas. Instead of concealing its cyberattack capabilities until a real crisis arose, the Kremlin tipped its hands and attacked Estonia's infrastructure over the removal of a minor monument from one site to another. Aware on an intellectual level that a nuclear-armed Iran is a far greater threat to Russia and its interests than to Europe or North America, the Kremlin nonetheless sold dangerous technology to Tehran in deals whose profits were slight compared to the existential risks involved—helping Iran was another way to poke the West and, especially, Washington in the eye. Of late, Russia has been staging military provocations against Georgia, a tiny state that poses no threat to Moscow, but whose nascent democracy and rejection of Russian suzerainty is viewed as an affront by the Kremlin's masters.

Russia may produce brilliant mathematicians and chess masters, but its foreign policy has been driven by emotional self-interest, not rational calculation. The Schadenfreude Russians feel they are teaching the West a lesson. But how rational is it to scrape up spare parts to get two antique bombers into the air and fly them toward a U.S. Navy carrier? What does Russia gain in practical terms? We know their military is in a disastrous state, and they know that we know it. But such gestures make them feel good.

For our part, the U.S. Realpolitik quickly foundered on passionate national liberation movements then broke up on the rocks of reawakened religious fervor. Our diplomats are survivors clinging to rafts and driftwood. Our cherished explanations just don't work. And yet we keep squeezing every new analytical problem into the old cookie press of material or political advantage. This is the behavior of the certifiably insane: the endless repetition of the same failed action in the expectation of a different outcome next time.

Suicide bombers. One of the most dismaying experiences I've had in Washington since September 11, 2001, (that's quite a standard) came a few years ago after a briefing at the National Counter-Terrorism Center. A senior analyst dismissively told me that Islamist suicide bombers were never motivated by religion. "Research has shown" that most had practical grievances, a mistreated relative, or personal reverses. And that was that. The point that many of us have personal grievances but that few Western Christians, Jews, or atheists become suicide bombers was lost on him. Nor did the logic faze him that taking revenge for a grievance need not involve suicide— why not just emplace a bomb and scram?

The analyst, who had little personal exposure to Muslim societies, could not grasp that religion isn't solely about personal faith, but also pervades the social environment, setting the parameters of acceptable behavior even for those who shrug at belief. The proud mother of the suicide bomber didn't factor into that analyst's equation, since she didn't fit. Yet it has been the atmosphere of encouragement and approval, of admiration for the sacrifice of self-immolation, that has fostered the cult of the suicide bomber. While offense given to a sister or the imprisonment of a cousin might have awakened the impulse, it was ultimately the sense of emotional satisfaction, of anticipated catharsis and the admiration of others that compelled the suicide bomber to walk into a marketplace or a clinic and detonate himself.

Logic doesn't work here. Suicide bombing is an emotional act. The puppet masters above the bomber may have cynical goals (along with their religious zeal), but suicide bombing doesn't make sense in a Cartesian universe—the obvious point being that human beings don't operate according to strict Cartesian logic even in the West, and when we expect them to do so, we call it wrong.

Suicide bombing isn't a logical act. It's a selfish one.

The bring-the-troops-home-now movement. If you need an example closer to home of how emotional satisfaction trumps rational self-interest in human affairs, you need look no further than the current mindset of the leave-Iraq-now advocates in the United States.

Over the past eighteen months, the situation in Iraq has turned around remarkably, and, while challenges remain, every major indicator has turned positive. A strictly logical analysis would suggest that, at this point, a premature withdrawal of our forces would pose enormous risks to Iraq, to the region, and to our own security. Furthermore, with casualties down and "peace breaking out," there are no compelling logical arguments for a swift retreat. According to the rational-self-interest model, activist politicians and voters should have changed their positions. Yet there has been no shift at all in the position of antiwar activists in the face of the evidence that the surge succeeded, that Iraqis are making rapid progress, that al Qa'eda has suffered a catastrophic defeat, that Iranian designs have been frustrated, and that an objective assessment suggests that the odds now favor a reasonably positive outcome. Given the proven threat that al Qa'eda has posed to our citizens and our interests, the terrorist organization's loss of potency and status alone would argue that our efforts are not wasted, while a premature evacuation would allow al Qa'eda to claim victory and recover. In terms of rational self-interest, we should stay—hands down.

But rational self-interest was never in play for most of the activists. Empirical data are irrelevant. The movement was always about emotional satisfaction, about acting out, about an emotional rejection of our involvement in Iraq as a symbol of their perceived political and social nemeses. One only has to turn on the television to hear yet another political activist deny that the surge has made any difference. The behavior is that of a child shutting his eyes and clamping his hands over his ears to make reality go away.

This isn't a matter of whether we should or should not have gone into Iraq. Responsible citizens can disagree about that. The point is that emotional self-interest, the need to be right at all costs, trumps both reason and our collective self-interest—and we're supposed to be the rational actors on the world stage.

The closest thing we have witnessed in our own country to rational self-interest in the behavior of individuals has been the drop in sales of SUVs during the current fuel-cost crisis. On the other hand, it wasn't rational calculation that drove the huge sales of SUVs over the past decade but emotional self-interest, the satisfaction of projecting a certain image in the dangerous wilds of suburbia.

The purpose of this essay is not to argue against objective analysis but to expand the scope of our analysis to include a consideration of our opposite number's emotional needs. Identifying an enemy's emotional composition is essential to predicting his strategic course: In the ineffectual shock-and-awe campaign against Saddam Hussein's regime, we expected him to respond according to our desires and we ignored his own emotional makeup; the result was that our "rational analysis" proved to be irrational, a case of wishful thinking carried to a strategic extreme. It was a repetition of our analysis in 1990, when our diplomats and their advisers reasoned that Saddam would not be irrational enough to invade Kuwait—we looked at the dictator's world through Western lenses and failed to see what was happening, literally, before our eyes in Iraqi divisional assembly areas on the border.

We rely on analytical methodology that fits our own prejudices comfortably, rather than on techniques suited to the strategic climate. That, too, is an emotional choice.

We need not totally discard rational analytical models, but we must stop relying on them exclusively. In Iraq, Afghanistan, Pakistan, Sudan, the West Bank, Russia, and on, ad infinitum, we can witness, on any given day, how powerful emotion can be as a galvanizing factor, how dominant emotional self-interest is in human affairs, and how passion trumps practicality, while pride overrules rational self-interest.

It isn't the human mind that's the killer. It's the human heart.

Fighting Words

Armed Forces Journal

October 2008

If our troops shot as wildly as our politicians and bureaucrats fire off words, we'd never win a single firefight. The inaccurate terminology tossed about by presidents and pundits alike obscures the nature of the threats we face, the character of our enemies, and the inadequacies of our response. If we cannot, or will not, label our opponents, their cause, and their motivations correctly, how can we forge an efficient and effective national strategy?

Let's begin with the most-abused word in Washington, "ideology." Flocks of Potomac parrots in Brooks Brothers suits tell us, again and again, that we're in a "war of ideologies," or a "contest of ideologies" with the terrorists we face. The speakers—not one of whom seems to have thought the issue through—appear to believe that ideology can be used as a pleasant euphemism for religious fervor, that ideology has been with us since the days of cave paintings and really bad hair days, and, oddest of all, that we ourselves are fighting for an ideology.

In fact, political ideologies are a relatively new phenomenon in the bloody pageant of history. If you open Samuel Johnson's dictionary, published in London in 1755 (and still my favorite dictionary), you will not find the word "ideology." The term first appears as "ideologie" in 1796, in Paris, in the noisy aftermath of the French Revolution. The word and what it represents are products of the madly misnamed Age of Reason, when human beings discovered vast new horizons of causes about which they could behave unreasonably.

How does the current *Oxford English Dictionary* define "ideology"? The pertinent entry runs as follows: "A system of ideas or way of thinking pertaining to a class or individual, esp. as a basis of some economic or political theory or system, regarded as justifying actions and esp. to be maintained irrespective of events." That's a fine definition of communism, Maoism, Nazism, fascism, anarcho-syndicalism, Trotskyism, Fourierism, and on through the -ism of the individual malcontent's choice. However, it does not describe Islamist fanatics determined to sacrifice their lives to honor their god.

Religion is a deeper, far more enduring factor than ideology. Ideologies come and go, often making quite a mess along the way, but the remarkable thing about successful religions—those that survive over millennia—is their galvanizing resilience. They may evolve or devolve, adapt or mutate grotesquely, but they last and continue to inspire. In historical terms, ideologies are closer to fads, to deadly hula hoops. Religion, on its mundane side, may develop subordinate ideologies—such as liberation theology or other passing militancies—but no ideology has ever produced a religion.

Religion and ideology are essentially antithetical. Religion is not "a system of ideas," but a matter of faith subduing and transcending reason. Religion may give birth to ideas, but ideas never give birth to a religion. So our devout enemies—and they are, indeed, devout—are not engaged in a battle of ideas or ideologies with us. They are driven by unreasoning faith, by passion, by furies, by a perverted vision of eternity.

And what about us? Are we fighting for an ideology? Absolutely not. Democracy isn't an -ism. Democracy is a technique of human governance that uses the tool of elections. In the United States, ideologies in their true sense only exist on the extreme margins of the political spectrum (where they belong, to the extent they belong anywhere). We are not fighting for an American ideology. There's no American equivalent of Marxism or fascism, and we should be very glad of it. We're fighting to defend our values.

Now the relevant definition of "values" from the *Oxford English Dictionary* is: "The principles or moral standards of a person or social group; the generally accepted or personally held judgment of what is valuable and important in life."

The "American way of life" and the values that have made it a
success are a matter of national consensus that transcends our individual differences; an ideology is the opposite of a consensus
approach to society—it's dictated, one way or the other. Our consensus has developed organically, by trial and error. Ideology is artificial,
constructed by an individual or small group and foisted on a society.
There is no American ideology with its *Das Kapital,* Mao's *Little Red
Book,* or *Mein Kampf.* The nature of this confrontation—between the
all-or-nothing religious fanaticism driving our enemies and the cherished values motivating us, between a merciless interpretation of a
god's will and an ongoing experiment in human freedom—is yet
another asymmetrical aspect of postmodern conflict.

If we were simply in a duel of ideologies, our task would be a lot
easier.

The Timeless Fanatic

We desperately want our enemies to be reasonable, to operate from
motives we can nail down neatly and explain without too much dis-
comfort. But religious extremists are, by definition, not reasonable.
The fanatic is driven by faith in a greater reality than that which our
senses identify in our waking hours. And what is faith? I know of no
better definition for our purposes than that proposed three centuries ago by Jonathan Swift and cited in Johnson's magisterial dictionary:

"Faith is an entire dependence upon the truth, the power, the
justice, and the mercy of God; which dependence will certainly
incline us to obey him in all things."

In other words, there is no truth but your god's truth, no power
comparable to his, and his is the only justice, while mercy is also his
alone. Above all, faith is not to reason, but to obey "in all things."

Unlike political ideologues, religious fanatics have been with
us since the infancy of history. For Johnson, a "fanatick" was "a
man mad with wild notions of religion," while the *Oxford English
Dictionary* defines a "fanatic" as "a mad person; a religious maniac."
Those seem rather more appropriate descriptions of men who saw
the heads off living prisoners to please their god or who walk into a
marketplace crowded with fellow believers and detonate a suicide
bomb.

Nonetheless, various U.S. government outlets and agencies, from military publications through intelligence organizations, have been discouraged or forbidden outright from bringing religion into their analysis of our enemies, or from using terms such as "Islamist terrorist," because we would rather avoid giving the least offense than accurately describe the ambitious murderers we face. It's a bit like banning the word "Nazi" when describing Hitler.

Political correctness has no place in the intelligence world and no place in (what should be) hard-headed government documents. If your enemy declares himself an Islamist and your enemy is a terrorist self-avowedly motivated by his religion, then it hardly seems unjust to describe him as an "Islamist terrorist."

Nor does political correctness infect only the left. The conservative version simply obsesses on different terms. For example, some well-meaning (and some downright nutty) internet activists on the right have argued that we should never use the terms "jihad" or "jihadi" when referring to al Qa'eda, the Taliban, and their ilk. In a bizarre confluence, those on the hard right find themselves sharing common ground with the extreme left, both agreeing that "jihad" isn't really about war at all, but about an unarmed personal struggle (somewhere between morning-after guilt and a bowel obstruction).

This is nonsense. A personal struggle is an anomalous and far lesser form of jihad. Since the first conquering Arab armies exploded out of the desert thirteen centuries ago, "jihad" has consistently described warfare waged on behalf of the faith. Were the hand-wringers to inspect the historical record, they would find "jihad" used from the start to describe campaigns against unbelievers, against schismatic Muslims, against Crusaders, against Byzantines, against Slavs, Austrians, Hindus, the British, the French, Americans in the Philippines, the Israelis, the Soviets, and, now, the West in general. An armed struggle waged on behalf of the faith of the Prophet is a jihad. Period.

Nor is there a supreme terrestrial authority who can give a jihad the thumbs-up or thumbs-down: Jihad is practically "every mullah for himself." While only the Pope could declare a Crusade in the pre-Reformation West, Islam is not only divided between Sunni and Shi'a, but is a semi-anarchic collection of diffuse institutions that seldom agree on much. When it suits their whims, the Saudi royal family may be able to influence domestic clerics to declare a given jihad invalid, but that won't stop Islamist extremists who view the entire Saudi establishment as corrupt and illegitimate. If a cleric of middling standing can persuade a sufficient number of people to launch a jihad, it's a jihad. And those who wage it are jihadis.

The notion that non-Muslims have sufficient authority to declare that jihadis aren't real jihadis reaches heights of absurdity rarely encountered outside of the House of Representatives. Do we really think that the Muslims of the Middle East hang on the words of our domestic pundits? If an American scholar of Anglo-Saxon heritage writes a carefully footnoted article "proving" that al Qa'eda isn't engaged in a jihad and that its members don't conform to classical Koranic values, can we really believe that al Qa'eda gives a damn? If a Saudi, Egyptian, or Iranian authority declared that our soldiers and Marines fighting in Iraq and Afghanistan were not true Christians, just how seriously would we take it? We're babbling for our own consumption—our enemies are not impressed. The terrorist enemies we face view themselves as jihadis and they are viewed as jihadis by many millions of Muslims (even by many who don't approve of their actions—just as our domestic left accepts that a Marine is a Marine, like him or not).

The inability or unwillingness to speak clearly generally arises from the inability or unwillingness to think clearly. Our slovenly use of terminology—whether from intellectual sloth, political correctness, or both—is a serious obstacle to understanding our enemies and fighting them effectively. We continually describe the enemies we want to face, rather than those who are determined to kill as many of us as possible.

If we lack the judgment and courage to speak plainly, where shall we find the strength to defeat men of such passion and will as those jihadis? No enemy has ever been defeated by a heavy barrage of euphemisms.

Good Dr. Johnson, who understood the value of specificity as well as any English-speaking man, gives us this definition of "folly": "Act of negligence or passion unbecoming gravity or deep wisdom."

Our official blasts of inaccurate terminology are folly, indeed. But that negligence only masks Washington's deeper foolishness—the refusal to think honestly.

Trapping Ourselves in Afghanistan

and Losing Focus on the Essential Mission

Joint Forces Quarterly

3rd Quarter 2009

Afghanistan doesn't matter. Afghanistan's just a worthless piece of dirt. Al Qa'eda matters. To a lesser degree, the hardline elements within the Taliban matter. Pakistan matters, although there is nothing we can do to arrest its self-wrought decay. But our grand ambition to build an ideal Afghanistan dilutes our efforts to strike our mortal enemies, mires our forces in a vain *mission civilatrice*, and leaves our troops hostage to the whims of venomous regimes.

Afghanistan is the strategic booby prize. Even a perfect success in Kabul (which we shall not achieve) influences nothing beyond the country's largely imaginary borders. No other state looks to Afghanistan—a historical black hole—as an example. Political partisanship blinded many Americans to the importance of Iraq in our effort to get at the roots of terror. Addressing topical symptoms rather than deep causes, we decided that Afghanistan was vital because our enemies, al Qa'eda's lethal gypsies, had based themselves there when they wore out their welcome elsewhere. The more important issue was the "why?" behind al Qa'eda. That *why* leads to the Arab Middle East, not Afghanistan, and the emotional heart of the Arab world lies in Baghdad. While Saddam Hussein's Iraq was not a safe haven for al Qa'eda, its archetypal problems formed the foundation for Islamist terror: the comprehensive failure of Arab attempts at political modernity, resulting in the estrangement of frustrated individuals who turned to stern Islam as an alternative to secular strongmen and preyed-upon societies.

Positive changes in Iraq, however imperfect, will resonate throughout the Middle East (if not as swiftly as the neoconservatives
hoped). Progress in Afghanistan is a strategic dead end.

Even the assumption that, if we do not "fix" it to Western specifications, Afghanistan will become a terrorist base again misreads the
past. Afghanistan became a terrorist haven because we refused to
attack the terrorists we knew were there. Osama bin Laden could
have been killed. Al Qa'eda training camps could have been
destroyed. The Taliban could have been punished. Instead the Clinton administration simply hoped the threat would fade away. Our
problem was fecklessness, not the neomedieval lifestyle of villagers
in remote valleys. We have embraced a challenge of marginal relevance, forgetting that al Qa'eda was a parasite on the Afghan body
and choosing to address an Arab-fathered crisis by teaching our values to illiterate tribesmen who do not speak Arabic.

Even if we could persuade Afghan villagers that our values and
behaviors are superior, if we could reduce state corruption to a
manageable level, if we built thousands of miles of roads, elimi-
nated opium growing, and persuaded Afghans that women are fully
human, it would have no effect on al Qa'eda. The terrorists who
attacked our homeland were not Afghans. Afghanistan was just a
cheap motel that was not particular about asking for identification.
Even a return to power of the Taliban—certainly undesirable in
human-rights terms—does not mean that September 11, Part Two,
then becomes inevitable. The next terror attack on the West will not
be launched from Afghanistan.

Pause to consider how lockstep what passes for analysis in Washington has become. The Taliban's asymmetric strategy is not to
defeat us militarily, but to make Afghanistan ungovernable. But
what if our strategy, instead of seeking to transform the country into
a model state, were simply to make it ungovernable for the Taliban?
Our chances of success would soar while our costs would plummet.
But such a commonsense approach is unthinkable. We think in
terms of Westphalian states even where none exist.

We buy into so many unjustified-but-comfortable assumptions
that it is bewildering. There is no law, neither our own nor among
international statutes, that commands us to rescue every region

whence attacks against us originate. Our impulse to lavish aid on former enemies was already a joke in the 1950s. By the 1960s, our "send money" impulse had grown so wanton that it began to destroy allies. In Vietnam, our largesse corrupted our local partners. For their part, the North Vietnamese enjoyed the strength of their poverty: As South Vietnamese officials and officers grabbed everything they could, North Vietnam concentrated on grabbing South Vietnam. Today, we are repeating that strategic decadence, deluging an ethically inept government with so much aid that we only anger the frustrated population while enriching those in power. And, of course, we hardly give a thought to what the Afghan people truly want or do not want.

Nor are we willing to recognize that the Taliban, or something like it, will always exist in those forbidding valleys. Unlike al Qa'eda in Iraq, the Taliban is an indigenous movement (its rise accelerated by aid from Pakistan's Inter-Services Intelligence). The hold of religion—and the paralyzing social customs upon which faith insists—is powerful beyond our ken. We wish it away, pointing out the corruption among mullahs or the hypocrisy of believers willing to stone women to death for human foibles while enjoying the forbidden delights of pederasty themselves. But if hypocrisy negated the power of religion, there would be no religion anywhere. The human mind grows supple when self-interest and power come into play—even the mind chock full of religious doctrine. *Do as I say, not as I do* is an appropriate motto for faiths of all complexions—but that does not make religion any less potent. A "holy man" can rationalize personal monkey business in any number of ways but still believe implacably in the destiny of his faith. The Taliban's rank and file are not draftees, after all. Yes, social pressures exist, and, for some, fighting is a job (and not an unwelcome one). But subtract religion from the equation and we have no Taliban (or al Qa'eda).

A modern state as we wish to see it rise cannot coexist with Afghanistan's traditional values. The distance between Afghanistan and Iraq is not twelve hundred miles, but twelve hundred years—give or take a few modern weapons.

This circles back to the prime thesis of this essay: Even if everything broke our way in Afghanistan, so what? Afghanistan is a sideshow to its eastern neighbor, Pakistan, and to its western neighbor, Iran. We are renovating, at great cost, the outhouse between two blazing strategic mansions.

When Washington dramatically increases aid to a troubled country—as we are doing with Pakistan—we might as well put the death notice on the international obituary page. Pakistan, which has well over five times Afghanistan's population and a nuclear arsenal, cannot be rescued by American efforts. Why? Because Pakistan does not *want* to be rescued. A succession of demagogues (including the late Benazir Bhutto) turned the country into an anti-American bastion by blaming Washington for every jot of suffering in Sindh and each increase in poverty in the Punjab. Pakistan cannot serve up its favored elements within the Taliban (although the military is willing to take on other elements of that complex network of fundamentalist organizations). Ever obsessed with India, Pakistan views Afghanistan as providing strategic depth and sees "its" Taliban as a useful auxiliary force. Now having underestimated the power and will of Islamists, Pakistan's government and military watch helplessly as terror groups gnaw into the country's vitals. Pakistan is the new ground zero of terror.

And it is our lifeline.

Criminal Irresponsibility

Even if Afghanistan were important to our security, we would still be foolish to deploy ever more troops in the nebulous hope that things will somehow break our way. We have reached—indeed, passed—a point where our military's can-do attitude and our government's nice-to-do impulses have put our troops in the worst position they have faced since the autumn of 1950 in Korea, if not since December 1941 in the Philippines.

While I recognize that, given the time and resources, our troops can defeat (although not destroy) the Taliban and keep a Kabul government in office indefinitely, the problem is not the quality or even the quantity of our Armed Forces, but the vagueness and relative pointlessness of the tasks assigned: Our men and women in uniform will do what they are asked and do it well, but decision makers should ask them to do sensible, useful things.

As I write, we are sending twenty-one thousand additional American troops to Afghanistan, with the prospect that more will follow. It is appalling—and a gross dereliction of duty—that no senior officers have spoken out against the violation of fundamental military principles involved in this troop increase.

In order to roll more Afghan rocks uphill, we are ignoring the *essential* requirement to secure supply lines adequate to the mission. Even if Afghanistan were worth an increased effort, the lack of reliable, redundant lines of communication to support our forces would argue against piling on. In the wake of 9/11, it was vital to send Special Operations Forces and limited conventional elements to Afghanistan to punish al Qa'eda and its hosts despite the risks. Indeed, we might usefully have sent more soldiers in those early months. But instead of striking hard, shattering our enemies, then withdrawing—the one military approach that historically worked in Afghanistan—we put down roots, allowing ourselves to become reliant upon a tortuous fifteen-hundred-mile lifeline from the Pakistani port of Karachi northward through the Khyber Pass to various parts of Afghanistan. We have put ourselves at the mercy of a corrupt government of dubious stability with an agenda discordant with ours. Strategically, our troops are Pakistan's hostages.

And Islamabad already has taken advantage of our foolishness. While milking us for all the military and economic aid it can extract, Pakistan's security services recently demonstrated just how reliant we are on their good will. In the wake of the Mumbai bombings—sponsored by a terror organization tacitly supported by Pakistan's government—attacks on our convoys transiting the Khyber Pass, as well as raids on supply yards in Peshawar, swelled in number and soared in their success rate. This could not have occurred had the Pakistanis not given the green light to the attacks. Pakistan was strong-arming us into getting an angry India under control. And we did.

Serious strategy requires balancing potential rewards with inherent risks. Above all, it demands a clear recognition of what is doable and what is not, as well as the ability to differentiate between what is merely nice to do and what is essential. A strategic goal may be desirable in itself but not worth the probable cost. To put fifty thousand or more U.S. troops at risk demands a no-nonsense analysis of the dangers weighted against the potential strategic return. That analysis has not been done. We are arguing over tactics and thinking, at most, in terms of operations, while missing the critical strategic context.

Meanwhile, the belated awareness that our troops are de facto prisoners of war to Pakistan has led to the even greater folly of contemplating a four-thousand-mile supply line from the Baltic Sea through Russia and various Central Asian states to provide nonlethal goods to our troops and those of the North Atlantic Treaty Organization (NATO). Even though the evidence is irrefutable that Moscow bribed Kyrgyzstan to deny our continued access to Manas Air Base—a critical support node—elements within the U.S. administration actually argue that, in the interests of "resetting" our relationship with Russia, it is essential to "expose" ourselves to risk to show the Russians that we trust them. These are serious arguments made by American officials. One suspects they do not have children serving in our military.

Few strategic calculations are more obvious than Prime Minister Vladimir Putin's ploy to addict us to a Russian-controlled supply line. With a domestic economic crisis on his hands (during which he still managed to promise Kyrgyzstan $2.5 billion to close Manas to us), he senses that he will need to create foreign diversions and that the time is right to back an electoral *putsch* in Ukraine and to force regime change in Georgia. Putin calculates that we would accept these moves (protesting vigorously and briefly) in order to keep the supply line open. We are walking into *this* trap with our eyes willfully shut to the obvious peril.

Other voices have suggested bargaining for an ambitious supply route across China into the Afghan panhandle, crossing some of the roughest country on Earth. There are even whispers about opening a line of communication through Iran, an exemplary case of leaping out of the frying pan into the fire.

The logistics problem should have shaped our strategy in Afghanistan. After the late spring of 2002—when we had done what *needed* doing in Afghanistan—our further goals and the means allocated to achieve them should have been determined by one iron-clad criterion: What size force could be deployed, sustained, and, if need be, evacuated *in its entirety* by airlift? One vehicle beyond that calculation is one vehicle too many.

Even beyond the logistics debacle, we lack an integrated strategy, either specific to Afghanistan or regional. We have picked the wrong country to "save." We are sending more troops, without clearly defining the endstate they are to achieve (echoes of Vietnam there). And the problem is where we are *not*—in Pakistan and, to an even greater extent, on the Arabian Peninsula. Indeed, there are serious opportunity costs worldwide, including in our own hemisphere, that are bewilderingly absent from the national debate—to the extent Washington allows a serious debate.

Yes, we *can* make Afghanistan a better place, for us and for the Afghans, if we are willing to remain for a full generation while immobilizing a substantial slice of our battle-worn Armed Forces (it is astonishing that, as Mexico degenerates under the impact of a savage narco-insurgency, our military officers are agonizing over the moods of toothless village elders on the other side of the world; the crisis is on our border here and now, and it is fueled by an array of other drugs, not opium).

Even if we hang on in Afghanistan, giving our all as we bribe cynical foreign powers to let us feed our troops, what ultimate benefit will make the mission worthwhile? Be specific: What do we get out of it?

Can we even define the mission in plain English?

What Makes Sense
Historically, our military has taken risks with its logistics under three types of circumstances: when we had no choice, as in the desperate efforts in the North Atlantic or the Pacific in the first years of our involvement in World War II; when the gamble was carefully calculated to achieve a clearly defined end *and* was of limited duration, as in Winfield Scott's march on Mexico City or the culminating maneuvers of Ulysses Grant's Vicksburg campaign; or when we grew overconfident and careless, which led to the Bataan Death March and the collapse of the thrust toward the Yalu in Korea. The fragile lines of communication supporting our forces and those of our allies in Afghanistan do not fit the first two models.

Any serious strategic analysis would recognize that Pakistan is the problem, not part of the solution. Our natural ally in the subcontinent is India, but developing a closer relationship with New Delhi will be strained by our need to warn India off from retaliating after Pakistani-sponsored or Islamabad-condoned provocations. Pakistan has no incentive to stop its rabble-rousing efforts to embarrass India over Kashmir or other matters, since Islamabad is convinced that we will keep an angry India in check. (Were we completely honest with ourselves, we would recognize that a nuclear exchange between India and Pakistan, however grim in human terms, would not only leave India the clear victor, but might solve quite a number of strategic problems.) Under the current conditions, Pakistan, a state that cannot control its own territory, is our regional boss.

And every troop increase in Afghanistan strengthens Pakistan's grip on us. Or, God help us, Russia's hold, if we really get it wrong.

Another obstacle to a more rational approach to Afghanistan is the difficulty that U.S. officers, once given responsibility for a problem, have in admitting that there may be no solution. Our military is not good at cutting its losses. So now we have flag officers who, protesting all the while that Afghanistan is not Iraq, appear intent on applying the techniques that worked in Iraq to Afghanistan: troop surges, security for the population, train up the local security forces, and so forth. While the situational differences are so great that it would require another article of this length to enumerate them, the basic proposition is that Iraq is a semimodern society that wants to get better, while Afghanistan is a feudal society content with its ways and impatient with our presence (in large part thanks to the cynical populism of President Hamid Karzai). In Iraq, religious extremism was imported. In Afghanistan, it sprouts from the soil with the ease of poppies.

And, decisively, Iraq matters.

To determine which strategy makes sense going forward, we need to have the mental discipline to distinguish between what we need to do for our own security and what merely appears desirable to idealists. We *do* need to continue to hunt al Qa'eda and to prevent Afghanistan from becoming a safe haven for global-reach Islamist terrorists again. We do *not* need to pursue the disproportionately expensive and probably futile mission of creating a modern state in the Hindu Kush. Indeed, a fundamental problem we face is that Afghanistan was never an integrated state in which a central government's writ ran to each remote valley. Afghanistan has always meant the city-state of Kabul, with tributary cities along caravan routes and tribal regions that coexisted under various terms of compromise with the government and their neighbors. Iraq at least has a nascent, if not yet robust, sense of national identity. Beyond a few Western-educated figures, Afghanistan does not and will not.

If we accept the need to continue the pursuit of our sworn enemies, but abandon the self-imposed requirement to build a modern state where none existed, the dimensions of the problem shrink and our requirements become sustainable. A sound strategy with realistic goals would look different from our present approach, though. Roughly outlined, the strategic goals and means from which we might choose are these:

Enemy-focused Approach #1. Concentrate on the continued attrition of al Qa'eda and the prevention of an outright Taliban takeover. Cease development efforts. Turn domestic security requirements over to "our" Afghans, reversing our hapless attempt at being an honest broker in favor of supporting those figures and groups willing to fight against the radical Islamists. Reduce our footprint to a force that can, if necessary, be sustained entirely by air (fifteen thousand troops or less). Establish a mothership base at Bagram, with a few subsidiary bases distributed around the country. Design our residual force around special operations capabilities reinforced by drones, conventional attack, and rotary-wing aircraft, and sufficient conventional forces for local defense and punitive raids. Ask all NATO forces that do not contribute directly to the core mission of destroying our mutual enemies to leave the country. Ignore the opium issue. Instead of attempting to foster governance, concentrate on rendering provinces ungovernable for the most extreme Taliban elements, striking fiercely whenever they come out in the open to exercise control of the population.

Enemy-focused Approach #2. While less desirable than the first approach, a complete withdrawal of our forces from Afghanistan—while continuing to strike our enemies with over-the-horizon weapons and supporting anti-Taliban Afghan factions to keep the Pashtun provinces ungovernable by our enemies—would still be preferable to an increase in our present forces. Allow Afghanistan to further disintegrate if that is its fate. Let an unfettered India deal with Pakistan.

The past and persistent tragedy of our involvement in Afghanistan began with our unwillingness to accept that punishing our enemies is a legitimate military mission and need not be followed by reconstruction largesse. We never sense when it is time to leave the party, so we wind up drunk on mission creep. At home, a polarized electorate defined our simultaneous commitments solely in domestic political terms: For the left, Iraq was Bush's war and, therefore, bad. But those on the political left felt the need to demonstrate that they, too, could be strong on national security, so Afghanistan became the good war by default. It has been impossible to have an objective discussion of the relative merits, genuine errors, appropriate lessons, and potential returns of each of these endeavors.

In this long struggle with Islamist terrorists, our focus should not be on holding territory, but on the destruction of our enemies. That is a lesson we should have taken from al Qa'eda's disastrous engagement in Iraq. Thanks to its own grave miscalculations, al Qa'eda suffered a colossal strategic defeat as millions of Sunni Muslims turned against it. Its error was to believe that a terrorist organization could and should hold ground. Al Qa'eda immobilized itself by seeking prematurely to administer cities and districts, forsaking its flexibility and losing the war of popular perceptions. In Afghanistan, we are in danger of making a parallel mistake as we assume that physical terrain still matters.

Throw away the traditional maps. Chart the enemy. Our focus should be exclusively on his destruction.

As the Obama administration attempts to come to grips with the Afghan morass, it must begin with the strategist's fundamental question: "What's in it for *us*?"

The Last (Mini) Empire
Understanding Why Pakistan's Such a Problem

Armchair General Magazine

January 2011

At the culminating point of his spectacular journey of conquest across Asia, Alexander the Great reached the Indus River. Unlike the politicians and pundits of our own time, he recognized that great barrier for what it was and remains: the dividing line between two profoundly different and hostile civilizations.

As the British fled from their "jewel in the crown," India, territories with nothing in common but Islam were slapped together to create the instant state of Pakistan—to allow Muslims their own country. Passing over the million or so civilians murdered during the abrupt partition of India, the issue always has been that Pakistan just doesn't work. It isn't a nation—its ethnic groups are too diverse and entrenched in tradition to coalesce. It isn't even a coherent state, since not all provinces count equally (four decades ago, a savage civil war ended with the secession of East Bengal—today's Bangladesh).

Pakistan's a last, miniature empire. Today's tribal insurgencies and terrorism leap into focus if you view this dysfunctional space on the map through Alexander's Macedonian eyes: The Indus River, which divides Pakistan in two as it flows north to south, forms the frontier between two civilizations historically uncomfortable with each other. To the east, Muslim or not, you meet the culture of the subcontinent: India's food, dress, manners, values, and so on. On a long drive down from the Khyber Pass, crossing the Indus eastward at Attock Fort, you suddenly enter a different, richer realm.

The western territories you left behind belong to the civilization of Central Asia, the lands of Tamerlane and Babur, now much diminished in their power to conquer. To the east, you have a sophisticated culture; in the west, tribes. The eastern provinces of Punjab and Sindh, with their great, near-chaotic cities, are the rulers today. Those states are the "real" Pakistan, the home ground of the country's business community and political base (Punjab, with its long military traditions, also supplies a disproportionate number of military officers).

West of the Indus, the vast, sparsely-populated and impoverished province of Baluchistan has seen decades of on-and-off insurgency. Why? Because it's a colony by another name, and its natives view the Punjabis and Sindhis as occupiers. The same goes for the Northwest Frontier Province (Khyber-Pakhtunkhwa), the Federally Administered Tribal Areas, and all the refuges and hotbeds of Islamist fanaticism in this Central Asian borderland. East of the Indus, Islam is complex, Sufi-influenced, and often mystical. West of the river, the faith is uncompromising, tradition-lashed, and cruel. Punjabis and Sindhis view their western co-citizens as hillbillies (although the Pashtun tribes supply a good number of soldiers, as they did under the Brits). The Baluchis and Pashtuns, in turn, see the easterners as revenuers—and enemies.

Pakistanis from east of the Indus are the overlords. And they're seen that way by their "colonial subjects." Today's west-of-the-Indus separatist movements and Islamist rebellions aren't new—they've always been there. That's why forts line the Indus and the Grand Trunk Road to the Khyber. Now, though, the spirit of rebellion is supercharged by the global Islamist movement.

The problem for us is that Pakistan seeks to exploit these unruly tribal lands to extend Islamabad's empire: Afghanistan's the prize (even if it proves to be a booby prize). Pakistan's generals think in pre-WWII imperial terms, strategically and militarily. They want strategic depth for a war with India, as if nukes weren't in the equation. Recent revelations about Afghanistan's potential mineral wealth make the place still more attractive to them.

The problem for the Pakistanis is that they've opened a fundamentalist Pandora's Box they'll never be able to close. Should the United States and NATO leave Afghanistan, Pakistan might enjoy a brief period of hegemony, but the next target of all those insurgents would be Pakistan itself. Pakistan has sown the wind, and will reap the whirlwind.

Watch: Pakistan's efforts to work a deal that empowers the "good" Taliban backed by Islamabad.

Crisis Watch Bottom Line: After nearly ten years in Afghanistan, we still don't understand what the fighting's really about.

Charisma and Victory

Armchair General Magazine

May 2011

Some commanders have it, others don't. Some men acquire it, others won't. Charisma, the special magic that adds so much to command authority, remains a great riddle: We know it when we feel it, but can't fully explain it. Certain men and women are born with a quality that exerts magnetism over others, but we don't yet understand the neurobiology. Physical stature or attractiveness may help, but aren't nearly enough. Some of history's most charismatic military leaders—not least, Napoleon—were short men. Prince Eugene, the greatest soldier of his generation, was dwarfish and downright ugly. Frederick the Great was homely, heartless, and, on at least one occasion, cowardly—yet he mesmerized millions.

We may never fully understand this gift, but we can categorize the varieties of the complex phenomenon we call "charisma." In signals intelligence parlance, we can "read the externals." When we take pains to do so, three different forms of charisma emerge, none exclusive of the others, but each distinct.

Shakespeare possessed an uncanny sense of soldiering (and captured charismatic leadership in Henry V's famed Agincourt speech), but he was writing in a different vein when one of his characters declared that "some are born great, some achieve greatness, and some have greatness thrust upon 'em." He might have been speaking about charisma: Some men (and women) are born with it, others acquire charisma through their achievements, while others are assigned the charisma of office.

Nor is charisma always a good thing. The leader born with charisma may turn out to be a selfless Jose de San Martin, the South American hero of independence, or a Mao—a murderer of tens of millions. Personal charisma may empower a successful leader of men, such as Francis Marion, the "Swamp Fox," or instill too much confidence in someone like George B. McClellan, the Union general who could do everything well but fight. The other forms of charisma may go awry and do great damage, but the naturally charismatic figure is the one who seems to come out of nowhere to become either a national saint or a deadly charlatan, a Washington or a Hitler.

In contrast, the battlefield captain who owes his charisma to professional achievement, who has "earned his spurs" and built an inspiring reputation, is often the most dependable manipulator of charisma. He may disappoint in the end but usually has acquired the technical skills to avoid catastrophe. Plain as a stump, Ulysses S. Grant was the sort of man who goes unnoticed in a crowd, yet his Civil War victories in the west let him come east wrapped in an aura of irresistible success. In the opposing camp, John Singleton Mosby was a smallish, unimpressive man whose courage and canny sense of guerrilla tactics turned him into a legend as the "Gray Ghost."

Finally we have the commonest form of charisma, the artificial charisma associated with an office or rank. This variant overlaps heavily with celebrity, our common agreement that someone is special because he wears a crown or a general's stars, sits in the Oval Office or appears on television. Met in person, such an individual may be a terrible disappointment. Publicly he may fail utterly, if he proves no match for the crisis that eventually faces his kingdom, country, or army (or network). He may rise to the occasion, as did Harry Truman, our "accidental" president, or fail miserably, as did Czar Nicholas II, whose weakness damned an empire. The charisma of robes, rank, or crown, the authority of a captain's bars or a field marshal's baton, can only give a leader a chance to serve effectively; he must find within himself the additional qualities leadership requires for success.

The charisma of position is a contract between followers and a leader: If the company commander or the prime minister can't cut it, the magic quickly fades. This assigned charisma guarantees that our troops will cheer any visiting president, thanks to the halo that surrounds the office. But it doesn't guarantee that they'll vote for him or his party, if he doesn't deliver.

Of course, these forms of charisma don't have firewalls between them. Some leaders, such as generals Robert E. Lee, George S. Patton, and John Churchill, First Duke of Marlborough, fused all three forms in their persons and careers. Others, such as General and President Dwight D. Eisenhower, combined the charisma of achievement and position. President Barack Obama possesses great personal charisma and the charisma of office, but lacks the charisma (and effectiveness) of experience. The point in identifying three different forms of charisma isn't to draw neat lines, but to color in our understanding of this phenomenon that has, so often, changed history.

Born With It

Oliver Cromwell is a classic example of a leader born with charisma—and few other advantages—who used it to change history. The greatest of all Englishmen, Cromwell engraved religious toleration and freedom of conscience on his country's traditions of government, insuring that no future monarch would attempt to impose continental absolutism on English-speaking men and women. After Cromwell, English kings knew their limits and only the requirements of public order restricted private consciences. Vilified for centuries by royalist propagandists and those who romanticized the Cavaliers—who fought for a bad king and worse principles— Cromwell has been rehabilitated by historians, but not in the popular mind. This man, who struck the greatest blows for freedom of any of his kind between Queen Boadicea's revolt against Rome's legions and the American Revolution, is still portrayed in popular culture as cold, cruel, and selfish, even paranoid. Cromwell was none of those things. He was, though, a military commander to rival the later Duke of Marlborough or the Duke of Wellington.

How did Cromwell begin? He was ugly. His most flattering portraits show us a man with pockmarks and toadstool moles. He had no personal wealth, but worked hard as a gentleman-farmer in that distinctly English social wedge between the yeoman and the minor aristocracy. He cared nothing for the trappings of success and paid a fine rather than allow himself to be knighted by King Charles I, who was forcing knighthoods on Cromwell's peers as a means of taxation (there was a fee if you took on a "Sir" before your name and a fine if you didn't). Even at the zenith of his power, when he ruled England as Lord Protector, Cromwell lived simply, enjoying the company of the family he adored or listening to music while sharing good English ale with close companions. Above all, he loved God—but never sought to force his form of worship on others.

Contrary to wildly inaccurate portrayals of Cromwell as a religious fanatic, he opposed, in turn, the attempt of Anglican bishops to force their religious forms on all Englishmen, the efforts of Scottish Presbyterians to impose their Covenant on all Englishmen, and radical Protestant demands that Anglicans and Presbyterians be suppressed. Cromwell opened the door for Jews to return to England and winked at the private celebration of the Catholic mass. His only failure was his inability to persuade a stubborn, conniving king to honor his obligations to Parliament and the people.

In addition to his robust love of God, Cromwell displayed great strength of will and a fine ability to judge men and the times. Still, those qualities alone would not have been sufficient to thrust him upward past the great nobles of the land, past archbishops and a king. From his early maturity, Cromwell radiated a near-magical charisma that transcended his physical unattractiveness. In his rural haunts, men looked to him to protect their ancient rights. In Parliament, others gravitated toward him. On the battlefield, even those of higher rank obeyed him. He commanded men not just through his orders, but through a gift that made men believe in "Oliver."

In taking political decisions or weighing matters of state, Cromwell was deliberate, even slow, weighing the evidence as he mastered his famous temper. But on the battlefield, he was decisive. He had the faculty of seeing into the heart of a tactical (or strategic) problem in an instant, giving the right orders, then leading by example.

With no professional military experience, he had the born warrior's gift. Rising quickly from a captain to a colonel of horse, he rapidly assessed the problem with Parliament's cavalry arm and impressed his will on the troopers under his command. Able to joke with common soldiers, he was nonetheless a firm disciplinarian—especially, when it came to fighting. In an age when cavalry formations were good for only one charge and, perhaps, a pursuit, Cromwell taught his horsemen to maintain order or, if order was lost in a melee, to promptly reestablish their lines or columns. This allowed him effectively to double his cavalry's strength in battle, since his dashing, murderous opponent, Prince Rupert, never managed to exert a similar discipline on his own riders. The scattered Royalist horse became easy pickings for a countercharge by Cromwell's Ironsides. From Marston Moor to Worcester, Cromwell demonstrated better tactical control of cavalry than any other officer of his age.

As a general, he also displayed an uncanny grasp of strategy and sense of the enemy's psychology. His victories added the charisma of achievement to his innate charisma as he shattered Royalist, Scottish, and Irish armies. He could make a brilliant strategic march to concentrate against enemies caught piecemeal at Preston, or sense the point of weakness in a Scottish and Royalist force twice the size of his own at Dunbar. Again and again, he defeated professional commanders who were veterans of the Thirty Years' War on the continent. He credited God and his hand-picked subordinates for his victories, and his willingness to praise others served him well. Even as Lord Protector, when Cromwell no longer took part in combat himself, the senior officers he had chosen performed superbly in a naval war with the Dutch—who possessed the finest maritime force in the world in the mid-seventeenth century.

Cromwell ended with the charisma of office, too, in addition to his inherent charisma and that of achievement. This plain man raised England from the disorder of civil war to make her a respected imperial power sought as an ally by her traditional enemies, France and Spain. When Cromwell died in office, a king returned to the English throne—but despotism never did. Our Founding Fathers may have admired the Romans of the Republic, but the true roots of our freedom lie in the England of Oliver Cromwell.

Earning It

Unlike Cromwell, Ulysses S. Grant was not a naturally charismatic man. "Sam" Grant was the sort who blurs into a crowd. At West Point, his one distinction was his horsemanship—he set equestrian records that stood for decades. In the war with Mexico, his service was solid but undistinguished. A few years later, he showed great courage and leadership while shepherding a party of soldiers and civilians across the Panamanian Isthmus during a gruesome cholera epidemic, but upon reaching the garrisons of our wild Northwest, he went to seed as an officer.

Grant drank. Common knowledge. But the circumstances under which he drank have gone unnoticed. Lieutenant Grant fell in love with Julia Dent, a belle from a prosperous Missouri family. Winning her, he lost a part of himself, the independence that had let him float cargo down the Midwest's mighty rivers while still a boy. Because the only photos we see of Julia Dent Grant show us a stout old matron, we don't envision the couple's romantic passion. Yet the Grants had one of the great love stories in American history. Sam Grant adored his wife, and she never lost faith in him—even after he resigned from the Army to come back to her and found himself reduced to hawking firewood in the streets of St. Louis.

Grant drank when he was separated from his beloved wife. He couldn't bear to be apart from her. It's that straightforward. Isolated posts on the far frontier were too much for him. During the Civil War, Grant's drinking binges were fewer than legend has it—but they always occurred when he had been separated from Julia for too long. Later in the war, when his wife was able to join him at his headquarters, the drinking stopped (although the cigar-smoking that would kill him continued). I have found no recorded instance of Grant being drunk in his wife's company.

When the "War of the Rebellion" broke out, Grant was helping keep shop in Galena, Illinois. But he had kept up with military affairs, studying the campaigns in Italy and explaining the Battle of Solferino to acquaintances on the porch of the store where he worked. He was liked, but a nobody. Applying for a commission, he hoped that his West Point education and former service might get him command of a regiment in the instant army the North needed to create.

Then Grant began to do what no other northern leader seemed able to accomplish: He won battles. After fighting to a mixed result at Belmont, he rode through various skirmishes until, in an otherwise dark season for the Union, he took Ft. Donelson, giving the Union control of the Tennessee and Cumberland Rivers. Surprised while encamped a few months later, he shored up his battered lines to bleed his opponents so ferociously that Confederates lamented, "The South never smiled after Shiloh."

He took Vicksburg. Grant's mind had always been sharper than his appearance—he preferred the commonest of uniforms—and he'd drawn lessons from his experiences that eluded the war's early luminaries, North and South. From his boyhood adventures on the Ohio and Mississippi, he'd internalized a sense of how those superhighways of the age brought the land together—and divided it. From Winfield Scott's stunning march to Mexico City, he took the lesson that a well-led force could cut loose from its base, as long as it maintained the initiative (when Grant decided to risk severing his lines of communication during the Vicksburg campaign, his friend, William Tecumseh Sherman, told him he was mad—but just as Grant learned from Scott, Sherman learned from Grant . . . his March to the Sea was the Vicksburg campaign writ large).

After the fall of Vicksburg, Grant rescued Rosecrans at Chattanooga in the wake of the Chickamauga bloodbath. His presence electrified the troops so powerfully that a limited attack expanded into a spontaneous general assault as regiments in blue stormed up Missionary Ridge, sending the besieging Rebels running in what was truly a "soldiers' battle."

Grant was now wrapped in the charisma of achievement, the radiant cloak of the victor. Yet he still had no personal charisma when unrecognized. Summoned east by President Lincoln, Grant walked from his train to Washington's Willard Hotel and politely asked if a room was to be had. Confronted with a poorly shaven, mild-mannered fellow in an old frock coat, the clerk disdainfully assigned his guest a small room in the attic. Without objection, Grant signed the hotel register.

The clerk's manners improved when he read the signature. *General* Grant got the finest suite available, along with lavish attention from the management. The charisma was there—but in the reputation, not the person.

At Appomattox, Grant asked Lee if he remembered their meeting years before. Lee didn't recall Grant and eased away from the question. But, once again, a flashing Cavalier had been subdued by a drab Roundhead.

After the war, Grant's charisma of achievement—his reputation and fame—carried him into an ill-fated presidency (although his terms in office were better than their reputation). The charisma of achievement may get you a higher position, but it won't guarantee you'll succeed there.

Another example of the charisma of achievement is today's General David Petraeus. He illustrates a variation on the charisma of achievement, the determined construction of an image, a brand. Smart, dedicated, competitive, boundlessly energetic, and ambitious, Petraeus set his sights on a general's stars while still at West Point. In every assignment, he strove to be first among his peers. Despite some awkwardness connecting with enlisted soldiers, Petraeus outperformed the competition at every level, building a reputation as the sharpest, fittest, most hardworking officer in any given unit or on any staff. In intimate settings, Petraeus projects energy . . . but no charisma, no common touch (the first time I encountered him, he seemed like just another bright staff officer). His effect works best on large groups or among his acolytes.

His first tour in Iraq, with the 101st Airborne Division, appeared successful, but had few lasting effects; his second tour, as a trainer of Iraqi soldiers, was a failure. But the brand was strong, he was aggressive, and he had the right answers for Washington at a critical moment. His third and final tour in Iraq was a stunning success, if for more complex reasons than the media would have it.

Now General Petraeus has both the charisma of achievement and of position. He may rise still further from his current position heading our effort in Afghanistan. An impeccable soldier on the battlefront and the home front, it will be interesting to see how far his blend of talent and earned charisma will take him—and what effect it will have on our country's strategic situation.

Overall, today's U.S. Army shuns charismatic leadership at the highest levels, preferring quiet corporatism. The Marines, by contrast, aren't afraid of charismatic leaders. General Jim Mattis, the Bulldog of Fallujah, is a Cromwellian example of innate charisma. Short and plain as a fencepost, his charisma is nonetheless immediate and unmistakable: Marines love Mattis and would follow him anywhere. We don't understand the magic of such men.

Crowned With Charisma

Frederick II of Prussia was not a charismatic man. Scrawny and bird-faced, he spent his youth rebelling ineffectually against his military-minded father, who made the teenage prince watch from a barred window as his best friend was beheaded for aiding him in an attempt to run away (amid a probable homosexual relationship). When Frederick came to the throne in 1740—he would reign for forty-six years—he was noted primarily for his interest in music and litera-ture. Even his father doubted Frederick's capacity for leadership.

In the beginning, the cold-blooded monarch who would become famed as Frederick the Great possessed only the artificial charisma of kingship. Since the days of myth, kings and potentates had recognized the importance of pomp and circumstance, of out-ward displays of majesty, not only for impressing subjects and oppo-nents, but also to lend authority to weak members of a dynasty. Until a serious crisis occurred, heavy robes and a crown could prop up a nonentity, in Babylon, Byzantium, or Berlin. His subjects and foreign rivals respected the office to which Frederick was raised, but expected precious little of the man.

Frederick exploited the charisma of office to stun the world. Building upon the foundation of his absolute authority—and the well-drilled army his father had bequeathed him—Frederick would turn poor, backward Prussia into a major European power. Along the way, he would acquire a charisma of achievement second to no military figure of his age.

If Frederick lacked muscles and a parade-ground voice, he had a superb mind and an iron will. Heartless when it came to his sol-diers, pity never weakened him. His men were there to die for him. And he understood that Prussia could not prosper with its discon-nected territories. He set out promptly to build a geographically coherent realm.

Embarking on the first of his three wars, the War of the Austrian Succession (1740–1748), he marched to seize the rich province of Silesia from Austria, where the young Empress Maria Theresa was struggling for her throne. At first, though, Frederick's strategic vision was not matched by tactical savvy. In his first major battle, Mollwitz, he fled the field when the tide ran against the Prussians. His generals turned the situation around to win the day, but Frederick would long be haunted by the charge that "the only living thing toward which he ever felt gratitude was the horse that carried him away from Mollwitz."

Spurred on by his first taste of war, Frederick proved a swift learner. He mastered not only tactics, but also a regal air of imperturbability amid the carnage of eighteenth-century battlefields. At a later low point in his fortunes, when Russian Cossacks rode into his capital, he had the fortitude to go on fighting—and ultimately win (a far lesser creature, Adolph Hitler, would summon him as an example as the Red Army closed in on Berlin). At various points in his wars, Frederick faced coalitions that included Austria, Russia, France, Sweden, and neighboring Saxony, with only England and a few German principalities as his allies. Given the odds against him, it was inevitable that he would suffer battlefield defeats, as he did at Kolin, Kunersdorf, and elsewhere. But Frederick always came back.

Able to operate on interior lines against his encircling opponents, Frederick was not afraid to take risks and laid down the dictum for his generals that "to attempt to be strong everywhere is to be strong nowhere." He marched hard to concentrate against a single foe, then applied his famed oblique order of attack to destroy one wing of the enemy's force while fixing the other in place. And he multiplied the effectiveness of his smaller forces by drilling his men ruthlessly on the principle that they needed to fear their officers more than they did the enemy. On the battlefield, his men could march and counter-march, change front and fire volleys more rapidly than any other soldiers of the day. His greatest victories—Rossbach, Leuthen, and Hohenfriedberg—passed into military legend. And this puny, bent-spined king's presence on the battlefield gave his troops an aura of invincibility. In Frederick's case, the assigned charisma of office proved a devastating tool.

After the high points and low points of the Seven Years' War (1756–1763), Frederick's final military adventure, the War of the Bavarian Succession (1778) amounted to little. By then, though, his mystique was great enough to keep the Prussian army feared throughout Europe for two decades after his death, until military affairs moved past the Frederician model and the forces of another genius, Napoleon Bonaparte, destroyed Prussia's "clockwork" regiments at Jena-Auerstadt.

Combination Plays

As evidenced by Frederick—and so many others—one form of charisma can be parleyed into another; in Frederick's case, the charisma of office set the conditions for his ultimate charisma of achievement. Throughout history, stellar military leaders, from Julius Caesar to Erwin Rommel, parleyed the charisma with which they were born into that of achievement and, finally, of high rank. General Douglas MacArthur fused the charisma of character and that of career achievement so powerfully that his catastrophic errors in 1941 were overlooked by a nation desperate for heroes. Like Patton, MacArthur was a master of the theatrical aspects of command—which may be mocked, but can be powerfully effective with troops and the public alike.

In other cases, though, we meet the limits of charisma. General "Fighting Joe" Hooker had personal charisma in spades, but led the Army of the Potomac to a needless disaster at Chancellorsville. Mexico's Santa Anna exuded powerful personal charisma, but brought his country devastating defeats that cost it over half its territory. Few in the last century were more charismatic to their native audiences than Benito Mussolini—and we all know how his military ambitions ended.

There are two bottom lines on charisma and command. First, we still don't understand the personal magic some human beings exercise over others. Second, charisma is a sharp, but two-edged sword. A charismatic leader who also possesses talent, courage, and moral balance may prove the savior of his people or of the entire free world. But charisma in the person of a fool leads to disaster.